Transforming Cinema with Artificial Intelligence

Uğur Kilinç
Ondokuz Mayıs University, Turkey

IGI Global
Scientific Publishing
Publishing Tomorrow's Research Today

Vice President of Editorial — Melissa Wagner
Managing Editor of Acquisitions — Mikaela Felty
Managing Editor of Book Development — Jocelynn Hessler
Production Manager — Mike Brehm
Cover Design — Phillip Shickler

Published in the United States of America by
IGI Global Scientific Publishing
701 East Chocolate Avenue
Hershey, PA, 17033, USA
Tel: 717-533-8845
Fax: 717-533-8661
E-mail: cust@igi-global.com
Website: https://www.igi-global.com

Library of Congress Cataloging-in-Publication Data

Names: Kılınç, Uğur (Film historian), editor.
Title: Transforming cinema with artificial intelligence / edited by Uğur Kılınç.
Description: Hershey, PA : IGI Global Scientific Publishing, 2025. | Includes bibliographical references and index. | Summary: "This book seeks to provide a comprehensive understanding of how AI technologies like Machine Learning, Deep Learning, Reinforcement Learning, and Natural Language Processing are revolutionizing the film industry"-- Provided by publisher.
Identifiers: LCCN 2024053613 (print) | LCCN 2024053614 (ebook) | ISBN 9798369339169 (hardcover) | ISBN 9798369352199 (paperback) | ISBN 9798369339176 (ebook)
Subjects: LCSH: Motion pictures--Technological innovations. | Motion picture industry--Technological innovations. | Artificial intelligence. | Motion pictures--Production and direction. | LCGFT: Essays.
Classification: LCC PN1995.9.T43 T73 2025 (print) | LCC PN1995.9.T43 (ebook) | DDC 791.4302/32028563--dc23/eng/20250101
LC record available at https://lccn.loc.gov/2024053613
LC ebook record available at https://lccn.loc.gov/2024053614

British Cataloguing in Publication Data
A Cataloguing in Publication record for this book is available from the British Library.

Editorial Advisory Board

Table of Contents

Detailed Table of Contents

Artificial intelligence (AI) is rapidly transforming various industries, and filmmaking is no exception. This research paper explores the future trends and impacts of AI on filmmaking, drawing on insights from expert interviews with industry professionals. The analysis reveals a multifaceted picture, highlighting both the potential benefits and challenges associated with AI integration. AI tools hold promise for enhancing creativity by suggesting story ideas, streamlining workflows through casting and production automation, and optimizing budgets. However, ethical considerations arise regarding potential bias in AI algorithms and the homogenization of filmmaking if AI is overused. The paper concludes that AI serves as a powerful tool to empower human creativity, but human judgment and artistic vision will remain central to the filmmaking process. Responsible development and implementation of AI are crucial to ensure a future where AI complements, rather than replaces, the human touch in creating a vibrant and emotionally engaging cinematic landscape.

This research focuses on Artificial Intelligence's current and future potential in art. Applying a systematic literature review method and bibliometric analysis, the paper reveals the main trends and technologies that define AI in art. It conducts a literature search using an SLR and bibliometric analysis to identify key authors and clusters of research. It gives a good overview of the current state; it is more formal. Several new trends are identified in the context of the discussed findings, including the symbiosis of human artists and AI, AI-customized artistic experiences, AI's impact on cultural,

Artificial intelligence (AI) technologies are revolutionising the cinema industry. AI, which offers significant innovations especially in sound production and editing, enriches the film atmosphere. Deep learning models produce realistic sound effects, reducing the need for manual foley and facilitating synchronisation. AI provides higher quality sound effects while saving cost and time in film production. The quality of dialogue and the naturalness of sound effects are also improved with AI. AI stands out as an important technology that will shape the future of sound in cinema.

Artificial Intelligence uses personalised content curation to make recommendations that are specifically tailored to each individual user's watching preferences based on their viewing history, reviews, and interactions and what it implies for our future. In this chapter, we are going to explore the multitudes of effects of AI in visual media. From the enchantment of special effects that defy the boundaries of reality to the nuanced artistry of colour grading, we aim to unravel the intricate dance between technology and storytelling. Our chapter aims to take our readers on a journey to learn more about AI in animation, character generation, CGI, and many more. From enhancing cinematography to streamlining post-production, AI not only revolutionizes the technical aspects of filmmaking but also contributes to a deeper understanding of audience preferences and engagement.

concluded that generative artificial intelligence applications can be successful in producing movie posters.

The study employs a documentary method from qualitative research methods through a literature review. Different examples are used within the scope of purposive sampling to demonstrate the synthesis of artificial intelligence and editing: The selected examples show how artificial intelligence technologies are used in different areas and how they affect the editing processes. Examining each example will help to better understand the impact of the synthesis of artificial intelligence and editing on the film industry. It can be stated that studies on the synthesis of artificial intelligence and editing offer an important perspective on how future storytelling and visual art may be shaped. The aim of this study is to reveal the potential to further optimize creative processes, develop new opportunities for artists, and provide more impactful experiences for audiences

The art of cinema is in a constant process of change and development depending on technology. While theorists are trying to create new narrative techniques, studios are trying to market their films as a commercial product. It can be said that artificial intelligence is used instead of or in support of human power within the collective structure of cinema. Box office results are one of the most important indicators of success for the producers of films, in which more than one department is involved in the production process. ScriptBook is an artificial intelligence software that uses movie scripts as data. It reveals the possible success or failure of films at the box office by analyzing the elements in their scripts. In the study, the working principles of the software and its contribution to the film industry will be examined.

Sophisticated recommendation systems are crucial in the dynamic digital content consumption environment to improve user engagement and content discoverability. This work provides an in-depth analysis of different recommendation models such as User-based Collaborative Filtering, NMF-based Content Filtering, and a Hybrid Model. It uses a detailed dataset of user interactions with a streaming platform to evaluate their performance.We utilized User-based Collaborative Filtering to utilize similarities among users for content recommendations, NMF-based Content Filtering to break down the user-item interaction matrix and reveal hidden features, and a Hybrid Model that combines the advantages of both methods to offer more tailored and precise recommendations. The results demonstrate the intricate strengths and weaknesss of each model, with the Hybrid Model displaying a favorable combination of customisation and accuracy. The findings from this work provide valuable contributions to the discussion on recommendation systems and also have practical implications for streaming platform

Preface

WHERE DOES ARTIFICIAL INTELLIGENCE STAND IN CINEMA?

In the ever-evolving cinematic landscape, the integration of Artificial Intelligence (AI) represents a pivotal moment in the history of storytelling, production, and audience engagement. This book, Transforming Cinema with Artificial Intelligence, explores the transformative synergy between AI and the art of filmmaking. By analyzing AI-driven advancements across scriptwriting, editing, sound design, cinematography, and audience analytics, this volume offers a multidimensional view of how technology is reshaping cinema's creative and technical processes. As AI continues to blur the boundaries between human ingenuity and machine precision, the implications for storytelling, production efficiency, and audience interaction are profound and far-reaching.

Cinema has always been a medium that reflects the technological zeitgeist of its time. Today, we are witnessing an unprecedented confluence of AI technologies with cinematic practices driven by machine learning, deep learning, and natural language processing advancements. AI is no longer a distant futuristic concept but an active participant in every film production and distribution stage. From automating labor-intensive processes like editing and color grading to enhancing creative outputs in screenwriting and visual effects, AI is a force reshaping the industry. In an era where streaming platforms dominate media consumption and personalization is critical to audience retention, AI-driven algorithms can analyze viewer behavior, recommend tailored content, and predict commercial success. This convergence highlights the importance of understanding AI's role as a tool and collaborator in cinematic creation.

This book is written for a diverse audience comprising scholars, practitioners, and enthusiasts at the intersection of film and technology:

- **Scholars and Students**: Those in film studies, media and communication, artificial intelligence, computer science, and related disciplines seeking to understand the theoretical and practical implications of AI in cinema.
- **Industry Professionals**: Filmmakers, producers, and post-production experts eager to incorporate AI tools into their workflows to enhance creativity and efficiency.
- **AI Developers and Technologists**: Professionals in AI and machine learning working on tools and applications for the cinematic domain.
- **Cultural Analysts and Critics**: Individuals exploring how AI influences the socio-cultural dimensions of storytelling and audience experiences.
- **General Enthusiasts**: Readers fascinated by the intersection of art and technology, and how AI is transforming the way stories are told and experienced.

The following chapters provide a detailed exploration of these themes, each focusing on a specific facet of artificial intelligence's integration into cinema—from its transformative influence on storytelling and technical workflows to its implications for audience engagement and ethical considerations.

"Lights, Camera, AI: Lights, Camera, AI: The Future Trends and Impacts of Artificial Intelligence in Filmmaking" explores the transformative potential of artificial intelligence in revolutionizing the filmmaking industry. By analyzing the integration of AI into areas such as scriptwriting, casting, editing, and audience analytics, the chapter highlights both the opportunities and challenges posed by this technology. While AI enhances efficiency and reduces production costs, the chapter critically examines its limitations, such as the inability to replicate human creativity and emotional depth in storytelling. By combining expert interviews with qualitative research, this chapter provides a nuanced perspective on how AI can complement human creativity in filmmaking rather than replace it. The insights offered serve as a valuable guide for industry professionals, policymakers, and creatives navigating the future of AI-enabled cinema.

"AI and the Evolution of Artistic Expression: AI and the Evolution of Artistic Expression: Impacts on Society and Culture" explores the transformative role of artificial intelligence in reshaping the creation, consumption, and understanding of art in the contemporary era. By drawing parallels with previous technological revolutions, such as photography and digital art, the chapter situates AI within a historical continuum of innovation that challenges traditional notions of creativity and authorship. Case studies and a systematic literature review demonstrate how AI democratizes artistic expression, introducing accessibility and diversity while raising critical ethical and philosophical questions about originality and cultural sensitivity. The chapter highlights AI's dual capacity as a tool for groundbreaking creativity and a force that redefines the relationship between technology and culture.

“Artificial Intelligence In Screenplay, ChatGPT Application” investigates the use of ChatGPT as a tool for screenplay writing, examining its strengths and limitations within the context of classical narrative structures. Analyzing AI-generated scripts highlights the challenges posed by creativity and originality, especially within genre-specific constraints like science fiction. While ChatGPT effectively utilizes basic narrative frameworks such as introduction, development, and conclusion, its outputs often need more depth, nuance, and emotional resonance found in human-written scripts. The study also reveals that AI tends to rely on predictable character development patterns and needs help integrating multiple characters into cohesive narratives. Furthermore, superficial descriptions, limited visual and auditory detailing, and repetitive thematic elements are emphasized. Despite these limitations, the chapter underscores the potential of AI as a complementary tool in the creative process and calls for ongoing research to evaluate advancements in AI capabilities over time. This critical assessment contributes to the dialogue on the evolving relationship between AI and storytelling, offering valuable insights for filmmakers and researchers exploring AI-driven creativity in cinema.

“Revolutionizing Malayalam Cinema: AI Powered Scripting And Creative Brainstorming With ChatGPT” explores the transformative impact of ChatGPT in revolutionizing the scriptwriting and creative processes of Malayalam cinema. By integrating AI-driven tools into traditional filmmaking practices, the chapter highlights how ChatGPT is a collaborative ally for writers and filmmakers, aiding in brainstorming, plot development, and character creation. With its ability to generate culturally resonant and authentic narratives in Malayalam, ChatGPT bridges technology with local storytelling traditions. The chapter delves into its potential to enhance pre-production efficiency, enrich narrative depth, and foster a collaborative community among creators.

“The Digital Transformation of Sound and Music Cinema Experience with AI” explores how artificial intelligence is reshaping sound design, dubbing, and music composition in the film industry. By analyzing the evolution of sound technologies from the early days of cinema to the current AI-driven landscape, the chapter highlights how tools like deep learning models and voice cloning have enhanced creative possibilities while streamlining production processes. AI-powered platforms enable more efficient workflows, such as generating high-quality foley effects, automating dubbing, and composing emotion-driven soundtracks tailored to specific scenes. At the same time, the chapter critically examines challenges related to job security, copyright issues, and ethical considerations arising from the widespread adoption of AI in sound production. By addressing these dualities, this chapter provides a balanced perspective on how AI contributes to the evolution of cinematic soundscapes while reshaping the industry's cultural and technological framework.

"Illuminating the Path from Script to Screen Using Lights, Camera, and AI" delves into the transformative integration of artificial intelligence in visual effects, cinematography, and storytelling, highlighting its profound impact on filmmaking. Through innovative techniques like volumetric animation, AI-powered rendering, and neural style transfer, the chapter examines how AI enhances filmmaking's technical and creative aspects, enabling filmmakers to achieve unprecedented realism and artistic expression. Additionally, it addresses the ethical and creative challenges posed by AI, including the risks of over-reliance, potential homogenization of content, and copyright and job security issues. By exploring case studies like Pixar's Elemental and the broader implications of AI-driven storytelling, this chapter provides a nuanced analysis of how AI redefines cinema's visual and narrative paradigms. The insights presented guide stakeholders in navigating the evolving cinematic landscape while balancing innovation with ethical considerations.

"Cinema & Artificial Intelligence: Charting Its Role In the Indian Film Sector" examines the transformative influence of artificial intelligence on the Indian film industry, illustrating its integration across production, distribution, and audience engagement. The chapter highlights how filmmakers navigate the interplay of traditional practices and technological innovation by leveraging AI tools for scriptwriting, actor selection, special effects, and audience analytics. It emphasizes AI's role in democratizing access to filmmaking, empowering diverse narratives and underrepresented voices while addressing critical ethical concerns, such as algorithmic bias and socio-economic impacts on industry professionals. Through structured interviews and interdisciplinary analysis, the chapter provides actionable insights into balancing technological augmentation with human creativity and emotional depth. By exploring both the opportunities and challenges, this chapter offers a roadmap for the Indian film sector to harness AI's potential, enrich storytelling, and redefine audience experiences in an increasingly digital and inclusive cinematic era.

"Research on the Potential of Digital Image-Generating Artificial Intelligence Applications in Movie Poster Production" examines the transformative potential of artificial intelligence in creating movie posters, using a case study focused on Hayao Miyazaki's award-winning films. Through semiotic analysis of visuals generated by AI tools like Ideogram and Gemini, the study explores how these technologies replicate professional-quality designs with thematic consistency, effective typography, and aesthetic balance. The analysis encompasses six iconic Miyazaki films—*Princess Mononoke*, *Spirited Away*, *The Walking Castle*, *Ponyo*, *The Wind Rises*, and *The Boy and the Heron*—highlighting their universal themes, cultural richness, and artistic storytelling. By narrowing its scope to these celebrated works and employing select AI applications, the study identifies how AI accelerates design processes and introduces new creative possibilities while addressing challenges such as originality, emotional resonance, and prompt-dependent outputs.

"The Synthesis Between Artificial Intelligence and Edit Stories of the Future" examines the transformative role of artificial intelligence in the evolution of video editing, presenting a comprehensive review of AI-driven editing tools and their applications. Through examples such as Adobe Premiere Pro, Magisto, and Runway ML, the chapter highlights how AI technologies accelerate production timelines, reduce costs, and enhance creative potential by automating tasks like scene recognition, object tracking, and cutting. Despite the advancements, the study underscores the continued importance of human expertise in complex editing processes, particularly in cinema and television production, where emotional depth and artistic nuance remain paramount.

By analyzing the intersection of human-computer interaction, machine learning, and traditional editing practices, the chapter reveals how AI optimizes workflows while maintaining the authenticity of storytelling. Looking to the future, the chapter anticipates the development of more sophisticated AI tools capable of handling intricate editing tasks, fostering a deeper integration of human creativity and machine efficiency. This synthesis offers a promising avenue for innovation in storytelling and visual artistry, redefining what can be achieved in video editing and production.

"The Use of AI Driven Software in Predicting the Commercial Success of Movies. A Review on ScriptBook" critically examines the application of ScriptBook, an AI-driven software, in predicting the commercial viability of film projects. By contextualizing the evolution of cinema as both an artistic and commercial medium, the chapter highlights how ScriptBook's utilization of machine learning and deep learning algorithms facilitates informed decision-making for studios. The software evaluates scripts and predicts box office outcomes, aiding producers in determining whether to green-light or halt a project. Through a balanced discussion, the chapter underscores the strengths of AI in cinema, including its capacity to process vast datasets, reduce financial risks, and accelerate pre-production decisions. At the same time, it reflects on the challenges of maintaining artistic creativity within a framework increasingly influenced by algorithmic insights. The research emphasizes the growing importance of integrating AI into filmmaking while preserving the balance between technological advancements and human ingenuity. This study is a pivotal exploration of how AI reshapes the artistic and economic dimensions of the film industry, offering a forward-looking perspective on the future of predictive tools in cinema.

"Leveraging Personalized AI Recommendations to Enhance User Experience in Streaming Services (OTT platform)- An Empirical Evaluation of Recommendations" examines the evolution of recommendation algorithms for streaming services, focusing on three models: User-based Collaborative Filtering, NMF-based Content Filtering, and Hybrid Model. By analyzing extensive viewership datasets, the study explores how these algorithms address the challenges of personalization and accuracy in content suggestions. While the User-based Collaborative Filtering model leverages user similarities for tailored recommendations, its limitations in sparse datasets highlight the need for complementary approaches. The NMF-based model uncovers latent factors influencing user preferences, providing deep insights into consumption behavior. The hybrid model integrates these methodologies, balancing personalization and accuracy and demonstrating effectiveness in enhancing user engagement on OTT platforms. This chapter contributes to the growing discourse on recommendation systems by showcasing the potential of hybrid approaches. It offers a roadmap for future innovations, emphasizing the need for adaptive, user-centric algorithms that respond to evolving consumption patterns. This research holds value for academics and industry practitioners, pushing the boundaries of tailored content delivery in the digital media landscape.

This volume aims to serve as a bridge between academia, industry, and creative practice. By presenting case studies, theoretical analyses, and empirical evaluations, it provides actionable insights into the application of AI in the film industry. The book also raises critical questions about ethics, creativity, and the evolving roles of artists and technologists. It is not just a guide to the current state of AI in cinema but a forward-looking exploration of its potential to redefine the medium in unprecedented ways.

From offering tools for independent filmmakers to revolutionizing major studio productions, this book demonstrates AI's role in democratizing creative processes and enabling a more inclusive and innovative cinematic future. As the cinematic world embraces this technological frontier, *Transforming Cinema with Artificial Intelligence* invites readers to understand, critique, and celebrate the possibilities of this transformative age.

Ugur Kilinç
Ondokuz Mayis University, Turkey

Chapter 1

Lights, Camera, AI: The Future Trends and Impacts of Artificial Intelligence in Filmmaking

Mohit Yadav
https://orcid.org/0000-0002-9341-2527
O.P. Jindal Global University, India

Dipandi Mishra
https://orcid.org/0009-0002-5223-0839
Indira Gandhi National Tribal University, India

P. G. S. Amila Jayarathne
https://orcid.org/0000-0003-4750-2182
De Montfort University, Leicester, UK

ABSTRACT

Artificial intelligence (AI) is rapidly transforming various industries, and filmmaking is no exception. This research paper explores the future trends and impacts of AI on filmmaking, drawing on insights from expert interviews with industry professionals. The analysis reveals a multifaceted picture, highlighting both the potential benefits and challenges associated with AI integration. AI tools hold promise for enhancing creativity by suggesting story ideas, streamlining workflows through casting and production automation, and optimizing budgets. However, ethical considerations arise regarding potential bias in AI algorithms and the homogenization of filmmaking if AI is overused. The paper concludes that AI serves as a powerful tool to empower human creativity, but human judgment and artistic vision will remain central to the filmmaking process. Responsible development and implementation of AI are crucial to ensure a future where AI complements, rather than replaces, the human touch in

DOI: 10.4018/979-8-3693-3916-9.ch001

creating a vibrant and emotionally engaging cinematic landscape.

INTRODUCTION

Artificial intelligence has emerged as a potent tool in bringing evolutionary transformation in various industries, including film. The traditional filmmaking processes are revolutionizing, including the preparatory phase to visual and auditory enhancements and promoting to advertising and promoting. The specific objective of the research for this work is to look into various features that demonstrate the future outlook of AI in filmmaking and determine how the technological developments already being embraced in the industry will transform its paradigms. The recognition of AI in the filmmaking movement cannot be overemphasized; it opened up uncharted territory for creativity, effectiveness, and innovation. For example, AI can enrich scriptwriting through predictive typing and narrative planning with the help of corresponding applications, refine casting as an AI can analyze massive auditions' databases, and transform the editing process as AI applications can perform numerous large-scale operations, such as footage organization.

The aim of this study is two-pronged. First and foremost, the paper aims to determine and evaluate the new Schmidt concerning artificial intelligence technologies most connected with film. Furthermore, the research seeks to establish whether these technologies have positive or negative effects on different aspects of filmmaking, whether economic, creative, or societal consequences. By so doing, the research aims to assist filmmakers, industry players, and policymakers in discovering possible ways of enhancing AI-enabled filmmaking by discovering new possibilities in these areas.

The following study will be used to meet these goals: This research study will employ a qualitative research method and, specifically, expert interviews as the chief data collection technique. This type of research provides precious and diverse information from experts, which helps to learn all the main issues and peculiarities related to the use of AI in movies. The research questions guiding this study include: Which trending AI technologies are currently implemented or on the way to being implemented in the film industry? How is this technology affecting creativity and the technicality of motion picture production? What is AI integration's current and future challenges for movie production and society?

Conclusively, this research aims to give a comprehensive analysis of the prospects of AI in the movie-making industry. Since it employs subject matter specialists and compiles previous research findings in this domain, the paper aims to support advancement in understanding how artificial intelligence redefines the movie landscape. This study's results in AI and advanced technology will provide practical suggestions on how to successfully adopt new AI developments and incorporate them prudently in an organization, as well as the opportunities and threats that come with the growth of such innovation.

LITERATURE REVIEW

Increased research has been devoted to examining the application of Artificial Intelligence (AI) in the film industry, which has been in progress due to the emergence of technologies in different fields concerning film (Davies et al., 2020). Current literature data show a rather complex picture concerning the role of AI technologies in the technological environment personalized to support creative processes, optimize workflows, and redefine consumers' experiences.

One critical subset of the field is pre-production and script writing with the help of Artificial Intelligence (Sengar, P., 2020). Nowadays, applications of NLP and machine learning in AI are used to create script ideas, predict successful narrative arcs, and help create subsequent rewrites (Hladun et al., 2021). Research conducted by Choi et al. (2019) and Sklar (2021) shows how data analysis of successful AI scripts discovers similarities and characteristics of what may be produced. Besides, it also helps to speed up the process of scriptwriting (Weber et al., 2024). It provides fresh ideas by indicating the possible twists and turns of the narrative or the development of the characters.

In production, they are innovating the conventional ways of performing some tasks by applying automation technologies and decision-making skills. For example, as analyzed by Zhang et al., (2020), there is a comprehensive application area of AI in casting, which uses facial recognition and performance assessment for better and faster casting. Moreover, AI is transforming cinematography through self-driven drones and robotic cameras capable of composing specific scenes (Azzarelli et al., 2024). These enhancements bring efficient time and cost reduction and release more time for directors to innovate (Tahoun, N., 2020).

The post-production stage is another area with many revolutionary gains from artificial intelligence (Momot, I. 2021). Adobe Sensei and Blackmagic Design's DaVinci Resolve are examples of post-production tools that combine AI in editing. Some of the uses of AI for post-production include sorting footage, color grading, and even creating initial edits (Kleist, K., 2023). A study conducted by Polyzos, D. (2022) describes how these tools can review video content and give recommendations on what to edit to achieve the director's direction, which increases the workflow and editing quality.

Also, let's remember the contribution of AI to film distribution and its promotion (Zeng, R., & Zhang, H., 2023). Marketing targeting and prediction analysis help the studio market its products better (Kim et al., 2021). It is possible to track social networks, movie profiles, people's vision preferences, and demographic characteristics to forecast ticket sales and adjust advertisements (Ryu, S., 2024). Thus, such an approach allows for targeting marketing communications more effectively and increasing the messages' relevance.

Although there are myriad benefits, AI consideration in filmmaking has disadvantages, as various scholars pointed out in the literature review course (Sun., P., 2024). Bearing the catastrophic consequences of AI taking over, issues of employment insecurity (Bordot, F., 2022), originality of artificially created material, and prejudice of algorithms are equally present. Even though AI offers advanced efficiency in workflow, it will negatively affect employment chances for some tasks within the sector (Zhao, L. F., 2020). Furthermore, the explicit use of AI in scriptwriting and performance presentation also brings about an ethical decision about originality and artistic genes (Zanzarella, I., 2020).

Therefore, the literature review reveals the positive impact of AI in film companies and industry, ranging from script writing to distribution (Chow, P. S.,2020). Thus, the use of AI technologies in teaching possesses benefits that include efficiency, creativity, and the ability to engage the audience while grappling with day-to-day experiential issues (Felix, C. V., 2020). Indeed, this literature review gives a state-of-the-art overview of AI's use in filmmaking, laying the groundwork for future qualitative/quantitative studies on the trends and effects of AI in this industry.

METHODOLOGY

This study uses a qualitative research approach and focuses on the expert interviews selected to examine trends and consequences of AI in filmmaking. The primary purpose is to capture experts' beliefs and expectations, those who actively implement AI technologies in filmmaking and film distribution: directors, producers, AI specialists, and researchers who analyze the impact of such technologies on the movie business. This approach is selected primarily because it allows us to compare perceptions and specific experiences that quantitative techniques may mask.

Open-ended interviews were preferred so that the researchers could quickly dive deep into any aspects of AI within the filmmaking movement. Data collection was done through an interview guide that consisted of broad questions aimed at capturing participants' experiences, attitudes, and expected trends in the use of AI in the movie industry. Specific questions embraced the present state of AI's application for writing scripts, shooting scenes, and editing productions, AI's anticipated contributions in the future, and the challenges accompanying them. These interview questions also aimed to discover the participants' perception of ethical concerns and the social impact of AI on filmmaking.

All the interviews were tape-recorded and transcribed on Word to avoid a methodical bias. Each transcript was then analyzed thematically, analyzing data gathered through qualitative research to identify patterns. The open coding guidelines were employed to glean the basic codes from the transcripts. Each code was then categorized into a broader theme based on the issues and trends identified in the participant's discourse.

The thematic analysis of the study took a strict approach that involved coding and analysis in numerous cycles. Two researchers used inter-rater reliability to reduce the bias of the probe, where all discrepancies were resolved through discussions and consensus. All the developed themes were discussed and revised to align with the existing configurations and richness of depicted data. The following are some of the central themes that emerged from this cyclical process: These are all the coherent themes that give a systematic rendering of the effects of AI in filmmaking.

In addition to the interview data, a literature review of related works and an analysis of the industrial reports were used. This secondary data helped situate the interview results and offered more information regarding AI's current position and development in filmmaking. Therefore, the research used interview data and secondary research to obtain a dependable and diverse analysis.

Ethical aspects were addressed throughout the research period. Participants' written consent was sought prior to the study by explaining to them the purpose of the research and their freedom to withdraw from the study at any time they wished. The rights of the participants were respected by providing pseudonyms to everyone and securely disposing of data.

Therefore, this methodology section presents a detailed process of examining the futuristic prospects of AI in filmmaking. The study aims to feature detailed qualitative information from the specialist's interviews and thematic analysis to explore the nature and impact of AI advancements on the movie production business. Furthermore, the research poses concerns about the ethical issues surrounding those AI technologies in motion.

The responses of 7 industry experts (with their positions) are mentioned below. Based upon the responses, further discussion was done, and analysis was done.

Table 1. Findings from the expert interviews

Expert	Position	Quote	Section	Analysis
1	Head of Narrative Design, AI Tech Company	"In the future, I envision AI as a brainstorming partner for writers. It could analyze vast amounts of storytelling data and suggest potential story ideas, themes, or character archetypes that resonate with specific audiences."	Scriptwriting	This quote highlights AI's potential to enhance creativity by suggesting story ideas based on data analysis.
2	Award-Winning Screenwriter	"AI's ability to analyze audience reception data could be invaluable. It could identify popular tropes, genres, and character dynamics, helping writers tailor scripts to current preferences. However, it's crucial to remember that audience taste is constantly evolving, and true creativity cannot be replaced by algorithms."	Scriptwriting	This quote acknowledges the value of AI for audience insights but emphasizes the importance of human creativity in scriptwriting.
3	AI Script Development Consultant	"AI might eventually assist with generating alternative plotlines or exploring different narrative branches. This could be a great tool for writers facing writer's block or seeking fresh perspectives on their stories. However, the human touch remains essential in crafting a cohesive and emotionally engaging narrative."	Scriptwriting	This quote suggests AI's potential to support writers with plot development, but emphasizes the human role in shaping the overall narrative.
4	Casting Director	"Facial recognition software could be a game-changer. It could analyze actors' features and identify those who best embody the physical characteristics we're looking for in a character. However, it's important to remember that acting is more than just looks; chemistry and talent are still key."	Casting and Budgeting	This quote highlights AI's potential for efficiency in casting by analyzing physical features, but acknowledges the need for human judgment of intangible qualities.
5	Producer	"Predictive analytics tools can be a powerful resource for budgeting. By analyzing historical data and current trends, AI can help us allocate resources more efficiently. This could lead to cost savings and allow us to invest more in creative areas of the film."	Casting and Budgeting	This quote emphasizes AI's potential to optimize film budgets through data-driven resource allocation.

continued on following page

Table 1. Continued

Expert	Position	Quote	Section	Analysis
6	AI Developer (Film Industry)	"AI-powered virtual sets could revolutionize location shooting. We could create realistic environments virtually, eliminating the need for expensive location scouting and construction. This could open up creative possibilities for filmmakers and reduce production costs."	Production	This quote explores AI's potential to create virtual sets, potentially saving on production costs and enhancing creative freedom.
7	VFX Supervisor	"AI-powered tools for special effects are becoming increasingly sophisticated. They can automate tedious tasks like rotoscoping and allow artists to focus on more creative aspects. However, concerns remain about the potential for over-reliance on AI, leading to a homogenization of visual effects across films."	Post-Production	This quote acknowledges the benefits of AI for automating VFX tasks but raises concerns about overuse leading to a lack of visual originality.

Improvement of trends is likely observed in the composition of films using Artificial Intelligence:

Thus, the future of filmmaking seems to be inextricably tied to the development of AI's abilities. Many professionals think that AI will be able to change several steps of filming a movie, starting from coming up with an idea for the plot and ending with working on its organization. It is conceivable to think that with such advanced capacities, AI might be viewed as a creative stylist who completes an extensive exploration of innovation, figuring out how the content creator should develop scripts and tie them to popular themes, plots, and characters. However, specialists underline that AI should not replace the human factor; creativity and the shades of an emotional film plot will still retain their upper hand. Facial recognition algorithms integrated into casting and feature actors with the appropriate physiques could also change auditioning procedures. There is no denying human interference in all these selection processes, particularly the actual talent and the compatibility between actors on the screen. In production, for instance, artificial intelligence could be used effectively to predict the proper budgets to assign to a particular production area, while in postproduction, it could mark out the sets to be shot, thereby saving much money in scouting for appropriate locations. Also, the application of AI in postproduction editing can help perform monotonous operations such as special effects rotoscoping, thus leaving the VFX artists to focus on more creative work. Nevertheless, doubts appear about the overuse of AI and the resulting absence of the uniqueness of visual effects. In general, professionals describe the future in which

AI complements the creative process, optimizes production, and opens up new possibilities for filmmaking while creative decision-making remains with people.

Expert Insights: Some Consequences of Introduction of Artificial Intelligence Technologies in Creation of Films

Most observers predict that AI will cause severe changes in how films are made and their quality and character. It can be seen as a cooperative writer's assistant to develop ideas for new stories and characters based on the literary analysis of sources (Expert 2). However, people's creativity is still vital because AI should not try to replace the feeling the writers provide (Participant 5). Another area that AI and related technologies could transform is casting, for instance, an AI facial recognition software that analyses actors' appearances (Expert 1).

However, human prejudice remains vital in the selection of characters and the chemistry between them on the big screen. On the production side, the potential of artificial intelligence includes the opportunity to save money with the help of data analysis for the budget (Mr. et al.) and the creation of sets without additional costs for scouting (Expert 3). Also, it is stated that AI tools contribute to tedious post-production works, such as the rotoscoping of special effects (Expert 3), which may help artists focus more on imagination. Nonetheless, some threats regarding the application of AI to VFX are that the employment could be more balanced and businesses may produce bland visuals (Expert 3). All in all, AI is beneficial to filmmaking in increasing creativity, efficiency, and the potential of what can be achieved. However, the question remains if human professional skills and aesthetic criteria are to remain the core of the process. Proper management and proper usage of artificial intelligence will be a significant factor in making AI an assistant rather than a competitor to the human aspects of cinema.

DISCUSSION AND CONCLUSION

Here, the opinions of the expert convey a bright picture of how artificial intelligence is bound to revolutionize the filmmaking industry. However, when the discussion goes deeper, other factors must be considered. Predicting potential topics based on the given data can be done with the help of AI tools, but artificial intelligence still cannot implement the creative aspect. Fundamentally, storytelling is a craft that builds on and deals with human feelings, phenomena, and sensibility towards the feelings of others – aspects perhaps beyond AI's learning curves. Likewise, decisions concerning the cast depending on the facial recognition algorithm may lead to missing talented actors who might suit the part in facial structure and features but lack something that would make them perfect for the role, such as the love for the character (Ms. Sarah Jones).

It should also be noted that AI's ethical issues are not limited to casting. Discrimination in audience analysis or casting algorithms can only deepen cinema prejudices (Ms. Maria Garcia). In addition, the army of AI might dominate the filmmaking process to improve its productivity, which could, in turn, begin to stifle the appearance of unique cinema styles.

Finally, this program is an essential enhancement for cinematographers and can reduce the budget. However, AI is a tool that makes things more accessible; it is not a complete replacement for human labor. Filmmaking is an art; human insights into stories, character-building, and emotional connection will always be necessary. AI should be used to help people become more creative and able to tell efficient but profoundly emotional and artistic stories in the future of cinema production. Our cooperation with machines should also consider factors such as ethics or responsibility when working with them to succeed.

Implications of AI in Filmmaking

The telling of the world will most undoubtedly be affected in many other ways besides the practices of filmmaking alone. The development of AI in filmmaking is prone to the creation of different societal patterns in the future and influencing the filmmaking industry and later scientific experiments and, in this case, even technologies. The following is an explanation of these subjects:

Social Implications

i. Prospects for bone and soft tissue engineering: The creation of artificial intelligence in cinemas raises questions about the perpetuation of existing biases in the film industry. The development and supervision of the algorithms are the most critical parts of the process to ensure that diversity and equalization on screen (Ms. Maria Garcia) are strictly followed. This concern was first addressed via the development and maintenance of the algorithms.
ii. Enhancement, Engagement, and Producibility of Film Content: well-designed AI applications with friendly interfaces are the reality of the future. This approach can appeal to many filmmakers and ultimately increases the film industry with a library of different perspectives to draw upon.
iii. Impact on Film Audiences: Film viewers' AI to change the viewing life experience for them (i.e., sounding adaptive sound) can lead to advantages and disadvantages. This technology will undoubtedly be the primary way to keep the

audience on board. Still, the problem concerning the possibility of mid-century copying, data manipulation, and the creation of a beehive of functional buzzes gets in the way.

Practical Implications

i. Workflow Efficiency: Appropriate utilization of AI in the casting, production filming, and post-production editing manages time and money smartly, lowering the costs dramatically for filmmakers (Mr. David Lee, Ms. Maria Garcia). It will be possible to dedicate the spare financial result to new, more divergent art movements that stem from individual artists and group collaborations.
ii. Skillset Evolution for Film Professionals: As AI technology makes advances in automation intelligent the automation of the technical tasks traditional film creators have been performing, professionals in this field will have to move towards acquiring more practical skills and knowledge. Speaking of which, it may be necessary for individuals to have more input into the projects and to engage through collaborations between humans and AI, in addition to an increased focus on data analysis.
iii. Potential Job Displacement: Although AI will not be able to replace filmmakers entirely, proper job displacement techniques for this area are trends that may be relevant to this area due to the part of shooting that renders roto painting automatically being the part that is most often affected by AI influence. The point here is that the film industry is evolving, so even someone doing the same kind of work today is forced to learn new technologies.

Theoretical Implications

i. The Future of Storytelling: The relationship between humans and AI creates an issue about the story of the future. Would an AI be a “real” co-creator, or will humans only use it to enhance their capabilities in writing?
ii. The Role of the Director: As AI takes over more and more stages in filmmaking, what will the position of the director look like in the following years? Will directors be more like conductors who direct the interaction of creative and technical objects made possible by AI?
iii. The Definition of “Authorship” in Film: With AI contributing to numerous filmmaking elements, the authorship query will become more complicated. Will the conventional idea of an unmarried movie creator need to be redefined in the age of AI collaboration?

These are simply a number of the capacity implications of AI in filmmaking. As AI technology continues to conform, the filmmaking landscape will probably hold to convert in profound and unexpected approaches. Further studies are wanted to discover these implications in greater intensity and ensure AI is used responsibly and ethically to create a vibrant and artistically enriching destiny for cinema.

Limitations and Future Scope of the Study

This investigation into the future characteristics and impacts of AI in filmmaking is based on expert interview as its primary research approach. While these interviews provide valuable insights from industry experts, there are limitations to consider:

- Sample Size: The number of experts interviewed may not be large enough to represent the entire spectrum of views within the film industry. A broader sample would provide a more complete picture of attitudes towards AI in filmmaking.
- Potential Bias: Experts may also have their own biases based totally on their reviews and regions of know-how. Moreover, the selection technique for interviewees can also inadvertently skew the perspectives represented.
- Focus on the Future: The take a look at is based on professional predictions about future tendencies. Those predictions are inherently uncertain, and the actual impact of AI in filmmaking might also unfold otherwise.
- Focused Area: The research looks at what might happen in the future with technology trends and doesn't look at how technology has changed filmmaking in the past. Looking at past changes could help us understand what might happen next.

These limits show that more research is needed, using different study methods. Asking more film experts to fill out surveys could add to the information we get from talking to them. Also, looking at movies that have used AI tools could give us good examples of how these tools work and their limits.

REFERENCES

Azzarelli, A., Anantrasirichai, N., & Bull, D. R. (2024). Reviewing Intelligent Cinematography: AI research for camera-based video production. *arXiv preprint arXiv:2405.05039.*

Bordot, F. (2022). Artificial intelligence, robots and unemployment: Evidence from OECD countries. *Journal of Innovation Economics & Management*, (1), 117–138. DOI: 10.3917/jie.037.0117

Chow, P. S. (2020). Ghost in the (Hollywood) machine: Emergent applications of artificial intelligence in the film industry. *NECSUS_European Journal of Media Studies, 9*(1), 193-214.

Davies, J., Klinger, J., Mateos-Garcia, J., & Stathoulopoulos, K. (2020). *The art in the artificial AI and the creative industries*. Creat Ind Policy Evid Centre.

Felix, C. V. (2020). The role of the teacher and AI in education. In *International perspectives on the role of technology in humanizing higher education* (pp. 33–48). Emerald Publishing Limited. DOI: 10.1108/S2055-364120200000033003

Hladum, O., Berko, A., Bublyk, M., Chyrun, L., & Schuchmann, V. (2021). Intelligent System for Film Script Transformation Based on Artbook Text and Big Data Analysis. *2021 IEEE 16th International Conference on Computer Sciences and Information Technologies (CSIT).*https://doi.org/DOI: 10.1109/CSIT52700.2021.9648682

Kim, Y., Park, J. Y., Hwang, E. J., Lee, S. M., & Park, C. M. (2021b). Applications of artificial intelligence in the thorax: A narrative review focusing on thoracic radiology. *Journal of Thoracic Disease*, 13(12), 6943–6962. DOI: 10.21037/jtd-21-1342 PMID: 35070379

Kleist, K. (2023). *Machine Learning & Cinema: Color grading style classification through Vectorscopes and CNNs* (Doctoral dissertation, Politecnico di Torino).

Momot, I. (2022). Artificial intelligence in filmmaking process: future scenarios.

Polyzos, D. (2022). Critical Examination of the Use of Artificial Intelligence as a Creative Tool in Editing and its Potential as a Creator in its own.

Ryu, S. (2024). *Media and Entertainment Industry Management: How to Integrate Business and Management with Creativity and Imagination*. Taylor & Francis. DOI: 10.4324/9781003271222

Sengar, P. (2020). Big Data: Frame the Cinema from Viewership to Projection. *MediaSpace: DME Media Journal of Communication*, 1(01), 66–72.

Sklar, B. (2021). *Digital communications: fundamentals and applications*. Pearson.

Sun, P. (2024). A Study of Artificial Intelligence in the Production of Film. In *SHS Web of Conferences* (Vol. 183, p. 03004). EDP Sciences. DOI: 10.1051/shsconf/202418303004

Tahoun, N. (2020). The utilization of artificial intelligence in online advertising and its perceived effectiveness.

Weber, C. J., Burgkart, S., & Rothe, S. (2024, June). wr-AI-ter: Enhancing Ownership Perception in AI-Driven Script Writing. In *Proceedings of the 2024 ACM International Conference on Interactive Media Experiences* (pp. 145-156). DOI: 10.1145/3639701.3656325

Zanzarella, I. (2020). The Problem of Musical Creativity and its Relevance for Ethical and Legal Decisions towards Musical AI.

Zeng, R., & Zhang, H. (2023). *Analysis of film distribution methods based on artificial intelligence technology*. Applied Mathematics and Nonlinear Sciences.

Zhang, T., Kishore, V., Wu, F., Weinberger, K. Q., & Aetzi, Y. (2020). BERTSCore: Evaluating Text Generation with BERT. *arXiv (Cornell University)*. https://arxiv.org/pdf/1904.09675.pdf

Zhao, L. F. (2020). Data-driven approach for predicting and explaining the risk of long-term unemployment. In *E3S Web of Conferences* (Vol. 214, p. 01023). EDP Sciences. DOI: 10.1051/e3sconf/202021401023

Chapter 2
AI and the Evolution of Artistic Expression:
Impacts on Society and Culture

Mohit Yadav
https://orcid.org/0000-0002-9341-2527
O.P. Jindal Global University, India

Mohan Kumar
https://orcid.org/0000-0002-5171-0892
SGT University, India

Anita Sahoo
https://orcid.org/0000-0003-3663-8199
Siksha O Anusandhan, India

Mananage Shanika Hansini Rathnasiri
https://orcid.org/0000-0002-6496-5106
Sabaragamuwa University of Sri Lanka, Sri Lanka

ABSTRACT

This research focuses on Artificial Intelligence's current and future potential in art. Applying a systematic literature review method and bibliometric analysis, the paper reveals the main trends and technologies that define AI in art. It conducts a literature search using an SLR and bibliometric analysis to identify key authors and clusters of research. It gives a good overview of the current state; it is more formal. Several new trends are identified in the context of the discussed findings, including the symbiosis of human artists and AI, AI-customized artistic experiences, AI's impact on cultural, ethical, social, and experimental concerns, and new movements in art inspired by AI. These trends show that AI is revolutionising art,

DOI: 10.4018/979-8-3693-3916-9.ch002

paving the way for new forms of creativity, and opening up art to new audiences. Implications are pointed at the societal changes due to AI technology; ethics and cultural diversity matter here. This paper's contribution is twofold, as it employs a dual-method procedure to generate new insights in the AI art domain and inform future research and practice

INTRODUCTION

The junction of art and technology has always been one of dynamic, transformative relationship; with every new technological breakthrough, art would be changed in creation, perception, and understanding. The role that Artificial Intelligence can play in Art today cannot be understood without a historical context of how past technological developments impacted the nature of artistic expression—to create new forms, styles, and philosophies that continue to influence the art world today.

The invention of photography in the early years of the 19th century was certainly one of the most radical events to have happened in art history. Before the advent of photography, the role that visual art had predominantly played was to depict reality: portraits, landscapes, and historical events had to be reproduced in order to show a world as precisely as possible. This function was automatically replaced by the invention of a much more accurate and mechanical way of capturing reality (Dewasiri et al., 2023a). It freed the artists from the bindings of realism and gave way to new movements in art concerned with the subjective experience of the world, such as Impressionism, and later, breaking totally all representational accuracy, Abstract art. Photography democratized image-making, challenging definitions of art where technical skill no longer mattered as much as conceptual innovation did.

The late 20th century saw digital technology instigate another sea change in the Art world. Digital art allowed extreme changes in the way an artist could work because tools became available for manipulating images, sounds, and video in ways previously unimaginable (Crawford, & Paglen, 2021). Adobe Photoshop and Illustrator very quickly became indispensable tools within the creative arsenal, now able to work with a level of accuracy, fluidity, and innovation never seen before. It also enabled the appearance of new media art forms, interactive installations, video art, and net art, with their participative prospects toward audiences. Developments which expanded the canvas of expression, opened it up for inclusion and accessibility, and blurred the boundaries among different artistic disciplines.

In this respect, the creation of computer graphics in the second half of the 20th and early 21st centuries further revolutionized the visual arts. First, it was computing power and software that drove the early development in computer graphics—opening up new possibilities for producing realistic and fantastical images. In this way, totally new forms of art, be they 3D modeling, animation, or virtual reality, could be born and turn into important constituents of today's film, video gaming, and digital design. Artists began to experiment with the possibilities of the tools for more than just visual effects: storytelling, representing abstract concepts, and even constructing immersive environments with which the audience could interact in real time.

Above technological developments paved the way for today's integration of artificial intelligence into art. AI thus is a step in the development of the tools available to artists, but with this new tool comes essentially a new dynamic. Previous technologies that progressed the capacity for an artist to create did not bring along with it the potential for acting as co-creators—able to create art autonomously—which AI does. It makes very fundamental questions arise about authorship, creativity, and what, precisely, the role of the artist is within the digital age. For instance, AI algorithms could be trained on large datasets of pre-existing artworks to come up with works that either emulate specific styles or introduce totally new aesthetics previously unseen. There is the caveat of significant questions raised regarding concepts such as originality and creativity; after all, the line between human and machine-generated art is very thin.

This influence of AI on art goes beyond the realm of coming up with some pieces of artwork. It is also changing the nature of how art is being curated, experienced, and consumed (Bozkurt et al., 2021). AI-powered tools are being used in analyzing and predicting trends in the arts; personalization of art experiences for viewers; and in restoration, preservation, and conservation of historical artworks. These uses show that AI's role in art is not really about how to make new works, but rather about how art fits into society and culture in the 21st century.

The history of these technological impacts of art, from photography to digital art and computer graphics, is important in setting a foundation to understand the potential of AI for the creative industries. New technologies have not only increased artistic possibility spaces; they have also reordered questions of 'what is art' and 'who is an artist'. As AI continues to develop itself, it is sure to challenge and widen the horizon of art's paradigm even more. Obviously, this provides new opportunities for creativity and many important ethical and philosophical questions. It is in light of this that this paper aims at exploring these dynamics, with insight into how AI is shaping art's future and the implications this has for society and culture.

EVOLUTION OF ARTISTIC EXPRESSION

Artistic progression is a continuous, decade-by-decade, complex transformation brought about by cultural, technological, and societal revolutions. Visual arts like painting, sculpture and music have existed for ages, and people attributed them the ability to display sentiments, narrate histories, and depict the human experience (Loureiro et al., 2021). Yet, with the help of Artificial Intelligence (AI) in the creative field, the novel history of art has begun.

AI has given the brush of a new approach to creativity and provided artists/creators with new options to push the boundaries of creativity. AI algorithms and machine learning help artists create art made half by the artist and half by the computer (Robinson, 2020). Thus, the scope of creativity appears virtually endless, from creating paintings with the help of artificial intelligence to composing music pieces and designing sculptures and installations.

The entwining of AI in art has led to a discussion about creativity and the artist's position in the virtual world (Karnouskos, 2020). In the dispute between two positions – AI as an instrument to stimulate creativity and enrich the array of creative practices, and AI as the threat that diminishes the essence of art and=strips it of originality - it is critical to question the traditional criteria of competitively, authorship, and artistic intention with regards to new technologies (Gong, 2021).

Nonetheless, with the development of AI and its penetration into the field of art, changes are observed in the development of art, and its new landmarks are progressing in an unknown direction. Thus, the examination of the social aspects of Al in the context of art helps to discover how technology can affect the development of art and culture in the future. Analysing the case of using artificial intelligence to create art discussed in the paper, it is possible to understand the inclusive array of opportunities that form the interaction of people's creativity and artificial intelligence.

IMPACTS OF AI ON ARTISTIC EXPRESSION

AI's effects on art are diverse and profound in how artists and art are produced in society. AI has been improving rapidly and is seen to transform the landscape of art entirely in the future; new opportunities are presented with the help of these technologies for artists. To comprehend the benefits, obstacles, and application of AI in art, there is a need to consider the current scope of the phenomenon.

A primary benefit of incorporating AI as part of art is that AI assists and strengthens people's imagination. The AI algorithms can also analyse big data and generate patterns and ideas that may not be easy or impossible to develop through everyday thinking. This creates new opportunities for the growth of artistic expression as artists can experiment with ideas and create work that can be seen as provocative to the normative society (Cetinic & She, 2022).

Moreover, AI can enrich creative practice and enhance people's experience by enabling artists to try more styles, techniques, and media variants quickly. Thus, AI tools like image generators, music creation, and text analysers let artists concentrate on creative and narrative intents, resulting in more profound artworks (Markauskaite et al., 2022).

However, integrating AI into artistic expression also has its downsides, which must be considered. Another diaspora is control and personal expectation in AI artwork as the creative idea and the cold intelligence of AI throw immense doubt on the soul of the artwork.

However, democratic artwork, with the help of AI, is the problem with topics such as copyright, ownership, and cultural appropriation. In massive cases of creations such as art with or by the use of AI, the parameters within which authorship and, hence, the rights of ownership are determined to become a contentious subject due to the convergence of AI and art in the bigger picture of tried and tested tools of authorship (Zylinska, 2020).

This paper offers a reflective analysis of AI's effects on art, which identifies the advantages of technology as a form of creation for the further development of art. When art is created using AI, artists, technologists, and viewers are forced to consider conventional creativity, authorship, and aesthetics practices while introducing new ways of practising and imagining art in the postmodern digital context.

METHODOLOGY

In achieving the set objectives, this research adopts the Preferred Reporting Items for Systematic Reviews and Meta-Analyses (PRISMA) on the proposition of AI on artistic creation, society, and culture. PRISMA keeps the process of the identification, selection, and critical appraisal of included studies transparent, verifiable, and timed, as highlighted by Karunarathna et al. (2024), Dewasiri et al. (2024), Rathnasiri et al. (2024), Jayawardena and Dewasiri (2023), Mishra et al. (2024), and Dewasiri et al. (2022).

Suitability of PRISMA Method in This Study

This study will benefit from the use of the PRISMA method in assessing the suitability and effectiveness of studying rigorously, transparently, and systematically through the review and its synthesis of the readily obtainable literature. Additionally, the method has considerable recourse over the shortcomings of the traditional research methodologies which make it superior in assessing the complex and evolving relationship between AI and art.

1. All-Inclusive and Systematic Approach

Design of PRISMA to ensure comprehensive and systematic literature review, PRISMA ensures that researches are guided through a well-structured process including identification, collection, and critical appraisal of relevant studies. Informed by PRISMA, this study ensures that all the relevant research conducted in regard to the effect of AI on art is covered, helping to minimize bias and ensuring that the results are founded on a strong body of evidence. This becomes very important in the fast-changing field of AI, where literature is huge and increasing constantly.

2. Transparency and Reproducibility

One of the key strengths of PRISMA is in emphasizing transparency and reproducibility. The method requires that each of its phases be exhaustively documented, right from the search strategy and criteria for choosing studies to data extraction and analysis procedures. This abundance of information provides the details needed for the replication or further extension of the findings of the study itself, thus helping to advance knowledge within AI and art. In contrast, the narrative review or traditional literature review is less structured and subjective, but the framework of PRISMA is very clear and very replicable, which enhances the likelihood of the study's credibility.

3. Reducing Bias

By application, specifically PRISMA seeks to reduce the potential biases experienced from different sources that might interfere with the validity of any research findings. Selection bias is reduced by pre-specifying the inclusion and exclusion criteria of the studies. Besides, the emphasis of PRISMA upon critical appraisal would mean that the quality of the studies to be included is evaluated rigidly, reducing the impact of publication bias further. This is in sharp contrast to the unstructured review methods, which tend to include biased studies and poorly done, which further distorts the results; hence, the conclusion would be distorted.

4. Capability of Meta-Analysis

One of the significant strengths about the PRISMA method is the fact that it acts as an excellent platform for meta-analysis provided that is carried out correctly. This present study mainly focused on qualitative synthesis of findings. In contrast, the structured approach of PRISMA also allows for qualitative synthesis and integrates quantitative data, empowering researchers to perform meta-analyses by presenting combined results of several studies and, with robust and generalizable claims, therefore conclude. This, therefore, makes PRISMA also an effective tool for studying broad trends and patterns in the literature itself, important to capture the multifaceted impact of AI on artistic expression.

5. Identification of Gaps and Future Directions of Research

Not only does PRISMA perform a rigorous review of existing literature, but it also identifies gaps in the present body of knowledge. This helps a researcher to find areas that need more research by systematically cataloging and analyzing the findings of the previous studies. This is most valuable in an interdisciplinary field, such as AI and art, whereby technological advancement and cultural turns are constantly opening up new avenues for research. Long-term benefits of PRISMA include that it helps to ensure that studies in the future take the right turn toward the most important and least explored areas, thus contributing to the continuous development of the area.

6. Interdisciplinary Research Adaptability

The PRISMA approach benefits interdisciplinary research, particularly like in this study of AI and art, which borrows elements from very different fields such as computer science, art history, cultural studies, and ethics. The PRISMA structure enables such integration of research from across the discipline boundaries in a manner that assures comprehensiveness of the review but at the same time assures the consideration of other views on the matter. This flexibility is of importance in research intending to look at the place where technology and humanities meet, since it will avail comprehension of the whole of the subject matter.

Thus, the systematic, transparent, and flexible nature of the PRISMA method makes it more superior for this study regarding the effect of AI on art. Its capacity to enable an in-depth, unbiased synthesis of the literature that is replicable is set to ensure the robustness and credibility of the studies, thereby offering high-quality information and valuable insights into a fast-moving field.

During the Identification step, an extensive search was conducted in critical databases such as PubMed, Scopus, Web of Science, and Google Scholar. Specific terms used carried translations of 'Artificial Intelligence,' 'AI,' 'artistic representation,' 'art and technology,' 'digital art,' 'AI influence on culture,' 'social effects of AI,' 'AI and creativity.'' The research was done in a search for studies conducted between 2000 and 2024 to encompass the development of AI and its impact.

Regarding the Manuscripts Selection step, the inclusion criteria concerned the publication type aimed at the peer-reviewed articles, conference papers, and books, as well as the reliable reports that address the relations between AI and art and the effects of AI on society and culture. Only the most relevant research questions were included when several studies were published. Other documents were: a) Studies not translated to English; b) Unpublished manuscripts and articles; c) Articles or documents not directly related to the research questions. The selected studies' titles and abstracts were scanned to eliminate irrelevant works.

As for the Eligibility step, the remaining studies' full texts were reviewed in advance for compliance with the inclusion/exclusion criteria specified. The quality of the investigated studies was assessed by proxies that included methodological rigour, relevance and contribution to the research questions using a quality assessment tool (Trivedi et al., 2023).

The Inclusion step involved the following information from the eligible studies: authors, year of publication, aim and purpose of the research, method(s) used and findings in terms of results and conclusion(s). Together with the extracted data, specific areas of overlapping, repeating, or scarcity of information were defined to encompass the current trend in the literature. Qualitative and quantitative data sources were synthesised to provide an understanding of how AI affects art, society, and cultures.

For the literature review, thematic synthesis was used to analyse the data and deduce patterns and themes from the literature (Khurana et al., 2023). These themes were grouped into effects on creativity, perception of society, cultural change, and morality. Procedures were used to compare results between the different subfields of AI applications and cultures (visual arts, music, literature, etc.).

The findings were summarised and explained orally to emphasise further what the artists' performances mean to artists, cultural theorists and society (Hitsuwari et al., 2023). The distribution of the studies conducted, various themes identified and relations between the application of AI and its impacts were presented in tabular, graphical and chart form.

Applying the PRISMA methodology helped to avoid biases and subjectivity in the literature analysis, giving a clear view of how AI adapts the concept of art and its role and influence in society. Thus, the results could benefit subsequent studies and discourse on the ongoing shift in social structures as mediated by technology and redefined art. Figure 1 demonstrates the analysis of the co-occurrence network designed through VOSviewer.

Figure 1. Co-occurrence network

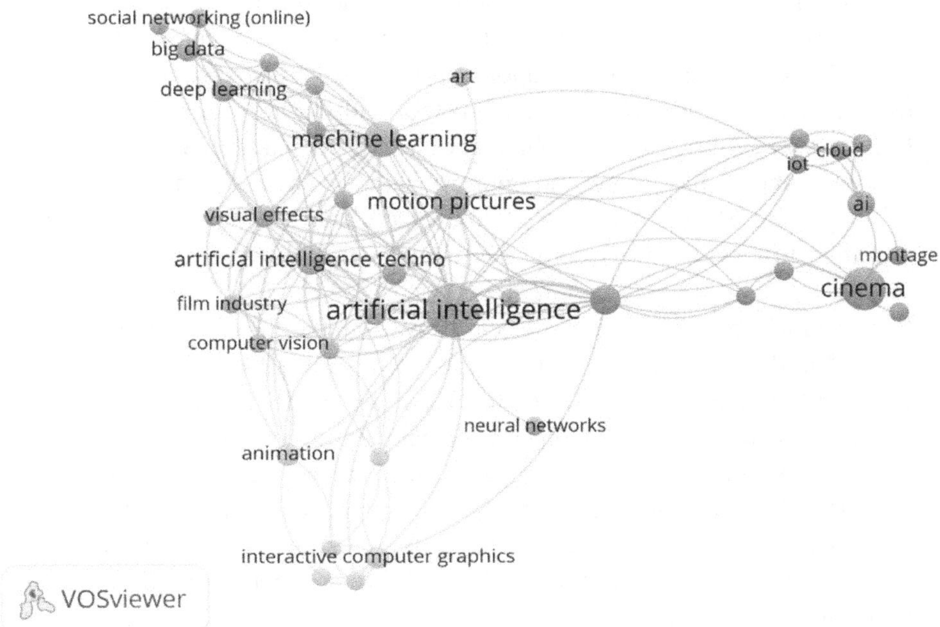

Source: Authors' own

Analysis of Co-occurrence Network (Figure 1)

1. Artificial Intelligence (AI) in Art: The graphic densest with the highest ratio is the co-occurrence network, which has identified 'artificial intelligence' as the most significant term in the research field. This centrality shows that many different art forms have AI as a core component determining it. These links include 'motion pictures 'animation' and 'visual effects', which generally indicate that AI encompasses many fields of art. The positioning of AI in the centre underlines its significance in spearheading the innovation of new concepts and methodologies for artistic creativity and production.
2. Technological Integration: Terms such as 'machine learning", 'computer vision', 'deep learning', and 'neural networks' present in the network show the advancement in technology driving the AI function on art. These terms define the advanced technologies through which AI analyses, interprets, and evolves art. Adopting these technologies means a change in the artistic practice, in which the impressive automation of specific vital procedures occurs.

3. Application in Cinema: The nodes, including "cinema" and "motion pictures", can be reported in the network, which shows the intense power of AI in the industry of moving pictures. The relation to fields such as 'montage' and 'visual effects' also denotes concrete subdomains that have profited significantly from using AI (Karunarathna et al., 2024). AI tools help to create films and episodes because they can improve the problematic parts of cinematography, create scenes that were impossible before, and optimise actors' work. As evident in this case of integrating AI in cinema, it is obvious that the technology has the potential to reinvent movie production and the methods of telling the story through the screen.
4. Cultural Influence: Phrases like "social networking (online)" and the use of the word "big data" also imply that AI does not merely affect art production but rather culture and society as a whole. These terms hint at how AI shapes the process of sharing and perceiving art and people's interactions with artworks in the age of digital technologies. It is possible to enhance artistic engagement by implementing AI technologies into social networks and analysing the big data to recognise the trends in the audience's preferences. This aspect of cultural influence demonstrates how the infusion of AI is deep-rooted in the consumption of art in today's society.
5. Emerging Technologies: These aspects are expressed through words like 'cloud' and 'IoT' (Internet of Things), indicating further inclusion of developing trends into the art network. It emerged that these technologies can present new forms and approaches to artistic works, which may change existing art ideas. Cloud computing can offer ample resources for complex models for AI, and IoT devices can provide immediate interaction with the experience of art (Yadav et al., 2023). The coupling of these technologies with AI implies that art could be even more creative in the future and more open and engaging.

Analysing the nature and development of the connection between AI and art is a multifaceted process that confronts this field's technological, cultural, and social aspects. Figure 2 demonstrates the analysis of the co-occurrence network designed through VOSviewer.

Figure 2. Co-Citation Network

Source: Authors' own

Analysis of Co-Citation Network (Figure 2)

1. Key Contributors: The co-citation network also points to notable authors and researchers, the large nodes being 'Minsky M." And 'Scorsese M." These nodes depict several influential scholars that have extensively contributed to the production of base theories and proficiency in the AI and art category. Their work can be considered the key to further research within this field and is regarded as interdisciplinary.
2. Interdisciplinary Influence: The variety of authors indicates that the issues investigated in the network relate to artificial intelligence and art and embrace perspectives from different fields such as artificial intelligence, film, art, and culture. The intersectionality of these disciplines shows that the focus is on analysing how AI integrates and influences art-making, art production, and art reception. Thus, incorporating both disciplines is mutually beneficial to advancing knowledge and enhancing analytical tools and tricks.
3. Research Clusters: By observing the colours the network has assigned to each cluster, one can understand how works that are in a way related are found clustered together. These clusters suggest microdomains like AI tech, film, culture, etc. Such an arrangement also presents an understanding of the networking of

these subfields, to and from, that is, how progress in one subfield acts as the foundation for further developments in other subfields. This clustering also aids in determining the key trends and moving target areas of focus in the sizeable overall discussion of AI and art.

4. Prominent Studies: Nodes with greater size gather all the works that have received many more citations, which makes it easier to understand their influence in the research world. These marked publications can be considered reference works for academic and professional researchers, pointing at the works which laid the convention or are seminal. These papers were highly cited due to their contribution to exploring and promoting further knowledge and discussions of AI in art.
5. Collaborative Networks: The links and nodes in the network imply the interaction and scholarly cooperation between the researchers. These links prove a sense of collaboration in researching the application of AI in the sense of art and culture. Networking entails various methods, such as communicating new ideas, research techniques, and discoveries, making the research more robust and prosperous. They also embody the modern and progressive character of the academic discipline; this is the teamwork of multidisciplinary teams who advance human experience and research.

The analysis of the co-citation network shows a complex structure of the submitted papers that reveals connections between AI and art and breaks down the relations between the authors and their works, their collaboration, and their influences upon one another.

These diagrams help to get acquainted with the state of research on AI in art, focusing on the developments in the field, cinematographic impacts, and the cultural shift. Sharing the same context as biodiversity conservation, the co-citation network also reveals this research area's leading actors and interdisciplinarity.

The PRISMA methodology allowed for the systematic and structured approach to examining the identified sources and presented the key findings on how and in what way AI influences art, along with potential social and cultural consequences. The research results enhance the methodology of analysing the shifts in the interaction between technology and art and contribute to scholarly and policy discussions.

Case Studies

and value. A look at case studies is an essential way of getting acquainted with real-life contexts and the consequences of adopting AI in art. Therefore, detailing some of these projects and initiatives will make it easier to notice the possibilities and problems created when technology is intertwined with artistry. Here are a few case studies that highlight the diverse ways in which AI is shaping artistic expression: Here are a few case studies that highlight the diverse ways in which AI is shaping artistic expression:

1. *The Painting Fool:* The Painting Fool by an artist cum computer scientist, Simon Colton, is an AI program which paints original artworks based on algorithms. Through painting analysis and applying various methods and styles, The Painting Fool produces paintings that conflict with current artistic conventionalities of authorship and painting purpose. Such a project provokes multiple concerns about the artist's place in the creation process and the possibility of developing AI systems to create pieces that emotionally affect people.
2. *Google's Magenta Project:* Magenta is an open-source research project at Google that aims to learn melding Creativity and AI, particularly regarding music and art. Typically, via Magenta, researchers and artists develop models based on AI for creating compositions in music, paintings, etc., and poetry. Thus, as Magenta opens sources of AI tools and resources to more artists and creators, the agency advances the capabilities of AI by creating more opportunities for art and challenging the limits of machine learning.
3. *The Next Rembrandt:* The Next Rembrandt is combination between the advertising agency J. Walter Thompson and Microsoft. The Next Rembrandt project used algorithms to create a new painting by analysing Rembrandt's paintings. Concerning the main aspects of the AI system, by analysing Rembrandt's micro-stroke patterns and the content of his typical portraits, the AI system produced a work that appeared highly reminiscent of the artist's style. This project demonstrates how AI octaves imitate the artistic styles of the past and can raise some important questions concerning the issue of originality in AI Art.
4. *AI Art Auctions:* Recently, an art market has witnessed the emergence of AI art, and paintings created with the help of algorithms were sold at auctions for relatively large amounts of money. Collectors and those interested in art can now buy art made by artificial intelligence; this has necessitated the creation of portraits, as well as abstract pieces, by AI. This trend demonstrates people's readiness to buy and sellers' willingness to offer AI creations as art and points to the characteristic change in the definition of art in the age of artificial intelligence.

Through such cases and other similar studies, we can grasp how AI affects art-making by subverting conventional ideas of creativity and authorship, as well as the potential of extending the range of creative possibilities in culture and art. Therefore, case studies offer a beneficial perspective in addressing AI's effects and potential in the twenty-first century's social context of contemporary art and cultural industries.

IMPLICATIONS

Ethical Implications

The mere implementation of artificial intelligence in the field of art promises to bring about certain issues related to authorship, biases in algorithms, and general implications for creativity and cultural integrity.

1. Authorship and Creativity

One of the most pressing ethical issues is the question of authorship. Traditionally, art would be considered something deeply human, through which the identity of the artist, their intention, and the act of creation itself are deeply embedded in the value and meaning of the artwork. AI-generated art blurs the boundaries. AI will itself be in a position to attach data sets to outputs that can compete with human creativity. This raises some really hard questions: Who authored the work—the programmer, the machine, or the dataset it was trained on? This ambiguity questions existing definitions of intellectual property and copyright and may lead to cleavages over rights and attribution in the artistic community.

2. Algorithms with Bias

Another major cluster of ethical issues related to AI is the bias of algorithms. AI systems are trained with vast amounts of data, which most of the time contain already existent biases and prejudices within society. Examples could be misrepresentation in the art produced, stereotyping in many cases, or even silencing communities. It may impose some kind of cultural predominance—for example, an AI trained on a curriculum that is based largely on the art and history of the West. Homogenization of art can happen and can reinforce existing power structures in art, thereby affecting diversity and inclusivity in cultural expressions.

3. Impact on Human Creativity

The advent of AI in art also raises some ethical questions: its impact on human creativity. As much as AI can help improve artistic production with new tools and new possibilities, there is a threat that it will overshadow or diminish the role of a human artist. In some contexts, the increased independence in producing work of top quality from AI devalues human creativity or maybe even makes it replaceable at such levels. In the future, a cultural shift could take place where more attention is paid to the technological process over the human experience and emotion connected to art.

4. Cultural Appropriation and Integrity

The ability of AI to analyze and mimic cultural styles has been seen as a threat to cultures. But there really is this danger that the AI-created art attributing to cultural motifs or traditions will be out of context or there is no sensitivity in the representation of such cultural value. This may then commoditize cultural heritage: representations of age-old, hallowed heritage may just sugarcoat sacred or particular meanings, hence nullify their powerful meaning and importance. Moreover, these very creators of AI systems often do not belong to the cultures from which they're borrowing, so their consent and the ethics of using their cultural knowledge could be questioned.

5. Ethical Use of Data

Literature has it that indeed, there also lies a challenge in the integrity of the data used in training these art-based AI systems. Most of training datasets in respective projects, include some sort of copyrighted images or works created without explicit consent of original artists. This obviously poses questions about the ownership of data and the ethics surrounding the use of creative works in training AI models. Then there is the issue of privacy, particularly when AI systems are using data containing personal or sensitive information, which could be leveraged to create art that potentially has ramifications on individual rights.

This forms a large, complex, and multilayered set of AI ethics in art, throwing questions of authorship, bias, cultural integrity, and responsible data use. AI is on the way to enter art creation and its dispersion; this is happening every day. These ethical issues in art should be a concern of technologists, artists, and policymakers. In other words, the future of AI within the art world will depend on how its adoption can be effected in ways ensuring the technology will enhance, and not compromise, human creativity, respect cultural diversity, and engender fairness and consent principles.

Societal Implications

In the case of art, one may easily observe societal aspects related to the use of artificial intelligence (AI) in artworks, such as accessibility, perception, and ethical issues that will shape our culture in the future. Given that AI is gradually seeping into artwork creation, analysis, and appreciation, society must inevitably address how that might affect it.

Regarding AI and artistic creation, one of the social consequences is that it affects the concept and meaning of art and creativity. AI art interrogates the notions of creative genius and skill, forcing the West and the culture outside the West to develop new ways of identifying art and who gets to decide what is acceptable or desirable. Since the AI generators can generate artworks that are a framework of those produced by professional artists, there is a blurring of who is a creator and, thus, what art is beginning to change.

Besides, democratising art through AI in the artist's work can also increase art availability to the commoner. AI makes art accessible for people to consume and share, allowing laypeople and various talented individuals to develop artistic skills. This democratisation of art not only helps to destroy prejudices in art and the diversity of people in it but also opposes the authorities and monopolies that have always ruled over art.

However, integrating AI technologies into art raises a concern that needs to be considered. As AI challenges artistry, artists, critics, and audiences begin to wonder if AI art is genuine or own, or even authored in the first place. Problems of cultural appropriation, copyright, and the industrialisation of art in the context of information technologies in the learning process framework should be discussed thoroughly to analyse AI-based art regarding the ethical norms it complies with and the rights of the authors and communities it violates.

In uncovering the impact of AI on art, one learns about how technology alters culture by portraying new paradigms. In the meantime, society is forced to deal with questions of identity and representation and question who has the authority to create within the sphere of art. This approach means that AI-generated art will be critically and ethically discussed so that inclusive opportunities offered by technology in the cultural field will make any artistic experience more diverse and unconventional and open the gates to a brighter artistic perspective.

Cultural Impacts

AI in art entails social implications that give a new form to the generation, use, and understanding of art in modern society. Thus, as AI technologies enter the artwork creation process, they also impact culture, its norms, values, and practices by altering the paradigms of art and perception.

One-way cultural changes are affected by AI inserted into art is the introduction of new styles and subgenres of art. The power of AI is its capability to process extensive datasets from various cultural contexts, thus helping artists consider many influences and traditions that should be included in the artwork. It also becomes apparent how the blending could be a positive phenomenon of popularity that not only enlivens creativity and contributes to cultural and ethnic interchange in a general sense but also be able to bring about more professionalism and multicultural representation within art.

Also, AI art is a focal point of new possibilities for the distribution of culture by giving the floor to the voiceless people and minorities. Hence, by enabling individuals, regardless of race or social status, to develop their work and display it to the public, AI helps balance the power in the art world and forces the elites to stop discouraging independent thinking.

At the same time, the concerns are also there about the maestro of AI art on cultural heritage, the aesthetic and creative originality in contemporary society. When machines create art based on the aesthetic replication or sampling of cultural tropes and aesthetics, there are issues of authenticity and value of cultural products when faced with technological advancement. Integrating creative and technical qualities alongside saving and fostering culture means that the relations between innovation and tradition, creation and cultural assets become challenging when artists face AI art problems.

When critically analysing the effects of culture on AI in the framework of art, it is possible to ponder the role of technology in evolving and defining culture and worth. As the social relations through which art and culture are being created and consumed are being transformed by Intelligent technologies, society is forced to question the values of cultural originality, representation, and proprietorship in the digital age. Thus, we can make the proper and correct-willed use of AI in the art to celebrate various cultures and allow people to allow other cultures to exist and be diverse and rich in the forthcoming generations.

FUTURE DIRECTIONS

Reflecting on the possible trends of AI in art is a way to look at the future of creatives along with technology and culture. With the developments of the upcoming AI technologies and their interconnections with the arts, new trends and issues arise, inextricably influencing the future of art and culture. Here are some potential future directions for AI in artistic expression: Here are some potential future directions for AI in artistic expression:

1. AI-Enhanced Collaboration: Possibly further in the future, there is likely to be closer integration of human artists and artificial intelligence systems where artists use the artificial intelligence systems to improve, further and extend the possibility of art. By integrating human creative feelings and thoughts with

analytical ability and the generative nature of AI art, artists can create a piece of art beyond the scope of intellect and technology (Dewasiri et al., 2023a).

2. AI-Driven Personalization: AI applications can adapt an artistic performance to the specific audience and emotions of the viewers and their culture or ethnicity. They can use data regarding the viewers' responses to the art to generate art that relates to viewers and provide them with artistic experiences that are captivating, kind, and even adaptive to the individual.
3. Ethical and Cultural Considerations: Ethical as well as cultural factors will become more significant as AI is further integrated into the creation of artwork: there is a need to address possibilities of AI algorithms' bias, cultural sensitivity, and effects of AI on traditional art practices and conventions with artists, technologists, and regulators.
4. AI as a Tool for Social Change: AI, therefore, can be a great assistant in fighting for social change and activism in arts, where artists will be able to discuss issues affecting society, give a voice to the voiceless and make statements that go against the norm in the society. Thus, artists could leverage technology to help them create art that opens people's eyes and makes them stand up and fight for a cause that is dear to them, such as creating art that brings awareness to a specific social issue.
5. AI-Generated Art Movements: It is possible to predict that in the future, there could be completely new styles and trends in art which will be created by artists with the help of AI technology. In the foreseeable future, having chosen the methods and opportunities of AI in developing and producing artworks, artists could create a new movement in the art world. The following are hypothetical art movements generated by AI that could change the face of art and the practice of art for many more decades.

Thus, the further development of the program opportunities discussed can give an idea of the specific impact of technological tools on the artistic future. Therefore, with the steady progress of the AI movement and its interaction with the arts, artists and technologists, along with the audiences, are prompted to reconsider both the possibilities and the horizons of art and creativity as they form the basis for the Developments in the Digital Ages for the artistry.

CONCLUSION

The role of AI in the art world is, therefore, one of transformation: it is changing how art is created, consumed, and understood in the contemporary era. Continuing to progress, AI technologies now offer authors—for the very first time—the opportunity to create singular innovative and genuinely unique artworks, challenging classic notions of creativity and authorship. But this technological turn raises some very relevant questions: What does art come to mean in a digital age with issues of originality, ethics, and what, in fact, does an artist do?

This research reflects on the impact that AI is having on the concept of art by underscoring the opportunities brought forward and the challenges. AI democratizes artistic creation, by making it accessible and diverse. AI challenges long-standing cultural and aesthetic habits in societies. Drawing from the case studies and the systematic literature review conducted in this research, AI will exert a strong impact on the art world—from changing a creative process to the definition of the relations between technology and culture.

With this in view, the future of AI in art opens up all the impulses for breakthroughs of the mind, which will awaken much creativity and so much power for cultural innovation. However, it now calls for great concern for the ethical and cultural considerations this integration comes with. And so, as the artists, technologists, and the viewers embark on this rising synergy of AI and art, it is important to tread into this evolution in art with a commitment to ethical practice, cultural sensitivity, and an acute sense of the transforming power of AI.

In the end, further research and incorporation of AI in art will help to bring about a more pluralistic, inclusive, and more imaginative art world—one in which human creativity merges with technological innovation as a possible source of new forms of artistic expression and cultural dialogue. The future of art in the age of AI needs to be one of co-creation, exploration, and redefinition, promising to transform the art world and the broader cultural landscape on their own.

REFERENCES

Bozkurt, A., Karadeniz, A., Baneres, D., Guerrero-Roldán, A. E., & Rodríguez, M. E. (2021). Artificial intelligence and reflections from educational landscape: A review of AI Studies in half a century. *Sustainability (Basel)*, 13(2), 800–812. DOI: 10.3390/su13020800

Cetinic, E., & She, J. (2022). Understanding and creating art with AI: Review and outlook. [TOMM]. *ACM Transactions on Multimedia Computing Communications and Applications*, 18(2), 1–22. DOI: 10.1145/3475799

Crawford, K., & Paglen, T. (2021). Excavating AI: The politics of images in machine learning training sets. *AI & Society*, 36(4), 1105–1116. DOI: 10.1007/s00146-021-01301-1

Dewasiri, N. J., Baker, H. K., Banda, Y. K. W., & Rathnasiri, M. S. H. (2022), "The Dividend Decision Model: A Possible Solution for the Dividend Puzzle", Rana, S., Sakshi and Singh, J. (Ed.) Exploring the Latest Trends in Management Literature (Review of Management Literature, Vol. 1), Emerald Publishing Limited, Leeds, pp. 249-267. https://doi.org/DOI: 10.1108/S2754-586520220000001013

Dewasiri, N. J., Dharmarathna, D. G., & Choudhary, M. (2024). Leveraging Artificial Intelligence for Enhanced Risk Management in Banking: A Systematic Literature Review. Singh, R., Khan, S., Kumar, A., & Kumar, V. (Ed.) Artificial Intelligence Enabled Management: An Emerging Economy Perspective, De Gruyter, pp. 197–213, Berlin, https://doi.org/DOI: 10.1515/9783111172408-013

Dewasiri, N. J., Karunarathne, K. S. S. N., Menon, S., Jayarathne, P. G. S. A., & Rathnasiri, M. S. H. (2023a). Fusion of Artificial Intelligence and Blockchain in the Banking Industry: Current Application, Adoption, and Future Challenges; Saini, A. and Garg, V. (Ed.) Transformation for Sustainable Business and Management Practices: Exploring the Spectrum of Industry 5.0, Emerald Publishing Limited, pp. 293-307, Bingley, https://doi.org/DOI: 10.1108/978-1-80262-277-520231021

Dewasiri, N. J., Pigera, A. K. M., Karunarathne, K. S. S. N., & Rathnasiri, M. S. H. (2023), "Financial Services Employee Engagement and Attitude Toward Artificial Intelligence: Evidence From Sri Lanka", Saini, A. and Garg, V. (Ed.) Transformation for Sustainable Business and Management Practices: Exploring the Spectrum of Industry 5.0, Emerald Publishing Limited, Leeds, pp. 231-245. https://doi.org/DOI: 10.1108/978-1-80262-277-520231017

Gong, Y. (2021). Application of virtual reality teaching method and artificial intelligence technology in digital media art creation. *Ecological Informatics*, 63, 101304. DOI: 10.1016/j.ecoinf.2021.101304

Hitsuwari, J., Ueda, Y., Yun, W., & Nomura, M. (2023). Does human–AI collaboration lead to more creative art? Aesthetic evaluation of human-made and AI-generated haiku poetry. *Computers in Human Behavior*, 139, 107502. DOI: 10.1016/j.chb.2022.107502

Jayawardena, N. S., & Dewasiri, N. J. (2023). *Food Acquisition and Consumption Issues of South Asian Countries: A Systematic Literature Review and Future Research Agenda*. FIIB Business Review., DOI: 10.1177/23197145231194113

Karnouskos, S. (2020). Artificial intelligence in digital media: The era of deepfakes. *IEEE Transactions on Technology and Society*, 1(3), 138–147. DOI: 10.1109/TTS.2020.3001312

Karunarathna, K. S. S. N., Dewasiri, N. J., Singh, R., & Rathnasiri, M. S. H. (2024). What Does Artificial Intelligence–Powered ChatGPT Bring to Academia? A Review. Singh, R., Khan, S., Kumar, A., & Kumar, V. (Ed.) Artificial Intelligence Enabled Management: An Emerging Economy Perspective, De Gruyter, pp. 3-13, Berlin, https://doi.org/DOI: 10.1515/9783111172408

Khurana, R., Yadav, M., Quttainah, M., Srivastava, A. P., Baludi, A., & Singh, P. K. (2023, November). Neural Networks in Recruitment: Trends and Future Directions. In *2023 International Conference on Ambient Intelligence, Knowledge Informatics and Industrial Electronics (AIKIIE)* (pp. 1-5). IEEE. DOI: 10.1109/AIKIIE60097.2023.10390017

Loureiro, S. M. C., Guerreiro, J., & Tussyadiah, I. (2021). Artificial intelligence in business: State of the art and future research agenda. *Journal of Business Research*, 129, 911–926. DOI: 10.1016/j.jbusres.2020.11.001

Markauskaite, L., Marrone, R., Poquet, O., Knight, S., Martinez-Maldonado, R., Howard, S., Tondeur, J., De Laat, M., Buckingham Shum, S., Gašević, D., & Siemens, G. (2022). Rethinking the entwinement between artificial intelligence and human learning: What capabilities do learners need for a world with AI? *Computers and Education: Artificial Intelligence*, 3, 100056. DOI: 10.1016/j.caeai.2022.100056

Mishra, U., Rathnasiri, M. S. H., & Dewasiri, N. J. (2024). Net-Zero Economy and Energy Sustainability: A Nepalese Perspective. In Singh, R., Khan, S., Kumar, A., Luthra, S., & Chokshi, H. (Eds.), *Net Zero Economy, Corporate Social Responsibility and Sustainable Value Creation. CSR, Sustainability, Ethics & Governance* (pp. 145–161). Springer., DOI: 10.1007/978-3-031-55779-8_9

Rathnasiri, M. S. H., Dewasiri, N. J., & Kumar, A. A. (2024). Policy Framework and Implementation Strategies for Sri Lanka's Transition to a Net-Zero Economy. In Singh, R., Khan, S., Kumar, A., Luthra, S., & Chokshi, H. (Eds.), *Net Zero Economy, Corporate Social Responsibility and Sustainable Value Creation. CSR, Sustainability, Ethics & Governance* (pp. 43–60). Springer., DOI: 10.1007/978-3-031-55779-8_3

Robinson, S. C. (2020). Trust, transparency, and openness: How inclusion of cultural values shapes Nordic national public policy strategies for artificial intelligence (AI). *Technology in Society*, 63, 101421. DOI: 10.1016/j.techsoc.2020.101421

Trivedi, S. K., Vishnu, S., Singh, A., & Yadav, M. (2023). Research trends in sustainable E-payment systems: A study using topic modeling approach. *IEEE Transactions on Engineering Management*, 71, 7511–7525. DOI: 10.1109/TEM.2023.3280216

Yadav, M., Khurana, R., Vihari, N. S., Mittal, A., Balodi, A., & Srivastava, A. P. (2023, November). Virtual Reality in Human Resource Management: Past, Present and Future Trends. In *2023 International Conference on Recent Advances in Science and Engineering Technology (ICRASET)* (pp. 1-5). IEEE. DOI: 10.1109/ICRASET59632.2023.10420290

Zylinska, J. (2020). *AI art: machine visions and warped dreams* (p. 181). Open humanities press.

Chapter 3
Artificial Intelligence in Screenplay: ChatGPT Application

Sevcan Sönmez
Yaşar University, Turkey

ABSTRACT

Artificial intelligence (AI) is a field which is advancing rapidly. Its use has become increasingly prevalent in various industries, from robotics to communication. The purpose of this study is to explore the innovations that AI bring to the cinema industry, as well as to investigate the possibilities offered by current AI applications in cinema. Cinema is an industry and art form that can potentially utilize various AI capabilities, benefit from innovations in mass communication and creative technologies. This study examines scriptwriting process using ChatGPT. Designed as a case study, the research conducts scriptwriting experiments with ChatGPT based on given genre, themes, and keywords. The limitations of the research include the use of ChatGPT, with ten research attendees -Scriptwriting class students-, using specific prompts. The results of the study will provide insights into how artificial intelligence contributes to screenplay writing both currently and over time, revealing its shortcomings, benefits, conveniences, and potential areas for development.

INTRODUCTION

Artificial intelligence has entered our lives as a rapidly rising technology in recent years, and its use has become widespread in many areas. Artificial intelligence is a versatile technology used in many different fields and is constantly evolving. Therefore, its usage areas and applications are expanding day by day. This technol-

DOI: 10.4018/979-8-3693-3916-9.ch003

ogy is used to provide human-like intelligence features to computer systems. This technology enables computers to perform tasks such as data analysis, learning, decision making and problem solving.

Artificial intelligence; In order to model human intelligence, it can give the computer or machine abilities such as reasoning like a human, making meaning, making generalizations, and learning from past experiences. (Yılmaz, 2022). "The aims of AI are to imitate human rational activity as much as possible through machines, normally electronic machines, and perhaps ultimately improve human rational activity ability" (Penrose, 1997, pp. 11). The development of artificial intelligence has come to this day as a result of very long and detailed studies. When talking about artificial intelligence, machine learning takes its place as the main subject in this field. "Machine learning, involves teaching a computer to recognize patterns, rather than programming it with specific rules. The training process involves feeding large amounts of data to the algorithm and allowing it to learn from thar data and identify patterns" (Elnoshokaty, pp. 11). Over time, every set of information in the digital field has progressed in machine learning with increasing data, and AI continues to develop in every field with serious support from the database. Artificial intelligence, whose use is becoming more widespread day by day in the financial field, automatic vehicles, health field, entertainment field, and visual and audio production field, has quickly entered the agenda of producers and artists in the field of cinema, art and design.

While discussing the situation and expectations regarding artificial intelligence in the cinema industry, Elnoshokaty asks as: "The learning Machin can write like Shakespeare yes it can do that but how can do the same wording the same style but create an emotional story or play can it? or humans can like that or any passed away writer can the scientists create text to text deep learning machine learning from all of his production, style, wording, pattern plot, form and his own character it easy to do that right now it is the Eternity. to be or not to be that is the problem" (p. 142). This question is quite meaningfully a comprehensive question regarding the field of literature, poetry, aesthetics and visual arts. Whether the content produced with artificial intelligence is technically and formally correct, but where the content is in terms of emotion, originality and authenticity is an important question. Artificial intelligence programs and applications open up a wide range of users and creators in the cinema industry, in areas such as visual special effects, image editing, sound design, dubbing and script writing. There are many websites and applications related to these areas. However, the advantages and disadvantages of these programs and applications are still a matter of debate and research. As Hilal (2024) mentions; "AI tools have had a significant effect on film making and production phases, as AI technologies are integrated into the film production process throughout multiple stages (pre-production, production, and post-production)" (p. 320). Studies conducted in this field in recent years have shown that the use of AI gives more obvious and better results in the production and post-product parts. What Hilal also reveals and analyzes in her study is that artificial intelligence is used extensively in the fields of spatial design and set production conceptual design in the films. Tools such as Midjourney and DALL-E are among the most popular and successful results in this field (2024, pp. 322). Discussions continue with the idea that the Hollywood system will perhaps change radically with artificial intelligence programs, and that robots will offer a creation that will completely reorganize this field, and on the contrary, underlining the deficiencies regarding the originality part. However, there are not yet enough studies on scientific research as a case study in this field. In this study, research is carried out on what kind of content can be achieved in script writing with artificial intelligence and where these contents stand on the literary, aesthetic, original and authentic side.

Narration is an important act that has existed in fairy tales, myths, literature, theater and cinema for centuries, since the beginning of human existence. Man's innate and innate desire to tell, which takes on various genres and artistic forms, is a field whose foundations were laid by Aristotle with the classical story. He used narrative, story, literature and cinema to make sense of human existence, to transfer his life experience to future generations, to reflect himself and humanity with a playful tendency, sometimes to manipulate reality, sometimes to create fantasies. If we look at the scenario that is the subject of this study, the scenario itself has certain rules and criteria within the framework of theoretical narratology. In this study, the scenario in cinema is discussed within the framework of the classical narrative form. AI's scenario writing is evaluated with the classical narrative structure. This perspective is also due to the fact that the inputs that form the basis of AI's learning model, such as machine learning and deep learning, are more concentrated in this area. It is quite common in AI studies in the field of cinema to provide data with popular and mainstream content. Below, we will first look at what research has been done with AI in cinema and studies focused on developing AI. However, short films made with the use of AI will be briefly mentioned, as they are the pioneers of this field. In the study, after briefly discussing the basic meaning of scenario and narrative through narrative theory, the findings and the result of the study will be presented.

A Short History of AI in Cinema

Movies have a significant role for people that firstly informed about AI. With the movies such as *I Robot, Chappie, Blade Runner* or *Ex Machine*, we saw the robots, intelligent machines, human-like machines and their different existence styles. As movies take this theme, this topic as a main plot people started to think about what is the future of these robots or this technology. By the way the movies which came with magnificent visual developments, such as visual effects, modeling, animated images, huge artificial environments opened a new ground breaking audio visual window for both the audiences and the creators. So, for years people are watching AI themed, AI generated movies when the producers, the filmmakers are focused on every new detail of AI developments in the industry.

According to Kılınç, who evaluated the current situation of artificial intelligence in the cinema industry, “it is possible to say that the developments in artificial intelligence technologies have greatly affected today's cinema industry. Many programs supported by artificial intelligence-based tools and software offer various opportunities in production processes such as pre-production, production and post-production” (2023, pp. 108). As Nasrullah puts; “Using AI in storytelling has been a new transformative phase of storytelling. This unique blend offers a new realm of storytelling possibilities that are more adaptable, interactive, and captivating” (2023, pp. 25). It is also seen that artificial intelligence was initially used in cinema, mostly in the field of consultancy and box office analysis on various issues, but today it also affects the search for a new language and production processes (Anadolu, 2019, pp. 53). Both academic and scientific studies on the widespread use of artificial intelligence in cinema, as well as studies on films produced with artificial intelligence, show that we have a wide area in front of us to understand the current situation.

The first production in which artificial intelligence took on the role of screenwriter was the initiative of British filmmaker Oscar Sharp and artificial intelligence researcher and artist Ross Goodwin in 2016. The artificial intelligence program named Benjamin was developed with the support of Recursive Neural Network (RNN) and Long-Short-Term Memory Network (LSTM). (Quoted Kılınç, 2023, pp. 101). *Sunspring* is the first AI written short film that the machine named Benjamin wrote. Duration of the movie is 09.02’’, it is a experimental science fiction short movie. Sharp and Goodwin showed this short at Sci-Fi London’s 48hr Film Challenge3. These two entrepreneurs make another attempt a year later. The second short *It's No Game*, offers a narrative on the possibility of replacing striking screenwriters with artificial intelligence writers which’s genre is post-apocalyptic and thriller. The work and the film developing phase of this AI filmmakers is described as; “they trained four new long short-term memory (LSTM) recurrent neural network models on subtitles from David Hasselhoff’s 1980s TV shows, Shakespeare, Golden Age Hollywood films, and Aaron Sorkin. In addition, they used a context-free grammar loaded with words from a ballet dictionary to make a choreography generator, and re-used an LSTM recurrent neural network from “Sunspring” to produce Hasselhoff’s final soliloquy. The process required the use of New York University’s supercomputer for training, and a Razer Blade laptop outfitted with a high-performance graphics processing unit (GPU) for text generation.” (URL 1)

The duo's other attempt, *Zone Out* (2018), is an attempt made by placing the faces of today's actors on old film footage. However, this attempt only presented a visuality in which the images were not well integrated into each other. (URL 2). Another AI made movie was done in 2022, named The Safe zone is another important experiment which used the technology in both script writing and directing. "AI entrepreneur and literal rocket scientist Aaron Kemmer and his co-producer made another film by using every possibility of AI. Kemmer said; "We used OpenAI ChatGPT to WRITE and DIRECT a film in a weekend," said AI entrepreneur and literal rocket scientist Aaron Kemmer on Twitter." (Deruvo, 2022). "Using an AI chatbot, Kemmer and his cohorts were able to come up with over 100 ideas and then 50 scripts for a short film in under an hour. The chatbot used artificial intelligence to further refine each idea when asked for more details until the complete idea had been hatched." (URL 3).

Through the prompt of the producers, ChatGPT was able to produce a 4-minute script and a shot list that the actors and the crew used in the production of this film. We were also able to ask ChatGPT to suggest specific instructions for the Director of Photography and camera operators (choice of camera lenses, camera movements and lighting requirements), recommend wardrobe preferences, and even give us specific prompts to let Dall-E 2 create a full storyboard" (URL 3).

> *"According to Juan, the goal of the film is to showcase the collaboration between humans and AI in the creation of quality content. It will also give a glimpse of the potential for AI and humans to work together in the creative field" (URL 4).*

The common feature of the films *Sunspring, It's No Game and The Safe Zone*, which are in the fiction genre and strive to be based on a narrative, is that they are all in the science fiction genre and contain experimentation or some absurdity. Absurdity is most evident in the first movie, *Sunspring*. The lack of flow of events, the absence of a narrative structure such as introduction, development and conclusion, the absurd artificiality of the dialogues, and the disconnection of meaning in the film are quite evident. In the other two films, the plot could be established to some extent. However, the superficiality of the dialogues and characters is still evident. *It's No Game* seems to make some sense as a situation movie. However, *The Safe Zone* movie has the feature of being a scene of a movie rather than a short film in itself.

Despite some negative criticism, these four short films have already gone down in history as the first examples in the history of AI cinema. In the coming years, looking back, these films will always remain important as the first steps of AI cinema, and perhaps years later they will stand in a place similar to where we put the films of the Lumiere Brothers.

In the evaluation of these films made by/with AI, it is seen that the learning of AI has actually improved. The inputs and outputs of various studies conducted with these tools, which use machine learning and deep learning models, that are the main learning models of artificial intelligence, also give an idea of how the developments in this field continue and how they will progress. There are studies that have serious diversity in the field of cinema and examine the progress in this field by uploading new data to AI. One of these is the study conducted by Makarand Tapaswi et al. (2016) based on the question-and-answer method, which tried to make artificial intelligence make sense of movie visuals. Researchers focused on the potential of matching relationships between characters through the database using 408 subtitled movies and their extended summaries on Wikipedia. Although artificial intelligence matches some of the relationships correctly, there is a need for a larger database. In the study, in which a question-and-answer method was applied, some deficiencies of artificial intelligence in interpretation were revealed. Another deep learning study on the development of literary understanding and language through cinema and literature is the study put forward by University of Toronto and MIT researchers. In this study, the researchers say, "A truly intelligent machine needs to not only parse the surrounding 3D environment, but also understand why people take certain actions, what they will do next, what they could possibly be thinking, and even try to empathize with them. In this quest, language will play a crucial role in grounding visual information to high-level semantic concepts." In this study, which aims to correctly code the cinema narrative both textually and visually, the film image, subtitles and texts from the book are discussed together. (Zhu, Kiros et al., 2015)

Various experimental studies like this reveal how AI interprets visual and textual meanings with cinema. While all these studies, whether analyzing movies, understanding movie scripts and providing answers to the content, reveal what kind of processing ability AI has today, they also contribute to the development of this technology with constantly uploaded data. Dhajero and his friends also say in their paper that; "AI technologies such as natural language processing (NLP) and AI authorship have significantly impacted scriptwriting by providing advanced character development and narrative creation tools. NLP has enabled scriptwriters to analyze extensive text data, including scripts, novels, and screenplays, to gain valuable insights into dialogue patterns, character interactions, and storytelling techniques" (Dhajero, Memon, Dayo, 2023, 28).

With this huge study in this field, AI and cinema interaction have been walking hand in hand in recent years. AI in scriptwriting field except from Chatgpt there are many apps and websites which is claimed to writing scripts, developing story, dialog and scenes. These apps can give content by paid or to some degree free. The most well-known scenario apps are; AI ScreenWriter, Plotdot, Squibler, Scene One, NolanAI, Jasper, AI Magic Writer.

Scenario and Classical Narrative

A scenario is a piece of writing that serves as the foundation for a play, movie, television show, or other kind of visual or audio art. A scenario which is called a written version of a story or work of fiction that includes characters, dialogue, scenes, and other significant elements is called a scenario, is a kind of structure that engages and affects viewers and can evoke powerful emotional responses. A theoretical analysis of the situation reveals that the traditional narrative structure is essentially predicated on. Aristotle laid the groundwork for classical narrative theory. According to Aristotle: "Tragedy is the imitation of an action. The imitation of an action is a story (mythos). Every story is a cohesive whole of words, ideas, music, and characters. The crucial component is the proper connection between the events" (1987, 25-26). According to this theory, known as the Principle of Three Unities, which Aristotle proposed as the foundation for tragedy, a play, or other theatrical production, must have unity in time, space, and action. According to this theory, the main events, a location, and a particular time period should all be at the center of a story. Nonetheless, the introduction, development, and conclusion structure of a classical narrative is its most crucial component (Aristotle, 1987).

The Russian folklorist Vladimir Propp examines the fundamental structures of folktales and fables in his 1985 book The Morphology of the Tale. Propp identifies these elements and makes the case that fairy tales have certain archetypal roles and events. It demonstrates how specific roles are assigned to heroes in fairy tales and how behaviors can be broadly classified (Propp, 1985). Propp's schematic analysis of stories, tales and heroes in this way was later taken up by Campbell in *The Hero with a Thousand Faces* (2008) and, after Campbell, by Vogler (2009) in the same vein. Characters, archetypes of characters, myths, fairy tale narrative structures, and the ways in which they evolve all share structurally similar basic schemes. These are the elements that form the basis of the classical narrative structure.

According to Chatman (1978), a structuralist in the field of classical narrative theory, narrative events have a radical relationship, unfold in a sequential fashion, and ultimately lead to one another ever since Aristotle. Conventional reasoning implies that the events are not merely linear, but rather causal. Causality can be explicit, overt or implicit, implied. (1978, 41). "Each event is connected to the next in a cause-and-effect relationship, and the results cause other results," said Chatman, who highlighted the significance of cause-and-effect relationships in classical narrative structure. Even if two different events do not appear to be in an obvious relationship with each other, we infer that there may be a relationship and, as a more general rule, we discover this relationship later" (1978, 42). Once more, as Chatman points out, a scenario's events happen in a hierarchical order. While some events, referred to as main events or core events are more significant than others, side-satellite events work in tandem with the core to support the main event. (1978, 49).

In his book Story, Robert McKee also discusses what and how the fundamental elements of a movie scenario ought to be: Storytelling is about uniqueness, not repetition. Narrative emphasizes thoroughness over expediency. Story is not about stereotypes, but about archetypes. The goal of a story is to elevate the art form, not to speculate about market trends. Story is not about formulas; it is about eternal, universal forms." (1997, 3-9). These fundamental components of McKee's approach can be thought of as the primary steps in the process that will turn a film into a good film with a variety of features.

Of course, when we discuss cinema and films, we are not limited to discussing the genre and technique of classical narrative. With today's new media possibilities, a new film language has emerged for avant-garde, experimental, modern, and Brechtian narratives and the narrative structure is also evolving and changing in the world of digitalization. Many theorists and writers agree that the *classical narrative,* with all its new forms, experimental and modern structures, has been the basic narrative from the very beginning of human existence. However, the basis of cinema, which is an industry and mass art, is Hollywood, popular films and classical narrative. For this reason, this study focuses on the classical narrative structure. The development of artificial intelligence in the creation of movie content, scenario writing, the inputs and data utilized in the learning phase of artificial intelligence programs, and the process that artificial intelligence structurally follows and advances in production are all based on classical narrative, despite the study's stated objectives. As previously discussed, Hollywood films based on classical narratives are the subject of research on artificial intelligence's analysis of various contents; visual, aural, and textual during the machine learning process, when corroborated by literary works, it appears that classical narratives are once again prevalent. Consequently, it has been noted that artificial intelligence also uses the classical structure to process information.

Considering that AI is a crucial stage in the screenwriting process and employs a "groundbreaking" technique, it is critical to obtain data from Chatgpt on screenwriting, which serves as the study's foundation, in order to comprehend the procedures AI uses to write a screenplay. The question "How to write a scenario" was posed to ChatGpt at this point, the answer and the sequential steps for writing a scenario are as follows...

Writing a film script involves several key steps. Here's a simplified guide to get you started:

1. Conceptualize Your Story: Develop a clear idea of what your film will be about. This includes the plot, characters, setting, and themes. Consider what message or emotion you want to convey to your audience.

2. Outline Your Story: Create a structured outline outlining the key events and plot points of your story. This will help you organize your thoughts and ensure your script has a cohesive narrative arc.

3.Develop Your Characters: Flesh out your characters by giving them backgrounds, motivations, and personalities. They should feel like real people with strengths, weaknesses, and quirks.

4. Format Your Script: Familiarize yourself with screenplay format, including proper formatting for scene headings, action lines, dialogue, and transitions. Software like Final Draft or Celtx can help you with this.
5. Write the Script: Start writing your script based on your outline. Focus on writing visually and economically, using concise language to convey the action and dialogue. Show, don't tell.
6. Revise and Rewrite: Once you've completed a draft, go back and revise it. Look for areas where the pacing is slow, dialogue feels unnatural, or the plot needs clarification. Rewrite as necessary to improve the overall quality of the script.
7. Get Feedback: Share your script with trusted friends, family, or colleagues for feedback. Listen to their suggestions and be open to making changes based on their input.

8.Finalize Your Script: After incorporating feedback and making final revisions, your script should be ready to go. Make sure to proofread it carefully for any errors before submitting it to potential producers or production companies.

Remember, writing a film script is a creative process, and there's no one right way to do it. Experiment with different techniques and find what works best for you.

FINDINGS

Chatgpt's headings for the stages of scriptwriting list the methods used in dramatic narrative, but offer a basic explanation that does not go into the depth of the subject. In addition, it underlines that scenario writing is a creative process and emphasizes that the user should use own point of view and creativity in this process. Thus, in this case study focusing on Chatgpt scenario writing, a study was conducted with 10 students in the scenario writing course. Writing a short movie scenario in science fiction genre was requested. Progress was made with prompts such as adding characters, developing the character, adding dialog, changing the events performed by the character, extending the end of the scenario, etc. to improve the first texts obtained. In the study, 5 scenarios in Turkish and 5 scenarios in English were tested. In this way, the outputs in the two different language options were also compared.

The scripts obtained as a result of the request to write a short film scenario are primarily 1 and a half to 2 pages. All scenarios are more of a brief summary than a detailed scenario from start to finish. The scenes are mostly structured in the form of scene summaries. The scripts consist of 6 or 7 scenes, with short events in each scene.

There is no clear plot, conflict, climax and resolution, or main events and side events, or symbolic expressions. A situation around one or two characters within the framework of a certain subject develops quickly and ends quickly. In these scenarios, which do not have a detailed plot, there are no side events. Similar to the sterility of the plot and story development, the characters are also sterile. Chatgpt, who gave a one-character scenario in the first attempt, continues by adding a rather artificial and forced side character upon request to add a side character. When we want things to deepen between two characters, some events develop, but they evolve into a complex situation. For example, the story tried to create conflict by having characters directly oppose each other through orders or commands; however, this approach felt superficial and didn't lead to a well-developed or meaningful clash

The resulting scenarios use all the clichés of the science fiction genre. Movie titles and content are very similar across all trials. If we look at the movie titles, these are the titles: Time Traveler, Parallel Fall, Infinite Discovery, Lost Planet, Echoes of Eternity, Parallel Times... However, in the 10 essays, the main character is a famous scientist and the movie begins in a large laboratory when the scientist makes an interesting and potentially future-threatening discovery. It is observed that the characters are stereotypes and remain quite superficial within the scenario. It is also possible to talk about the clichés of the genre spatially; films that open with futuristic cityscapes and chaotic city scenes are similar. The atmosphere of a dystopian future is the same in the 5 scenarios that emerged in the study. In the wastelands, deserts and desertified areas, the war and struggle of different species have emerged in a spatially and contextually similar way.

Table 1.

Opening Scene	Numbers of movies	Second scene	Numbers of movies
Laboratory	5	Parallel universe/different time planes	4
Desert, desolate wasteland	2	Passing from Desert to Lab From Lab to Desert	1 1
Futuristic/dystopian city	3	Passing from the futuristic city to the desert	2
		Continue in the city or in space	2

The significant difference between Turkish and English scenario writing is stylistic. In Turkish, scene numbers and only scene titles are given, whereas in the English scenario, scene location/time/cutting/continuation information is also given. In Turkish scenario writing, in the first attempt, scene content is given without dialog, and then dialog is added on the dialog insertion command. However, in English, it can also give dialogues in its first scenario attempt. In Turkish, the scenario in the first output is mostly one character, while in English it is more prone to produce two-character content.

Dialogues are also very important in the theoretical perspective on characters and their realism in a screenplay. However, there is a lack of dialog in ChatGpt. Monologue is used more than dialog. The dialogues are superficial and bookish sentences.

As an example, from the outcomes of the scripts, opening scene at a laboratory:

Title: Echoes of Tomorrow

INT. ABANDONED LABORATORY – DAY

The camera pans across a dusty, dimly lit laboratory filled with broken equipment and flickering screens. A lone figure, ANDY, 30s, cautiously enters, carrying a small device.

ANDY (whispering to himself) This has to work.

INT. LABORATORY- CONTINUOUS

Andy approaches a large, dormant machine in the center of the room. He attaches the device to a panel on the machine and activates it. Lights begin to flash as the machine hums to life.

ANDY Come on, come on...

Suddenly, a surge of energy erupts from the machine, enveloping Andy in a blinding light.

In this example it is seen that he movie opens in a laboratory, there is a scientist who deals with a machine. (The machine is a time travelling machine by the way, which is a common pattern in nearly %60 of the scenarios). There is only one character who speaks to himself. İnstead of dialog the movie starts with the character's monolog.

Another outcome starts as;

Write me a science fiction script

ChatGPT

Title: "Echoes of Eternity"

FADE IN:

EXT. FUTURISTIC CITY - NIGHT

A sprawling metropolis gleaming with neon lights and holographic displays. Flying cars zip through the sky, while bustling crowds move along the futuristic streets.

CUT TO:

INT. APARTMENT - NIGHT

In a dimly lit apartment, ALEX, a weary ex-soldier, sits alone, nursing a drink. His face bears the scars of battles long past.

In the development of a script, side characters and side events are important to reinforce the main story. When ChatGpt was given the command to add a side character to this scenario, the scenario appeared as follows.

Title: Parallel Times

Boundary Between Dream and Reality:

Daniel wakes up in his bed and looks around for a moment. Although the apartment seems familiar, he senses that something is different. Suddenly, he realizes he is in the dream world. The surroundings are different from the real world and filled with strange symbols. Daniel (to himself): "Is this a dream?"

Discovery of Parallel Universes:

In the real world, Daniel accelerates his research and discovers a connection. He realizes that the symbols in the dream world are linked to events in the real world. To understand this connection, he refers to his past notes and research. Sarah, a supporting character, assists Daniel during this process and together they investigate the interdimensional connection. Sarah (to Daniel): "How can I help you?"

CONCLUSION AND COMMENTS

In this study, scenario writing was tested using Chatgpt. Due to their extensive length, the specific details of the experiments and their outcomes are documented in separate two case studies, which are beyond the scope of this discussion. Just as the knowledge gained by giving commands to artificial intelligence is limited, creativity in scriptwriting is limited. In the limitation of the genre, an experiment was made on the science fiction genre and cliché examples of the science fiction genre emerged. The narrative incorporates well-established science fiction concepts, including journeys through time, the existence of parallel universes, humanity establishing a home amongst the stars, conflicts against extraterrestrial forces vying for

Earth's domination, and the ethical complexities of human replication When given commands about these topics, it was observed that the content could not go to a very different point and simple variations of the same basic story could be produced.

It is seen that Chatgpt wrote a scenario format in the form of scene numbering and scene titles without following the scenario writing format. This is especially the case in Turkish scenario writing. It was observed that scene distinctions and descriptions were formatted more accurately in the request for English scenario writing. In the scenario, it is seen that the AI makes more generalizations in terms of style and expression. Although he divides the scenario into scenes and uses the classical structure of introduction-development-conclusion, he fails to make a detailed expression in a staged sense. It was observed that he created a scenario in the form of a treatise. The expressions in the scenes lack visual and auditory expression. There is a narrative expression. However, in a scenario, the event or situation that is intended to be described in the scenes is written down as it can be visualized. At this point, Chatgpt tends to summarize the events of the scenes with a superficial narrative.

Apart from this, for example, character development in classical narrative structure, the contribution of side characters to the story or the contribution of side events to the story are important in a film narrative. However, when using AI, the initial prompt dictates a scenario where events unfold for a single character at a time. Attempts to introduce additional characters, whether as sidekicks or more complex roles, resulted in them being superficially inserted into the existing plot without any significant development of their motivations or personalities. Specifying the character's role as protagonist or antagonist resulted in the AI following predictable patterns when adding to the scenario, this approach makes it challenging to develop characters with depth and nuance

Another important result is that similar content with similar themes and keywords is reached even if the desired content is created by different people. As each user's command differs during the intervention and development phase of the scenario presented to them by the AI, the resulting story flow may change, but in the resulting scenario, the narrative turns into a jumpy content with no organic meaning ties to each other.

This study highlights the limitations of artificial intelligence in screenwriting given current technological advancements. We get scenarios with very little creativity and mechanical and structural content in place of emotion and emotional connections. In a field of technology where machine learning is evolving daily and becoming more diverse, it is crucial to conduct similar studies again in order to track developments, store data, and assess whether and to what degree there is development and change.

REFERENCES

Anadolu, B. (2019). *Dijital Hikâye Anlatıcılığı Bağlamında Yapay Zekanın Sinemaya Etkisi: Sunspring ve It's No Game Filmlerinin Analizi*. Erciyes İletişim Dergisi / Journal of Erciyes Communication.

Aristoteles. (1987). Poetika. (Çev. İsmail Tunalı). Remzi Kitabevi.

Campbell, J. (2008). *The Hero with a Thousand Faces*. New World Library.

Carter, J. (2018). How artificial intelligence is creating new ways of storytelling. https://www.techradar.com/news/how-artificial-intelligence-is-creating-new-ways-of-storytelling

Chatman, S. (2008). Öykü ve Söylem. Filmde ve Kurmacada anlatı Yapısı. (Story and Discourse: Narrative Structure in Fiction and film) Cornell University Press, 1978.

Dayo, F., Memon, A. A., & Dharejo, N. (2023). Scriptwriting in the Age of AI: Revolutionizing Storytelling with Artificial Intelligence. *Journal of Media & Communication*, 4(1), 24–38.

Deruvo, J. (2022). This Film Was Written and Directed by AI—Here's the How and What You Can Learn. https://nofilmschool.com/ai-generated-movie

Elnoshokaty, I. (2021). Cinema industry and artificial intelligency dreams. Prof. Ibrahim elnoshokaty.

Mckee, R. (1997). *Story: Substance, Structure, Style and the Principles of Screenwriting*. Regan Books.

Penrose, R. (1997). *Bilgisayar ve Zeka*. Kralın Yeni Usu. Tübitak Yayınları.

Propp, V. (1985). *Masalın Biçimbilimi. (Çev. Mehmet&Sema Rifat)*. Bilim/Felsefe/Sanat Yayınları.

Tapaswi, M., Rainer, S., Antonio, T. (2016). MovieQA: Understanding Stories in Movies through Question-Answering. Computer Vision and Pattern Recognition (CVPR), Conference Paper. https://www.researchgate.net/publication/286513348_MovieQA_Understanding_Stories_in_Movies_through_Question-Answering

Vogler, C. (2009). *Yazarın sonsuz Yolculuğu*. Okyan Us Yayınları.

Yılmaz, A. (2022). *Yapay Zeka*. Kodlab.

Zhu, Y., Kiros, R., & Richard, Z. Ruslan Salakhutdinov et. (2015). Aligning Books and Movies: Towards Story-like Visual Explanations by Watching Movies and Reading Books. https://arxiv.org/pdf/1506.06724

Chapter 4
Revolutionizing Malayalam Cinema:
AI-Powered Scripting and Creative Brainstorming With ChatGPT

Vishnu Achutha Menon
https://orcid.org/0000-0003-4028-3685
Institute for Educational and Developmental Studies, India

ABSTRACT

This study examines how AI-powered scripting, particularly through ChatGPT, is changing Malayalam cinema. Interviews with 30 prominent scriptwriters provide insights into the integration of AI into the scripting process. The findings highlight ChatGPT's role as a collaborative tool, aiding in brainstorming, character development, and script refinement. The findings underscore ChatGPT's significant role as a collaborative partner, assisting scriptwriters in brainstorming ideas, developing complex characters, and refining scripts to enhance narrative coherence.

INTRODUCTION

Scripting is the foundational process in filmmaking, wherein a written document, often referred to as a script, is meticulously crafted to outline the narrative, dialogue, and directions for a film or any other visual production. Serving as a blueprint, it guides directors, actors, and the entire production team in bringing a cinematic vision to life. The script provides both the structural and creative framework, dictating the flow of the story, character interactions, and the overall visual and emotional experience for the audience. AI-powered scripting refers to the integration of artificial intelligence (AI) technologies into the traditional scriptwriting process. This involves

DOI: 10.4018/979-8-3693-3916-9.ch004

utilizing machine learning algorithms and natural language processing to assist or enhance various aspects of script creation. AI can contribute to idea generation, plot development, character analysis, and even suggest creative elements based on patterns learned from vast datasets. The aim is to augment human creativity, streamline the writing process, and potentially introduce innovative elements that might not have been considered through conventional methods.

The emergence and utilization of ChatGPT among scriptwriters in Kerala signifies a notable evolution in the realm of scriptwriting technology. This shift reflects a departure from traditional methods, indicating an increasing reliance on sophisticated tools. The positive implication on creativity is evident, as scriptwriters leverage ChatGPT to enhance their ideation processes and overcome creative hurdles. The collaborative dynamics between human intuition and AI capabilities become apparent, potentially resulting in a synergistic approach that introduces innovative storytelling methods. However, this collaborative trend also prompts critical considerations, such as questions about the originality of AI-generated content and concerns related to data privacy. The objective of this study is to investigate and demonstrate the transformative impact of AI-powered scripting and creative brainstorming through ChatGPT in the context of Malayalam cinema. By exploring the integration of artificial intelligence in the filmmaking process, the study aims to analyze the enhancements brought to scriptwriting, collaborative creativity, and overall cinematic storytelling. It seeks to evaluate the ethical considerations, challenges, and future prospects associated with revolutionizing Malayalam cinema through the innovative application of AI technology. This study aims to explore the integration of artificial intelligence (AI) tools, specifically ChatGPT, in the creative processes of narrative development within the film industry. The focus is on understanding how AI can enhance story development, character creation, and script refinement in both general and regional contexts, such as Malayalam cinema. The research investigates various AI-driven methodologies and tools that assist filmmakers and writers in overcoming creative challenges, generating innovative ideas, and ensuring narrative coherence and authenticity. The study also examines the ethical considerations of AI usage in creative fields, particularly concerning the balance between automation and human creativity.

REVIEW OF LITERATURE

AI can't replace human intelligence and creativity in educational contexts" has been supported by Vicente-Yagüe-Jara et al. in 2023. This statement underscores the unique qualities of human cognition and creativity, suggesting that while AI may have its merits, it cannot fully replicate the nuanced understanding, empathy, and creative problem-solving abilities inherent in human intelligence within educational settings. However, it's worth noting that AI tools have demonstrated significant advantages in certain domains. For instance, Niloy et al. (2024) highlight the merits of AI in the realm of writing. AI-powered writing assistants can aid in tasks such as grammar correction, language translation, and even generating text based on provided prompts. While these tools can enhance productivity and accuracy in writing tasks, they do not possess the holistic understanding and creative ingenuity that humans bring to the writing process. Similarly, Al-sa'di & Miller (2023) argue that AI tools can indeed improve the efficiency and creativity of user interfaces (UI). By leveraging AI algorithms, UI designers can automate repetitive tasks, personalize user experiences, and even generate novel design concepts. However, despite these advancements, the human touch remains indispensable in crafting UI designs that resonate with users on emotional and intuitive levels.

The research by Ritala et al. (2024) underscores ChatGPT's role in enhancing human agency within knowledge work, signifying a significant shift with far-reaching implications for both individuals and companies. By harnessing AI capabilities, individuals can streamline their workflow, swiftly access relevant information, and generate innovative solutions to complex problems. For companies, integrating ChatGPT into knowledge work processes can enhance productivity, encourage creativity, and facilitate informed decision-making. Sudirman & Rahmatillah (2023) demonstrate how AI-powered tools, including ChatGPT, can enrich students' learning experiences, especially in the domain of app development. By utilizing AI-generated insights and suggestions, students can refine their ideas, tackle challenges, and develop viable mobile applications. This not only enhances their technical skills but also nurtures their problem-solving abilities and creativity. Maher et al. (2023) highlight how access to ChatGPT empowers students to take charge of their learning journey by facilitating constructive work on their own schedules. This flexibility allows students to delve deeper into subjects of interest, seek clarification on complex concepts, and engage in self-paced learning experiences tailored to their individual needs. Lai (2023) emphasizes the potential of AI writing technologies, such as ChatGPT, to serve as powerful complements to human creativity. By offering suggestions, refining drafts, and providing inspiration, these tools can amplify the creative output of individuals while preserving the authenticity of their voices and ideas. Silva & Janes (2021) underscore ChatGPT's ability to deliver personalized and interactive learning experiences, catering to the unique preferences and learning styles of each student. Through adaptive feedback, tailored content recommendations, and real-time assistance, ChatGPT enhances engagement and understanding among learners. Murad et al. (2023) posit that ChatGPT has the potential to facilitate open education by serving as a guiding companion for self-directed learners. By offering assistance, guidance, and feedback, ChatGPT empowers individuals to pursue their educational goals autonomously, breaking down barriers to access and promoting a culture of lifelong learning.

The use of AI-powered scripting and creative brainstorming via ChatGPT has significantly changed various established domains, as highlighted by Luan et al. (2023). This innovation has not only streamlined processes but also sparked new approaches to problem-solving and idea generation. Biswas (2023) identifies several potential applications of ChatGPT within the film industry, indicating its ability to enhance screenplay writing, character development, and even audience engagement strategies. By utilizing AI-generated insights and suggestions, filmmakers can refine their narratives, optimize storytelling techniques, and create more immersive cinematic experiences. Vasconcelos & Santos (2023) propose ChatGPT and Bing Chat as powerful tools to revolutionize STEM education through a constructionist lens. By providing interactive and adaptive learning experiences, these platforms empower students to explore, experiment, and construct their understanding of scientific concepts, and critical thinking skills. Kiy (2023) demonstrates the advantage of using ChatGPT for exploring information relevant to various topics. Whether conducting research, brainstorming ideas, or seeking inspiration, individuals can utilize ChatGPT's capabilities to access pertinent information swiftly and efficiently. Schmidt et al. (2023) assert that combining human and AI creativity can expedite the generation of content ideas in content marketing. By utilizing AI-powered tools like ChatGPT alongside human insights and expertise, marketers can develop compelling content strategies, resonate with their target audiences, and drive engagement effectively. Fischer et al. (2023) predict that AI applications such as ChatGPT will fundamentally change the way businesses operate. From customer service and market analysis to product development and strategic planning, businesses across industries stand to benefit from integrating AI technologies into their workflows, unlocking new opportunities for innovation and growth.

Yudono (2023) discusses AI's constraints in crafting horror short stories, noting limitations in generating titles, constructing realistic conversations, incorporating intrinsic elements, and utilizing olfactory imagery. These shortcomings underscore the challenges AI faces in replicating the intricacies of human creativity and the nuanced understanding of horror fiction. Bin-Hady et al. (2023) highlight ChatGPT's potential in enhancing learners' language skills. By providing personalized feedback, generating contextualized prompts, and offering language practice exercises, ChatGPT can facilitate language acquisition and proficiency development in learners of all levels. Peres (2024) emphasizes the importance of examining the potential of AI-based technologies like ChatGPT in the realm of academic writing. As academic writing and scientific knowledge dissemination evolve, there is a pressing need to critically evaluate how AI-mediated processes impact the integrity, accessibility, and effectiveness of scholarly communication.

Tran (2023) suggests that ChatGPT can assist authors in efficiently producing high-quality work. By offering suggestions, refining drafts, and providing creative prompts, ChatGPT streamlines the writing process and enables authors to focus on crafting compelling narratives and engaging content. Habeb Al-Obaydi et al. (2023) note that the use of ChatGPT can complement language learning strategies and contribute to the development of linguistic and social skills. When integrated with other learning methods, ChatGPT facilitates interactive language practice, nurtures communication skills, and promotes cultural understanding among learners. Gervacio (2023) reports that international TESOL students perceive Chat AI positively. By providing personalized language assistance, cultural insights, and conversational practice opportunities, ChatGPT enhances language learning experiences and promotes confidence in communication skills. Irfan et al. (2023) highlight the benefits of integrating AI tools like ChatGPT into classroom environments. These tools encourage students to engage in in-depth analysis, collaborate on projects, and refine their writing skills through iterative feedback and support. Lee (2023) suggests that collaborating with conversational artificial intelligence can offer a novel self-understanding and introduce a unique writing experience that enhances critical and analytical thinking. By engaging with AI-generated texts, writers are prompted to reflect on language usage, narrative structure, and thematic development, enhancing their writing proficiency and cognitive abilities.

Al-Zaghir et al. (2023) note ChatGPT's proficiency in producing linguistically accurate samples, showcasing its capability to generate text that adheres closely to grammatical rules and linguistic conventions. Clayphan et al. (2014) suggest that interactive tabletops hold potential for enhancing brainstorming sessions, offering a collaborative and intuitive platform for generating and organizing ideas. Chinonso et al. (2023) highlight ChatGPT's ability to provide rapid and immediate responses to search queries, demonstrating its efficiency in retrieving relevant information and assisting users in accessing desired content quickly. Loos et al. (2023) observe that ChatGPT is capable of generating text that closely resembles human-written content, showcasing its advanced language generation capabilities and its potential to produce natural-sounding dialogue and narratives. Duc et al. (2023) propose that the text processing and generation capabilities of ChatGPT have the potential to bring about significant changes across various domains. From content creation and communication to data analysis and information retrieval, ChatGPT's capabilities hold promise for revolutionizing numerous areas of human endeavor.

Bekeš & Galzina (2023) assert that AI-powered chatbots hold the potential to transform the accessibility, creation, comprehension, and implementation of educational content. This suggests a paradigm shift in how individuals engage with and utilize educational materials, with AI-driven technologies playing a pivotal role in facilitating learning experiences.Anderson et al. (2023) highlight ChatGPT's versatility in assisting with content generation and problem-solving tasks. By providing insights, generating ideas, and offering solutions to complex problems, ChatGPT enhances productivity and creativity in various contexts. Tenhundfeld (2023) notes ChatGPT's ability to deliver remarkably accurate responses to factual questions, write functional code across multiple programming languages, and generate text passages that closely resemble human-authored content. These capabilities underscore ChatGPT's proficiency in a wide range of tasks, from information retrieval to creative writing. Wegerif et al. (2010) describe how the emergence of new perspectives in graphical dialogue maps can be identified using a coding scheme supported by a machine pattern-matching algorithm. This approach enables moderators to recognize and highlight evolving discussions, providing valuable insights and awareness indicators within collaborative learning environments. Sundar & Liao (2023) illustrate how AI-powered scripting and creative brainstorming, facilitated by ChatGPT, have captured the popular imagination in the context of Malayalam cinema. This suggests that AI technologies are reshaping creative processes and narrative development within the film industry, leading to innovative storytelling approaches and engaging cinematic experiences.

Mannarsamy (2023) observes that AI is increasingly becoming an integral part of our literary landscape, indicating a significant shift in how artificial intelligence is shaping the field of literature and creative expression. Fernandez (2023) highlights the deep learning model as a crucial component that drives the functionality of ChatGPT, underscoring its importance in enabling the chatbot to generate contextually relevant responses and engage users in meaningful conversations. Ren et al. (2023) regard the proliferation of ChatGPT as a milestone in the normalization of artificial intelligence applications in education. This suggests that the widespread adoption of ChatGPT reflects a broader acceptance and integration of AI technologies into educational settings, paving the way for innovative learning approaches and experiences. Ram & Verma (2023) outline various aspects of AI research, including reasoning, knowledge representation, planning, learning, natural language processing, perception, and manipulation of objects. These areas of study highlight the diverse range of capabilities and applications within the field of artificial intelligence. Tran (2023b) suggests that ChatGPT can enhance various aspects of academic research, offering researchers valuable assistance in data analysis, literature review, and idea generation. Susanto et al. (2023) discuss the different roles that language models play in helping student writers become more creative. By offering prompts, suggesting revisions, and providing feedback, language models like ChatGPT support students in exploring new ideas and refining their writing skills. Hawanti & Zubaydulloevna (2023) find that AI chatbot-based instruction can reduce students' anxiety about learning English writing. By providing personalized support, guidance, and feedback, AI-powered chatbots create a supportive learning environment that enhances confidence and engagement among students. In a recent experimental study, 180 media students participated in a project where they were tasked with writing a script for a short film using a virtual reality (VR) environment, facilitated by Oculus Head-Mounted Displays (HMDs). This setup aimed to explore the potential of VR and AI technologies in enhancing creative writing and storytelling skills. The participants, selected through purposive sampling to ensure a diverse representation, interacted with ChatGPT, an AI-based conversational agent, within the VR space. This integration allowed students to receive real-time suggestions and dialogue prompts, helping to shape their scripts. To assess the effectiveness of this approach, the Virtual Experience Questionnaire developed by Tcha-Tokey was used, measuring aspects like immersion, presence, and user satisfaction (Kunnumpurath, Menon, et al., 2024).

Fraiwan & Khasawneh (2023) describe ChatGPT as a type of artificial intelligence language model that utilizes deep learning algorithms to produce responses akin to those generated by humans when prompted with text-based queries. This technology represents a significant advancement in natural language processing, enabling more fluid and contextually appropriate interactions between humans and machines. Tseng & Warschauer (2023) discuss the unique challenges posed by AI-generated writing tools like ChatGPT for second language educators. While these tools offer opportunities for language practice and skill development, they also require educators to adapt their teaching methodologies to effectively integrate AI technologies into language learning curricula. Sanjay et al. (2023) note that ChatGPT, developed by OpenAI, is emerging as a leader in the field of AI-driven conversational agents, surpassing other competitors such as Bard AI, Bing AI, ChatSonic, OpenAI playground, LaMDA, and Socratic. This suggests that ChatGPT's advanced capabilities and user-friendly interface have positioned it as a preferred choice among consumers and developers alike. Wang & Li (2018) highlight the effectiveness of intelligent agents in online brainstorming, particularly in the realm of idea generation. By facilitating collaboration and providing prompts for creative exploration, intelligent agents like ChatGPT enhance the efficiency and productivity of brainstorming sessions. Singer et al. (2023) point out that ChatGPT cannot be held ethically responsible for the content it generates, as the output is ultimately determined by the user's input. This underscores the importance of ethical considerations and human oversight when utilizing AI technologies for content creation and communication. Tholander & Jonsson (2023) suggest that generative machine learning models, including ChatGPT, can play a significant role in creative design processes such as ideation, early prototyping, and sketching. By generating diverse and innovative ideas, these models augment the creative capabilities of designers and facilitate the exploration of novel design concepts. Dyer et al. (2023) propose that AI-powered scripting and creative brainstorming with ChatGPT, particularly in the context of Malayalam cinema, can enhance learning experiences. By simulating real-world scenarios and encouraging experimentation, ChatGPT digs deeper understanding and engagement among learners. Yeh & Chang (2007) introduce a controlling agent known as the Playwright Agent, developed for implementing adaptive scripts. This technology enables the customization of scripts based on user interactions and feedback, enhancing the adaptability and responsiveness of automated systems in various applications.

METHODOLOGY

In order to comprehensively explore the impact of AI-powered scripting and creative brainstorming in the Malayalam film industry, the researcher conducted in-depth interviews with 30 prominent script writers who have significantly contributed to the cinematic landscape. These interviews serve as a primary source of valuable insights and firsthand experiences, shedding light on the perspectives, challenges, and innovations that arise when integrating artificial intelligence, specifically ChatGPT, into the scripting process. The diverse narratives and viewpoints gleaned from these interactions will be meticulously examined and discussed in the subsequent chapters of this study. By exploring into the thoughts and experiences of these scriptwriters, the study aims to capture a nuanced understanding of how AI technology, particularly ChatGPT, is influencing and revolutionizing the creative aspects of Malayalam cinema. The themes extracted from these interviews will be intricately woven into the contents, providing a rich and multifaceted exploration of the intersection between artificial intelligence and the artistry of scriptwriting in the Malayalam film industry.

Enhancing Story Development

In the study by Yao et al. (2019), it was found that the narratives produced through a process involving comprehensive planning exhibited greater diversity, coherence, and relevance to the intended topic compared to narratives generated without such meticulous pre-planning. This method involved the utilization of autonomous characters whose actions served as the driving force behind the development of the plot. However, despite the autonomy granted to these characters, their actions were still governed by overarching plot requirements, ensuring a semblance of structure within the generated narratives. As a result, the narratives produced under this approach were characterized by their enriched storyline, logical progression, and adherence to the central theme, thus showcasing the effectiveness of incorporating a full plan into the narrative generation process.

In the research conducted by Riedl and Young (2010), a groundbreaking refinement search planning algorithm was introduced, demonstrating its superior capability to enhance audience understanding of character intentions when compared to plans generated through conventional partial-order planners. This innovative algorithm employed a systematic approach to iteratively refine plans, ensuring a more coherent and comprehensible depiction of character motivations and actions within a narrative context. By meticulously analyzing and adjusting the sequence of events, the refinement search planning algorithm effectively minimized ambiguity and inconsistencies in character behavior, thereby facilitating a clearer portrayal of their intentions and objectives throughout the narrative. Consequently, the narratives crafted through this refined planning process were characterized by their heightened clarity, enabling audiences to more readily empathize with and comprehend the motives driving each character's decisions and actions. This pioneering approach marks a significant advancement in narrative planning methodologies, promising to elevate the quality and accessibility of storytelling in various interactive and entertainment mediums.

In the exploration conducted by Szilas (2007), a two-pronged approach was delineated for the generation and selection of narrative actions, enhancing the meaningfulness and relevance of generated narratives. Firstly, a rule-based component was introduced to govern the generation of narrative actions, ensuring that each action contributed meaningfully to the unfolding storyline. This component operated on a set of predefined rules that guided the selection and execution of actions within the narrative framework, thereby imbuing the generated narratives with coherence and purpose. A user model was devised to facilitate the ranking and selection of these narrative actions based on their perceived relevance and significance to the user. This model leveraged insights into user preferences, expectations, and engagement patterns to assign a rank to each potential action, thus enabling the system to prioritize actions that were most likely to resonate with the user. By incorporating this user-centric approach into the action selection process, the system aimed to tailor the narrative experience to individual user preferences, promoting more immersive and engaging storytelling environment. Through the integration of a rule-based component for narrative action generation and a user model for action ranking and selection, Szilas (2007) presented a comprehensive framework for the creation of meaningful and personalized narratives.

ChatGPT has been a game-changer for us. One instance that comes to mind is when we were stuck on a crucial dialogue scene in our cinema. We turned to ChatGPT for inspiration, and it provided us with fresh perspectives and dialogue options that *perfectly captured the essence of the scene. It helped us break through the creative block and elevate the quality of our script. (Participant 10, 2024)*

The participant describes how ChatGPT served as a pivotal resource during a challenging phase of script development, particularly when they encountered a creative block while working on a crucial dialogue scene for their cinema project. The participant's characterization of ChatGPT as a "game-changer" emphasizes the profound significance of the tool in their creative endeavors. This suggests that ChatGPT has fundamentally altered their approach to scriptwriting, indicating its substantial role in shaping their creative output. The mention of being "stuck" on a crucial dialogue scene underscores the specific challenge faced by the participant and their team. This highlights the critical nature of the scene within the larger narrative framework and the importance of overcoming creative obstacles to ensure the script's coherence and effectiveness. The participant's decision to turn to ChatGPT for inspiration reflects their confidence in the tool's ability to provide valuable insights and solutions. By leveraging ChatGPT, they sought to break through their creative block and generate fresh ideas that would resonate with the essence of the scene. The testimonial further elucidates how ChatGPT delivered on its promise by providing "fresh perspectives and dialogue options" that perfectly captured the scene's essence. This indicates ChatGPT's versatility in offering diverse and relevant suggestions, thereby facilitating the exploration of new narrative avenues. Ultimately, the participant attributes their ability to break through the creative block and elevate the script's quality to the assistance provided by ChatGPT. This highlights the tangible impact of the tool in enhancing the craftsmanship and effectiveness of the script, underscoring its value as a creative aid.

In our latest film, we wanted to create a compelling backstory for one of the main characters. We used ChatGPT to brainstorm ideas, and it helped us flesh out the character's background in a way that resonated with the audience. The depth and authenticity brought by ChatGPT added layers to the storytelling, ultimately enhancing the overall impact of the film. (Participant 24, 2024).

In their latest film, the filmmakers aimed to craft a captivating backstory for one of the main characters, turning to ChatGPT for assistance in generating ideas. Through this collaboration with artificial intelligence, they successfully fleshed out the character's background in a manner that resonated with the audience. The depth and authenticity brought forth by ChatGPT added intricate layers to the storytelling, ultimately enriching the overall impact of the film. This creative integration of AI into the filmmaking process demonstrates a harmonious blend of human ingenuity and technological innovation.

It has significantly improved the user experience of our films by allowing us to craft more engaging and relatable narratives. For example, in our recent romantic drama, we used ChatGPT to fine-tune the dialogues and interactions between the lead characters. This attention to detail enhanced the emotional resonance of the film, resulting in positive feedback from viewers who felt deeply connected to the storyline. (Participant 26, 2023)

The participant notes that integrating ChatGPT into their filmmaking process has notably elevated the user experience of their films, allowing for the crafting of more compelling and relatable narratives. They exemplify this by detailing its application in a recent romantic drama, where ChatGPT was utilized to fine-tune the dialogues and interactions between the main characters. This meticulous attention to detail resulted in heightened emotional resonance throughout the film, eliciting positive feedback from viewers who felt deeply connected to the storyline.

Customization for Malayalam Context

ChatGPT writes in Malayalam through a sophisticated process known as natural language processing (NLP). Initially, it undergoes training on a vast dataset consisting of Malayalam text from diverse sources like articles, books, and online content. During this training phase, ChatGPT comprehends the grammar rules, vocabulary, and syntax of the Malayalam language, along with understanding contextual nuances. When prompted with a Malayalam input, ChatGPT utilizes its acquired knowledge to generate text that adheres to the language's conventions. By predicting the most probable next words or characters based on the input, ChatGPT ensures coherence and relevance in the generated text. ChatGPT may undergo further refinement through fine-tuning on specific Malayalam datasets, enhancing its proficiency in the language. Interaction with users provides a feedback loop for ChatGPT to learn and adapt, continually improving its ability to write fluently and accurately in Malayalam.

It writes in malayalam well, as it requires correct command. (Participant 30, 2023)

This quote reflects the participant's observation regarding the proficiency of ChatGPT in generating text in the Malayalam language. The participant highlights that ChatGPT demonstrates competence in writing in Malayalam, attributing this capability to the requirement of correct command. However, a correct command is required to write.

Ethical Considerations

Ethical considerations surrounding the use of artificial intelligence (AI) have become increasingly prominent as AI technology continues to advance and integrate into various aspects of society. In the realm of AI ethics, there are several key concerns that arise. One primary concern is the potential for AI algorithms to perpetuate biases, whether through the data they are trained on or the decision-making processes they employ. This raises questions about fairness, accountability, and transparency in AI systems, particularly in sensitive areas such as hiring, lending, and law enforcement. There are ethical dilemmas surrounding AI's impact on employment and the economy, as automation threatens to displace human workers and widen socioeconomic inequalities. Privacy and data security are also critical ethical considerations, as AI systems often rely on vast amounts of personal data, raising concerns about surveillance, consent, and data protection. As AI technology continues to evolve, it is essential for stakeholders to address these ethical considerations proactively, ensuring that AI is developed and deployed in a responsible and ethical manner that prioritizes the well-being and rights of individuals and communities.

> *Integrating AI into cinema raises important ethical considerations regarding the balance between automation and human creativity. While AI can streamline certain aspects of the filmmaking process, such as generating dialogue or suggesting plot twists, it's essential to ensure that human creativity remains at the forefront. As filmmakers, we must be mindful of maintaining artistic integrity and authenticity in our work, even as we leverage AI technology to enhance efficiency. (Participant 15, 2023)*

The participant addresses the integration of AI into filmmaking, acknowledging its potential to automate tasks like generating dialogue and suggesting plot twists. However, they stress the importance of upholding human creativity as paramount. Despite the efficiency gains AI offers, the participant emphasizes the preservation of artistic integrity and authenticity. They urge filmmakers to remain mindful of the balance between leveraging AI technology and maintaining the unique human touch in their work. This stance raises ethical considerations regarding the impact of AI on the creative process and the industry as a whole, prompting reflection on how to navigate this intersection responsibly.

> *AI has a profound impact on every stage of filmmaking, from pre-production to post-production. In pre-production, AI tools can assist with script analysis, character development, and even predicting audience preferences. During production, AI-enabled cameras and editing software can automate tasks such as color correction and visual effects, streamlining the filmmaking process. However, this automation raises questions about the role of human creativity and expertise in traditional workflows. Filmmakers must strike a balance between harnessing AI's capabilities and preserving the artistry and craftsmanship inherent in the filmmaking process. (Participant 23, 2023)*

The quote underscores the significant influence of artificial intelligence (AI) across all stages of filmmaking, spanning from pre-production to post-production. In pre-production, AI tools play a pivotal role in assisting filmmakers with tasks like script analysis, character development, and predicting audience preferences, thereby shaping the foundation of the film's narrative and audience engagement strategies. During production, AI-enabled cameras and editing software streamline tasks such as color correction and visual effects, enhancing efficiency and precision in the filmmaking process. However, the automation facilitated by AI prompts critical reflections on the evolving role of human creativity and expertise within traditional workflows. Filmmakers are tasked with navigating a delicate balance between harnessing the capabilities of AI technology to optimize production workflows and preserving the artistry and craftsmanship inherent in filmmaking. This tension between automation and human ingenuity raises profound questions about the future of the industry and underscores the need for filmmakers to approach AI integration with mindfulness and ethical consideration.

User Experiences and Success Stories

Some of the user experience and success stories mentioned by the script writers are as follows.

In one of my recent projects, I was tasked with writing a gripping thriller with intricate plot twists. I hit a roadblock in the middle of the screenplay, unsure of how to seamlessly tie together various subplots. That's when I turned to ChatGPT. By inputting key plot points and character arcs, ChatGPT generated several plausible scenarios that not only resolved the plot but also added layers of complexity that I hadn't considered (Particpant 5, 2023).

The participant recounts a specific instance where they encountered a challenge while writing a thriller screenplay, struggling to seamlessly connect multiple subplots within the narrative. Faced with this roadblock, they turned to ChatGPT for assistance. By inputting key plot points and character arcs into the AI system, ChatGPT generated several plausible scenarios that not only resolved the plot dilemma but also introduced additional layers of complexity to the story. This showcases how AI can serve as a valuable tool for writers, providing innovative solutions and inspiring fresh perspectives that may not have been initially considered.

In one of our recent Malayalam films, we encountered a creative block while developing the climax sequence. We turned to ChatGPT for inspiration, and it provided us with innovative ideas and plot twists that completely transformed the scene. This creative breakthrough not only elevated the quality of our film but also garnered critical acclaim and resonated with audiences on a profound level. (Participant 1, 2023)

The participant recounts a specific instance where they faced a creative challenge while developing the climax sequence of a recent film. In need of inspiration, they turned to ChatGPT for assistance. The AI system provided them with innovative ideas and plot twists that sparked a creative breakthrough, completely transforming the scene. This infusion of fresh perspectives not only enhanced the quality of their film but also led to critical acclaim and resonated deeply with audiences. The participant's experience highlights the valuable role of AI in facilitating creative problem-solving and promoting artistic innovation within the filmmaking process.

In one of my recent projects, we were exploring a historical drama set in colonial-era Kerala. Researching the period and ensuring historical accuracy was paramount, but weaving a compelling narrative around it was equally challenging. ChatGPT became our ally in this journey. By inputting historical facts, cultural nuances, and character motivations, ChatGPT generated rich dialogues and plot developments that seamlessly blended with the historical backdrop. It not only accelerated the writing process but also added authenticity to the narrative, resonating deeply with audiences and critics alike. (Participant 8, 2023)

The quote highlights the significant role of artificial intelligence, specifically ChatGPT, in the creation of a historical drama set in colonial-era Kerala. The participant outlines the challenges they faced in balancing historical accuracy with the need for a compelling narrative. They describe ChatGPT as an invaluable tool in this endeavor, leveraging its ability to generate rich dialogues and plot developments that seamlessly integrate with the historical backdrop. This use of AI not only expedited the writing process but also enhanced the authenticity of the narrative, resulting in resonance with both audiences and critics. Critically analyzing this statement, it exemplifies the potential benefits of AI in creative endeavors, particularly in scenarios requiring extensive research and adherence to historical accuracy. By inputting relevant information into ChatGPT, the filmmakers were able to harness its capabilities to augment their storytelling, adding depth and authenticity to the narrative. However, it is important to acknowledge potential limitations and ethical considerations associated with AI integration in creative processes. While AI can offer valuable assistance, there may be concerns about over-reliance on technology and its potential to replace human creativity and intuition. There could be questions regarding the accuracy and cultural sensitivity of AI-generated content, particularly in historical contexts where nuance and context are critical.

CONCLUSION

ChatGPT serves as a collaborative tool for filmmakers, writers, and creative minds in Malayalam cinema by offering a unique blend of innovation and inspiration. In the dynamic realm of filmmaking, where storytelling is paramount, ChatGPT emerges as a versatile ally, aiding creators in various stages of the creative process. For writers, ChatGPT serves as a brainstorming companion, generating ideas, plot twists, and dialogue snippets that spark creativity and fuel narrative exploration. Its ability to understand and generate text in Malayalam enables seamless integration into the local creative ecosystem, ensuring authenticity and cultural resonance in storytelling. Filmmakers leverage ChatGPT's capabilities to streamline pre-production tasks, such as character development and script refinement, while also utilizing its insights to navigate creative challenges and enrich narrative depth. Moreover, ChatGPT's collaborative potential extends beyond individual projects, encouraging a community of creators who share insights, exchange ideas, and collaborate on collective storytelling ventures. By facilitating collaboration, stimulating creativity, and expanding storytelling possibilities, ChatGPT emerges as an invaluable tool for filmmakers, writers, and creative minds in Malayalam cinema, shaping the future of storytelling in the region.

REFERENCES

Al-sa'di, A., & Miller, D. (2023). Exploring the Impact of Artificial Intelligence language model ChatGPT on the User Experience. *International Journal of Technology* [IJTIM]. *Innovation and Management*, 3(1), 1–8. DOI: 10.54489/ijtim.v3i1.195

Al-Zaghir, Z., Matroud, A. A., Abdalgader, K., & Alnaqbi, N. (2023). Exploring opportunities and challenges of using ChatGPT in professional writing instruction. *2023 IEEE International Conference on Teaching, Assessment and Learning for Engineering (TALE)*. DOI: 10.1109/TALE56641.2023.10398234

Anderson, N., McGowan, A., Galway, L., Hanna, P., Collins, M., & Cutting, D. (2023). Implementing generative AI and large language models in education. *2023 7th International Symposium on Innovative Approaches in Smart Technologies (ISAS)*.

Bekeš, E. R., & Galzina, V. (2023). Exploring the pedagogical use of AI-powered chatbots educational perceptions and practices. *2023 46th MIPRO ICT and Electronics Convention (MIPRO)*.

Bin-Hady, W. R. A., Al-Kadi, A., Hazaea, A., & Ali, J. K. M. (2023). Exploring the dimensions of ChatGPT in English language learning: A global perspective. *Library Hi Tech*. Advance online publication. DOI: 10.1108/LHT-05-2023-0200

Biswas, S. (2023). *Role of ChatGPT in the film industry: According to ChatGPT*. Qeios., DOI: 10.32388/NABVHA

Chinonso, O. E., Theresa, A. M.-E., & Aduke, T. C. (2023). ChatGPT for teaching, learning and research: Prospects and challenges. *Global Academic Journal of Humanities and Social Sciences*, 5(02), 33–40. DOI: 10.36348/gajhss.2023.v05i02.001

Clayphan, A., Kay, J., & Weinberger, A. (2014). ScriptStorm: Scripting to enhance tabletop brainstorming. *Personal and Ubiquitous Computing*, 18(6), 1433–1453. DOI: 10.1007/s00779-013-0746-z

Duc, A. N., Lønnestad, T., Sundbø, I., Johannessen, M. R., Gabriela, V., Ahmed, S. U., & El-Gazzar, R. (2023). *Generative AI in Undergraduate Information Technology Education — Insights from nine courses*. DOI: 10.48550/ARXIV.2311.10199

Dyer, T., Steele, J., & Mandernach, J. (2023). Three student-centered approaches to integrate ChatGPT in the online classroom: Effective eLearning (special series). *ELearn, 2023*(7). https://doi.org/DOI: 10.1145/3609266.3594546

Fernandez, P. (2023). "Through the looking glass: Envisioning new library technologies" AI-text generators as explained by ChatGPT. *Library Hi Tech News*, 40(3), 11–14. DOI: 10.1108/LHTN-02-2023-0017

Fischer, H., Dres, M., & Seidenstricker, S. (2023). *Application of ChatGPT in Design Thinking*. AHFE International. DOI: 10.54941/ahfe1004312

Fraiwan, M., & Khasawneh, N. (2023). *A review of ChatGPT applications in education, marketing, software engineering, and healthcare: Benefits, drawbacks, and research directions*. DOI: 10.48550/ARXIV.2305.00237

Gervacio, M.Jr. (2023). Breaking barriers in academic writing: The uses of Chat AI models in empowering international TESOL students. *International Journal of Asian Education*, 4(4), 256–264. DOI: 10.46966/ijae.v4i4.361

Habeb Al-Obaydi, L., Pikhart, M., & Klimova, B. (2023). ChatGPT and the general concepts of education: Can artificial intelligence-driven chatbots support the process of language learning? [IJET]. *International Journal of Emerging Technologies in Learning*, 18(21), 39–50. DOI: 10.3991/ijet.v18i21.42593

Hawanti, S., & Zubaydulloevna, K. M. (2023). AI chatbot-based learning: Alleviating students' anxiety in english writing classroom. *Bulletin of Social Informatics Theory and Application*, 7(2), 182–192. DOI: 10.31763/businta.v7i2.659

Irfan, M., Murray, L., & Ali, S. (2023). Integration of artificial intelligence in academia: A case study of critical teaching and learning in higher education. *Global Social Sciences Review*, VIII(I), 352–364. DOI: 10.31703/gssr.2023(VIII-I).32

Kiy, H. (2023). A study on writing experience with ChatGPT of college students. *Culture and Convergence*, 45(9), 853–868. DOI: 10.33645/cnc.2023.09.45.09.853

Kunnumpurath, B., Menon, V. A., & Paul, A. (2024). ChatGPT and virtual experience. In *Advances in computational intelligence and robotics book series* (pp. 32–50). DOI: 10.4018/979-8-3693-4268-8.ch003

Lai, Y. (2023). The impact of AI-driven narrative generation, exemplified by ChatGPT, on the preservation of human creative originality and uniqueness. *Lecture Notes in Education Psychology and Public Media*, 26(1), 121–124. DOI: 10.54254/2753-7048/26/20230865

Lee, J. (2023). A case study on writing a self-introduction letter in university liberal education using ChatGPT. *Culture and Convergence*, 45(9), 193–208. DOI: 10.33645/cnc.2023.09.45.09.193

Loos, E., Gröpler, J., & Goudeau, M.-L. S. (2023). Using ChatGPT in education: Human reflection on ChatGPT's self-reflection. *Societies (Basel, Switzerland)*, 13(8), 196. DOI: 10.3390/soc13080196

Luan, L., Lin, X., & Li, W. (2023). *Exploring the cognitive dynamics of artificial intelligence in the post-COVID-19 and learning 3.0 era: A case study of ChatGPT*. DOI: 10.48550/ARXIV.2302.04818

Maher, M. L., Tadimalla, S. Y., & Dhamani, D. (2023). An exploratory study on the impact of AI tools on the student experience in programming courses: An intersectional analysis approach. *2023 IEEE Frontiers in Education Conference (FIE)*.

Mannarsamy, N. (2023). Scripting imagination: The AI revolution in creative writing. *Shanlax International Journal of English*, 12(1), 33–36. DOI: 10.34293/english.v12i1.6727

Murad, I. A., Surameery, N. M. S., & Shakor, M. Y. (2023). Adopting ChatGPT to enhance educational experiences. *International Journal of Information Technology and Computer Engineering*, 35(35), 20–25. DOI: 10.55529/ijitc.35.20.25

Niloy, A. C., Akter, S., Sultana, N., Sultana, J., & Rahman, S. I. U. (2024). Is Chatgpt a menace for creative writing ability? An experiment. *Journal of Computer Assisted Learning*, 40(2), 919–930. DOI: 10.1111/jcal.12929

Peres, F. (2024). Health literacy in ChatGPT: Exploring the potential of the use of artificial intelligence to produce academic text. *Ciencia & Saude Coletiva*, 29(1). Advance online publication. DOI: 10.1590/1413-81232024291.02412023 PMID: 38198321

Ram, B., & Verma, P. (2023). Artificial intelligence AI-based Chatbot study of ChatGPT, Google AI Bard and Baidu AI. *World Journal of Advanced Engineering Technology and Sciences*, 8(1), 258–261. DOI: 10.30574/wjaets.2023.8.1.0045

Ren, X., Tong, L., Zeng, J., & Zhang, C. (2023). AIGC scenario analysis and research on technology roadmap of Internet industry application. *China Communications*, 20(10), 292–304. DOI: 10.23919/JCC.fa.2023-0359.202310

Riedl, M. O., & Young, R. M. (2010). Narrative Planning: Balancing Plot and Character. *Journal of Artificial Intelligence Research*, 39, 217–268. DOI: 10.1613/jair.2989

Ritala, P., Ruokonen, M., & Ramaul, L. (2024). Transforming boundaries: How does ChatGPT change knowledge work? *The Journal of Business Strategy*, 45(3), 214–220. DOI: 10.1108/JBS-05-2023-0094

Sanjay, M., Vikas, S., & Prashant, D. (2023). ChatGPT: Optimizing text generation model for knowledge creation. *I-Manager's Journal on Software Engineering*, 17(3), 21. DOI: 10.26634/jse.17.3.19469

Schmidt, L., Piazza, A., & Wiedenhöft, C. (2023). "augmented brainstorming with AI" – research approach for identifying design criteria for improved collaborative idea generation between humans and AI. In *Frontiers in Artificial Intelligence and Applications*. IOS Press.

Silva, A. de O., & Janes, D. dos S. (2021). The emergence of ChatGPT and its implications for education and academic research in the 21st century. *Review of Artificial Intelligence in Education*, 2(00), e06. DOI: 10.37497/rev.artif.intell.education.v2i00.6

Singer, J. B., Báez, J. C., & Rios, J. A. (2023). AI creates the message: Integrating AI language learning models into social work education and practice. *Journal of Social Work Education*, 59(2), 294–302. DOI: 10.1080/10437797.2023.2189878

Sudirman, I. D., & Rahmatillah, I. (2023). Artificial intelligence-assisted discovery learning: An educational experience for entrepreneurship students using ChatGPT. *2023 IEEE World AI IoT Congress (AIIoT)*.

Sundar, S. S., & Liao, M. (2023). Calling BS on ChatGPT: Reflections on AI as a communication source. *Journalism & Communication Monographs*, 25(2), 165–180. DOI: 10.1177/15226379231167135

Susanto, H., Woo, D. J., & Guo, K. (2023). *The role of AI in human-AI creative writing for Hong Kong secondary students*. DOI: 10.48550/ARXIV.2304.11276

Szilas, N. (2007). A computational model of an intelligent narrator for interactive narratives. *Applied Artificial Intelligence*, 21(8), 753–801. DOI: 10.1080/08839510701526574

Tenhundfeld, N. L. (2023). Two birds with one stone: Writing a paper entitled "ChatGPT as a tool for studying human-AI interaction in the wild" with ChatGPT. *Proceedings of the Human Factors and Ergonomics Society ... Annual Meeting. Human Factors and Ergonomics Society.Annual Meeting, 67*(1), 2007–2012. DOI: 10.1177/21695067231192916

Tholander, J., & Jonsson, M. (2023). Design ideation with AI - sketching, thinking and talking with generative machine learning models. *Proceedings of the 2023 ACM Designing Interactive Systems Conference*. DOI: 10.1145/3563657.3596014

Tran, N. V. (2023a). How to edit a manuscript with assistance of ChatGPT. *TTU Journal of Biomedical Sciences*, 2(1), 51–64. DOI: 10.53901/tjbs.2023.08.art06

Tran, N. V. (2023b). Utilizing ChatGPT in the process of crafting a research paper: A comprehensive guide. *TTU Journal of Biomedical Sciences*, 2(1), 41–50. DOI: 10.53901/tjbs.2023.08.art05

Tseng, W., & Warschauer, M. (2023). AI-writing tools in education: If you can't beat them, join them. *Journal of China Computer-Assisted Language Learning*, 3(2), 258–262. DOI: 10.1515/jccall-2023-0008

Vasconcelos, M. A. R., & dos Santos, R. P. (2023). *Enhancing STEM learning with ChatGPT and Bing Chat as objects to think with: A case study*. https://doi.org/DOI: 10.48550/ARXIV.2305.02202

Vicente-Yagüe-Jara, M. I., López-Martínez, O., Navarro-Navarro, V., & Cuéllar-Santiago, F. (2023). Writing, creativity, and artificial intelligence. ChatGPT in the university context. *Comunicar*, 31(77). Advance online publication. DOI: 10.3916/C77-2023-04

Wang, C.-H., & Li, T.-Y. (2018). Design of an Intelligent Agent for Stimulating Brainstorming. *Proceedings of the 2018 10th International Conference on Machine Learning and Computing*. DOI: 10.1145/3195106.3195119

Wegerif, R., McLaren, B. M., Chamrada, M., Scheuer, O., Mansour, N., Mikšátko, J., & Williams, M. (2010). Exploring creative thinking in graphically mediated synchronous dialogues. *Computers & Education*, 54(3), 613–621. DOI: 10.1016/j.compedu.2009.10.015

Yao, L., Peng, N., Weischedel, R., Knight, K., Zhao, D., & Yan, R. (2019). Plan-and-write: Towards better automatic storytelling. *Proceedings of the ... AAAI Conference on Artificial Intelligence.AAAI Conference on Artificial Intelligence, 33*(01), 7378–7385. DOI: 10.1609/aaai.v33i01.33017378

Yeh, Y.-P., & Chang, T.-W. (2007). Playwright agent as adaptive scripts for organization-communication. In *Human-Computer Interaction. HCI Applications and Services* (pp. 816–824). Springer Berlin Heidelberg. DOI: 10.1007/978-3-540-73111-5_91

Yudono, K. D. A. (2023). Keterbatasan Cerita Pendek Horor Karya Artificial Intelligence (AI) pada Perangkat Lunak ChatGPT. *DIDAKTIS: Jurnal Pendidikan Bahasa Dan Sastra Indonesia*, 1(2), 51–56. DOI: 10.33096/didaktis.v1i2.306

Chapter 5
The Digital Transformation of Sound and Music Cinema Experience With AI

Ufuk İnal
https://orcid.org/0000-0001-8638-0662
Ondokuz Mayıs University, Turkey

ABSTRACT

Artificial intelligence (AI) technologies are revolutionising the cinema industry. AI, which offers significant innovations especially in sound production and editing, enriches the film atmosphere. Deep learning models produce realistic sound effects, reducing the need for manual foley and facilitating synchronisation. AI provides higher quality sound effects while saving cost and time in film production. The quality of dialogue and the naturalness of sound effects are also improved with AI. AI stands out as an important technology that will shape the future of sound in cinema.

INTRODUCTION

Today, artificial intelligence (AI) technologies are revolutionizing the movie industry. In particular, AI applications play an important role in sound production and editing. Sound design and editing are critical to create the atmosphere of movies and draw the audience deeper into the movie. In this context, the new possibilities

DOI: 10.4018/979-8-3693-3916-9.ch005

provided by AI technologies enable sound engineers and artists to increase their creativity and deliver more immersive and realistic sound experiences.

The film production process is multi-stage and complex. In addition to images, sound recordings must also be produced in high quality. However, it is a common problem that the sounds cannot be recorded in the desired quality during shooting or that the sound recordings are incomplete due to various reasons. This situation necessitates a process called foley, which requires the subsequent addition of sound effects appropriate to the scene. Foley artists produce sound effects using various objects and materials to enrich the atmosphere of films. However, this process is time-consuming and costly.

AI technologies offer innovative solutions to overcome this challenge. In particular, deep learning models provide significant advantages in producing realistic sound effects. These models reduce the need for manual foley production and make audio synchronization easier by ensuring that fake sounds are close to the real thing.

AI-powered sound production systems not only save filmmakers cost and time, but also deliver higher quality and consistent sound effects. While AI applications deliver results close to expectations in filmmaking, they need to be tested for more complex scenes.

In the movie industry, sound is not limited to soundtracks; the quality of dialog and the naturalness of sound effects are also of great importance. AI technologies offer innovative solutions in these areas, minimizing the artificiality of manually produced sounds. Studies emphasize that some manually added sounds seem artificial, while AI-generated sounds are more natural.

This study will question the impact of artificial intelligence on cinema today through these issues.

Sound Use Experiments in Cinema

With the development of the cinema industry, many innovations have started to emerge. While cinema has developed its own structure, it has also led to the formation of new structures. One of these formations is film music. The emergence of film music started with movie screenings. The first known soundtrack was used by the Lumiere brothers during the first movie screenings. During the film screening at the Grand Cafe on Boulevard Des Capucines in Paris on December 28, 1895, a piano accompanied the film. Soon after, it was shown at the Lumiere brothers' public shows in England, in various theaters in London on February 20, 1896 and again in April of the same year, this time accompanied by an orchestra. At the request of the Pathe brothers, Camille Saint-Saens composed the first film music (score) for the film "L'Assassinat du Duc de Guise" in 1908. After that, Joseph Weiss for "Der Student von Prag" in 1913, Ildebranda Pizzetti for "Cabirio" in 1914 and Victor Schertzinger for "Rapsoda Sanatica" prepared special movie scores (Erdoğan, 2005: 76).

When it comes to the techniques used in cinema, the idea that the image is the primary source and the sound is the secondary source has been a subject of debate for many years. The effect of reality created by the first sound film proved that this debate was unfounded (Weis and Belton, 1985: 46). At first, no relationship was observed between the music played in movie theaters and the images (Özön, 1964: 290). However, it did not take long to realize the value of sound. With Jazz Singer, the impact of music in cinema was experienced in a historical sense. With this film, sound in cinema received the value it deserved within the narrative structure (Verscheure, 1995: 264). The 1930s witnessed the establishment of IATSE, the first sound-based union in the first production department. During this period, models of categorization, standardization and hierarchy among workers began to emerge in sound work. It was during this period that the regular structure was built, where employees coming from studio apprenticeships tended to specialize in a single field such as sound editing and sound mixing (Moore, 2017: 2).

With the advent of sound cinema, music, like other sounds, was included in the soundtrack and could be used in harmony with the images. However, this technical development did not lead to a major change in the way music was used in cinema; music was still used as a kind of depiction of images. This method, which worked well for still photographs, could have negative or even comical consequences in story-driven films. Nevertheless, it remains the most common use of film music even today (Özön, 1964: 290).

Functions of Music in Cinema

With the advent of sound cinema, music began to play an important role in cinema. During the silent film era, music was used to protect movie audiences from disturbing noises and to create an emotional atmosphere, but after a while it became a tradition to play certain pieces of music for certain scenes. Over time, original music composed specifically for films became widespread and the functions of music in cinema became more diverse. Berg (1976) lists the reasons for the presentation of silent films with musical accompaniment as follows (Erdoğan, 2005, p. 75): elimination of disturbing noises, elimination of stagnation, immobility and silence, mediating the continuity of the film phenomenon, illustrating the images of the film and commercial reasons.

In addition to these reasons, the need for pianists to adapt to images has led to a tradition of playing certain pieces in certain situations. Some well-known pieces were even played to illustrate certain situations. For example, fast and cheerful pieces were preferred for moving scenes, while emotional and slow pieces were preferred for slow scenes. Production companies began to distribute manuals with the movie, explaining the general tempo of the movie and the pieces that should be played in certain scenes. Italian Giuseppe Becce prepared a list of pieces that could be used in certain scenes by classifying all classical pieces under the name "Kinothek". However, in time, it became widespread to prepare original music composed directly for the film (Özön, 1964: 290).

We know that music is a tool for revealing emotions. Accordingly, every society, every period and every experience has a different music. Since we experience joy, sadness and enthusiasm through music, we shape our dreams with music. In this context, music describes the landscapes in our minds and takes us to new horizons. Music has similar functions in cinema. While we are affected by the image we see, we enter the emotional dimension of the moment with the music. Film music has many functions like this. Different sources put forward different opinions about these functions.

According to Maas, who explains his view based on basic sources including the works of Adorno and Eisler, Maas and Schudack on film music, the functions of film music can be categorized under four headings. Firstly, in tectonic functions, music can provide announcement and ending tension as a structural element outside the film formation, or it can be used entirely within the framework of the film's formation, such as in a revue film. Secondly, as an element of narrative structure, music in sequential functions can bring scenes to a climax, separate real and imagined formations, or connect processes in the succession of scenes. Thirdly, in semantic functions, music can be charged with ideological or connotative meaning; it can enhance the emotionality of scenes, accompany emotions, double the action or psychologically stimulate the audience. Finally, in the mediatization function, music leads the audience to temporary associations and makes them accept the film. For example, the use of a popular piece of music in a teen movie or the use of a well-known motif in a detective movie. The soundtrack establishes the connection between the audience's sociocultural experience of film music and the film (Erdoğan, 2005, p. 60).

Bertolt Brecht, in his note in the Contemporary Cinema magazine, comments on the functions of film music as follows: Music increases the appreciation of art. The soundtrack pre-flames the emotions that the events on the screen should give rise to and makes the audience experience these emotions. Music tries to express the storm of emotions that the events of the movie should have generated and perhaps never did. Another function of music is to ensure the invisibility of cinema. Music hypnotizes the audience and makes them forget that cinema is cinema. Furthermore, music is used to cover up the mavericks, leaps and incongruities of the actions in the movie. Seemingly unrelated events can be connected by music, contradictory events can be directed in a certain direction (1975, p. 47).

According to Arslantepe, music is used to enhance images. It gives the spirit of the movie and helps the audience to better reflect emotions such as excitement, tension, romance or fear in a scene. It often appears as an element that creates atmosphere. The relationship between cinema and music can be seen in two ways: 'film for music' and 'music for film'. A movie for music is a movie that tells the life of a musician or composer or a movie story that focuses on a musician. The phenomenon of music in cinema finds its true meaning in music for film. Music in a movie can be categorized under two main headings: credits music and background/bottom music. The credits music is the music played during the introductory credits of a movie and gives information about the mood of the movie. Background music is the music heard in the background during the movie. The use of popular, well-known music that can be evocative can be detrimental to the film. Background music can provide additional information, strengthen the emotional structure of a scene and reveal the psychological structure of people. Music does not always have to be in harmony with the scene; sometimes incompatible uses are encountered. Different uses can be made according to the context of the movie. A great sadness can be accompanied by joyful music, which can be a means of irony (2012: 40).

According to Pudovkin, the role of music in film is to provide an objective perception of visual events, while music provides a subjective evaluation of this objectivity (1965: 210). Onaran, on the other hand, discussed the functions of music in a comprehensive manner. According to Onaran, music can be used in film in various ways: By substituting music for a real sound, for example, by using music instead of effects such as explosions or footsteps; by representing a sound that someone is thinking or remembering, such as an old worker remembering his old days; as a continuation of a shout or a noise, such as a joyful music heard after the joyful cries of a child seeing the sea for the first time. Music can also be used to reflect a person's psychological state, expressing joy or sadness. The use of a particular musical theme when the same person or situation recurs, a technique known as a leitmotif, also serves an important function, especially in situations such as the development of a character or the progress of a police investigation. Finally, by providing background music, it creates a backdrop to scenes; however, he notes that such use is often unnecessary and ineffective (1986: 54).

Cinema refers to a space in the entertainment industry where reality is reproduced. The closer what we see and hear is to reality, the more successful our moviegoing experience is.

ARTIFICIAL INTELLIGENCE AND SOUND DESIGN

The phenomenon that substances that create vibrations in the air transmit these vibrations to us as sound reveals that we need a source in the formation of sound. In the art of cinema, where real life appears as a fiction within the framework of various purposes and rules, the sound, just like the image, must be transformed into a unique form. The sounds that exist in this fictionalized world turn into an effective tool that serves a specific purpose regardless of its primary feature. Recent developments in artificial intelligence technology show that this form of fiction filtered through the human mind can be realized in different forms in computer-mediated environments.

The way in which thinking prescriptions originating from human intelligence are read and reproduced by computer environments refers to the technology model we call artificial intelligence today. One of the basic structures produced for computer systems to behave like humans is the Neural Network, which is inspired by the human brain and, according to Mitchell (2019: 32), is the most successful tool of modern artificial intelligence. Researchers have produced important studies on how to command machines using components that behave like biological neurons. The Neural Network functions to classify patterns and patterns and to classify these components (Picton, 1994: 1). Russell and Norvig argue that this technology, which has been studied for a very long time and called "Electronic Super Brains", is a competent invention that can play chess using logical reasoning techniques, write poetry by imitating emotions, or produce solutions for diagnosing diseases in the medical field. According to them, this process goes back much further than previously thought. In fact, the fact that the analytical machine produced by Lord Byrron's daughter Ada Lovelace in the 1800s had the ability to compose music is an example of the idea that machines can be programmed (1995: 4).

In this period when technology is used more intensively than ever to facilitate human life, it can be said that machine algorithms and human life have become intertwined. Hayles explains this situation, that is, the forms of cognition that merge with the social world, with the theorem he calls cognitive fusion. This structure seems to have almost reached its peak with artificial intelligence. Hayles' theorem states that such an intertwining of algorithms with human nature leads to new techniques and new models of cognition. Chubb and Beer (2024) reduce this structure to the field of music and express it through the example of the term counterpoint, which is used to describe the relationship between two or more musical formations. According to them, this relationship arising from the integration of human and machine is explained through the concept of counterpoint through sound texture. In their inquiry through the concept, they concluded that artificial intelligence applications in the use of sound in cinema are useful for human productions, especially in terms of using the audience's emotions and thoughts as a guide.

The subject of sound and music has been a structure that has grown together, starting with computer technologies and continuing with artificial intelligence algorithms. Today, sound and music technologies are used in almost all entertainment sectors. Just like the visual universe offered by cinema, the main goal of these technologies in the sound and music universe is to touch human emotions in the most effective way. Considering that the process of music creation requires a mental effort, it has recently become clear that this artistic endeavor, which was unique to humans until recently, can also be designed with artificial technologies. Recently, artificial intelligence technologies have been used to meet different functions in the field of sound and music in the cinema ecosystem.

Sound Effect Production: Digital Foley Technique

Foley is a sound creation technique that was introduced in the 1920s by radio broadcasting, whose biggest trump card was sound, to help people design the world in their minds. Named after Jack Foley, this technique started to be used at Universal Studios in the 1930s (Ghose and Prevost, 2020: 1). In this system, Foley tried to create the sounds created by different objects in real life from the sounds of many things around him by using association. This technique has been used by Foley artists for many years in both visual and auditory works in order to impress the audience and listeners by using the power of sound.

Foley production is not only a successful system but also a system that requires time and effort. The production phase of the sounds is provided by the movements of the object as a result of the performances of foley artists through microphone sets in manual recording rooms. In this process, the correct use of recording devices is as crucial as the success of the artist's performance. A noisy, ineffective or unsuccessful recording can cause the foley artist's performance to be dysfunctional.

Ghose and Prevost (2020: 12) draw attention to two issues for the artificial intelligence-supported Foley model developed with the deep learning model for adding sound effects to videos. These are related to the matching of the processes expressed as Frame Sequence and Frame Relation Network with sounds. What determines the working principle of these models derives from correctly used examples taught to artificial intelligence systems. In this way, the artificial intelligence system is inspired by the examples consisting of audio and video pairs that have been previously defined to it and makes predictions about the expected products. The soundtracks planned to be used for the specified scenes were commanded to be created in previously taught formats in accordance with the movie frame. It is stated that these models are successful in analyzing complex data and thus have a much higher success rate compared to previous studies. In this study, the sounds of breaking, car, step, cutting, fire, horse, rain, keyboard keying, gun, lightning, waterfall and clock were used as samples. A questionnaire was used to test the naturalness of the sounds. In the questionnaire, it was stated that the sounds obtained were played to people and more than 73% of the participants gave the opinion that the sounds produced were original human production.

Another remarkable development in the field of sound production is the Pixel player, a neural system product developed by MIT researchers after long-term studies. This program works with the motivation of learning voice and instrument sounds from images in videos. It finds the sound-producing regions of images and separates these sounds into a set of representations. The program works by self-monitoring without the need for a human. The fact that it works without the need for humans to classify the sounds obtained from both visual and auditory sources is seen as an important development for the future of these systems (Zhao, H. Et al. 2019: 1-14).

Artificial intelligence-based software, which takes on the role of the artist in the Foley system, eliminates a process that requires a long time and effort in the manual system. In this sense, it can be said that this system, which brings many advantages, also has some disadvantages. As with many AI-based applications, there are also user-based concerns about the loss of authenticity in these applications. On the basis of this concern, there are also discussions that AI-supported foley applications go through similar learning processes and therefore will recommend similar products using a similar recommendation mechanism.

Human Voice Cloning

There are two different trends in the use of the human voice in artificial intelligence technologies. The first of these is the use of human emotions as an example for machines. The second use is the exact copying of human voices. This structure, known as voice cloning, is based on three different structures. These are Text to Speech, Speaker Recognition and Zero-shot technologies. This system, which converts written text into spoken vocalizations, has been used in computers for many years. So it can be said that the voice cloning technique is a trained version of the TTS model. It has limited voice cloning capability and derives from a pre-existing learned voice without fine-tuning. Apart from TTS, another method for voice cloning is the Zero-shot learning process. This model aims to fill in the gaps in the knowledge of non-existent voices with the support of various descriptions. Speaker Recognition, on the other hand, analyzes the sound waves of the speaker and creates a unique profile of the person (Pecora, 2023:4- 18).

Inamdar et al. (2023: 426) found that the HiFi-GAN model, which utilizes deep learning and natural processing processes in voice cloning technology, is more successful in identifying and influencing emotions than any other production model. In this model using deep neural networks, speech synthesis and transformations are very close to reality and emotionally meaningful productions are in question. According to them, as this technology continues to produce more and more successful voice clones, it becomes inevitable to find a solution to ethical and consent issues in voice cloning technology.

While such developments are taking place in production. On the industrial side, it is seen that these technologies are put into the service of users in a short time. Microsoft Research announced that it has developed an artificial intelligence tool called VALL-E 2 by taking software such as LibriSpeech, VCTK and ELLA-V, which were previously on the market, to a more advanced stage. It was stated that this application is much more natural and realistic than the others. The company stated in its statement that they were concerned about potential misuse due to the success of the product in voice cloning and did not put the application into use for this reason alone (wenewsenglish, 2024).

One of the most well-known examples of audio cloning in the movie industry is Respeecher, which is also used in Star Wars productions. For the program to work successfully, at least 30 minutes of quality audio is required. After this audio is processed into the system with the deep learning method, cloning can be used successfully (Respeecher.com).

Emotional Voice Synthesis

Emotional sound synthesis is one of the most frequently used techniques of AI-supported sound technologies in cinema. In Foley technique, music is created for the scenes preferred in the visual. However, it is known that in order to achieve the desired effect on the audience in the recorded scene, it needs sound as much as visuals. Purves and his colleagues state that different parts of the brain must work in harmony in the formation of reactions such as happiness, surprise, anger, fear and sadness, which are daily emotions. The source of the stimuli that initiate the process of signaling to the brain are bodily sensations such as sight and hearing. In addition, they state that the frontal part of the brain, which processes these emotional systems, performs functions such as decision-making, interpreting social behaviors, and making moral judgments (2004: 706).

Considering that cinema aims to create an emotional impact on the audience, the importance of the correct use of sound in creating the right effect emerges. Sound designers in the cinema industry state that sound is the most important element in terms of creating emotional impact in cinema. According to them, it is a fact that music directs and manipulates the audience's emotions (Chubb & Bira, 2023).

The sounds produced by humans in various situations such as laughing, crying and being scared are important for artificial intelligence applications to make the right suggestions. In this process, known as emotional state identification, machines are given emotion descriptions through human voices. It is very common for people to be able to recognize which emotion they are in during their speech. Just as humans learn by experiencing it, the machine needs to go through similar processes (Marechal, 2019: 312).

In the training process of AI-supported applications in the movie industry, visuals, scenes and sound frequency ranges in the scenes are used for emotion teaching. Even small changes between voice tones and pitches are taken into account in order to achieve accurate results in emotion and sound matches. Huang's (2024:6) research revealed that sound has an important role in identifying emotions. According to the research, using voice to predict the emotions of the audience gives much more specific results than using visuals. This is a promising development in terms of increasing the success of artificial intelligence applications that are more successful in learning and applying complex emotions every day.

Another directional development in learning is related to background sounds. Marechal (2019: 312) draws attention to the use of sound isolated from background noise in order to create the desired emotional impact on the audience. As Huang emphasizes, even the slightest changes between tones and pitches are important for learning. Therefore, this situation reveals the necessity of isolating the sample sounds used in the learning process from the background sounds, which are referred to as noise. This has a direct impact on the successful teaching and production process.

Shan et al. stated that music plays an important role in reflecting emotions to the audience in movies. This necessitates minimizing inaccuracies in the correct identification of music recommendations. For this purpose, they selected 107 soundtracks, including 20 animated films where emotions are more prominent than other genres. In their research on these movies, they produced a model to produce music suggestions for emotions. According to this model, they tested that the accuracy rate of the suggestions was 85% (2009: 7673).

One of the first examples of AI-powered audio technology in the movie industry is Morgan (2016), directed by Luke Scott. The trailer of the movie was realized through IBM's Watson computer. The program modeled the scenes visually and aurally using machine learning. Hundreds of trailers of similar movies were analyzed to enable machine learning. The role of the AI in the creation of the trailer was to determine the most emotionally effective sound and image patterns, like an editor, and present it to the editing team. It took Watson 24 hours to review the 90-minute movie, select the most effective scenes and reduce it to a 6-minute trailer (Nofilmschool, 2016).

At this point, it cannot be said that artificial intelligence sound technologies are always successful in influencing human emotions in the desired direction with sound and images in cinema productions. Meltzer (2024) states that this issue stems from traditional human-made techniques. In this sense, he states that AI-supported music designs can design music suitable for the emotions of each scene and, if necessary, revise the sound editing from start to finish.

Improvement in Recording Technologies

Recording sound in cinema productions is a job that requires competence in itself. In the process of recording the sound of speech or the sound of any object, many unwanted sounds can be recorded due to the microphone shape, technical deficiencies of the microphone or the geography of the recording. Some techniques are tried in applications such as adobe audition to isolate these unwanted sounds, which technicians call background sound, external sound, noise, etc., from the sound we want to use. The success of these techniques is measured by the ability to minimize unwanted sounds while preserving the recorded sound as much as possible. In this sense, artificial intelligence applications seem to end this difficult process, which technicians spend time and effort in analog efforts, with a single click of a button. Enhance Speech, an audio cleaning service designed by Adobe, has been very successful in isolating speech sounds from background noise.

It is known that artificial intelligence applications are taken into the training process in order to create the right emotion. Marechal et al. (2019:312) emphasized that for such applications to be successful, background noises should not be included in the deep learning process. It is expected that productions that are isolated from any noise objects or, in other words, isolated from background sounds will give realistic results in terms of detecting the correct emotion. In addition, it can be said that blocking background noise will increase the clarity of dialogs and sound effects. It can be said that this feature, when used correctly, will also facilitate the work of sound engineers in challenging recording conditions in the recording geography (Townsend, 2024).

Today, there are many applications that bring the function of an AI-supported foley system, which can produce in computerized environments, to the digital realm and guide sound engineers through the music creation process. Talking about the limits of these applications can be useful to see how recording technologies are being used in the final stage:

> Noisli[1] and Endel[2]: These two applications have a similar working principle. Both apps allow their users to create their own personal background sound design that they can listen to during work, sleep, rest, etc. As a marketing strategy, the apps market a soundscape to help reduce stress in the work environment. The apps can also be used as an alternative artificial intelligence tool to create background sounds for movies.

Audio Design Desk[3]: It is an application that contains more than 70 thousand royalty-free sounds and uses artificial intelligence in audio creation processes for videos. The application, which also includes audio editing and design features on its interface, is preferred by TV series, movie and documentary production companies. It has an audio content creation module used in Netflix, HBO Max, Amazon Prime and similar applications.

Aiva[4]: The application describes itself as a sound design assistant. The application, which offers the opportunity to produce music through the sounds it contains, leaves the copyright of these productions to the user. The application, which carries the references of companies such as Nvidia, Vodafone, TED, Animo Television, promises the user to produce new songs in more than 250 different styles within seconds.

OpenAI Jukebox[5]: This application is a neural net. Therefore, it contains sound profile sampling feature. This application symbolically generates music by determining the timing, pitch, speed and instrument of the note to be played. Since it bends to the task of predicting compressed audio codes, it can create virtual singers that mimic certain styles.

Magenta[6]: Magenta, a Google product, guides artists through machine learning. The application, which inspires the artist to create new music, works like an assistant in the music creation process. This application, which creates music syntheses through neural networks, uses deep learning and offers the Differentiable Digital Signal Processing library to its users. In this way, it creates many possibilities for the user, from virtual instrument creation to intuitive tone addition.

Suno[7]: The application known with the slogan "Make song about anything" promises to produce the song of the user's dreams. The program, which is a production of Cambridge MA musicians and artificial intelligence experts working together, can create music and sing vocals without the need for any instrument. The music produced in the program can be edited.

Mubert[8]: The program provides the opportunity to create music infrastructure for videos, podcasts, games and many similar productions. The company pays attention to the licensing of the created content and declares that it is one of the most powerful licensing platforms with more than 4000 musicians and more than one million samples. The company is also on a mission to bring musicians, creators and brands together in the same environment.

These software, which perform functions such as music composition and customization, digital sound effect creation, sound editing design and licensing, provide services using paid membership systems.

Generative Adversarial Networks in the Audio World

Generative Adversarial Networks is a model that improves the machine learning and natural language processing process used to ensure the authenticity of the products produced by artificial intelligence applications. This model, studied by Goodfellow et al. (2014:1), aims to improve machine learning and natural language processing in both the production and training phases of artificial intelligence applications. According to this model, it provides a contested production structure such as production and discrimination. Goodfellow explains this situation through the metaphor of counterfeit money. According to him, there is a competitor in the productive part. While the productive model aims to produce a counterfeit that is difficult to detect, the discriminative model works like a policeman trying to detect that the money is fake. This model, which is mostly evaluated through visual productions, has also been tested by different researchers for audio productions.

Film production is a multi-stage process. Producing sound recordings during the production of visuals requires a separate expertise. In some productions, it is a situation experienced in many plateaus that sound recordings cannot be used in scenes where the images are successful. This situation makes the use of foley necessary. When we go one step further, some video and film production teams do not record sound in the background while they are shooting images, which also leads to dependence on foley. It is known that the less sound is recorded during filming, the more performance is required in foley production. This situation necessitates a labor-intensive process not only in sound production but also in sound synchronization. Each of these processes creates a new cost item. One of the most important parts of film production is the high production costs. Ghose and Prevost (2021) state that the two preferred methods for solving such problems are the adaptation of previously recorded sounds to the scenes being shot or the establishment of foley sets suitable for the scenes being shot. Especially the second option increases the costs of film production. At this point, artificial intelligence-supported foley applications stand out as a new solution to reduce costs and minimize synchronization errors. In their study, Ghose and Prevost (2021), who are in search of a solution to this issue, started to test the success of sound formations created by artificial intelligence in the synchronization of sounds through a structure called Generative Adversarial Networks (GAN). The data they obtained shows that AI applications are close to meeting the expectations of filmmakers, but in order to make definitive judgments on this issue, AI-supported content produced for more complex videos should also be tested.

When it comes to sound in the movie industry, not only soundtracks but also dialogues and sound quality should be taken into account. Zhi et al. (2018) point out that some sounds added manually during the creation of music editing seem artificial compared to real sounds. They suggested that this is due to a modeling problem. Maayah et al. (2023) attempted to solve this problem. They state that the sounds used in GANs contain more complex patterns than visuals, so it is very difficult to extract a model to be taught. According to their research, making limited generalizations by keeping the sample learning information selected in the machine learning part to a minimum and choosing the frequency range that better represents human voice perception helps to obtain accurate results in the natural language processing part.

Sectoral Experiences, Opportunities and Concerns

On the music production side, it is known that artificial intelligence applications are an area that may be more preferred in the near future, as they provide advantages in terms of both time and cost. Many music companies around the world have been working on artificial intelligence forms for a very long time. Recently, the fruits of these efforts have started to emerge. Sony's artificial intelligence-based product Daddy's Car is an example of this. The song, whose lyrics were written through an artificial intelligence system called Flow Machines, is known as the first pop song created by artificial intelligence. Created in 2016, the song was released in 2017 with the touches of Youtuber Tryn Southern. He used programs such as Amper Music, Watson, Magenta and AIVA to turn the song into an album (Welsh, 2019).

In music production, there are many names that produce music through artificial intelligence applications. It is known that David Guetta used Eminem's voice through AI in a concert and rapper Mederios produced a Jay-Z voice. This issue has been met with harsh reactions from some musicians. The emergence of a debate on the topic of artificial intelligence replacing musicians, in which musicians such as Grimes and Zola were also involved on social media, has made the opinions of artists who use AI techniques in the production phase more valuable. One of the most well-known names in the field of music production through AI-supported applications is Holly Herndon. For her album Pronto this year, Herndon collaborated with artificial intelligence expert Jules LaPlace and a few other experts in the field to develop Spawn, which is designed for artificial intelligence music production. This design played an important role in the creation of the album. Herdon states that in music production with artificial intelligence, producers need rules in the fugue creation part, and at this point artificial intelligence can be used to create this rule set. Contrary to popular belief, he predicts that artificial intelligence will not completely replace musicians. As he experienced in his own album, he states that artificial intelligence techniques are very useful in learning the works of original music producers and suggesting alternative content to these productions. According to him, what makes humans valuable in this comparison is their ability to think independently. Therefore, the issue to be concerned about is the tendency of humans to become roboticized and predictable in their thinking (Minsker, 2019; Welsh, 2019).

Audio deepfakes are recently frequently encountered artificial intelligence productions in video music production. Deepfake is a concept that refers to the use of embedded audio and video production software. This application was recognized in 2017 with face-swapping videos. Thanks to this application, the sounds seen and heard in the video can be copied and replaced with the desired content (Paris & Donovon, 2019:2). In deepfake videos, which are frequently encountered on social media, especially the images of famous faces are manipulated for the purpose of laughter. This system, which is used with deep learning and technologies, has recently witnessed remarkable examples.

A musician named Ghostwriter produced a song called "Heart on My Sleeve" by manipulating the voices of The Weekend and Drake with artificial intelligence sound filters. This song, which was produced without the permission of Drake and The Weekend, was considered by listeners as a new partnership. After this song, Ghostwiter produced a single called "Whiplash" by using Travis Scott's voices without his permission. Ghostwiter, who calls these productions a genre of music produced by fans, states that AI-mediated music productions are a structure that can enable artists and songwriters to make more money. Stating that many songs that no one has heard yet have disappeared in the hands of producers and songwriters just because they do not adapt to the artist, Ghostwiter states that art will no longer be thrown away with a method like the one he has done. In addition, writers will be able to generate huge revenue streams by using the AI-generated voices of known singers. Stating that the song "Heart on My Sleeve" was written by Ghostwiter himself, the lyrics, music production, sound production and vocalization were done by himself, and only the vocals were manipulated. According to him, this structure represents the future of the music market. He predicts that in the future, all artists will be able to start licensing their own vocal similarities. With this system, it seems quite possible in the near future to listen to personalized birthday messages from singers' voices or to sing karaoke with the artist's voice (Time, 2023; Mashable, 2023).

One of the most prominent programs for voice cloning and manipulation in the film industry is Respeecher, a Ukrainian startup. The program made its name by voicing the character Luke Skywalker in the series version of the Star Wars series broadcast on the Disney Plus platform. This was necessitated by the fact that Mark Hamil, who played the character, is 68 years old and the character's 20-year-old self was performing. The surprising similarity of the voiceover to the original voice gave hope to the company and producers for the future. The voice archives of the Lucasfilm production company were used for the successful voice-over of the application (Miller, 2022). Jon Favreau, the director of the series, stated that no one realized that the character's voice was an artificial intelligence production during the

9 months it was on air. On the other hand, there is also a remarkable success of the application. The documentary "Event of Moon Disaster", in which a significant part of Richard Nixon's voice was produced by respecher, was awarded an Emmy award. In the statement made by the company, it was emphasized that the program offers time savings to the actors in high demand and financial savings to the producers in terms of easing their workload. On the other hand, the company stated that they are taking initiatives to prevent abuse of the program (Respeecher.com).

The Deepdub program, which is used in the field of dubbing in the media field and produced its first examples in the field of cinema in 2021, quickly entered the radar of producers. The program, designed to liberate media productions from the boundaries of language and therefore geography, was angel invested by names such as Kevin Reilly, an HBO Max executive, and Emiliano Calemzuk, former Fox Television Studios executive. Deephub made its name by being the first app to translate a feature-length movie into Spanish with the help of artificial intelligence. The app uses deep learning to dub in different languages while preserving the characteristics of the original voice. Under normal conditions, the dubbing of a 120-minute movie can take an average of 15 to 20 weeks, but the application reduced this time to around 4 weeks. In this respect, it can be said to be on the radar of producers. In 2021, the company partnered with Topic.com for English translation support. The company, which tries to eliminate borders in the dissemination of content in foreign languages, today defines itself as an organization that offers Hollywood-standard dubbing services (Warner, 2022).

These developments in the movie and music markets have caused concerns in the field of cinema, as in almost every field where artificial intelligence techniques are used. The use of ChatGPT in Hollywood writers' rooms as a cost-cutting tool for generating new plot ideas has forced writers to take a stand. Likewise, the widespread use of image-generation applications such as Midijourney caused concern among Hollywood writers and actors in the summer of 2023. Finally, these concerns peaked when studios attempted to use scanned copies of actors' bodies to reduce the cost of paying them. For these reasons, many employees have gone on strike against the use of these practices in order to avoid losing their jobs (Time, 2023). Similar concerns have been raised about the production and use of music, which is of crucial importance in cinema, especially in the post-production phase.

On the cinema side, many extras reported that they had recorded many times in the studio for 3D digital scanning, although they did not understand why. Since there was no legal obstacle in their contracts regarding this situation, the extras who continued the recordings realized that these recordings were made for the use of digital stunts. They stated that the companies used digital stunts and did not hire them. Digital stunt production has become widespread due to the lack of legal sanctions and the ability to produce low-cost work. In response, the Screen Actors Guild-

American Federation of Television and Radio Artists (SAG-AFTRA), a member of the International Federation of Actors, and record labels such as Universal Music Group (UMG) sought new ways to protect copyrights. SAG-AFTRA has taken the initiative to seek compensation sanctions for digital stunt producers. UMG, the most influential organization in the music world, worked with the Recording Industry Association of America on a new royalty scheme for the artists' union against the threat of AI. The coalition agreed that AI applications could be used with due regard to copyrights and artificial musician doubles. UMG CEO Lucian Grainge has expressed support for the use of AI to enhance human creativity for the benefit of musicians (Fastcompany, 2024; Telefonicatech, 2024; Time, 2023).

CONCLUSION AND EVALUATION

Since early in the history of cinema, the process of composing film music has been challenging, requiring time, cost and artistic freedom. During the silent film era, musicians would accompany films on the fly, while the development of synchronized sound technology in the 1930s allowed soundtracks to be added directly to films. While this opened up new opportunities for composers, it also set the stage for a challenging process. Composers had to work intensively to create original music suitable for movie scenes. Towards the end of the 20th century, the advancement of digital technologies brought significant changes to the music composition process. However, the real transformation took place in the 21st century with the rise of AI-supported music composition tools. By analyzing large databases of music, learning from different genres and creating original works, AI has been able to produce music that emphasizes certain emotions, scenes or plot points.

While AI-generated music was initially met with skepticism, the technology has shown its potential as a great aid to composers in creating customized music for film scenes. AI has played an important role in overcoming the shortcomings of traditional methods, allowing composers to be more creative, experiment with new sounds and quickly produce music that enhances the cinematic experience.

This collaboration between human creativity and AI-powered tools has created new opportunities in film music production. In the context of contemporary filmmaking, the incorporation of AI into the music composition process represents a harmonious fusion of technology and artistic expression. This historical process illustrates how technological and artistic innovations have come together in soundtrack production and transformed the cinematic experience.

Although the possibilities offered by artificial intelligence to its users make our lives easier in many respects, it is still difficult to reach clear statements about copyright and legal obligations. For example, no matter how much the work you create through Suno AI is your work, you will not own the right to paid use of the works created through a free account. Perhaps such issues, which do not concern us much today, may cause problems for users, even if they are undesirable, unless they are framed by legal boundaries.

On the other hand, Matt Panousis, CEO of MARZ, states that artificial intelligence applications have had a serious impact on the movie industry in terms of saving time. Panousis mentioned an application called Vanity AI, which completes the work that special effects artists complete in almost three working days in 20 minutes. According to him, such applications that save time and capacity are in strong demand in the movie industry. He even added that producers are looking forward to successful applications that meet Hollywood standards in terms of quality and reality. This situation indicates that in the future, the movie industry will turn into an area where many AI-supported platforms will be used.

The integration of artificial intelligence technologies into the film industry has the potential to reshape many areas of the industry. Especially in sound design, dubbing and soundtrack composition processes, the use of these technologies offers both opportunities and challenges. In the future, AI-enabled applications are expected to become more prevalent in film production processes.

Artificial intelligence plays a big role in voicing characters through voice cloning and manipulation techniques. For example, the Respeecher program was used to voice the younger version of Luke Skywalker and achieved great success. Deepdub, on the other hand, speeds up the dubbing process and provides time and cost advantages to producers. These technologies provide significant improvements in voice and dubbing processes.

In the movie industry, the use of digital stunts produced with artificial intelligence is becoming widespread in order to reduce actor costs. This has led to strikes by extras worried about losing their jobs. Organizations such as the International Federation of Actors (SAG-AFTRA) and Universal Music Group (UMG) are taking initiatives to regulate such practices in terms of copyright and job security. The use of digital stunts is generating considerable controversy in the film industry.

Artificial intelligence technologies are expected to become more widespread in the movie industry in the future. Applications such as voice cloning, personalized messages and karaoke songs produced from singers' voices are becoming possible. In addition, artificial intelligence can be used to make emotional descriptions by taking into account even small changes between sound frequencies and pitches. These predictions indicate that the impact of artificial intelligence in the movie industry will increase.

In conclusion, the increasing use of artificial intelligence technologies in the film industry is forcing many processes in the industry to transform. It seems that this transformation, while providing advantages in terms of cost and time, will also pose new challenges in terms of job security and copyrights. Therefore, it seems inevitable that in the near future, all stakeholders in the industry will make arrangements for the ethical and fair use of these technologies.

REFERENCES

Arslantepe, Mehmet (2012). Sinema Okuryazarlığı. Kocaeli: Umuttepe Yayınları

Brecht, B. (1975) “Sesli Sinema” Çağdaş Sinema Dergisi, Birlik Matbaası, Sayı 7: İstanbul.

Chubb, J., & Beer, D. (2023). *Establishing Counterpoints in the Sonic Framing of AI Narratives, AI and Ethics*. Springer.

Erdoğan, İ. (2005). *Sinema ve Müzik*. ERK Yayınları.

Fastcompany.com. (2024) Universal Music Group is Rewriting How Musicians are Paid in the AI era https://www.fastcompany.com/91041305/universal-music-group-most-innovative-companies-2024 (16.06.2024).

Ghose, S., & Ve Prevost, J. J. (2020). AutoFoley: Artificial Synthesis of Synchronized Sound Tracks for Slient Videos with Deep Learning. *IEEE Transactions on Multimedia*.

Ghose, S., & Ve Prevost, J. J. (2021). FoleyGAN: Visually Guided Generative Adversarial Network-Based Synchonous Sound Generation in Silent Videos. *IEEE Transactions on Multimedia*, V, 25. DOI: 10.1109/TMM.2022.3177894

Goodfellow, I. J.. (2014). Generative adversarial Nets. *Advances in Neural Information Processing Systems*, 3(11). Advance online publication. DOI: 10.1145/3422622

Huang, P. (2024). Decoding Emotions: Intelligent Visual Perception for Movie Image Classification Using Sustainable AI in Entertainment Computing. *Entertainment Computing*, 50, 50. DOI: 10.1016/j.entcom.2024.100696

Inamdar, M.. (2023). Voice Cloning Using Artifical Intelligence and Machine Learning: A Review. *Journal of Advanced Zoology*, 44-7(S7), 419–427. DOI: 10.17762/jaz.v44iS7.2721

Maayah, M.. (2023) “Using Context Specific Generative Adversarial Networks for Audio Data Completion” *Jordan International Joint Conference on Electrical Engineering and Information Technology*, Amman, Jordan. DOI: 10.1109/JEEIT58638.2023.10185733

Marechal, C.. (2019). Survey on AI-Based Multimodal Methods for Emotion Detection. In Kolodzjej, J., & Gonzalez-Velez, H. (Eds.), *High-Performance Modelling and Simulation for Big Data Applications*. Springer. DOI: 10.1007/978-3-030-16272-6_11

Mashable.com. (2023) "Ghostwriter, the guy behind the viral Drake/Weeknd Song, Thinks AI Music is Like Fanfiction" https://mashable.com/article/ai-music-ghostwriter-drake (20.06.2024).

Meltzer, A. (2024) "AI-Generated Music In Film: Enhancing Emotional Impact" https://cassetteai.com/blog/ai-generated-music-in-film-enhancing-emotional-impact (25.06.2024).

Minsker, E. (2019) Holly Herndon, Weighs in on Grimes and Zola Jesus' Debate About AI and the Future of Music" https://pitchfork.com/news/holly-herndon-weighs-in-on-grimes-and-zola-jesus-debate-about-ai-and-the-future-of-music/ (19.06.2024).

Moore, S. A. (2017). *The Rise of the Sound Designer: Northen California Film Sound in the 1960's and 1970's in Historical Journal of Film*. Radio and Television.

Nofilmschool.com. (2016) How IBM's Watson Used AI to the Trailer for Upcoming AI Thriller 'Morgan' https://nofilmschool.com/2016/10/ibm-watson-edits-morgan-trailer (21.06.2024).

Onaran, A. Ş. (1986). *Sinemaya Giriş*. Agora Kitaplığı/ Sinema Dizisi.

Özön, N. (1964). *Sinema El Kitabı*. Elif Yayınları.

Paris, B., & Donavan, J. (2019). *Deep Fakes and Cheap Fakes Them Manipulation of Audio and Visual Evidence*. Data and Society.

Pecora, A. E. (2023). *Data Driven: AI Voice Cloning*. Politecnico Di Torino Masters Degree in Data Science and Engineering.

Pudovkin, V. I. (1965). *Sinemanın Temel İlkeleri*. Bilgi Yayınevi.

Purves, D.. (2004). *Neuroscience*. Sinauer.

Respeecher.com. (t.y.) "Respeecher Synthesized a Younger Luke Skywalker's Voice for Disney+'s The Mandalorian" https://www.respeecher.com/case-studies/respeecher-synthesized-younger-luke-skywalkers-voice-disneys-mandalorian (30.06.2024).

Russel, S. J., & Ve Norvig, P. (1995). *Artifical Intelligence A Modern Approach*. Prentice Hall Englewood Cliffs.

Shan, M., Kuo, F.-F., Chiang, M.-F., & Lee, S.-Y. (2009). Emotion-based Music Recommednation by Affinity Discovery From Film Music [Elsevier.]. *Expert Systems with Applications*, 36(4), 7666–7674. DOI: 10.1016/j.eswa.2008.09.042

Telefonicatech.com. (2024) "Behind the Scenes Algorithms: Hollywood and the AI Technology Revolution" https://telefonicatech.com/en/blog/behind-the-scenes-algorithms-hollywood-and-the-ai-technology-revolution (21. 06.2024)

Time (2023) "4 Ways AI Transformed Music, Movies and Art in 2023" https://time.com/6343945/ai-music-movies-art-2023/ (19.06.2024).

Townsend, S. (2024) Exploring the Impact of AI on Film Production in 2024 https://medium.com/@channelasaservice/exploring-the-impact-of-ai-on-film-production-in-2024-f02da745af00 (19.06.2024).

Verschure, J. P. (1995) "The Challenge of Sound Restoration from 1927 to Digital" in Film History 7:3 pp.264-276.

Warner, A. (2022) AI-powered Localization Startup Deephub Raises 20 Million Dolars in Series A Funding" https://multilingual.com/deepdub-funding-milestone/ (24.06.2024).

Weis, E. And Belton J. (1985) "Film Sound: Theory and Practise" in Film Quarterly 39:1 pp.46-48.

Welsh, A. P. (2019) "Is AI making it easier for everyone to become a musician?" https://www.redbull.com/se-en/how-ai-will-make-everyone-a-musician (19.06.2024).

Wenewsenglish.pk. (2024) Microsoft Develops AI Tool for Perfect Human Voice Clonning https://wenewsenglish.pk/microsoft-develops-ai-tool-for-perfect-human-voice-cloning/ (21.06.2024).

Zhi, B. Et al. (2018) "Synthesizing Audio Using Genereative Adversarial Networks" CMSC723 University of Maryland Collgege Park fall 2018.

ENDNOTES

1 https://www.noisli.com/.noisli.com/

2 h ttps://endel.io/

3 h ttps://add.app/

4 https://www.aiva.ai/

5 https://openai.com/index/jukebox/

6 https://magenta.tensorflow.org/

7 https://suno.com/

8 h ttps://mubert.com/

Chapter 6

Illuminating the Path From Script to Screen Using Lights, Camera, and AI

Arjama Pal
https://orcid.org/0009-0001-8552-8693
VIT Bhopal University, India

Sakalya Mitra
https://orcid.org/0009-0006-8649-0072
VIT Bhopal University, India

D. Lakshmi
https://orcid.org/0000-0003-4018-1208
VIT Bhopal University, India

ABSTRACT

Artificial Intelligence uses personalised content curation to make recommendations that are specifically tailored to each individual user's watching preferences based on their viewing history, reviews, and interactions and what it implies for our future. In this chapter, we are going to explore the multitudes of effects of AI in visual media. From the enchantment of special effects that defy the boundaries of reality to the nuanced artistry of colour grading, we aim to unravel the intricate dance between technology and storytelling. Our chapter aims to take our readers on a journey to learn more about AI in animation, character generation, CGI, and many more. From enhancing cinematography to streamlining post-production, AI not only revolutionizes the technical aspects of filmmaking but also contributes to

DOI: 10.4018/979-8-3693-3916-9.ch006

a deeper understanding of audience preferences and engagement.

1. INTRODUCTION TO CINEMATOGRAPHY AND AI

We are no strangers to the usage of visual effects in cinema and the magic it bestows upon the audience. From the enchanting world of Pandora in Avatar to the mind-bending scenes of Inception, visual effects have become an integral part of modern cinema, captivating viewers worldwide. As we are hurling towards an unprecedented future of technology that heavily relies upon AI, we can observe everything around us evolve at an exponential rate, and the field of cinema is no exception. In our exploration, we aspire to unravel the intricate mechanisms through which AI and data recommendation algorithms wield their influence, particularly within viewer recommendation systems that are profoundly integrated into online entertainment platforms. These systems, omnipresent in the digital landscape, play a pivotal role in shaping audience preferences and consumption patterns, thereby shaping the future trajectory of cinema in the digital era.

Since the early days of civilization, visual media has been instrumental in portraying human experiences. The lens of a camera offers a perfect window to peek through and experience the ups and downs of humanity over time. Through meticulous framing, lighting, and composition, filmmakers create visual poetry that speaks directly to the soul. The harmony of light and shadow with the complexities of storytelling, complimented by thematic scores is often known to weave stunning movies that transcend the boundaries of entertainment and touch the hearts of millions, irrespective of their background, culture, or language.

According to Huang et al. (2014), the earliest evidence of visual media can be traced back to almost two centuries ago when cameras generated analog pictures by recording light on papers or photo-sensitive plates, which were then preserved on negative films. As we evolved, so did our techniques. The Lumière brothers were the first to project moving images to a paying audience in Paris, France, in December 1895, with their own gadget called the Cinématographe. It combined the functions of a projector, camera, and film printer, as stated by National Science and Media Museum (n.d). Since then, we have progressed more and more with time. Cinema evolved from silent films to “talkies,” from black and white to colour, continually captivating audiences with its ability to tell stories in new and innovative ways. Now that we are standing in the 21st century, at the threshold of a new era of Artificial Intelligence (AI), unprecedented modifications are about to be incorporated into this creative journey.

According to StudioBinder (2024), cinematography determines the narrative's tone by carefully measuring each shot, frame, and focus. It is an amalgamation of art and science to create a visual tapestry that conveys the intended mood, atmosphere, and themes through the craft of storytelling. Most importantly, this entire operation is not completed overnight but requires hundreds of artists' years of knowledge, practice, expertise, and manual labor. Thanks to AI, as we are progressing towards an era of automated procedures, it takes no genius to assume that AI will have a massive impact on how we create, consume, and experience the art of movies. Although it is imperative to address that no AI should be a replacement for the creative vision human beings possess, AI can definitely be a companion in streamlining repetitive tasks and simplifying time-consuming processes, helping filmmakers save on money and energy.

In this chapter, we aim to examine the many aspects of the filmmaking process, the elements of cinematography, and the implications of artificial intelligence on editing, visual effects, and other cinematography methods. The chapter aims to provide a holistic study of different processes involved in both the production and post-production stages of filmmaking and the integration of AI in each of them. Besides, we will also shed light on the ethical implications and societal considerations surrounding the adoption of AI technologies in the entertainment industry. By critically analyzing the impact of AI-driven algorithms on audience engagement, content curation, and cultural representation, our chapter seeks to stimulate thought-provoking discussions on the evolving role of AI in shaping the future of storytelling.

1.1 Historical Evolution of Visual Effects and AI's Transformative Role

Visual Effects or VFX have been around for centuries. Oscar Rejlander developed the first "special effects" image in history in 1857 by montaging a combination print, which was an amalgamation of 32 separate negative segments. In 1895, Alfred Clark invented what is regarded as the first motion picture special effects. History of VFX. (2022) stated that, using a mannequin to remove an actor's head during a beheading reenactment, he also created the first motion picture special effect known as the "stop trick," a method that dominated special effects creation for a century. However, the prolific French director Georges Méliès is frequently referred to as the "Cinemagician" because of his wizarding abilities to control and modify reality using the cinematograph for his films. His most famous film Le Voyage dans la Lune (1902) set the foundation for visual effects with its revolutionary effects using multiple creative and practical approaches like glass matte paintings, rewinding and reshooting unexposed negative, chemical manipulation, and so on, published Cram et al. (2012). In a study by Das et al. (2023), he mentioned that other contemporary filmmakers, including Willis O'Brien and Ray Harryhausen, followed similar practical approaches like stop-motion to create other-worldly imagery and bring life to their mythological visions.

As time progressed, so did the complexities of visual effects. The eras of the 1970s and 1980s saw massive prosperity of visual effects in cinematography, taking the craft to a new height. The advent of chroma keying, using a green or blue screen, brought a paradigm shift and opened whole new avenues of creativity. In his study, Das et al. (2023) als mentioned, that this technology, combined with optical printers, enabled directors to shoot cost-effectively and bring any idea into reality. The "Star Wars" franchise with its mind-bending intergalactic travel, 'The Abyss' with its underwater adventures, and 'Terminator 2: Judgement Day' with a fully computer-generated (CG) character paved the way for how visual effects impacted the narrative and visual storytelling in movies, beyond the realms of tangible reality, said Eldın et al. (2012).

In the 21st century, visual effects have become an essential component of filmmaking, appearing in almost all major motion pictures. As the technology developed further, expansive CG worlds and completely digital characters emerged. Over the past 20 years, the advancements in CGI have reached phenomenal levels which were previously deemed impossible. With computer graphics, hitherto unimaginable levels of realism and intricacy have been achieved. Movies like 'Interstellar', 'Avatar', and 'The Jungle Book' are living proofs of how CGI enabled filmmakers to dream, experiment, navigate into the territories beyond their comfort zones, and create timeless masterpieces.

The role of AI in visual effects is a more recent development and is quickly becoming transformative. According to Bermudez et al. (2021), AI-based technology is already being leveraged for rotoscoping, a time-consuming procedure that involves separating foreground from background features frame-by-frame. Moreover, AI-powered software assists directors in simulating intricate physical phenomena like fire and water and producing realistic textures. AI is simply the newest chapter in the ongoing narrative of innovation and with time, AI will unfurl its fullest potential to contribute further to the storytelling venture.

1.2 Different Stages of Filmmaking

1.2.1 Pre-Production

Pre-production refers to planning for the massive preparation needed to shoot a film. It is where the seeds of creativity are sown, laying the foundation of visual gems that are set to blossom later on the silver screen, expresses Johnson (2011). It includes arranging other necessary filming elements, choosing cameras, recruiting performers, and creating the plot, states Wu et al. (2021). This stage is extremely crucial as it determines the success of the movie.

- **Ideation:** Every good movie starts with an idea, a concept, or a theme someone wants to breathe life into. It could be a personal story, a biopic, a historical retelling, or an alien, alternate universe. Multiple brainstorming sessions and detailed and thorough research on the intended concept are required to ensure that the storyline is compelling, free of loopholes, historically accurate, and engaging for the audience. For setting the tone of the narrative and directing all the creative decisions, the ideation phase is extremely crucial.
- **Scripting and Plotting**: The ideas and the story of the conception are then given a narrative structure through the script-writing process. Characters are designed, personalities are mapped, and dialogues are written to bring dimension to the storyline and transform it to be more dynamic. This can involve multiple drafts and revisions as per the suggestions from producers and other collaborators.
- **Budgeting and Finances:** The next critical procedure in line is determining the expected expenses and gearing up for them. A comprehensive financial plan is developed, detailing all anticipated costs related to the cast, crew, locations, equipment, post-production, marketing, and standby funds. This step is crucial in ensuring that the production stays within budget and avoids any financial setbacks. By carefully planning and allocating resources, the project can proceed smoothly and efficiently toward completion minimizing financial risks. Once the estimate is finalized, it is time to gather the said funds from sources like producers, investors, production houses, grants, or even personal investment. The next step is to create a production plan that accounts for travel time, shooting days, and any delays.
- **Assembling the Crew:** The search for the ideal team starts with a strong screenplay, equipped with the estimated budget. Hiring important department heads like the casting director, production designer, costume designer, and director of photography is part of this. Next, each department head assembles a team of experts.
- **Casting:** Choosing actors appropriately for each role is extremely important for visualizing the story and embodying the characters. They are responsible for the precise representation of each personality and their motivations. The casting process involves auditions, callbacks, chemistry reads, and discussions with the director to ensure the right fit for each character. Once the cast is finalized, rehearsals and table reads are scheduled to build rapport and understanding among the actors.

- **Location Scouting:** The script comes alive with appropriate locations. Scouts are assigned the task of obtaining and securing shooting locations for the entire duration. Permits and permissions are obtained for filming in public places as well as at historical sites.
- **Organizing Props:** Actors are complemented by their costumes, props, and set design. Period pieces require historically accurate clothes, jewellery, and accessories to create an authentic atmosphere. Movies on space exploration need to have realistic spacecraft models, futuristic gadgets, and special effects to enhance the audience's experience. All props are carefully chosen and arranged to contribute to the overall visual storytelling of the film.
- **Storyboarding and Shot Lists:** Storyboards are visual representations of key scenes, helping the director and crew plan camera angles, movement, and shot composition. Shot lists detail every shot needed in the film, ensuring nothing significant is missed during filming.
- **Legal and Administrative Tasks:** Contracts are drawn up and signed by cast, crew, and vendors. Production insurance is obtained to cover accidents, equipment damage, and other liabilities. All necessary filming permits, location releases, and other legal clearances are secured.

1.2.2 Production

Production is the heart of the movie-making journey. It involves shooting and bringing the script alive. Here, the director is the commander of the ship and calls all the shots. It is a collaborative effort of hundreds of skilled individuals who put their blood, sweat, and tears into creating a piece. Although a set hierarchy is maintained, in this set, every single person — from the lighting director to the production assistant — has equal importance. Directors like Sanjay Leela Bhansali make sure every minute detail is properly executed. Script supervisors look after scene continuity and maintain wardrobes, hairstyles, and other props across the progression of the scene. Every member of the team, from actors delivering lines to camera operators catching the ideal image, contributes significantly to making the screenplay into a visual masterpiece. While it may be a stressful and fast-paced setting, it is also where a film's raw emotions, action, and storytelling magic come together.

1.2.3 Post-Production

It's arguably the most important and the last step of production in which a giant team of skilled professionals join their hands to give the final product the finishing touches. It involves a combination of multiple laborious processes like editing, implementing visual effects, applying CGI, adding animations if needed, colour correction, dubbing, giving any required voice-overs, creating the appropriate soundtrack, completing sound mixing, creating an interesting trailer, and marketing and promotional activities. Post-production processes are responsible for enhancing the overall quality of the film or project, ensuring that it meets industry standards and audience expectations. Additionally, post-production also plays a crucial role in creating a cohesive and engaging final product that resonates with viewers. The more efficient it is, the better it can create waves amongst both the audience and critics.

- The first and foremost process here is organizing and assembling the materials created in the production phase.
- Next comes the task of choosing the optimal shots, trimming the videos to maintain the perfect length, editing, combining them with smooth transitions, and adjusting the colour palette, taking inspiration from the story.
- Dialogues are edited, transcriptions are added, and captioning is also completed.
- Sound design and mixing come next where appropriate soundscapes are designed to set the tone for the story and narrative. Music and background scores determine the emotional impact of the movie.
- Advanced visual effects and appropriate CGI are integrated to give dimension to the story (according to the budget).
- The last step in this process includes creating a trailer to engage the viewers, creating promotional campaigns and generating distribution plans.

Figure 1. Stages of Cinematography

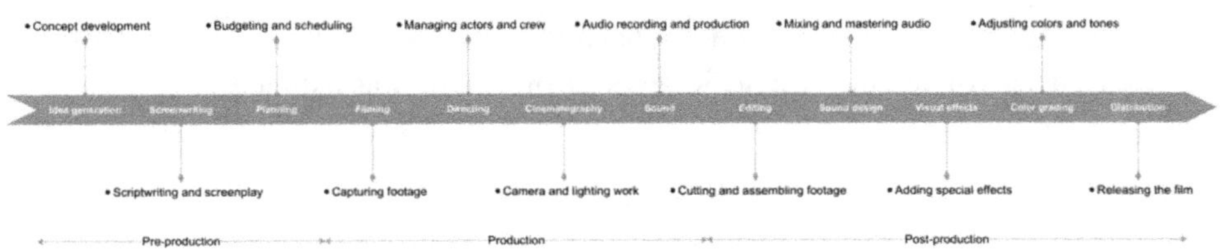

2. PRE-PRODUCTION

2.1 Exploring How AI Aids in Script Analysis, Pre-Visualization, Planning, Budgeting, and Casting

AI can be effective in accelerating and simplifying the aforementioned processes in pre-production and help one achieve better results quickly. Having an AI assistant can not only help a director save time, but it can also emerge as a cost-effective and more viable solution. Today, AI tools can aid in script-writing, picture visualization, budgeting, scouting places, set design as well as scheduling.

- **Script Writing and Analysis:** AI can analyze scripts quickly and provide valuable insights for improvements in pacing and characterization, saving time and enhancing the quality of the final product. Additionally, AI can assist in identifying potential issues in the script, such as plot holes, inconsistencies, or pacing problems, leading to a more polished and cohesive story. While a scriptwriter takes approximately 12 to 16 weeks to work on the first draft of a script, AI-based software can help to complete the same in typically a few hours, states Sun (2024). Though the quality of the dialogue and screenplay provided by AI are not exceptional at present, thanks to the enormous database and continuous development, we can expect AI to provide high-level, complex, and professional scripts soon, says Naji (2024). Moreover, script analysis and deconstruction are some of the most important pre-production processes which involve hours and hours of tedious and error-prone manual labour. Sun (2024) in his work states, by utilizing Machine Learning (ML) and Natural Language Processing (NLP), some software features can improve the accuracy and efficacy of script analysis, providing a more trustworthy and scientific level of production assistance.

Table 1.

Pros	Cons
1. According to Naji (2024), AI screenwriters can produce content at a rate of creativity that human screenwriters can't equal. 2. AI's massive database allows it to provide original ideas that writers would not have imagined, states Naji (2024). 3. Naji (2024) states that ML algorithms assess, analyze, and learn from large volumes of data, transforming book or movie scripts into novel ones, saving filmmakers significant time and money.	1. AI-generated scripts might lack human touch, says Sun (2024). 2. AI algorithms have not yet attained the complex nuances of emotional depth, flexible out-of-the-box thinking, and traditional cultural spirit, states Naji (2024).

There are multiple tools available for scriptwriting.

DeepStory: Anyone can generate high-quality content by using a Belgium-based software called DeepStory, which blends human creativity with artificial intelligence to produce AI-driven scripts and tales. According to DeepStory (n.d.), users may collaborate to co-create captivating films, role-playing games, short-form material, and stories of all kinds.
Squibler: Squibler is a supercharged AI writer designed specifically to assist with scriptwriting and screenplays, with features like script generation, storyboard creation, and AI-powered suggestions for dialogue and scene flow, states Squibler: AI Story Writer (n.d).
Jasper: According to Jasper (n.d),with its user-friendly, easy-to-use user interface enables scriptwriters to overcome writer's block and get the creative juices flowing.
TinyWoW: It is another online tool that caters specifically to YouTube screenwriting. According to TinyWow (n.d.), it also analyses SEO trends to boost video discoverability.
AI Writer: It has gone a step forward and offers style adaptability to its users, allowing them to generate scripts in any format and tone, from conversational to dramatic, states AI-Writer.comTM (n.d).

Case study: Director Oscar Sharp and Google's AI Researcher Ross Goodwin collaborated to use a Long Short-Term Memory (LSTM) recurrent neural network (RNN) named Benjamin to fully generate a script. The subsequent nine-minute-long movie called "Sunspring" was submitted as a 48-hour contest for a sci-fi London Film Festival, states Naji (2024). Benjamin produced a manuscript while following certain guidelines after studying hundreds of screenplays from films released in the 1980s to 1990s. In 2018, Benjamin advanced further and generated an entire movie called 'Zone Out', including screenplay and direction, and bagged third prize in the same festival, states Momot (2022). Momot (2022) also states that this time, AI-generated voice and face-swapping techniques were implemented, due to which the film had an odd, unattractive appearance, with computer-generated sounds that were hard to comprehend and horrifyingly flashing, dislocating features.

- **Picture visualization:** An AI system created for film storyboarding counts the number of shots in a screenplay and uses a text-to-image classifier to categorize the different shoot components. As per Naji (2024), then, it searches the archive database for images that best match the shot's requirements, generating a storyboard in the process. Users often have the option to build their own storyboards or adopt the system's suggestions. Key information pieces from the screenplay, such as characters and their interactions in the scenes, may be extracted using NLP approaches for text analysis and picturized accordingly, expresses Momot (2022).

There are multiple AI-based tools to assist filmmakers with this task:

Boords: According to Boords (n.d), they offer consistent AI image generation and one-click exports in multiple formats for easy sharing.
Shai Creative: According to Storyboard AI (2024), they offer consistent AI image generation and one-click exports in multiple formats for easy sharing.
Storyboarder.ai: This tool generates storyboards, screenplays, and even shot lists based on a simple script input, states Storyboarder.ai (n.d).
StudioBinder: It combines storyboard creation with scriptwriting, shot listing, call sheets, and other production tools. StudioBinder (2024) also states that it also allows users to upload images to generate a storyboard or use their builder for a more customized approach.

- **Budgeting, Casting, and More:** Another extremely significant part of the pre-production phase of filmmaking is estimating the expenses and planning for it ahead of schedule. Since movies are expensive endeavours, accurate budgeting helps the director to visualize how much everything will cost, from employing crews to building sets to visual effects. Instead of devoting weeks or months to the same, AI can streamline and decrease the chance of calculation mistakes in a much shorter duration. In a study by Ghiassi et al. (2015), on pre-production movie revenue forecasting using a Dynamic Artificial Neural Network (DAN2) proposed enhancements in financial planning and decision-making in the movie industry. It optimizes resource allocation, aids in project selection, and allows for early advertising and distribution strategies. In all such scenarios, AI can be particularly helpful as using a scenario, props, outfits, and other data in multi-level association forms, AI can alert the team to avoid financial risks if there is a possibility of going overboard.

NolanAI: It analyzes factors like character count, locations, special effects needs, and dialogue to generate a comprehensive budget breakdown.
Shortlister: It offers AI-powered cost estimation based on the script breakdown, factoring in industry averages and historical data.
Movie Magic Budgeting: This tool leverages AI to automate tasks like crew cost estimation and location scouting budget analysis, saving time and improving accuracy.
Cinelytics: It utilizes AI to provide real-time budget tracking and insights.

Casting plays a very vital role in determining the success rate of a movie. Instead of solely relying on intuition or past experiences, AI can analyze data from previous successful movies to suggest potential casting choices that align with audience preferences and market trends. This can ultimately increase the chances of a movie's success by ensuring the right actors are chosen for each role. According to Sun (2024), by compiling actor data into a database and deciphering attributes like gender, age range, and performance, AI can help filmmakers choose the right actors and actresses. This, in turn, can help the filmmakers to predict the box office figures more accurately, even before the shooting begins.

2.2 AI-Driven Animation and Character Casting

Just as much as we love watching real actors portraying iconic characters that get etched in our memories and steal our hearts, animated movies are no different. According to a finding by All Time Worldwide Animated Box Office. (n.d.), Frozen II, The Super Mario Bros Movie, The Toy Story Franchise, Zootopia, The Lion King, and Coco are some of the highest-grossing animated movies of all time, enjoyed by everyone from 8 to 80. Creating these movies is an equally painstaking process. From character design to drawing every frame meticulously, everything requires attention to detail and precision. The team of skilled animators and voice actors dedicated to each movie, therefore, can benefit from AI-driven automation.

2.3 Machine Learning Algorithms for Realistic Animation

- **Highly Realistic Transitions:** For animated scenes requiring high-level precision and life-like movements, Optical Flow Techniques and Convolutional Neural Networks (CNN) are particularly helpful. According to the Metavision SDK Docs 4.6.0 documentation. (n.d.), Optical Flow Techniques excel at analyzing object movements and translating the knowledge into animations. CNNs, on the other hand, are incredible at image manipulation and recognition. By training the algorithm on large databases of existing animation frames, it can learn the complexities of realistic movements and analyze our keyframes to generate smooth and authentic transitions.
- **Stylized Animation:** Each movie, each story, and each character require a unique animation style. No two characters are designed the same. For instance, Disney's classic Sleeping Beauty (1959) gave us the story of Aurora in one of the most gorgeous hand-drawn animations, says Valente et al. (2024). As per the Walt Disney Animation Studios (n.d.), on the other hand, Moana (2016) has incorporated hybrid animations as the style here is primarily focused on CGI, but also required for certain hand-drawn elements like water

effects and fire components. Hence, as the focus shifts to the distinct animation style, Variational Autoencoders (VAEs) appear particularly useful. A study by Sharma (2023) points out that, VAEs are trained on animation data for certain styles to understand patterns and correlations between poses, creating new frames fluidly throughout transitions while keeping a smooth flow. Neural Style Transfer is another technique that uses pre-trained algorithms to "transfer" the creative style of one picture or animation sequence to another, states Baheti (2021) in his study.

- **Complex Character Movements:** Complicated movements of an animated character can be challenging to animate. For instance, the movements of Disney princess Merida's hair strands or that of another Disney princess Ana's frozen cape have been almost bewitching to watch. To master the acts of those intricate movements, the assistance of Generative Adversarial Networks (GANs) can be taken. Through the back-and-forth training, the generator improves its ability to create extraordinarily realistic and fluid in-between frames, which is especially useful for complicated character movements with numerous limbs and quick position changes.
- **Motion Forecasting:** Deep Neural Networks (DNNs) increase animation control and efficiency by analyzing complicated patterns, training biomechanical models, delivering real-time feedback, customizing character movement, and allowing for scalability across several projects. A study by Dai et al. (2024) proposed that the 2D-AI-BM model outperforms other prominent approaches in accuracy (97.4%), computational efficiency (96.3%), motion control (95.4%), pose identification (94.8%), and scalability (93.2%), showing substantial improvements.

Other than these ML algorithms, NLP can be instrumental in translating visual descriptions into graphically animated sequences. Additionally, AI can interpret facial expressions into animated characters through motion pictures and facial recognition technologies, states Naji (2024). A study by Reddy et al. (2024) has examined the application of CNN in the well-known film 'Coco'. Despite identifying the model's parameters, the test set's accuracy remained pretty steady at around 59%. The result greatly improves the audiovisual quality and creative standards of film productions, while also supporting healthy and long-term growth in the industry. Another study by Cavazza et al. (2001) experimented with a prototype created using the Unreal gaming engine to animate storytelling using a sitcom framework. The Unreal environment offers essential user interaction elements for interactive storytelling, including navigation and interaction with virtual objects. However, training some ML algorithms, particularly GANs, can require significant processing power and be computationally expensive. While these algorithms have tremendous capabilities, human animators remain essential to fine-tune the transitions and give that unique touch of emotional depth and creative refinement, states Momot (2022).

2.4 Impact on Box-Office Success and Audience Engagement

The performance of a movie at the box office is determined by various factors including budgeting, casting, quality of script, current trends, and so on. The film industry has experienced multiple setbacks due to the issue of poor budgeting. In particular, between 2000 and 2010, 31% of the 3,453 films did not even earn domestically, with an average loss of 16.5 million per movie. Large volumes of comparable historical data on films may be analyzed by AI, which takes into account variables like cast, crew, location, and genre. This makes it possible to estimate costs for different production-related factors more precisely. According to the findings by Ghiassi et al. (2015), 75 films within the same time frame had deficits between their production budgets and gross domestic box office receipts that exceeded $50 million apiece, highlighting the detrimental effects of bad budgeting choices on the profitability of motion pictures.

Choosing the right actor for the right role is also very important to determine how the movie will be reviewed by the viewers. Though a single celebrity might not contribute to a film's success, an ensemble of high-level performers is often responsible for the movie's commercial success. However, that might not be a universal truth. A film's performance at the box office is very dependent on the audience's psychology and the current trends. Based on that, a movie with a remarkable script and storyline can outperform a movie with incredible casting but no story. Hence, determining and choosing the right decision often matters more than following the traditional way of casting through a meticulous process of hundreds of trials and errors.

Case Study: An article by Rose (2020) talks about multiple AI-based tools that provide incredible assistance in predicting the box-office performance of a movie. A Los Angeles-based startup called Cinelytic, Google's AI tool called Merlin, Belgium-based software named Scriptbook, and Israel's Vault AI have been proven to be incredibly useful and accurate in forecasting a film's success rate. While Cinelytic and Merlin analyze the patterns and objects in movie trailers, ScriptBook adapts a different approach and analyzes the script against 400 parameters. The accuracy of Cinelytic is 85%, that of ScriptBook is 83% and they are much more reliable than human-decision making where it has been successful in only 27% to 31% of times. Moreover, another doctoral dissertation by Gerges (2017) tested different ML techniques like Genetic Algorithms (GA), C5, Support Vectors Machine, K-Nearest Neighbors, Neural Networks, and Case-based reasoning against

4883 movies released in the USA between 2000 and 2017 and came up with their own GA with an accuracy of 90.5%.

However, since AI runs on a colossal amount of data, its predictions and suggestions are prone to be affected by bias. For instance, Rose (2020) points out that historically speaking, since female directors have won much fewer Academy Awards than their male counterparts, AI might predict that a movie directed by a woman is not going to make big numbers at the box office. After all, AI is just a tool that analyzes historical trends and hence, it's not free from the existing bias. Hence, AI-generated suggestions need to be accepted with a grain of salt.

3. PRODUCTION

3.1 AI Applications in Camera Technology, Set Design, and Live-Action Filming

As we move from the pre-production to the production phase of filmmaking, we will look at novel ways to implement AI in camera technology and live-action shooting. For example, AI can assist in optimizing camera angles, lighting, and even actor performances to enhance the overall quality of the film. By embracing AI in production processes, filmmakers can streamline workflows and achieve greater efficiency in bringing their creative vision to life on screen.

AI can be fruitful in optimizing camera angles and positioning to get the most stunning shots. Cameras, attached to a drone, can be controlled using AI during cinematography. This unusual "Seen MPG" technology employs AI to regulate camera settings, detect objects, focus, and monitor motions to ensure optimal shots, states Dhahir et al. (2022) in their study. This algorithm created by academics from the Universities of Zaragoza, Spain, and Stanford, USA, optimizes camera settings to produce the greatest outcomes in cinematography, improving the overall quality of aerial footage shot by drones. Moreover, AI-driven camera placements employ electronic handling to generate visually pleasing clip heights, thus improving the cinematographic experience by recording scenes from the most appealing viewpoints. Even robotization is employed to streamline camera movements and reduce manual labour. Robots can now operate cameras with preset settings, manufacture 3D objects, and carve props and sets. Automating tedious operations, synchronizing them with other processes, and achieving computational precision are key benefits of this procedure, states Momot (2022) in his findings. Another innovative way to shoot and create characters is by the method of deepfakes. Deepfakes are videos in which someone's real face is overlaid with an artificial one to produce a very lifelike film of someone talking or doing something they never did. For instance,

Luke Skywalker in "The Book of Boba Fett" is portrayed by an actor who has a younger Luke Skywalker deepfaked onto their face, as mentioned in a study by Murphy et al. (2023). However, though the intention of deepfakes is purely for fun and entertaining purposes, they can indeed be used for malicious purposes, and the implication of using deepfakes needs to be studied further.

3.2 AI-Enhanced Cinematography in Optimizing Shots and Angles

Case Studies: A study by Friedman et al. (2006) implemented a system called Mario which has the ability to convert screenplays, written in high-level formal language into an explicitly detailed set of instructions on camera positions, movements, and behaviours. The system depicts scenes as a chronology of activities, complete with spatial information such as item placements and gaze directions at various moments. Mario's architecture applies cinematic concepts to inputs such as scripts and floor designs, resulting in clear camera positioning and behaviour instructions. It employs a reasoning engine that turns domain-specific concepts into declarative rules, as well as automated reasoning to accommodate absolute, default, and arbitrary user options. The system is built using Common Lisp and Cake, a multi-layered reasoning engine developed by the researchers at MIT's Artificial Intelligence Laboratory.

Another paper by Azzarelli et al. (2024) compares and analyzes camera content acquisition in four types of production: General Production, Live Production, Virtual Production, and Aerial Production in the following manner:

Table 2.

Production	Key Technology	ML Algorithms
General Production	Automated camera calibration algorithms, machine learning models for workflow optimization, and computer vision systems for object tracking.	● Regression algorithms for camera calibration. ● Classification algorithms for object tracking. ● Clustering algorithms for workflow optimization.
Live Production	Machine learning algorithms for real-time video correction, computer vision systems for object tracking, and pose estimation models for human pose detection.	● Support Vector Machines (SVM) for video correction. ● Recurrent Neural Networks (RNNs) for object tracking. ● Pose estimation models based on keypoint detection using algorithms like OpenPose.
Virtual Production	Deep learning models for In-Camera Visual Effects (ICVFX), computer graphics algorithms for virtual asset integration, and real-time rendering engines for virtual stage production and automated 3D capture.	● Deep learning algorithms for image processing and rendering. ● Convolutional Neural Networks (CNNs) for virtual asset integration. ● Generative Adversarial Networks (GANs) for creating realistic virtual effects.
Aerial Production	AI-driven UAV control systems, computer vision algorithms for visual planning, and machine learning models for safety-first solutions in aerial cinematography.	● Reinforcement Learning algorithms for UAV control. ● Decision Trees for real-time camera planning. ● Anomaly Detection algorithms for safety protocols in aerial filming.

Although the use of AI is not too prominent in live-action shooting yet, we can only hope to see further inclusion of AI-driven technology to take the forefront in assisting film directors to ease their burden.

4. POST-PRODUCTION

Without proper organization, post-production procedures can get as chaotic and hectic as their previous phases have been. Each method employed here can get incredibly repetitive, monotonous, and tenuous for even the best in their fields. For instance, choosing the perfect shot among hundreds of takes, trimming the duration of videos, and combining them to create the most stunning visual can get frustrating. AI can help streamline these processes and automate choosing the best and most optimal shot, decreasing the overwhelm of the film editors.

4.1 Streamlining Post-Production Tasks with AI

- **Editing and Colour Grading:** Selecting the best shot among many, assembling the right ones, cutting them and adding smooth transitions to join them, colour grading, removing unwanted elements from the shot, correcting resolutions, and more such procedures are included in editing. It's what makes or breaks a film and sets the narrative and tone of the film. AI is well-equipped to help editors simplify this process and enhance the overall quality of the final product by offering suggestions and automating repetitive tasks. With AI assistance, editors can focus more on the creative aspects of their work and produce visually stunning films efficiently. Effective management of AI during early shooting may considerably reduce the editing department's workload in selecting items. Deep learning, image recognition algorithms, and NLP can prove to be time-efficient, as stated by Momot (2022). Deep learning algorithms can detect microphones, booms, and undesired elements like as coffee cups in large video datasets, replace them with background information, and produce a clean final shot by detecting and replacing them. Content-aware filling algorithms, on the other hand, can analyze the background and substitute items or people with the exact pattern or texture. AI-based software like Quikstories can accelerate video editing and reduce human errors. For instance, CCTV News' 2019 National Day coverage featured AI editing in a short video, expressed Sun (2024) in his work.

Figure 2. Colour grading changing the genre of the movie

Colour grading, on the other hand, refers to enhancing or altering the colour of the scenes to capture a certain mood. It involves changing the saturation, hue, tinge, and brightness to create a certain atmosphere and impact the storytelling. According to the study by Prajapat et al., AI algorithms can mimic colour grading methods or create unique colour schemes based on input from a large collection of professional-grade photos and videos. Algorithms like Generative Adversarial Networks (GAN), Autoencoders, CNN, and Style Transfer techniques learn the subtle nuances of colour correction, exposure adjustments, and other stylistic requirements and achieve the technicalities of colour balance and contrast enhancements.

- **Transcription:** Automatic Speech Recognition (ASR) and Text-to-Speech (TTS) algorithms can transcribe audio and dialogue pretty accurately and reduce human error and the exhausting manual labour of analyzing every frame of the movie and typing each word separately. These algorithms, equipped with metadata and NLP, can also translate the dialogues to multiple languages catering to viewers from diverse backgrounds. Additionally, according to a study by Jayanthiladevi et al. (2020), deep video analysis improves content nomenclature, tagging, and linkage accuracy, while machine-driven indexing and metadata tagging enable AI to automate content management while improving search and relationship accuracy.

- **Visual Effects and CGI:** Implementing visual effects is relatively easier these days with the advent of neural networks and generative algorithms. Incorporating 'Green Screen', which is otherwise known as 'Chroma Keying', is the concept of shooting against a uniform background, and later replacing the background with the appropriate details is the most prevalent canvas for storytelling. This process combines precise color sealing and spill correction to generate the most flawless effects. The process of chroma keying depends a lot on the understanding of lights and shadows, colour dilation, camera positions, and settings like its sensitivity to the green colour. However, a study by Palanimurgan (2024) masterfully demonstrates the challenges of using chroma keying in post-production. It highlights that irregular fringing edges and contaminant spillage are the chief challenges of this technique which does not allow the character to blend seamlessly with the background. This can be solved with proper colour correction and Despill algorithms which can detect spillage and remove them automatically.

CGI is an integral part of sci-fi movies. It allows filmmakers to create stunning visual effects that would be impossible to achieve otherwise. With advancements in technology, CGI continues to push the boundaries of what is possible in the world of filmmaking. For instance, the stylistic effect of a sequence in the movie 'The Matrix' popularly called "bullet time" has been adapted and replicated numerous times. The process included freezing time and capturing 360-degree images of the situation. For other AI-based CGI implementations, machine learning algorithms are used to analyze and predict movements in order to create realistic animations. AI is used to create realistic animation and visual effects by syncing 3D views, shading, dynamic texture creation, and realistic lighting. Anantrasirichai et al.(2022) in their study states that AI is also used to build lifelike digital individuals, known as Codec Avatars, in real-time by employing GAN-based style transfer and VAE to extract avatar properties.

- **Voice Recordings:** One important aspect of post-production is incorporating voice recordings and dubbing, wherever it's necessary. This is an equally time-consuming process. But it can be further simplified as AI can replicate someone's voice with a simple snippet of their voice. This process can enable voice actors to simply send a sample of their voice and AI can duplicate the tonal characteristics to complete the voice-over efficiently, states Naji (2024).

For instance, this cutting-edge technology is already being implemented by Open AI to allow users to interact with AI having realistic synthetic voices. Spotify, a popular music streaming platform, employs this technology to enable voice actors to translate their podcasts into multiple languages, serving a wider array of listeners.

- **Music:** Soundtracks are an inherent component of the storytelling journey which sets the tone for the movie. Using comedy music for a horror movie will significantly reduce the seriousness of the plot and may confuse or alienate the audience. Normally, composers produce the background score and create the atmosphere of the narrative by taking inspiration from the story. AI composers like AIVA, Flow Machines by Sony, Jukebox by Open AI, NSynth by Google AI can help create unique soundtracks by analyzing vast amounts of data and composing music based on specific criteria provided by filmmakers. Another software called Coconet employs CNN to fill the missing parts of music. Other than that, Long Short Term Memory (LSTM) is also very effective in generating creative music, states Anantrasirichai et al. (2022).

Other procedures like making trailers, designing advertisements, and other promotional activities can also be efficiently automated with AI. For instance, in 2016, IBM Supercomputer Watson created a trailer for a sci-fi thriller named "Morgan". According to the study by Nassar (2024), the model was trained with 100 trailers and the model analyzed audio to connect scenes, identify people, and study the composition style of the shots.

4.2 Advantages and Potential Challenges of Automated Post-Production

The use of automated post-production processes does not come without its fair share of limitations and challenges. AI-driven tools and ML algorithms intend to remove manual labor from cumbersome processes and streamline the workflow, but in turn, it might cause the removal of artists and experts completely from the creative process. A study by Momot (2022) also highlights that to handle novel technology, even the most experienced and proficient professionals might face skill discrepancies and might need to continuously improve themselves, which will prove to be quite a hassle. Another study by Ring et al. (2019) states that ML-based tools will be widely embraced if they provide artists equal power as they are accustomed to and allow the system to learn from its failures. The difficulty is to develop tools sensibly and provide algorithms that can update themselves based on user understanding. While on the one hand, the continuous improvement in technology will enable even small filmmakers to apply advanced visual effects, on the other hand, it raises severe concerns regarding the loss of individual artistic expressions. Hence, AI should be used as a resource, instead of giving it the power to decide and determine. The film industry will only benefit from these technologies if both human and machine factors work cooperatively with each other.

4.3 Contribution to Creating Immersive Virtual Environments

Augmented Reality (AR) and Virtual Reality (VR) are two of the most exciting emerging technologies being used to create immersive environments for movies. Going beyond the realms of spatial, temporal, and emotional immersion, AR and VR technologies bring the world of virtual immersion to their audiences. It places the user right in the middle of the environment and enables them to interact with the components in a more engaging way. While VR enables a viewer to engage in a completely virtual environment, AR enables the user to interact with virtual or digital objects placed in their physical environment, through mobile, iPad, or other gadgets.

Both AR and VR technologies require complex and expensive equipment. Professional photography equipment, such as 360-degree cameras, three-layered cameras, light field cameras, and motion capture frameworks capable of shooting in augmented reality, is essential for film and TV productions using VR technology, states Ming. Moreover, it requires users to wear a head-mounted device to participate and observe different incidents of the film. The price of the equipment, the psychological effect of the immersive world, and the lack of enough content prevent directors from using these technologies, states Anantrasirichai et al. (2022) in his study. Hence, though VR technology is a hot topic of innovation, implementation of the same in mainstream cinematography is still far from coming to reality.

5. AI VIEWER INSIGHTS AND THE EVOLUTION OF FILM IN THE DIGITAL ERA

In the ever-evolving landscape of digital media, AI has become a powerful tool for understanding audience preferences and shaping the future of filmmaking. By analyzing vast amounts of viewer data, AI provides filmmakers with deep insights into audience behavior, preferences, and trends. This enables a more tailored and engaging cinematic experience. The following sections explore the transformative impact of AI on viewer insights and its broader implications for the film industry, highlighting how these technological advancements are redefining both content creation and consumption.

5.1. AI's Influence on Viewer Insights and Preferences

Artificial Intelligence (AI) has significantly transformed the way the film industry understands and caters to its audience. By harnessing vast amounts of data from streaming services, social media, and other digital interactions, AI can discern patterns and preferences with remarkable precision. This section will delve deeply into the mechanisms and impacts of AI-driven analytics in shaping modern filmmaking.

5.1.1 Data Collection and Analysis

AI algorithms excel at collecting and analyzing massive datasets from a variety of sources to understand viewer behavior. The key to this process is the integration of data from multiple touchpoints to create a comprehensive picture of audience preferences.

- Streaming Service Logs: Streaming platforms like Netflix, Amazon Prime, and Disney+ continuously collect data on user interactions. This includes not only what shows or movies are watched but also detailed metrics like the exact time viewers start and stop watching, how often they pause, rewind, or fast forward, and their viewing schedules. For example, Netflix's AI algorithms analyze these logs to identify viewing patterns. If a significant number of viewers pause during a particular scene, it may indicate a confusing plot point or a lack of engagement.
- Social Media Interactions: Social media platforms provide a rich source of data on viewer sentiments and trends. AI can analyze likes, shares, comments, and hashtags to gauge the popularity of certain actors, genres, or films. For instance, the buzz generated by a new movie trailer on Twitter can be analyzed to predict the film's potential box office performance. Tools like sentiment analysis algorithms can categorize comments as positive, negative, or neutral, helping studios understand public perception in real-time.
- Biometric Data from Smart Devices: With the increasing use of smart devices like smartwatches and fitness trackers, biometric data such as heart rate and facial expressions during viewing can be collected. This data helps in understanding the emotional impact of different scenes. For example, a horror movie might be analyzed for scenes that elicit the highest spikes in heart rates, indicating effective jump scares or moments of high tension.

5.1.2 Personalized Recommendations

AI's ability to make personalized recommendations has revolutionized content consumption, making it easier for viewers to discover new content that aligns with their tastes.

- Predictive Models: Platforms like Netflix use complex algorithms to predict what content a user might enjoy based on their viewing history. These models consider factors such as genres, actors, and viewing times. For instance, if a user frequently watches romantic comedies, the AI might recommend a new release in that genre. Netflix's recommendation system, known as "Cinematch," analyzes patterns among millions of users to find similarities and suggest content accordingly.
- User Profiles and Viewing Habits: AI creates detailed profiles for users by analyzing their interactions with the platform. For example, Amazon Prime might notice that a user watches family movies on weekends and documentaries on weeknights. It will then recommend family-friendly content on Saturdays and Sundays while suggesting thought-provoking documentaries during the week. This tailored approach enhances user satisfaction and retention.

Spotify, although a music streaming service, employs a similar recommendation strategy that can be paralleled in film. Their "Discover Weekly" playlist uses AI to analyze users' listening habits and suggests new songs they might like. This strategy has proven successful in increasing user engagement and satisfaction, demonstrating the power of AI in creating personalized experiences.

5.1.3 Content Creation Decisions

AI not only influences what content gets recommended but also what content gets created. By providing insights into audience preferences, AI helps studios make informed decisions about new projects.

- Genre and Theme Analysis: AI can analyze trends to identify which genres and themes are currently popular or emerging. For instance, if data shows a growing interest in sci-fi thrillers with strong female leads, studios might greenlight more projects that fit this description. This ensures that new productions align with current audience interests, increasing the likelihood of commercial success.

- Casting Decisions: Insights from AI can also influence casting choices. By analyzing social media data and box office performance, AI can identify actors who are particularly popular with target demographics. For example, if an actor consistently draws high engagement on social media and positive box office results, they are more likely to be cast in upcoming projects. This data-driven approach can help studios maximize their return on investment.
- Script and Plot Development: AI tools can even assist in script analysis and development. By analyzing successful scripts and audience reactions, AI can suggest plot elements or character arcs that are likely to resonate with viewers. For instance, an AI tool might analyze thousands of scripts and find that certain story structures or character dynamics consistently perform well, guiding writers in their creative process.

Warner Bros. has partnered with Cinelytic, an AI-driven project management system, to predict the commercial success of films. This system analyzes data on genre trends, actor performance, and market conditions to help make informed decisions on what films to produce and how to market them. This approach exemplifies how AI can provide actionable insights that shape the future of filmmaking.

In conclusion, AI's influence on viewer insights and preferences is profound, enabling a more personalized and efficient content consumption experience while guiding the creative and business decisions in the film industry. This transformative impact ensures that the content produced not only meets but anticipates audience expectations, leading to greater engagement and success.

5.2. Exploration of How AI Contributes to the Evolution of Film in the Digital Era

As AI continues to integrate into filmmaking, it not only changes how films are made but also how they are distributed and consumed. This section explores the broader implications of AI on the film industry, examining how AI-driven tools and algorithms are revolutionizing various aspects of film production, marketing, and viewer engagement. By enhancing creative processes, optimizing distribution strategies, and personalizing viewing experiences, AI is reshaping the landscape of cinema in profound and unprecedented ways.

Virtual Reality (VR) and Augmented Reality (AR)

AI enhances VR and AR experiences by creating more immersive and responsive environments. This could revolutionize how audiences engage with films, offering interactive and personalized viewing experiences.

- **Creating Immersive Worlds**: AI algorithms are capable of generating highly detailed and interactive virtual environments. In VR, these environments can respond to the viewer's movements and interactions in real-time, creating a more engaging and realistic experience. For instance, in the VR game "Half-Life: Alyx," AI is used to manage the behavior of non-player characters and the environment, making the game world feel alive and responsive to the player's actions.
- **Personalization:** AI can tailor VR and AR experiences to individual users by analyzing their preferences and behavior. For example, an AI system could modify the narrative path or the difficulty of a VR experience based on the user's previous choices or skill level. This kind of personalization is seen in VR applications like "The Void," where the experience can be adjusted in real-time to enhance immersion and enjoyment.
- **Real-World Applications:** Beyond entertainment, AI-enhanced VR and AR have practical applications in fields like education and training. For example, AI-driven VR simulations are used for medical training, where the virtual environment adapts to the trainee's actions, providing a realistic and interactive learning experience. This technology is similarly being explored for film training, where aspiring filmmakers can practice in a simulated environment that mimics real-world conditions.

AI in "Half-Life: Alyx": The game utilizes AI to create dynamic interactions with the environment and non-player characters, making the VR experience feel lifelike. AI in "The Void": This VR experience adjusts in real-time to the user's actions, enhancing immersion and personalizing the adventure.

Enhanced Marketing Strategies

AI-driven analytics allow for more precise targeting in film marketing campaigns. By analyzing demographic data and viewer preferences, marketing efforts can be more effectively directed to potential audiences.

- **Targeted Advertising**: AI analyzes vast amounts of data from social media, streaming platforms, and other online activities to identify patterns in viewer preferences and behaviors. This enables studios to create highly targeted advertising campaigns. For example, if data shows a surge in interest for superhero movies among a particular demographic, targeted ads for the latest Marvel film can be shown to this group, increasing the likelihood of engagement and ticket sales.

- **Predictive Analytics**: AI can predict the success of marketing campaigns by analyzing historical data and current trends. Tools like IBM Watson's Predictive Analytics have been used to forecast box office performance and optimize release strategies. For instance, predicting the best release dates for movies based on historical box office data and current market conditions can significantly impact a film's financial success.
- **Social Media Monitoring**: AI-powered tools monitor social media in real-time to gauge public sentiment and engagement with film marketing campaigns. This allows marketers to quickly adjust their strategies in response to audience feedback. For example, AI-driven platforms like Crimson Hexagon can analyze millions of social media posts to determine how a film trailer is being received and identify key influencers who can help amplify the marketing message.

By analyzing viewing habits, Netflix tailors its marketing for new releases to specific audience segments, increasing engagement and viewership. IBM Watson's Predictive Analytics helps studios forecast box office success and optimize marketing strategies.

Content Customization

AI can tailor content not just at the recommendation level but also within the content itself. For example, interactive films like "Black Mirror: Bandersnatch" use AI to offer different storylines based on viewer choices. Viewers make choices that influence the film's storyline, demonstrating AI's role in interactive storytelling. Also in the movie, "The Elder Scrolls V: Skyrim": AI-driven characters and environments adapt to player actions, creating a unique narrative experience each time.

- **Interactive Storytelling**: AI enables the creation of interactive films where the narrative can change based on viewer decisions. "Black Mirror: Bandersnatch," a Netflix interactive film, is a prime example. Viewers make choices at key points in the story, leading to multiple possible endings. The next part is handled by AI: creating different branch of narratives, and ensuring that each of the choices lead to a coherent storyline.
- **Dynamic Content**: AI can generate content that evolves in real-time based on viewer interactions. This is seen in video games like "The Elder Scrolls V: Skyrim," where AI-driven non-player characters and environments react to the player's actions, creating a unique experience for each playthrough. Similar technology can be applied to films, where scenes might change based on viewer preferences detected through AI analysis.

- **Personalized Viewing Experience**: AI can analyze a viewer's past behavior and preferences to customize their viewing experience. For instance, AI could adjust the pacing of a film, recommend specific camera angles, or even alter the soundtrack to better suit the viewer's tastes. Personalization at such a level ensures enhancement in user engagement and satisfaction. Imagine a horror movie that tailors its scares to the viewer's fear profile, as inferred from their reactions to previous films.

6. CASE STUDIES AND EXAMPLES

6.1. In-Depth Analysis of Films Successfully Utilizing AI in Visual Effects

This section will present detailed case studies of films that have successfully integrated AI in their production, particularly in visual effects. By examining these groundbreaking projects, we will uncover how AI technologies have been harnessed to enhance visual storytelling, create realistic animations, and streamline production processes. These examples will illustrate the practical applications of AI, showcasing the innovative techniques that have set new standards in the film industry. Through these case studies, you can gain a comprehensive understanding of the transformative role AI plays in modern filmmaking.

Case Study-1: AI in the Creation of "Avatar" (2009)

James Cameron's "Avatar" leveraged advanced AI-driven tools to achieve its groundbreaking visual effects and lifelike animations. The film utilized AI for several key aspects:

1. **Motion Capture**:
    - Facial and Body Motion Capture: AI was instrumental in capturing the nuanced facial expressions and body movements of actors. High-definition cameras and sensors tracked the actors' performances, and AI algorithms translated these into the digital counterparts of the characters.
    - Real-Time Rendering: AI facilitated real-time rendering of these captures, allowing for immediate feedback and adjustments during filming. This technology was crucial in ensuring that the actors' performances translated seamlessly into the CGI characters.
2. **Environmental Simulation**:

- Pandora's Ecosystem: AI played a significant role in creating the complex and dynamic environment of Pandora. This included the intricate details of flora and fauna, which were generated and animated using AI algorithms. These systems ensured that the ecosystem responded naturally to interactions, adding to the film's realism.
- Procedural Generation: The landscapes and various environmental elements were created using procedural generation techniques powered by AI. This allowed for the creation of vast, detailed terrains without manual intervention, ensuring consistency and complexity.

Figure 3. Motion Capture using AI in Avatar

3. **Character Animation**:
   - Autonomous Movement: AI was used to animate background characters and creatures, providing them with autonomous behaviors and interactions. This reduced the need for manual animation and increased the realism of crowd scenes and wildlife movements.
   - Behavioral AI: Characters were programmed with AI to exhibit natural, lifelike behaviors, enhancing their believability and making the world of Pandora feel lived-in and organic.

"Avatar" set a new standard for visual effects in cinema. The film's AI-enhanced visuals were a significant factor in its critical and commercial success, contributing to its immersive experience. The innovative use of AI in motion capture, environmental simulation, and character animation not only advanced the field of CGI but also demonstrated the potential of AI in storytelling and film production.

The success of "Avatar" was largely driven by its pioneering use of AI technologies. By integrating AI into the production process, James Cameron was able to create a visually stunning and highly immersive cinematic experience. This approach has influenced subsequent films and continues to shape the future of animation and visual effects in the film industry.

Case Study 2: De-Aging the Irishman: AI's Role in Scorsese's Cinematic Time Travel

Martin Scorsese's "The Irishman" utilized advanced AI-based de-aging technology to make actors like Robert De Niro, Al Pacino, and Joe Pesci appear significantly younger. This involved several intricate steps:

1. **Facial Analysis**:
   - Archival Footage: AI algorithms analyzed extensive archival footage of the actors to understand their facial features and movements at various ages.
   - 3D Mapping: AI created detailed 3D maps of the actors' faces, capturing every wrinkle, contour, and expression to ensure accuracy in the de-aging process.
2. **Digital De-Aging**:
   - Algorithmic Adjustments: Complex AI-driven algorithms adjusted the actors' facial features frame by frame. This included smoothing out wrinkles, altering skin texture, and modifying other age-related characteristics while maintaining the actor's natural expressions and performance.
   - Machine Learning Models: Machine learning models were trained on large datasets of images and videos to predict how the actors' faces would have looked at younger ages, allowing for realistic and dynamic de-aging.
3. **Integration with Performances**:
   - Real-Time Monitoring: The de-aging process was integrated with the on-set performances of the actors. Real-time monitoring allowed the filmmakers to make adjustments and ensure that the de-aged faces matched the actors' live performances seamlessly.

- Post-Production Refinement: In post-production, AI was further used to refine the de-aged visuals, ensuring that every frame was polished and realistic.

The de-aging technology used in "The Irishman" was pivotal in storytelling, allowing actors to portray their characters across multiple decades without the need for different actors. This innovation demonstrated AI's potential in reducing costs and logistical challenges associated with casting and makeup, enabling a seamless narrative flow. The technology set a new benchmark for visual effects in filmmaking, showing how AI can transform traditional filmmaking techniques and open new possibilities for future productions.

"The Irishman" showcased the transformative power of AI in the film industry. By employing AI-driven de-aging technology, Martin Scorsese was able to bring his vision to life in a way that was previously impossible. This approach not only enhanced the film's storytelling but also pushed the boundaries of what can be achieved with AI in visual effects, paving the way for more innovative uses of technology in cinema.

Case Study 3: Marveling at AI: Behind the Scenes of "Avengers: Endgame" (2019)

Marvel's "Avengers: Endgame" utilized AI extensively to manage and integrate the vast array of CGI required for its epic scenes. Here are some key applications:

1. **Character Realism**:
    - Thanos' Facial Expressions: Digital Domain employed a machine learning software called Masquerade to capture and render Thanos' facial expressions based on Josh Brolin's performance. AI algorithms used low-resolution scans to create high-resolution facial animations, ensuring Thanos' expressions were lifelike and detailed. The system learned from numerous high-resolution scans to improve accuracy, automatically adjusting features like eyebrow movements and lip compressions.
2. **Scene Optimization**:
    - Real-Time Rendering and Integration: AI facilitated real-time rendering of complex battle scenes, which involved thousands of individual elements and characters. This allowed for seamless integration of CGI with live-action footage, maintaining high visual fidelity throughout the film.
    - Crowd Simulation: AI-driven tools were used to animate background characters and crowds, giving them realistic behaviors and movements.

This reduced the need for manual animation, making large-scale scenes more manageable and lifelike.

3. **Post-Production Efficiency**:
   - Automated VFX Processes: AI tools streamlined the post-production workflow by automating various VFX processes, such as lighting adjustments and texture mapping. This not only sped up production but also ensured consistency across different scenes.

The AI-enhanced visuals in "Avengers: Endgame" played a crucial role in the film's success. The ability to render realistic characters like Thanos and manage large-scale battle scenes contributed to its critical acclaim and commercial achievements. AI's role in automating complex tasks demonstrated its potential to revolutionize the filmmaking process, offering scalability and efficiency for blockbuster productions.

"Avengers: Endgame" showcased the transformative impact of AI in modern cinema. By integrating AI into special effects and post-production, Marvel was able to create a visually stunning and cohesive film. This use of AI not only enhanced the storytelling but also set a new benchmark for visual effects in the industry. Future films are likely to continue leveraging AI to push the boundaries of what is possible in cinematic experiences.

Case Study 4: "Elemental" Alchemy: Harnessing AI to Transform Animation Magic

The integration of AI in the production of Pixar's film "Elemental" was instrumental in creating the complex and dynamic visual effects seen in the movie. This application of AI encompassed several key areas:

1. **Volumetric Neural Style Transfer**: A standout AI application in "Elemental" was the use of volumetric neural style transfer for creating the character Ember, who embodies fire. Traditional fluid simulations, while dynamic and realistic, often lack the illustrative quality needed for animated characters. By using neural style transfer, Pixar could infuse the painted textures created by their artists into the fluid simulations, resulting in fire animations that are both dynamic and artistically stylized, capturing the essence of fire while maintaining a unique illustrative appearance stated Befores and Afters (2023).
2. **Volumetric Animation**: Unlike traditional animations that rely on geometry and texture maps, "Elemental" utilized volumetric animation, where each frame is a new simulation rather than a cached image. According to IBC (2023), this approach required significant computational power, provided by VAST Data's

storage solutions, enabling real-time access to massive amounts of data and ensuring that the render farm could handle the enormous workload efficiently.

3. **Character Animation and Effects**: AI played a crucial role in animating characters such as Wade, who represents water. The animation team had to simulate water's reflective and refractive properties, which was particularly challenging. They employed multiple layers and continuous adjustments to ensure that the characters looked and moved like water while retaining a cartoony appearance. As stated by Pixar Post (2023), the governing animation house in the creation of Elemental, AI helped in dynamically controlling the presence of bubbles and caustics within Wade's body, balancing realism with artistic needs.
4. **AI-Powered Storage and Processing**: The production of "Elemental" utilized more than 150,000 computing cores, a significant increase from previous Pixar films. This immense computational capacity was essential for handling the volumetric animations and AI-driven processes that generated unique simulations for each frame. The advanced storage solutions provided by VAST Data ensured that the data could be processed quickly, maintaining the efficiency of the creative workflow.
5. **Denoising and Image Enhancement**: Pixar also utilized machine learning algorithms to enhance the quality of rendered images. These denoising algorithms were trained on pairs of noisy and clean images from previous Pixar films, allowing for the automatic removal of noise from new renders. This application of AI ensured that the final images were of the highest quality without requiring extensive manual adjustments.
6. **Ethical Considerations**: In developing these AI tools, Pixar was mindful of ethical concerns. They ensured that the neural style transfer models were trained on internally created images to avoid intellectual property issues. This approach reflects a broader commitment within Pixar to ethically deploy AI technologies while respecting the work of artists.

The integration of AI into "Elemental" not only pushed the boundaries of what is possible in animation but also highlighted the need for advanced computational and storage capabilities. This blend of artistry and technology exemplifies how AI can enhance creativity while addressing the technical challenges of modern filmmaking.

7. CHALLENGES AND ETHICAL CONSIDERATIONS

As AI continues to revolutionize the visual effects industry, it brings not only unprecedented opportunities but also significant challenges and ethical dilemmas. Navigating these complexities is crucial to ensuring the responsible and sustainable use of AI in filmmaking. This section explores the multifaceted challenges posed by AI, including technical, financial, and creative limitations, and delves into the ethical implications that must be addressed to maintain the integrity and diversity of the visual effects landscape. By understanding these issues, stakeholders can better prepare for a future where AI plays an integral role in cinematic artistry.

7.1. Limitations and Challenges Associated with AI in Visual Effects

While AI offers numerous advantages in filmmaking, it also presents several challenges. Every budding technology or innovation, comes with its own advantages and drawbacks. And it is important to adhere and address those drawbacks to better leverage the technology, keeping the shortcomings in mind and ensuring mitigating policies to ensure protection against those. This section delves into the technical, financial, and creative limitations of AI in visual effects.

Technical Limitations

AI technologies, particularly in CGI and animation, require significant computational power and sophisticated software. The processing of complex algorithms and rendering of high-quality animations demand advanced hardware capabilities, which can be both expensive and energy-intensive. Moreover, the continuous evolution of AI models necessitates regular updates and maintenance of the software infrastructure to keep up with the latest advancements in the field.

- **High Computational Demand:** AI-driven visual effects need powerful hardware to process complex algorithms and render high-quality animations. For example, creating realistic character animations, like those seen in "Avengers: Endgame," involves extensive processing of facial capture data through machine learning models, which can be resource-intensive, says the report published by GoodworksLabs (2019). High-performance GPUs and large-scale computing clusters are often necessary to handle the processing demands of AI algorithms, particularly for tasks like real-time rendering and complex simulations. This requirement can create a barrier for filmmakers who lack access to such infrastructure, says the report from Mckinsey & Company (2021) as well as a report by APA (2021).
- **Specialized Software and Expertise:** Utilizing AI effectively in visual effects requires specialized software and technical expertise. According to GoodworksLabs (2019) and Mckinsey & Company (2021), developing and fine-tuning AI models for tasks such as motion capture or scene optimization

necessitates a deep understanding of machine learning techniques and visual effects software. This expertise is often limited to a few specialized teams or companies, making it less accessible to the broader filmmaking community.

- **Integration Challenges:** Integrating AI tools seamlessly into existing production workflows can be complex. Filmmakers must ensure that AI-generated content aligns with the artistic vision and technical requirements of the project, which can be a delicate balance to achieve, states Scientific American (2021).

Financial Constraints

The high cost of AI implementation can be prohibitive, especially for independent filmmakers or smaller studios. These costs are not limited to hardware and software but also include the expense of training staff to effectively use AI tools and integrate them into the production pipeline. Additionally, the financial burden can be exacerbated by the need for continuous updates and maintenance to keep pace with rapidly evolving AI technologies. The key financial challenges include:

- **Initial Investment**: The upfront costs of acquiring high-performance computing hardware, specialized software, and hiring skilled professionals can be substantial. Large studios like Marvel can afford these investments, but smaller studios may struggle to justify the expense.
- **Ongoing Costs**: Beyond the initial setup, maintaining and updating AI systems involves continuous financial investment. This includes costs related to software licenses, hardware upgrades, and ongoing training for staff to keep up with the latest AI advancements.
- **Return on Investment (ROI)**: For many filmmakers, the return on investment in AI technologies is uncertain. While AI can enhance visual effects quality and production efficiency, measuring the direct financial benefits can be challenging, particularly for projects with limited budgets.

Creative Limitations

Over-reliance on AI can sometimes stifle creativity, with filmmakers potentially leaning too heavily on AI-generated content rather than innovative storytelling. This reliance might result in a formulaic approach to filmmaking, where predictable algorithms replace imaginative and original ideas. As a consequence, the unique artistic vision that defines memorable films could be overshadowed by homogenized and less distinctive visual effects.

- **Standardization of Visual Effects**: AI tools can produce highly polished visual effects, but they may also lead to a homogenization of visual styles. When multiple films use similar AI technologies, there is a risk that visual effects across different projects may start to look alike, reducing the uniqueness and creative diversity in the industry. For instance, Sir Richard Taylor of Wētā Workshop while talking to the Virtual Producer. (2023), emphasized the irreplaceable value of human creativity and the nuances it brings to film, as stated in]. Similarly, Ben Grossmann, during his interview with Wired (2023), points out that while AI can enhance productivity, it might commoditize certain creative roles, potentially leading to a surplus of creativity that could devalue unique artistic contributions.
- **Reduced Human Touch**: AI-generated content may lack the subtle nuances and personal touches that human artists bring to visual effects. While AI can replicate certain aspects of human creativity, it may not fully capture the depth and emotional resonance that skilled artists contribute to a project.
- **Dependence on Technology**: Filmmakers might become overly dependent on AI, relying on automated solutions rather than pushing creative boundaries. This dependence can lead to a reliance on predictable, algorithm-driven outcomes rather than experimenting with novel and unconventional visual effects techniques.

While AI has significantly advanced the capabilities of visual effects in filmmaking, it is essential to acknowledge and address its limitations. Balancing the technical, financial, and creative aspects of AI implementation is crucial to harnessing its full potential while preserving the artistic integrity and diversity of the filmmaking industry. As technology evolves, continuous dialogue between technologists and creatives will be vital to ensuring that AI enhances rather than hinders the creative process.

7.2. Ethical Considerations Including Impacts on Industry Employment and Deepfake Issues

The integration of AI into the film industry is transforming production processes, enhancing special effects, and even assisting in scriptwriting. Despite these advancements, the technology also brings significant ethical concerns. Key issues include the potential displacement of industry professionals, the rise of deepfakes and their implications for misinformation, and inherent biases within AI algorithms. Addressing these ethical challenges is crucial to ensuring responsible and fair use of AI in filmmaking.

7.2.1 Impact of Employment

Job Displacement: AI-driven automation is poised to significantly impact employment within the film industry. Professionals in editing, animation, and visual effects, traditionally performed by human artists, are increasingly being replaced or supplemented by AI technologies. According to McKinsey & Company (2021), for instance, AI can now edit videos, create visual effects, and even animate characters, tasks that once required extensive human labor. While this can lead to increased efficiency and reduced costs, it also raises concerns about job security for many skilled workers, as expressed by Interesting Engineering (2023).

Adaptation and Retraining: The shift towards AI necessitates adaptation and retraining for the existing workforce. There is a growing need for professionals to acquire new skills to work alongside AI technologies. As per the findings of Wired (2023), the industry must invest in training programs to help workers transition to new roles that involve overseeing and interacting with AI systems.

7.2.2 DeepFakes and Misinformation

Creative Use vs. Misuse: AI-generated deepfakes can be a powerful creative tool in filmmaking, allowing for the seamless integration of actors into scenes or the creation of entirely new digital performances. However, the same technology poses significant risks when used unethically. According to the MIT Technology Review (2019), deepfakes can be employed to create misleading or false content, leading to misinformation and potentially severe consequences for public trust and privacy. According to a report by the Brookings Institution (2021), deepfakes can be particularly harmful when used to spread misinformation or manipulate public opinion.

Legal and Ethical Safeguards: There is a pressing need for legal and ethical frameworks to govern the use of deepfakes. This includes regulations to prevent misuse and guidelines to ensure that AI-generated content is transparent and accountable. Implementing such safeguards can help mitigate the risks associated with deepfake technology while still allowing its creative potential to be harnessed, said Brookings Institution (2021).

7.2.3 Representation and Bias

Algorithmic Bias: AI algorithms are often trained on data sets that reflect existing societal biases. If not carefully managed, these biases can be perpetuated and even amplified in AI-generated content. For instance, AI tools used in casting or scriptwriting may favor certain demographics over others, leading to a lack of diversity and fair representation in films, as found in Harvard Business Review (2020).

Ensuring Fair Representation: To combat this, it is crucial to develop AI systems that are trained on diverse and representative data sets. This involves actively curating training data to include a wide range of voices and perspectives. According to Forbes (2022), ongoing monitoring and adjustment of AI algorithms can help ensure that they do not reinforce harmful stereotypes or exclude marginalized groups.

The integration of AI in the film industry presents both opportunities and challenges. While AI can enhance creativity and efficiency, it also raises significant ethical questions that must be addressed. Ensuring fair employment practices, preventing misuse of deepfake technology, and managing algorithmic biases are critical steps towards a responsible and inclusive use of AI in filmmaking. By addressing these ethical concerns, the industry can harness the full potential of AI while safeguarding the interests of its workforce and the broader society.

8. FUTURE TRENDS AND INNOVATIONS

8.1. Speculation on the Future of AI in Visual Effects

Speculation on the future of AI in visual effects encompasses a broad range of possibilities, driven by rapid advancements in technology. As AI continues to evolve, its integration into visual effects could become even more seamless and sophisticated, potentially transforming the industry in unprecedented ways. Filmmakers may leverage AI to create more immersive and visually stunning experiences, while also streamlining production processes and reducing costs. However, this evolution will also require addressing the ethical and creative challenges that come with increased automation and machine learning in the creative process.

8.1.1 Real-Time Rendering

Advancements in AI hold the promise of revolutionizing real-time rendering, a process traditionally known for its time-consuming nature. AI-driven techniques like neural networks and deep learning have the potential to significantly accelerate rendering speeds while maintaining high-quality results. One notable advancement is the use of neural networks to predict the outcome of rendering processes, reducing the need for extensive computational power and time-consuming iterations.

According to NVIDIA (n.d.), their RTX technology, powered by AI-driven algorithms, has demonstrated real-time rendering capabilities previously thought to be unattainable. The RTX platform utilizes AI-enhanced rendering techniques like ray tracing to produce lifelike visuals in real-time, a breakthrough in the field of computer graphics.

8.1.2 Enhanced Interactivity

AI's role in visual effects extends beyond static imagery, with the potential to transform viewing experiences into interactive and personalized encounters. Through machine learning algorithms, AI can analyze viewer behavior and preferences in real-time, allowing for dynamic adjustments to storylines, character interactions, and visual effects. This level of interactivity could redefine audience engagement, offering viewers a unique and immersive journey tailored to their individual preferences.

Disney's (2022) research division has explored the integration of AI into storytelling, envisioning interactive narratives where viewer input influences the direction of the story. Their project "Storyliving" aims to create personalized storytelling experiences using AI algorithms that adapt the narrative based on audience feedback and engagement.

8.1.3 Photorealistic Animation

The pursuit of photorealistic animation has long been a goal in the visual effects industry, and AI is poised to take this pursuit to new heights. Machine learning techniques, such as generative adversarial networks (GANs) and neural rendering, are enabling artists to create animation that closely resembles real-life imagery. Through AI-driven processes, animation studios can achieve levels of detail and realism previously thought unattainable, blurring the line between computer-generated and real-world visuals.

Weta Digital, renowned for its groundbreaking visual effects work in films like "Avatar" and "The Lord of the Rings" trilogy, is leveraging AI to enhance the photorealism of its animation. Their research into neural rendering techniques aims to generate lifelike imagery by simulating the behavior of light and materials at a molecular level, resulting in animation that approaches the fidelity of live-action footage.

As AI continues to advance, these possibilities represent just a glimpse of the transformative potential it holds for the future of visual effects. From real-time rendering to personalized storytelling, the integration of AI promises to push the boundaries of creativity and immersion in filmmaking.

8.2. Exploration of Emerging Technologies That Could Further Revolutionize the Field

The future of AI in visual effects holds immense promise, with several emerging technologies poised to revolutionize the industry. These advancements are expected to significantly enhance the capabilities of filmmakers, pushing the boundaries of creativity and realism. Below, we delve into three key areas, out of the infinite possibilities brought by AI, where AI is anticipated to play a transformative role in the upcoming years:

8.2.1 Quantum Computing

The advent of quantum computing heralds a paradigm shift in computational power, potentially revolutionizing AI-driven visual effects. Quantum computers leverage quantum mechanics to perform computations at unprecedented speeds, surpassing the capabilities of classical computers. For visual effects, this means exponentially faster processing of complex algorithms, enabling the creation of incredibly detailed and realistic animations.

Quantum computing's impact on AI in visual effects is twofold. Firstly, it accelerates the training of machine learning models used in tasks such as character animation, scene rendering, and image processing. Secondly, it enables the exploration of computationally intensive algorithms that were previously impractical due to their complexity. While quantum computing for visual effects is still in its infancy, research and development in this field are progressing rapidly. Companies like IBM, Google, and D-Wave are actively pursuing quantum computing research, with potential applications in various industries, including entertainment.

8.2.2 Neural Networks and GANs

Generative Adversarial Networks (GANs) and advanced neural networks represent another frontier in AI-driven visual effects. GANs, in particular, have garnered attention for their ability to generate highly realistic images and videos by pitting two neural networks against each other: a generator network and a discriminator network.

In visual effects, GANs hold the potential to revolutionize character and environment generation. By training on vast datasets of real-world imagery, GANs can produce lifelike characters, detailed environments, and dynamic special effects with unprecedented realism. This technology could streamline the production pipeline, reducing the need for manual asset creation and speeding up the iteration process.

Moreover, advancements in neural network architectures, such as convolutional neural networks (CNNs) and recurrent neural networks (RNNs), continue to push the boundaries of what is achievable in visual effects. These networks excel at tasks like image recognition, semantic segmentation, and natural language processing, providing valuable tools for enhancing the efficiency and quality of visual effects production.

8.2.3 AI-Driven Storytelling

Beyond post-production, AI is poised to play a significant role in the creative process itself, particularly in storytelling. AI-driven storytelling involves the use of machine learning algorithms to assist in scriptwriting, plot development, and character creation, aiming to create more engaging and innovative narratives.

By analyzing vast troves of existing stories, AI algorithms can identify patterns, tropes, and narrative structures, providing insights to writers and filmmakers. This data-driven approach to storytelling has the potential to unlock new storytelling possibilities, helping creators craft more compelling narratives and resonate with audiences on a deeper level.

However, the integration of AI in storytelling raises ethical and creative considerations. While AI can offer valuable assistance, there is a risk of homogenization and formulaic storytelling if creators rely too heavily on algorithmic recommendations. Balancing the creative input of human storytellers with the capabilities of AI will be essential to preserve the diversity and richness of storytelling in film.

In conclusion, the future of AI in visual effects is brimming with possibilities, from leveraging quantum computing for unparalleled processing power to harnessing GANs and neural networks for lifelike character and environment generation. Moreover, the integration of AI into the creative process itself holds the potential to redefine storytelling in film. As these technologies continue to evolve, collaboration between technologists, filmmakers, and storytellers will be crucial to unlock their full potential while addressing ethical and creative challenges.

REFERENCES

A very short history of cinema | National Science and Media Museum. (n.d.). National Science and Media Museum. https://www.scienceandmediamuseum.org.uk/objects-and-stories/very-short-history-of-cinema#:~:text=The%20first%20to%20present%20projected,film%20printer%20all%20in%20one

AI-Writer.comTM - The only AI writing platform built to be trusted. (n.d.). https://ai-writer.com/

All Time Worldwide Animated Box Office. (n.d.). The Numbers. https://www.the-numbers.com/box-office-records/worldwide/all-movies/cumulative/all-time-animated

Anantrasirichai, N., & Bull, D. (2022). Artificial intelligence in the creative industries: A review. *Artificial Intelligence Review*, 55(1), 589–656. DOI: 10.1007/s10462-021-10039-7

APA. (2021). The promise and challenges of AI

Azzarelli, A., Anantrasirichai, N., & Bull, D. R. (2024). Reviewing Intelligent Cinematography: AI research for camera-based video production. arXiv preprint arXiv:2405.05039.

Baheti, P. (2021, September 8). Neural Style Transfer: Everything You Need to Know [Guide]. V7. https://www.v7labs.com/blog/neural-style-transfer

Befores & Afters (2023). The AI, volumetric and animation tools that helped make Pixar's 'Elemental' possible.

Bermudez, L., Dabby, N., Lin, Y. A., Hilmarsdottir, S., Sundararajan, N., & Kar, S. (2021). A Learning-Based Approach to Parametric Rotoscoping of Multi-Shape Systems. In *Proceedings of the IEEE/CVF Winter Conference on Applications of Computer Vision* (pp. 776-785). DOI: 10.1109/WACV48630.2021.00082

Boords. (n.d.). AI Storyboard Generator (Try for Free) | boords.com. https://boords.com/ai-storyboard-generator

Brookings Institution. (2021). How to regulate AI-generated deepfakes

Cavazza, M., Charles, F., & Mead, S. J. (2001, November). AI-based animation for interactive storytelling. In Proceedings Computer Animation 2001. Fourteenth Conference on Computer Animation (Cat. No. 01TH8596) (pp. 113-120). IEEE.

Cram, C. (2012). Digital cinema: The role of the visual effects supervisor. Film History. *International Journal (Toronto, Ont.)*, 24(2), 169–186.

Dai, F., & Li, Z. (2024). Research on 2D Animation Simulation Based on Artificial Intelligence and Biomechanical Modeling. *EAI Endorsed Transactions on Pervasive Health and Technology*, •••, 10.

Das, S. (2023). The Evolution Of Visual Effects In Cinema: A Journey From Practical Effects To CGI. Kolkata India, Journal Of Emergıng Technologies and Innovative Research (JETIR) s, 303-309.

DeepStory. (n.d.). https://deepstory.ai/

Dhahir, M. Q., AL-hakeem, M. A. M., & Alshadoodee, H. A. A. (2022). Automatic camera control and artificial intelligence in the future of cinematography. *International Journal (Toronto, Ont.)*, 7(1).

Disney Research. (2022). Storyliving

Eldın, N. M. S. (2012). Visual Effects Cinematography the Cinematographer's Filmic Technique From Traditional to Digital Era. *Turkish Online Journal of Design Art and Communication*, 2(2), 115–122. DOI: 10.7456/10202100/016

Forbes. (2022). How AI is changing the future of film production

Friedman, D., & Feldman, Y. A. (2006). Automated cinematic reasoning about camera behavior. *Expert Systems with Applications*, 30(4), 694–704. DOI: 10.1016/j.eswa.2005.07.027

Gerges, F. A. (2017). Pre-Production Movie Rating Prediction Using Machine Learning (Doctoral dissertation, LEBANESE AMERICAN UNIVERSITY).

Ghiassi, M., Lio, D., & Moon, B. (2015). Pre-production forecasting of movie revenues with a dynamic artificial neural network. *Expert Systems with Applications*, 42(6), 3176–3193. DOI: 10.1016/j.eswa.2014.11.022

GoodworksLabs (2019, May 2). How Machine Learning Gave "Thanos" a Soul in Avengers Endgame.

Harvard Business Review. (2020). AI bias: How to avoid it and ensure fairness

History of VFX. (2022, October 10). https://encyclopedia.pub/entry/28574

Huang, T., Le, V., Paine, T., Khorrami, P., & Tariq, U. (2014). Visual media: History and perspectives. *IEEE MultiMedia*, 21(2), 4–10. DOI: 10.1109/MMUL.2014.35

IBC (2023). Pixar's Elemental Lays Foundation for AI Powered Workflow.

Jasper | AI copilot for enterprise marketing teams. (n.d.). https://www.jasper.ai/

Jayanthiladevi, A., Raj, A. G., Narmadha, R., Chandran, S., Shaju, S., & Prasad, K. K. (2020, December). AI in video analysis, production and streaming delivery. [). IOP Publishing.]. *Journal of Physics: Conference Series*, 1712(1), 012014. DOI: 10.1088/1742-6596/1712/1/012014

Johnson, G. (2011). Spielberg your way to information literacy: producing educational movies and videos. In *Information Literacy* (pp. 151–183). Chandos Publishing. DOI: 10.1016/B978-1-84334-610-4.50007-0

McKinsey & Company. (2021). The real-world potential and limitations of artificial intelligence

Ming, X. M. Post-Production of Digital Film and Television with Development of Virtual Reality Image Technology-Advance Research Analysis.

MIT Technology Review. (2019). The ethical dilemma of deepfakes

Momot, I. (2022). Artificial intelligence in filmmaking process: future scenarios.

Murphy, G., Ching, D., Twomey, J., & Linehan, C. (2023). Face/Off: Changing the face of movies with deepfakes. *PLoS One*, 18(7), e0287503. DOI: 10.1371/journal.pone.0287503 PMID: 37410765

Naji, A. K. (2024). Employing artificial intelligence techniques to make films. Al-Academy, 171-180.

Nassar, S. (2024). Futuristic Scenarios: Utilization of AI Technological Settings to Foster the Filmmaking Visual Creation & Mass Production. *International Design Journal*, 14(2), 207–212. DOI: 10.21608/idj.2024.258755.1110

NVIDIA. (n.d.). *NVIDIA RTX: Ray Tracing*. Rendering, AI, & Deep Learning.

Optical Flow Algorithms Overview — Metavision SDK Docs 4.6.0 documentation. (n.d.). https://docs.prophesee.ai/stable/algorithms/optical_flow.html

PALANIMURUGAN, P. (2024). Challenges and Solutions in Green Screen Post-Production: A Narrative Review.

Pixar Post. (2023). *Elemental Fun Facts – 5 Things We Learned About the Film When Visiting Pixar*. And More Screencaps.

Prajapat, S., Singh, A. K., Banerjee, A., & Bhatnagar, K. Role of AI and Video Technology in Sci-Fi Cinema.

Reddy, V. S., Kathiravan, M., & Reddy, V. L. (2024). Revolutionizing animation: Unleashing the power of artificial intelligence for cutting-edge visual effects in films. *Soft Computing*, 28(1), 749–763. DOI: 10.1007/s00500-023-09448-3

Ring, D., Barbier, J., Gales, G., Kent, B., & Lutz, S. (2019, July). Jumping in at the deep end: how to experiment with machine learning in post-production software. In *Proceedings of the 2019 Digital Production Symposium* (pp. 1-5). DOI: 10.1145/3329715.3338880

Rose, S. (2020, January 16). "It's a war between technology and a donkey" – how AI is shaking up Hollywood. The Guardian. https://www.theguardian.com/film/2020/jan/16/its-a-war-between-technology-and-a-donkey-how-ai-is-shaking-up-hollywood

Scientific American. (2021). AI's Biggest Challenges Are Still Unsolved

Sharma, A. (2023, October 2). A Deep Dive into Variational Autoencoders with PyTorch - PyImageSearch. PyImageSearch. https://pyimagesearch.com/2023/10/02/a-deep-dive-into-variational-autoencoders-with-pytorch/

Squibler: AI Story Writer. (n.d.). https://www.squibler.io/

Storyboard, A. I. - The AI Storyboard Generator from Shai - Shai Creative. (2024, April 17). Shai Creative. https://shaicreative.ai/ai-storyboard-generator/

Storyboarder.ai – Revolutionize Your Storyboarding Process. (n.d.). Storyboarder.ai. https://storyboarder.ai/

StudioBinder. (2024, March 25) What is Cinematography? Defining the Art and Craft. https://www.studiobinder.com/blog/what-is-cinematography/

StudioBinder. (2024, January 30). Video, TV & Film Production Management Software | StudioBinder. https://www.studiobinder.com/

Sun, P. (2024). A Study of Artificial Intelligence in the Production of Film. In SHS Web of Conferences (Vol. 183, p. 03004). EDP Sciences. DOI: 10.1051/shsconf/202418303004

TinyWow. (n.d.). Free AI Writing Tools - No Sign-Up, No Limit - TinyWow. https://tinywow.com/tools/write

Valente, D., Strand, O., Kryza, A., & Singer, M. (2024, January 12). 50 Best Disney Movies Of All Time For Family Film Night With The Kids. Time Out Worldwide. https://www.timeout.com/film/the-best-disney-movies-of-all-time

Virtual Producer. (2023). Generative AI and the future of filmmaking

Walt Disney Animation Studios - The Role Of Hand Drawn Animation In Disneys Moana. (n.d.). Walt Disney Animation Studios. https://disneyanimation.com/publications/the-role-of-hand-drawn-animation-in-disneys-moana/#:~:text=The%20art%20direction%20of%20Moana,CG%20and%20hand%2Ddrawn%20elements

Weta Digital. (n.d.).. . *Technology*.

Wired. (2023). AI is making film. Will it steal human creativity soon?

Wu, X., & Wu, X. (2021). U.S. Patent No. 11,107,503. Washington, DC: U.S. Patent and Trademark Office.

Chapter 7
Cinema and Artificial Intelligence:
Charting Its Role in the Indian Film Sector

Saad Ullah Khan
https://orcid.org/0000-0002-3392-7844
Jamia Hamdard, India

Sadaf Khan
https://orcid.org/0009-0005-1348-0386
IEC College of Engineering and Technology, Greater Noida, India

Shivam Suryakant Ballewar
https://orcid.org/0000-0002-4753-884X
Symbiosis Institute of Media and Communication, Symbiosis International University, Pune, India

Jayendra Prabhakar Rane
https://orcid.org/0009-0009-5628-1626
Amity School of Communication, Amity University, Jaipur, India

Abdul Quadir Siddiquee
https://orcid.org/0000-0003-2889-6577
Centre for Media and Mass Communication Studies, Jamia Hamdard, India

ABSTRACT

This chapter critically assesses the transformative impact of Artificial Intelligence (AI) on the Indian film industry across its entire production spectrum, encompassing preproduction, production, and post-production phases. Within an increasing

DOI: 10.4018/979-8-3693-3916-9.ch007

technologically centric entertainment landscape, the convergence of AI and cinema signifies a crucial paradigm shift. Despite India's rich cinematic legacy, the assimilation of AI poses multifaceted challenges. Through a rigorous inquiry, this study probes AI's capacity to augment creative processes and operational efficiency, while also confronting pertinent ethical dilemmas. Drawing upon structured interviews and secondary source analysis, it offers a holistic examination of current AI practices, their implications, and anticipates future trajectories. By synthesizing insights from interdisciplinary domains, this chapter elucidates the complex interplay between technology and artistic expression, offering practical guidance for navigating technological advancements in Indian cinema.

INTRODUCTION

Within the contemporary cinematic milieu, the confluence of technological advancements and artistic endeavours has emerged as a central locus of scholarly inquiry, with Artificial Intelligence (AI) positioned as a transformative force reshaping traditional cinematic paradigms (Mahna, 2024). This convergence between cinema and AI delineates a multifaceted terrain characterized by a fusion of innovation and creativity, presenting both unparalleled opportunities and formidable challenges within the vibrant canvas of the Indian film sector. As AI permeates diverse facets of human existence, its incursion into the domain of filmmaking heralds a profound reconfiguration of established norms, heralding a redefinition of the very essence of cinematic artistry. In the dynamic landscape of the 21st century's globalized entertainment sphere, the fusion of AI and cinema emerges as a captivating narrative, driven by the demands of adaptation and innovation. With the rapid evolution of new media technologies and the expansive reach of globalization, this synergy epitomizes the transformative power reshaping both industries (Tamandehrou & Khan, 2015). As audience preferences evolve fluidly amidst exponential technological growth, the dynamic interplay between AI and cinema becomes a testament to the imperative of embracing change and harnessing innovation in this era of unprecedented connectivity and possibility. Within this dynamic milieu, the Indian film sector, renowned for its rich cultural heritage and multifarious cinematic traditions, stands at a critical juncture, grappling with the implications of AI integration while negotiating the delicate balance between artistic authenticity and commercial viability.

The present chapter investigates the multifaceted relationship between cinema and AI, with a particular emphasis on its profound ramifications for the Indian film industry. By deciphering the nexus of technology and creativity, it endeavours to illuminate the evolving role of AI as both a facilitator of artistic enhancement and a catalyst for narrative innovation. Against the backdrop of an expanding digital landscape characterized by data-driven insights and algorithmic decision-making, the cinematic medium undergoes a profound metamorphosis, challenging conventional conceptions of authorship and aesthetic autonomy. Through the harnessing of AI's computational prowess, filmmakers in India are endowed with novel avenues for experimentation and expression, enabling the realization of imaginative visions hitherto constrained by logistical or budgetary limitations. However, amid the allure of technological innovation, profound questions pertaining to ethical responsibility, cultural authenticity, and societal impact loom large, necessitating a rigorous interrogation of the ethical implications inherent in the integration of AI within the creative process.

Furthermore, the advent of AI-generated content engenders profound inquiries into the nature of artistic originality and the enduring relevance of human ingenuity within an increasingly automated landscape. As AI algorithms systematically analyse vast repositories of cinematic data to anticipate audience preferences and optimize marketing strategies, the traditional contours of film distribution and consumption undergo a seismic recalibration, prompting a revaluation of industry practices and regulatory frameworks (Khanna, 2024). Against this rich backdrop, the chapter charts a comprehensive understanding of the symbiotic relationship between cinema and AI, tracing its historical antecedents, probing contemporary manifestations, and prognosticating future trajectories within the Indian film sector.

Needless to state, in the contemporary scenario, AI has emerged as a disruptive force across sectors, including entertainment (Shah, 2023). However, within Indian cinema, the precise role and ramifications of AI remain relatively underexplored within scholarly discourse. This study bridges this knowledge gap by offering a comprehensive understanding of how AI innovations reshape Indian cinema's production, distribution, and consumption mechanisms. The outcomes of this investigation enrich academic dialogue and provide actionable insights for filmmakers, industry stakeholders, and policymakers, fostering informed decision-making and strategic advancements within the sector.

Aligned with this overarching aim, the study's objectives crystallize into four distinct focal points. Firstly, to describe the current landscape of AI utilization across different stages of film production within India, delineating existing practices and emergent trends. Secondly, to interpret AI's impact on creativity, efficiency, and cost-effectiveness in Indian filmmaking, discerning both tangible benefits and intangible consequences. Thirdly, to scrutinize the challenges and limitations inherent in AI's integration within the Indian film sector, probing ethical, cultural, and technical dimensions. Lastly, to investigate future trends and opportunities for AI-driven innovation in Indian cinema, envisioning plausible trajectories and transformative potentials.

To fortify the research endeavours, this study adopts a methodologically rigorous approach that integrates both primary and secondary data collection methodologies, thereby ensuring a robust triangulation of insights. This multifaceted methodological framework serves to enhance the validity and reliability of the research findings by drawing upon a diverse array of sources and perspectives. Structured interviews serve as the primary method, engaging specialists entrenched in pre-production, production, and post-production realms within Indian cinema. These interviews provide a systematic framework for data collection, affording flexibility to explore deeper into specific focal points of interest. Additionally, the study leverages secondary sources such as books, periodicals, and research papers to enrich its analytical framework and contextual understanding of the subject matter.

Moreover, through a synthesis of interdisciplinary perspectives drawn from the realms of film studies, artificial intelligence research, cultural studies, and media theory, this chapter endeavours to unravel the complex interplay of technological innovation, artistic expression, and socio-cultural dynamics shaping the cinematic landscape in India and beyond. By elucidating the myriad intersections between cinema and AI, this chapter fosters a comprehensive dialogue that transcends disciplinary boundaries, nurturing a deeper appreciation for the transformative potential and ethical imperatives intrinsic to the convergence of these two seminal domains. In so doing, it seeks to illuminate the emergent contours of a cinematic landscape characterized by innovation, experimentation, and an unyielding quest for creative transcendence amidst the inexorable march of technological progress.

REVIEW OF LITERATURE

Defining Artificial Intelligence (AI) presents a formidable challenge owing to the absence of a universally embraced elucidation of the concept. The landscape is riddled with myriad interpretations, engendering potential confusion. Hence, it becomes imperative to elucidate the usage of the term. The multiplicity of definitions does not stem from negligence but rather is intrinsic to the nature of AI itself (O'Shaughnessy, 2022). At its broadest expanse, AI is frequently synonymous with algorithms. However, algorithms predate the advent of AI and have pervaded domains beyond its purview. The term 'algorithm' traces its etymology to the Mohammed ibn Musa al-Khwarizmi (ninth-century Persian mathematician), denoting precise directives for problem-solving or computational tasks. Characterizing AI solely as algorithmic employment would encompass a plethora of other endeavours, ranging from the rudimentary operations of a handheld calculator to the procedural directives found within culinary recipes (Sheikh et al., 2023). Certain definitions augur into the cognitive faculties and tasks associated with AI. For instance, computer scientist Nils John Nilsson portrays AI as a technology capable of functioning aptly and anticipatively within its milieu. Others delineate AI as possessing perceptual abilities, goal-oriented behaviour, proactive initiation of actions, and the capacity for learning from feedback. Analogous delineations emerge from the High-Level Expert Group on Artificial Intelligence (AI HLEG) characterizes AI as systems that exhibit intelligent behaviour through the analysis of their surroundings and subsequent actions, executed with varying degrees of autonomy, all geared towards accomplishing predetermined objectives. (HLEGAI, 2019).

The historical trajectory of Artificial Intelligence traces its origins to the 1950s, when Marvin Minsky and John McCarthy first coined the term. Since then, AI has metamorphosed from a niche scientific pursuit into a transformative technological paradigm reshaping multifarious facets of society. The impetus provided by advancements in Big Data analytics and computational potency has propelled AI into quotidian existence, catalysing innovations like image recognition systems and autonomous vehicular navigation. Peering into the future, the trajectory of AI portends boundless potential for deeper entrenchment within commercial frameworks, refinement of decision-making frameworks, and augmentation of societal interactions. As AI undergoes continual evolution, ethical imperatives, regulatory frameworks, and imperatives for symbiotic human-AI coalescence will decisively sculpt its trajectory (Haenlein & Kalpan, 2019).

The burgeoning integration of Artificial Intelligence (AI) into the cinematic domain represents a veritable paradigm shift, transmogrifying sundry facets of the industry. AI's application spans script generation, trailer editing, visual effects enhancement, music composition, and editing tasks, among others. By scrutinizing vast datasets culled from extant scripts or literary works, AI aids filmmakers in crafting captivating narratives with heightened efficiency. Notably, AI algorithms adeptly parse earlier trailers to curate and splice together poignant moments, considerably truncating the editing temporality vis-à-vis human editors. In the realm of visual effects, AI-driven algorithms categorize and expedite the incorporation of computer-generated imagery, rendering the process swifter and more cost-effective. Moreover, AI's foray into music composition augurs a transformative era wherein AI-generated melodies resonate across cinematic oeuvres, exemplified by Sony's endeavours in generating original scores. Concurrently, AI facilitates a gamut of editing tasks encompassing colour correction, object removal, and image stabilization, democratizing video editing by furnishing user-friendly software suites catering to both neophyte and adept users. Such innovative deployments of AI redound to heightened productivity, amplified creative latitude, and the delivery of bespoke content to audiences (Ghosh, 2023).

AI's incursion into the cinematic milieu heralds a renaissance, marked by audience preference analysis, prognostication of cinematic triumph, and the genesis of digital simulacra. Future trajectories herald the advent of immersive storytelling modalities, including virtual reality and 360° video. As technology burgeons, augmented and virtual realities are poised to democratize content creation, precipitating a paradigm shift towards cloud-centric solutions for editing and visual effects. The cinematic landscape envisages a recalibration towards IT-centric methodologies, underscored by a predilection for cloud-deployed solutions catering to discerning audiences seeking superlative viewing experiences within the comforts of their abodes (Datta & Goswami, 2021).

Artificial Intelligence (AI) interfaces seamlessly with diverse echelons of the film production continuum, augmenting efficiency and creativity manifold. During pre-production phases, AI tools deftly sift through voluminous datasets to furnish actionable insights, thereby streamlining project selection and funding determinations. On-set, AI aids in virtual cinematography by proffering automated shot recommendations and facilitating scene construction, whilst concurrently exploring nascent frontiers in camera automation techniques. Post-production sees AI precipitate a renaissance in editing paradigms, rendering them more accessible to aspiring auteurs whilst revolutionizing visual effects through ingenious computational methodologies. By harnessing AI's prowess across these pivotal stages, filmmakers stand to reap the dividends of expedited workflows, fiscal prudence, heightened ingenuity, and augmented output quality (Sun, 2024).

The assimilation of AI into contemporary film production heralds a veritable panoply of opportunities and concomitant challenges. Foremost among the former include the automaton of rote tasks, enrichment of creative vistas through AI-derived insights, fiscal prudence via process streamlining, accessibility for indie filmmakers, and a quantum leap in visual effects and editing acumen. Nevertheless, navigating the labyrinth of integration complexities, ethical quandaries surrounding authorship and creativity, cognitive limitations vis-à-vis comprehending intricate decisions, data sovereignty concerns, and the spectre of attenuated human agency in creative decision-making represents a Herculean task. By deftly circumnavigating these challenges whilst leveraging the attendant benefits, filmmakers can indubitably harness AI's transformative potential to revolutionize their workflows and proffer immersive, captivating content to discerning audiences (Townsend, 2024).

Priya Chetan Parikh's seminal exploration into the realm of AI film aesthetics represents a pivotal investigation into the evolving syngamy of technology and cinema. Investigating into the representation of artificial intelligence within cinematic narratives, Parikh's study elucidates profound insights into this burgeoning intersection, shedding light on the distinctive features that characterize AI-infused films and their departure from traditional media paradigms. The research discerns

AI films as a nascent medium imbued with distinctive traits, notably manifested through their avant-garde digital construction, immersive virtual contexts, narrative focal points, and redefined authorial roles. Central to Parikh's discourse is the dynamic evolution of AI's role within film production, a process underscored by the profound implications it poses for the future trajectory of cinematic storytelling. Through systematic analysis, the study underscores the transformative impact of AI technologies on the creative landscape, prompting contemplation on the trajectory of narrative innovation and the ethical dimensions inherent in AI's integration within the industry. Interrogating the complex interplay between technology and artistic expression, Parikh's work showcases the recalibration of traditional film aesthetics within the milieu of new media, heralding a paradigmatic shift in the cinematic lexicon.

Furthermore, Parikh's inquiry navigates the contentious terrain of AI authorship, probing the peculiar conundrums surrounding the attribution of creative agency to artificial entities. By unpacking the subtleties of AI's contribution to the creative process, the study engenders discourse on the recognition of AI as a legitimate creative force and its attendant implications for intellectual property rights. This examination serves as a locus for deliberation on the reconfiguration of established notions of authorship within the digital epoch, precipitating a revaluation of conventional frameworks within the domain of film production. In parallel, the discourse extends to the cultural reverberations engendered by AI-infused cinema, illuminating its catalytic role in shaping online discourse and challenging entrenched paradigms of authorship and aesthetic valuation within the digital milieu. Parikh's analysis underscores the transformative potential of AI films as catalysts for cultural introspection, fostering a dialectic exchange that transcends traditional boundaries of artistic discourse (Parikh, 2019).

Expanding upon Parikh's foundational investigation, subsequent research by Chow underscores the seismic impact of AI integration within Hollywood's creative ecosystem. Highlighting the transformative role of AI tools in streamlining creative processes, Chow's discourse underscores the dialectic tension between efficiency and artistic integrity inherent within AI-driven production paradigms. Despite its potential to catalyse innovation, the infiltration of AI within Hollywood's creative apparatus precipitates a profound reckoning with ethical imperatives and the preservation of human agency in storytelling. Central to Chow's narrative is the industry's imperative to reconcile the imperatives of technological progress with the preservation of creative autonomy, foregrounding a discourse that transcends conventional binaries of man versus machine. As Hollywood grapples with the ethical and creative dimensions of AI integration, Chow's research serves as a clarion call for a systematic interrogation of the symbiotic relationship between technological advancement and artistic integrity within the cinematic landscape. In navigating this dialectic, the film industry stands poised at the precipice of a transformative juncture, wherein the harmonious fusion of human ingenuity and technological prowess promises to redefine the contours of cinematic storytelling for generations to come (Chow, 2020).

Mohammed Monirul Islam undertakes an in-depth examination of the integration of artificial intelligence (AI) within the landscape of Indian cinema, with a specific focus on the Hindi-language short film 'Anukul' directed by Sujoy Ghosh. The study elucidates the way Indian filmmakers navigate the terrain of ethical quandaries and legal complexities inherent in AI technology, as portrayed within the cinematic narrative of 'Anukul'. Through a cautious dissection of the AI-human interface depicted in the film, the scholarly discourse culminates in the assertion that 'Anukul' serves as an invaluable platform for contemplation upon the burgeoning interplay between humanity and intelligent machines within a paradigm characterized by posthuman attributes. The analysis underscores the imperative of conscientiously grappling with ethical conundrums, establishing robust legal frameworks, and discerning the evolving dynamics that delineate the relationship between humans and AI. Such reflections engender fervent dialogues pertaining to the delineation of boundaries and the subtleties underpinning interactions between these disparate yet increasingly interlinked entities (Islam, 2022).

Hardeep Singh elucidates the transformative prowess of artificial intelligence (AI) within the domain of film production, particularly accentuating its symbiotic relationship with machine learning (ML). The discourse accentuates the profound capacity of AI to redefine the cinematic creation process across multifarious stages, spanning from pre-production challenges to post-production finesse and eventual broadcasting endeavours. Through the seamless integration of AI technologies, filmmakers are poised to elevate the calibre of their cinematic endeavours, thereby fostering the prospect of augmented box office returns. A comprehensive survey conducted as part of the study endeavours to gauge the prevailing and prospective interest in the application of AI within the film industry, unveiling a resoundingly positive reception and signalling auspicious vistas for the continued entrenchment of AI within the cinematic milieu. The empirical findings gleaned from the survey delineate a discernible correlation between the deployment of AI and the amplification of production standards, thus underscoring the pivotal role of AI in streamlining processes and propelling triumph within the cinematic sphere. In summation, the research endeavour proffers a cogent testament to the momentous influence wielded by AI upon film production paradigms, delineating its versatility, proclivity for innovation, and salutary implications for the progressive evolution and maturation of the film industry (Singh, Kaur & Singh, 2023).

The landscape of contemporary filmmaking undergoes a profound metamorphosis catalysed by the integration of artificial intelligence, which mirrors human cognition and decision-making processes. This transformative paradigm shift is characterized by AI's multifaceted contributions spanning the entirety of the filmmaking pipeline. AI's capacity to elevate visual aesthetics empowers filmmakers with the capability to craft robust and hyper-realistic cinematic universes, exemplified through techniques such as actor de-aging and the utilization of deep fake technology. Moreover, AI-driven solutions streamline the post-production phase, automating an array of tasks encompassing editing, colour correction, budget management, and scheduling.

Recently, within this realm, a plethora of AI-enabled tools has emerged, serving diverse functions across different stages of filmmaking. Noteworthy mentions include screenwriting assistants such as Sudowrite and Squibler, which facilitate the conceptualization and refinement of narrative structures. Pre-production endeavours are bolstered by the likes of RivetAI and ShotPro, offering invaluable assistance in visualization and logistical planning. Furthermore, during the production phase, AI innovations like ARRI Stellar for lighting management and RTMotion Latitude for precision lens control optimize operational efficiency and technical precision (Chase, 2024). In the domain of post-production, AI's prowess is unmistakably evident in editing suites like Invideo and Filmora, which not only automate labour-intensive tasks but also enhance the overall visual fidelity of the final product (Fikri & Fitria, 2022). Similarly, tools like Colourlab AI and Pixotope emerge as indispensable assets for colour grading and visual effects, elevating image quality and fostering seamless integration of digital enhancements(McMillan, 2021).

The transformative influence of AI extends beyond the visual realm, permeating into the auditory domain through AI-generated music tools such as Mubert and AIVA. These innovative platforms offer composers unprecedented flexibility in crafting customizable musical compositions tailored to specific thematic subtilities and emotional resonances within cinematic narratives (Quthor, 2024). Furthermore, AI's impact on marketing and promotional endeavours is profound, as it enables the customization and optimization of outreach strategies to target audience segments with unparalleled precision and efficacy.

However, amid the undeniable benefits ushered in by AI integration in filmmaking, lingering apprehensions persist regarding its potential to encroach upon the realm of human creativity and expression. Particularly concerning is the perceived lack of sensibility inherent in AI-generated content, which raises concerns regarding its capacity to authentically capture the essence of scriptwriting and character development. Ethical considerations also loom large, with apprehensions surrounding the possibility of inadvertent plagiarism stemming from AI-driven content generation (Dayo, Memon & Dharejo, 2023).

Reflecting on the historical trajectory of AI's presence in cinema, its nascent origins can be traced back to the early 2000s with the advent of Computer-Generated Imagery (CGI), as evidenced in seminal works such as 'The Lord of the Rings' and 'The Matrix.' Moreover, the thematic exploration of AI as a central motif in films like '2001: A Space Odyssey,' 'The Terminator,' and 'Her' underscores its enduring significance as a narrative trope that transcends temporal and genre boundaries. Iconic cinematic depictions of AI entities, ranging from Robby the Robot in 'Forbidden Planet' to the enigmatic replicants in 'Blade Runner,' have indelibly shaped cultural perceptions and discourse surrounding the intersection of AI and humanity (Mathur, 2023).

These cinematic narratives serve as touchstones for subsequent explorations of AI's ethical, existential, and ontological implications, as evidenced in contemporary works like 'The Matrix' and 'I, Robot.' Looking ahead, the future trajectory of AI in filmmaking necessitates a delicate balance between technological innovation and the preservation of fundamental storytelling principles and emotional resonance. By serving as a complementary tool to human creativity and ingenuity, AI holds the potential to augment and enhance the filmmaking process, while safeguarding the intrinsic qualities that define the art of storytelling and its profound capacity to evoke empathy and introspection (Coleman, 2019).

The 2023 release of the iconic 'Indiana Jones' franchise presents an intriguing case study in the intersection of Hollywood and Artificial Intelligence (AI), as Harrison Ford's remarkably youthful appearance is attributed to advancements in AI and machine learning technologies. This cinematic portrayal not only serves as a testament to the evolving capabilities of AI-driven visual effects but also underscores the multifaceted concerns permeating the entertainment industry regarding the proliferation of AI (Bedingfield, 2023).

Against this backdrop, Hollywood finds itself embroiled in a labour dispute reminiscent of the tumultuous strikes of the 1960s, with actors and screenwriters taking a stand against perceived injustices relating to remuneration, working conditions, and the increasing prevalence of AI in creative processes. Central to these grievances is the apprehension surrounding AI's potential to disrupt traditional employment paradigms and fundamentally alter the nature of artistic roles within the industry (Coyle, 2023).

Of paramount concern are the complex legal and ethical ramifications surrounding AI's role in intellectual property rights. Debates surrounding the concept of 'fair use' in the context of training AI models, as well as the treatment of AI-generated outputs in terms of intellectual property and copyright, have emerged as contentious points of contention. Legal actions targeting technology providers further underscore the intensification of this ongoing debate.

The transformative potential of AI extends beyond mere visual enhancements, encompassing a diverse array of applications ranging from the creation of digital avatars capable of producing inclusive content to the cloning of voices through synthetic voice technology (Vilenkin, 2024). While these advancements present novel opportunities for enhancing creative expression and accessibility, they also engender concerns regarding the displacement of traditional roles and the erosion of artistic authenticity.

Furthermore, AI's capacity to automate repetitive tasks and streamline production workflows has been demonstrated through initiatives such as the AI-generated 'South Park' episode, exemplifying its potential to revolutionize content creation processes. Similarly, AI facilitates the seamless localization of content through multilingual releases, as evidenced by Hybe's collaboration with MidNatt to produce a song available in six languages (Salazar,2023).

Navigating the complex landscape of AI integration necessitates concerted efforts towards public-private collaboration aimed at addressing concerns and capitalizing on emerging opportunities. Initiatives such as the AI Governance Alliance endeavour to promote the development and implementation of safe, sustainable, and regulated AI systems within the entertainment industry, reflecting a collective recognition of the profound transformational potential AI holds for both producers and consumers alike (Li & Bantourakis, 2023).

The omnipresent influence of artificial intelligence (AI) within the cinematic sphere heralds a paradigm shift, permeating every facet of filmmaking from scriptwriting and visual effects (VFX) to music composition and editing. Its catalytic impact extends beyond mere augmentation, revolutionizing production workflows, fostering innovation, and concomitantly curbing operational costs. Yet, amid this transformative milieu, a confluence of ethical quandaries and apprehensions regarding the erosion of traditional creative roles looms large, complicating the industry's trajectory towards AI integration.

While AI's manifold benefits are indisputable, the film industry stands at a crossroads, tasked with navigating the interplay between technological advancement and the preservation of quintessentially human-driven storytelling. The imperative of striking a delicate balance between these competing imperatives necessitates a perpetual cycle of negotiation and adaptation, as stakeholders grapple with the ethical imperatives and existential ramifications attendant to AI's ascendancy.

Central to this dialectic is the immutable commitment towards fostering an ecosystem wherein human creativity remains the sine qua non of cinematic innovation, even as AI assumes an increasingly ubiquitous role within production pipelines. The exigencies of this transformative epoch mandate a proactive engagement with the ethical and philosophical dimensions underpinning AI's integration, illuminating pathways towards a future wherein technology augments rather than supplants the human creative spirit.

AI AND INDIAN FILM INDUSTRY: NAVIGATING THE TRAJECTORIES

Artificial Intelligence (AI) has emerged as a transformative catalyst within the Indian film industry, profoundly influencing diverse facets ranging from production to distribution. Traditionally dominated by major studios and blockbuster paradigms, AI has democratized access to sophisticated filmmaking tools, benefiting not only established entities but also regional cinema and independent auteurs. This paradigmatic shift represents a pivotal juncture where technological prowess intersects with creative ingenuity, fundamentally reshaping narrative frameworks and cinematic methodologies across India. At its core, AI's impact on Indian cinema manifests through its pervasive integration throughout the film production lifecycle. From script analysis to post-production, AI algorithms are harnessed to streamline operations and augment creative decision-making processes. For instance, leading production houses employ AI for script analysis and predictive audience behaviour analytics. This early adoption enables proactive adjustments in production strategies, optimizing resource allocation and narrative refinement based on empirical forecasts.

Moreover, AI's influence extends beyond mainstream Bollywood, permeating regional cinema where varied storytelling traditions and their on-screen adaptations are bolstered by technological facilitation (Sarkar, 2024). In South Indian cinema, AI-driven tools are pivotal in subtitle generation and dubbing processes, enhancing linguistic precision and expanding the global accessibility of regional films. Such integrative measures not only elevate viewing experiences for diverse audiences but also amplify market prospects for regional cinematic expressions.

Furthermore, AI empowers independent filmmakers and aspiring students within India's vibrant film academia by offering cost-effective alternatives to conventional production methodologies. Platforms such as Pixotope and Flair exemplify this trend, providing AI-driven solutions for virtual production and visual impacts, thereby enabling creators to achieve cinematic excellence on modest budgets. This democratization of technology is particularly transformative within India's independent film sphere, fostering narrative innovation alongside commercial viability.

A landmark achievement in this evolution is the incorporation of AI into educational curricula at esteemed film institutions and regional film schools. These initiatives equip emerging filmmakers with proficient AI competencies, preparing them to harness technological advancements effectively in their artistic pursuits. This educational paradigm not only cultivates future-ready talent but also nurtures a cohort of filmmakers' adept at synergizing artistic expression with cutting-edge technological tools.

Beyond production dynamics, AI plays a pivotal role in augmenting the distribution and marketing paradigms of Indian cinema. Streaming platforms such as Netflix and Amazon Prime Video leverage AI algorithms to personalize content recommendations based on user preferences, thereby enhancing the discoverability of diverse Indian films on a global scale. This data-driven approach optimizes audience outreach and fortifies the international footprint of Indian cinema amid evolving consumer landscapes.

Moreover, AI-driven analytics redefine audience engagement strategies by facilitating pre-release sentiment analysis and predictive modelling. Such insights enable filmmakers to gauge audience reception beforehand, enabling targeted promotional campaigns and strategic marketing initiatives. This data-centric approach not only mitigates financial risks but also heightens the potential for commercial success in an increasingly competitive industry milieu.

Looking ahead, AI's trajectory within Indian cinema is poised for further augmentation, driven by advancements in machine learning and natural language processing. Innovations like deepfake technology and AI-generated content offer novel avenues for narrative exploration and visual experimentation, albeit accompanied by ethical considerations and the preservation of creative integrity. Amidst these evolutions, the collaborative interplay between AI and human creativity continues to redefine the contours of cinematic expression in India.

From Script to Screen: Applications of AI in Filmmaking

AI has emerged as a pivotal catalyst for innovation within the Indian film industry, transcending traditional boundaries and democratizing access to advanced filmmaking tools. Its integration into pre-production, production, and post-production processes has revolutionized practices, offering filmmakers unprecedented creative and technical capabilities. Moreover, AI's inclusion in film education underscores its transformative potential, preparing the next generation of filmmakers to harness its power effectively.

I. Scriptwriting/ Screenplay: AI revolutionizes scriptwriting in the Indian film industry, transforming practices and enhancing creativity. Scripts go beyond narrative, shaping every cinematic element. AI tools like the 'Boords AI Movie Script Generator' redefine script development by boosting analysis, creativity, and efficiency, catering to a broad range of scriptwriters from professionals to amateurs. In a testament to its potential, the authors of this chapter have explored the capabilities of such AI tools for script generation, yielding a compelling and finely tuned screenplay. This intersection of technology and creativity underscores AI's burgeoning role in driving innovation within India's vibrant film industry, promising new horizons for storytelling and cinematic expression.

Figure 1. Inputs given to AI Script Generator to write a script for a film of five minutes duration

Figure 2. Screenplay by 'Boords AI Movie Script Generator' mentioning significant details

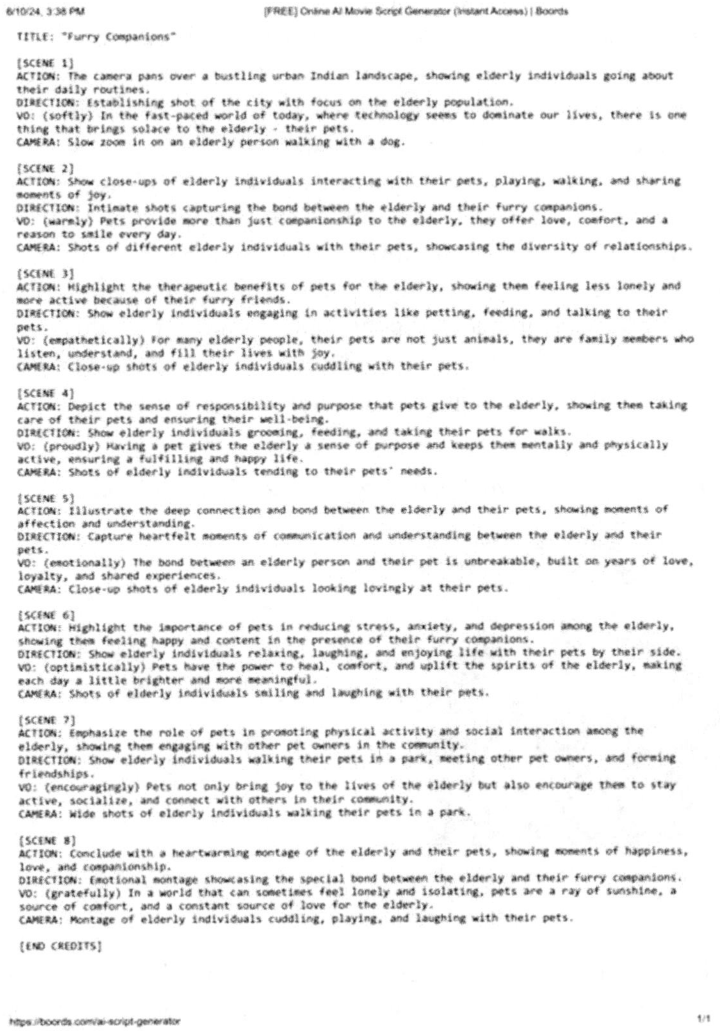

6/10/24, 3:38 PM [FREE] Online AI Movie Script Generator (Instant Access) | Boords

TITLE: "Furry Companions"

[SCENE 1]
ACTION: The camera pans over a bustling urban Indian landscape, showing elderly individuals going about their daily routines.
DIRECTION: Establishing shot of the city with focus on the elderly population.
VO: (softly) In the fast-paced world of today, where technology seems to dominate our lives, there is one thing that brings solace to the elderly - their pets.
CAMERA: Slow zoom in on an elderly person walking with a dog.

[SCENE 2]
ACTION: Show close-ups of elderly individuals interacting with their pets, playing, walking, and sharing moments of joy.
DIRECTION: Intimate shots capturing the bond between the elderly and their furry companions.
VO: (warmly) Pets provide more than just companionship to the elderly, they offer love, comfort, and a reason to smile every day.
CAMERA: Shots of different elderly individuals with their pets, showcasing the diversity of relationships.

[SCENE 3]
ACTION: Highlight the therapeutic benefits of pets for the elderly, showing them feeling less lonely and more active because of their furry friends.
DIRECTION: Show elderly individuals engaging in activities like petting, feeding, and talking to their pets.
VO: (empathetically) For many elderly people, their pets are not just animals, they are family members who listen, understand, and fill their lives with joy.
CAMERA: Close-up shots of elderly individuals cuddling with their pets.

[SCENE 4]
ACTION: Depict the sense of responsibility and purpose that pets give to the elderly, showing them taking care of their pets and ensuring their well-being.
DIRECTION: Show elderly individuals grooming, feeding, and taking their pets for walks.
VO: (proudly) Having a pet gives the elderly a sense of purpose and keeps them mentally and physically active, ensuring a fulfilling and happy life.
CAMERA: Shots of elderly individuals tending to their pets' needs.

[SCENE 5]
ACTION: Illustrate the deep connection and bond between the elderly and their pets, showing moments of affection and understanding.
DIRECTION: Capture heartfelt moments of communication and understanding between the elderly and their pets.
VO: (emotionally) The bond between an elderly person and their pet is unbreakable, built on years of love, loyalty, and shared experiences.
CAMERA: Close-up shots of elderly individuals looking lovingly at their pets.

[SCENE 6]
ACTION: Highlight the importance of pets in reducing stress, anxiety, and depression among the elderly, showing them feeling happy and content in the presence of their furry companions.
DIRECTION: Show elderly individuals relaxing, laughing, and enjoying life with their pets by their side.
VO: (optimistically) Pets have the power to heal, comfort, and uplift the spirits of the elderly, making each day a little brighter and more meaningful.
CAMERA: Shots of elderly individuals smiling and laughing with their pets.

[SCENE 7]
ACTION: Emphasize the role of pets in promoting physical activity and social interaction among the elderly, showing them engaging with other pet owners in the community.
DIRECTION: Show elderly individuals walking their pets in a park, meeting other pet owners, and forming friendships.
VO: (encouragingly) Pets not only bring joy to the lives of the elderly but also encourage them to stay active, socialize, and connect with others in their community.
CAMERA: Wide shots of elderly individuals walking their pets in a park.

[SCENE 8]
ACTION: Conclude with a heartwarming montage of the elderly and their pets, showing moments of happiness, love, and companionship.
DIRECTION: Emotional montage showcasing the special bond between the elderly and their furry companions.
VO: (gratefully) In a world that can sometimes feel lonely and isolating, pets are a ray of sunshine, a source of comfort, and a constant source of love for the elderly.
CAMERA: Montage of elderly individuals cuddling, playing, and laughing with their pets.

[END CREDITS]

https://boords.com/ai-script-generator 1/1

II. Storyboarding: Artificial Intelligence (AI) plays a pivotal role in storyboarding by automating layout suggestions through sophisticated script analysis and adherence to visual composition principles. This integration not only streamlines the creative process but also fosters heightened efficiency and creativity for filmmakers, providing dynamic tools that enrich scene visualization and elevate narrative coherence.

"The integration of Artificial Intelligence (AI) in storyboarding marks a significant leap forward for the film and animation sectors. AI algorithms systematically analyse scripts and propose visual layouts, boosting efficiency and creativity during pre-production. By automating the arrangement of scenes based on narrative structure and cinematic principles, AI empowers filmmakers to envision dynamic sequences and streamline storytelling. This optimization of initial scene visualization facilitates clearer communication of creative visions, expediting the development of compelling narratives on screen. AI-driven tools like BARD AI and Midjourney exemplify this transformation by providing seamless scene prompts and accurate sketches, revolutionizing visual planning. Innovations such as 3DFY in concept development further enhance efficiency by simplifying the design of props and environments, signalling AI's profound impact on contemporary media production and visual storytelling workflows." (G Puneet Kumar Reddy, Specialist in Storyboarding and visualization, personal communication, 24 May 2024).

Figure 3. Section of storyboard generated using Firefly AI and Microsoft BING integration with DALL•E

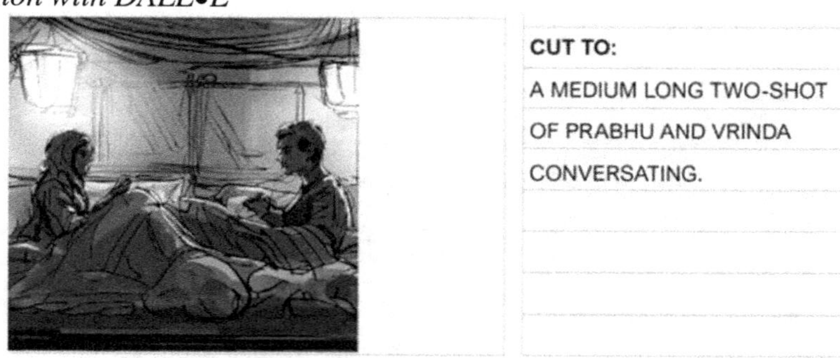

(Source: G Puneet Kumar Reddy's personal work, May 2024)

III. Casting: Artificial Intelligence (AI) is transformative in digitally matching actors with film projects, transcending traditional pre-production boundaries. By automating audition processes, AI accelerates casting procedures, ensuring precise and efficient casting choices. This integration not only streamlines operations but also elevates decision-making quality, fostering greater inclusivity and performance excellence across film, television, and theatre productions.

"Artificial Intelligence (AI) has started registering its presence in casting process within the Indian entertainment industry, gradually transforming conventional practices. By harnessing AI algorithms that analyse extensive datasets and social media profiles, casting directors can efficiently identify actors who are best suited for specific role requirements, considering attributes such as physical appearance, acting prowess, and audience appeal. This data-driven methodology not only expedites casting decisions but also promotes objectivity, mitigating biases and fostering greater diversity in casting selections. Furthermore, AI-powered tools leverage predictive analytics to evaluate an actor's potential success in a role, considering factors like past performances, audience reception, and current market trends. This predictive capability empowers casting professionals to make well-informed decisions that harmonize artistic vision with commercial viability, thereby enhancing the overall efficiency and effectiveness of the casting process. AI tools extensively aid actor recruitment across agencies. Largo.ai, for instance, links producers, casting directors, and actors by analysing scripts, character traits, and physical attributes. Notably, Largo.ai boasts an impressive 86% accuracy in predicting film earnings, marking a promising leap forward in AI's role within the casting process (Moviemaking Platform Largo.ai, 2021)." (Sadaf Khan, Educationist and Theatre practitioner, personal communication, 02 May 2024).

IV. Budgeting: Within the Indian film industry, the strategic allocation of budgets plays a pivotal role in shaping both economic efficiency and artistic outcomes. The financial architecture of a film exerts profound influence over the efficient utilization of resources and the ultimate realization of creative vision (Moore, 2019). Recent strides in artificial intelligence have heralded a new era, offering predictive models capable of accurately forecasting shooting schedules and generating comprehensive budgetary projections. These advancements facilitate the methodical generation of detailed expenditure analyses spanning multiple operational domains.

For film producers, these AI-driven tools represent more than just technological innovations; they serve as transformative catalysts, enabling a dual expansion of both financial and creative horizons. Empowered by these tools, producers can confidently embark on multiple projects concurrently, leveraging enhanced financial planning capabilities to optimize investment decisions and maximize their cinematic impact. This integration of technology marks a paradigm shift in the strategic management of cinematic enterprises, redefining how foresight in financial planning drives innovation and growth in the competitive landscape of Indian filmmaking.

The authors of this chapter have explored the transformative capabilities of AI-driven tools in crafting a detailed budget for their film project. Utilizing the 'Taskade AI Video Budget Generator', they applied advanced algorithms to develop a hypothetical yet comprehensive financial plan specifically tailored for their documentary. This innovative methodology not only illuminates the evolving significance of artificial intelligence within the realm of film production but also emphasizes its capacity to streamline resource allocation and promote financial transparency.

Figure 4. Inputs given to AI Video Budget Generator to frame a budget for documentary shooting

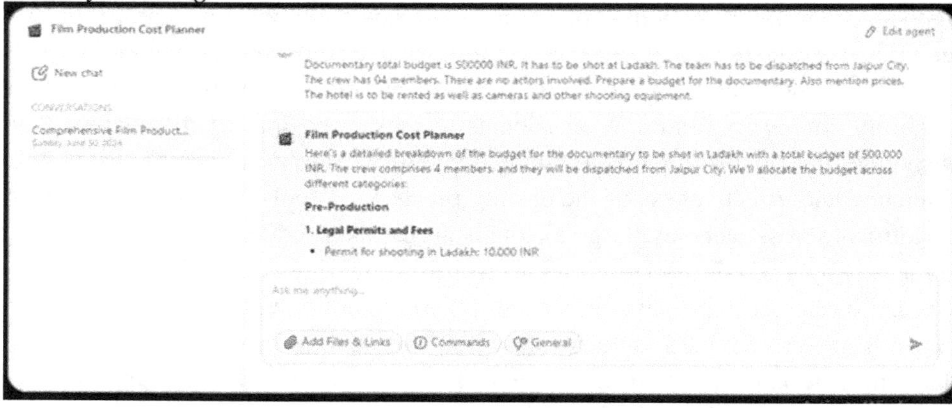

Figure 5. Documentary budget generated by 'Taskade AI Video Budget Generator' mentioning significant details (Part I)

6/30/24, 3:59 PM Workspace - Taskade

Film Production Cost Planner

Here's a detailed breakdown of the budget for the documentary to be shot in Ladakh with a total budget of 500,000 INR. The crew comprises 4 members, and they will be dispatched from Jaipur City. We'll allocate the budget across different categories:

Pre-Production

1. **Legal Permits and Fees**
   - Permit for shooting in Ladakh: 10,000 INR
2. **Location Scouting**
   - Location scouting fee: 15,000 INR (including travel)

Production

3. **Travel Costs**
   - Return airfare from Jaipur to Ladakh for 4 crew members: 10,000 INR per person
     - Total: 40,000 INR
4. **Accommodation**
   - Hotel stay in Ladakh for 4 crew members (for 1 month)
     - Estimated cost per night per room: 2,000 INR
     - Total: 2,000 INR * 30 nights * 4 rooms = 240,000 INR
5. **Transportation**
   - Local transportation (rental cars, fuel): 30,000 INR
6. **Equipment Rental**
   - Camera (e.g., RED or similar): 50,000 INR/month
   - Lighting equipment: 20,000 INR/month
   - Sound equipment: 15,000 INR/month
   - Miscellaneous filming gear (tripods, batteries, etc.): 10,000 INR/month
     - Total equipment rental: 95,000 INR
7. **Crew Salaries**
   - Director/Producer: 50,000 INR
   - Cinematographer: 40,000 INR
   - Sound Mixer: 30,000 INR
   - Production Assistant: 20,000 INR
     - Total salaries: 140,000 INR
8. **Catering and Miscellaneous Expenses**
   - Food and daily allowances for the crew: 500 INR/day per person
     - Total: 500 INR * 30 days * 4 crew members = 60,000 INR

Post-Production

9. **Editing**
   - Editing fees: 40,000 INR
   - Color grading: 15,000 INR

https://www.taskade.com/spaces/d7Li2yJKFPB2Nc2v/agents?onboarding-open-generate-agent=true 1/2

Figure 6. Documentary budget generated by 'Taskade AI Video Budget Generator' mentioning significant details (Part II)

6/30/24, 3:59 PM Workspace - Taskade

- Sound design and mixing: 10,000 INR
    - Total post-production: 65,000 INR

Miscellaneous

10. Contingency Fund

- Contingency (10%): 35,000 INR

Overall Budget Summary

- **Pre-Production**: 25,000 INR
- **Production**: 635,000 INR
- **Post-Production**: 65,000 INR
- **Miscellaneous**: 35,000 INR
- **Grand Total**: 760,000 INR

Given the total budget of 500,000 INR, the project exceeds the budget by 260,000 INR. We need to make adjustments to stay within the budget constraints. Here are some suggestions:

1. **Accommodation**: Look for cheaper accommodation or negotiate rates. Target accommodation cost to be reduced by 100,000 INR.
2. **Equipment Rental**: Negotiate or seek sponsorships for equipment rental. Target to reduce by 50,000 INR.
3. **Crew Salaries**: Negotiate salaries or find a way to reduce the crew size if possible. Target reduction by 40,000 INR.
4. **Miscellaneous Costs**: Reduce the contingency fund to 25,000 INR.

Adjusted Budget Summary

- **Pre-Production**: 25,000 INR
- **Production**: 445,000 INR (with targeted reductions)
- **Post-Production**: 65,000 INR
- **Miscellaneous**: 25,000 INR
- **Adjusted Grand Total**: 500,000 INR

By implementing these adjustments, you can stay within the budget constraints of 500,000 INR while still achieving the documentary's goals.

https://www.taskade.com/spaces/d7Li2yJKFPB2Nc2v/agents?onboarding-open-generate-agent=true 2/2

V. Image Generation: In the Indian context, Artificial Intelligence (AI) stands poised to revolutionize image generation across diverse sectors, notably within the vibrant landscape of the Indian Film Industry. Advanced AI technologies such as Generative Adversarial Networks (GANs) and neural networks are fundamentally reshaping the creation of visual content by enabling the rapid production of high-fidelity images with unparalleled efficiency. This transformative capability holds significant potential for Indian filmmakers, who navigate a rich tradition of cultural narratives and aesthetics. AI-driven image generation facilitates swift prototyping of scenes, augmentation of digital sets, and integration of sophisticated visual effects, thereby optimizing production costs and enriching cinematic storytelling. Furthermore, AI's capacity to simulate intricate lighting scenarios, generate realistic backgrounds, and automate routine tasks streamlines production workflows, allowing filmmakers to concentrate more deeply on creative direction and narrative intricacies. Beyond production phases, AI enhances post-production processes such as precise color grading, seamless integration of visual effects, and systematic editing, ensuring a cohesive and visually compelling cinematic experience. Embracing AI technologies not only strengthens the global competitiveness of the Indian Film Industry but also catalyzes innovation in visual storytelling, ushering in a transformative era characterized by cinematic excellence and enhanced cultural representation.

Figure 7. Figure created through Meta AI on WhatsApp, using provided prompts (Courtesy: Mr. S. U. Khan, June 2024)

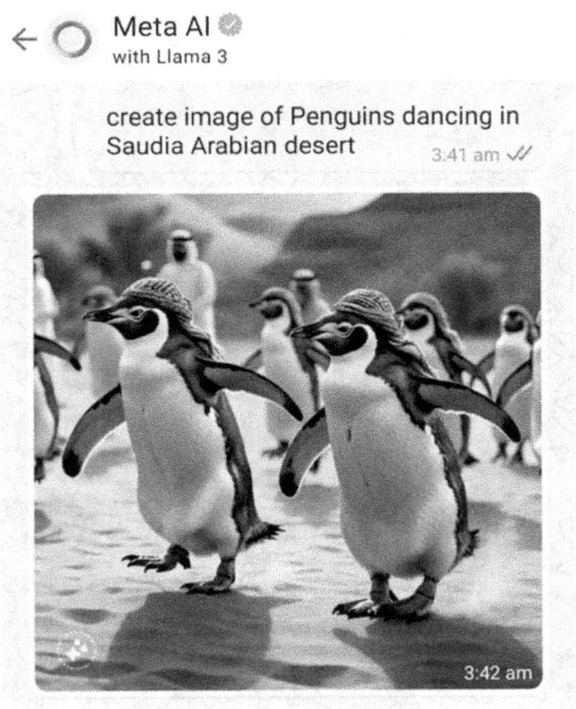

"AI has revolutionized image creation by swiftly generating highly accurate visuals from textual descriptions. Technologies like Meta AI have significantly advanced, allowing users to effortlessly produce photorealistic images by simply describing their desired scene. This innovation facilitates rapid ideation and visualization, particularly evident in platforms like WhatsApp, where diverse subjects can be explored with ease. In filmmaking, AI-generated images play a crucial role in enhancing visual storytelling by enabling filmmakers to prototype scenes, envision complex scenarios, and experiment creatively without the usual resource and time constraints. AI's ability to generate tailored images from specific prompts not only streamlines creative workflows but also enhances storytelling potential by offering precise visual articulation and conceptual refinement. As a result, AI tools, especially with advancements in Meta AI, are democratizing sophisticated imagery creation, making it accessible and immediate across creative industries." (Sana Ullah Khan, Graphic Designer & Content Creator, personal communication, 12 June 2024).

Figure 8. 'The penguins dance across the world' (Figure created through Meta AI, Courtesy: Mr. S. U. Khan, June 2024)

VI. Voice and Song Generation: AI has brought about a transformative impact on both voice and music creation, ushering in unprecedented capabilities in generating lifelike audio content. In the realm of voice synthesis, AI technologies can replicate human speech patterns and tones with remarkable accuracy. This breakthrough enables applications across virtual assistants, customer service automation, and accessibility tools. In music composition, AI algorithms leverage extensive music databases to craft melodies, harmonies, and lyrics across various styles and genres. This capability allows AI to mimic diverse musical traditions and innovate within established forms. Examples such as Suno AI and Udio exemplify this advancement in song generation. For instance, Suno AI recently composed a Punjabi-themed Bollywood-inspired song, accompanied by a video featuring 'Kala Chashma'. Despite minor synchronization issues, the nearly two-minute composition demonstrated Suno AI's autonomous musical composition prowess (Nair, 2024). Similarly, Udio and platforms like Muscify cater to a wide range of musical tastes and cultural preferences, particularly within India. By harnessing AI, these platforms efficiently meet the demands of millions by rapidly creating customized music compositions. These innovations underscore AI's role in shaping the future of music creation, democratizing sophisticated audio production and adapting it for global audiences.

VIII. Visual Effects: AI has fundamentally transformed the landscape of visual effects (VFX) in the Indian film industry, revolutionizing what was once a painstaking and time-consuming process. Previously, animators faced challenges like jerky movements, static backgrounds, and limited character expressions, as each frame had to be carefully crafted by hand, stifling creativity and consuming vast resources. Today, AI tools have reshaped VFX workflows, accelerating processes such as rotoscoping, inpainting, and camera tracking from months to mere weeks. Platforms like Arraiy, leveraging extensive VFX data for training, have streamlined tasks like rotoscoping, traditionally a labour-intensive process, into rapid and efficient operations. This acceleration allows filmmakers to review and potentially reshoot scenes within tight timelines, saving significant time and cost (Sathyan, 2023). With reference to usage of AI in context of visual effects generation, groundbreaking example in Indian cinema is the Tamil film 'Weapon', marking the first feature to integrate a two-and-a-half-minute AI-generated sequence. Using images of lead actor Sathyaraj as input, AI was employed in this film to create a younger digital version of him, showcasing the growing synergy between AI technology and filmmaking creativity.

Director S.S. Rajamouli exemplifies this transformative use of AI in his epic films 'Baahubali: The Beginning' and 'Baahubali: The Conclusion.' Here, AI and advanced VFX techniques were instrumental in bringing to life spectacular visuals such as massive armies, intricate palaces, and breathtaking landscapes. AI facilitated realistic simulations of crowd movements and battle sequences, enhancing the films' immersive quality while optimizing post-production tasks like colour correction and image stabilization. Rajamouli's integration of AI underscores its capacity to elevate cinematic storytelling by achieving levels of detail and realism that were previously arduous to attain. His films serve as a beacon for aspiring filmmakers and students alike, demonstrating how AI can augment creative vision to craft unforgettable cinematic experiences. As the industry continues to evolve, Rajamouli's pioneering use of AI sets a precedent for leveraging technology to innovate and enhance the art of filmmaking in India and beyond (K Kumar, 2024).

"In Indian cinema, Artificial Intelligence (AI) has revolutionized visual effects (VFX), fundamentally altering film production. AI is now deeply embedded in post-production workflows, from software like Photoshop to advanced platforms such as Premiere Pro, enhancing creative possibilities and streamlining processes. AI excels in VFX by mastering tasks from image manipulation to complex scene generation, achieving cinematic realism with unprecedented precision. This democratizes high-quality VFX, particularly benefiting independent and regional filmmakers constrained by budgets, enabling them to create visuals that rival big-budget productions on a global scale.

In film schools, AI is integrated into curricula, empowering students to innovate in VFX creation. This prepares them for industry demands while fostering ground-breaking storytelling techniques. AI's impact is marked by its ability to swiftly iterate and refine visuals, drastically cutting production timelines and costs. What once took extensive manual effort can now be accomplished in a fraction of the time, thanks to AI's computational power and advanced algorithms. Its efficiency and capability to interpret creative intent from minimal input consistently exceed human expectations. AI's integration into India's film VFX sector signifies a shift towards efficiency, accessibility, and innovation. As AI evolves, its role promises to redefine cinematic expression, equipping filmmakers with tools to craft compelling narratives and captivating visual experiences for global audiences." (Akshay Parashar, Film educationist specializing in advanced post-production filmmaking techniques, personal communication, 10 June 2024).

Figure 9. AI-generated visual effects for demonstrating the process of aging. (Courtesy: Mr. Akshay Parashar, June 2024)

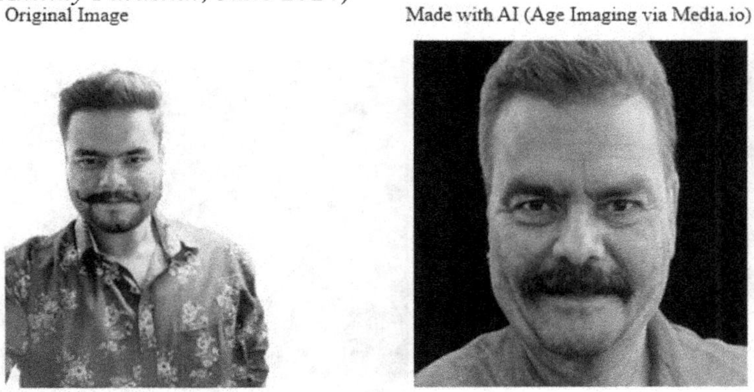

IX. Editing: The infusion of Artificial Intelligence (AI) into the film editing process marks a watershed in how movie trailers and editing overall are approached. AI algorithms play a pivotal role by assisting editors in identifying and emphasizing impactful movie scenes, particularly those rich in drama or action, thereby amplifying the emotional impact of trailers. Moreover, AI significantly contributes to comprehensive editing tasks through automation, such as scene analysis, character recognition, and story structure organization. This capability not only expedites editing workflows but also enhances precision and consistency. Beyond trailers, AI assumes a critical role in elevating visual effects (VFX) in films by optimizing the integration of VFX elements. Trained algorithms proficiently classify and apply effects, streamlining processes that traditionally demand substantial time and financial resources from VFX studios. This advancement not only enhances efficiency but also elevates the overall cinematic quality of films.

It is to be noted that AI revolutionizes filmmaking by automating and optimizing tasks such as editing, color grading, and visual effects enhancement. In editing, AI facilitates initial cuts, selects optimal takes, and suggests edits to refine pacing. For color grading, it ensures uniformity, applies stylistic enhancements, and enables real-time adjustments. AI-powered image extension can also streamline the editing process by providing editors and directors with more options and flexibility in manipulating visual elements. For example, it can enable editors to experiment with different visual compositions or enhance the quality of footage without relying solely on reshooting. As AI continues to advance, its impact on film editing promises to democratize access to sophisticated editing tools and enhance storytelling capabilities throughout the industry.

Figure 10. Usage of AI in image extension. (Courtesy: Mr. Akshay Parashar, June 2024)

“In the realm of editing, AI plays a pivotal role in not only minimizing time but also reducing costs significantly. Advanced tools like Adobe’s Sensei leverage machine learning to automate labour-intensive editing tasks, such as seamless object removal and precise scene stabilization. This automation not only accelerates the editing process but also enhances overall efficiency by allowing editors to focus more on creative decisions rather than repetitive technical adjustments. Furthermore, AI-driven capabilities in editing ensure consistent quality across projects, thereby improving the overall production value of films and other visual media. As AI continues to evolve, its integration into editing workflows promises to redefine industry standards”. (Eshan Harsh, Film Editor, personal communication, 03 June 2024).

X. Film Marketing & Distribution: Artificial intelligence (AI) has fundamentally reshaped the landscape of film marketing and distribution strategies, ushering in a new era where production houses engage audiences with unprecedented precision and efficiency. Traditionally reliant on static mediums such as billboards and television commercials, the industry in India has undergone a seismic shift propelled by Marketing Technology (MarTech), harnessing AI and data analytics to redefine promotional tactics from inception through to release. At the forefront of this transformation lies predictive analytics, a cornerstone of AI application in film marketing. By synthesizing vast datasets encompassing historical performance metrics, social media dynamics, and audience sentiment analysis, advanced AI models can forecast First Day Box Office (FBO) outcomes weeks in advance. This capability empowers studios to strategically allocate resources, optimize promotional campaigns, and tailor marketing efforts with a foresight previously unattainable through conventional methodologies.

Moreover, AI enables hyper-targeted marketing campaigns tailored to individual viewer preferences. Leveraging sophisticated algorithms to parse through extensive social media interactions and online behaviours, production houses can discern audience demographics and tailor content accordingly. This precision ensures that promotional messages resonate deeply, fostering heightened engagement and bolstering ticket sales. In tandem, AI-driven social listening tools have emerged as indispensable assets for monitoring audience sentiment and real-time reactions across digital platforms. These tools employ customized algorithms to track and analyse public discourse surrounding trailers, casting announcements, and promotional events. By gauging public sentiment swiftly and accurately, studios swiftly pivot marketing strategies in response to audience feedback, ensuring continuous relevance and resonance throughout the film's lifecycle.

Ethical Issues Concerning AI in Films

The integration of artificial intelligence (AI) into the Indian film industry represents a transformative shift with the potential to significantly enhance various aspects of filmmaking. AI's influence extends from scriptwriting and casting to visual effects and audience engagement, offering innovative solutions and efficiencies that were previously unattainable. However, this technological advancement also brings forth a host of ethical concerns that necessitate careful consideration. These concerns focus on the authenticity of creative works, ownership of intellectual property, the reinforcement of biases, and the preservation of cultural values. Addressing these issues is crucial to ensure that AI's integration into filmmaking enhances rather than compromises the integrity of artistic expression.

At the heart of the ethical debate surrounding AI in filmmaking is the issue of authenticity and ownership. Modern machine learning algorithms enable the creation of scripts, visual effects, and even the emulation of styles of iconic filmmakers by analyzing large datasets from existing films. This capability raises important questions about the originality of AI-generated content and the rights associated with it. The use of AI to replicate the distinctive techniques of renowned directors or scriptwriters blurs the boundary between homage and imitation, creating challenges related to intellectual property. The crux of the debate lies in determining whether the AI-generated works can be deemed original or merely a rearrangement of pre-existing artistic elements. Moreover, unresolved questions about copyright ownership persist—whether it should belong to the developers of the AI technology, the users who apply it, or the original artists whose styles have been emulated.

Another significant ethical concern is the potential for AI to perpetuate and even exacerbate existing biases and stereotypes. AI systems employed for audience analysis and targeted marketing analyze extensive datasets to predict viewer preferences and tailor content. While this approach can optimize marketing strategies, it also risks reinforcing and amplifying existing biases. AI algorithms trained on historical data might unintentionally perpetuate stereotypes by prioritizing content that aligns with preconceived notions about demographic groups. This can result in a narrow and skewed representation of diverse cultures and experiences, limiting the opportunities for marginalized voices. In the context of the Indian film industry, which is known for its rich tapestry of cultural narratives and traditions, there is a heightened risk that AI-driven decisions could undermine the industry's ability to represent its diverse audience with accuracy and sensitivity. Furthermore, the reliance on algorithmic predictions in content creation could lead to a homogenization of films, where artistic innovation is overshadowed by data-driven trends. Filmmakers might face pressure to conform to AI-generated predictions, potentially stifling creativity and diversity in storytelling.

Cultural sensitivity and preservation are also critical issues as the Indian film industry adapts to AI technology. The industry, renowned for its vibrant and diverse cultural expressions, must carefully balance technological advancement with the need to maintain cultural integrity. AI's capacity to generate content might prioritize global commercial appeal over traditional storytelling methods, risking the dilution of cultural authenticity. For instance, AI-generated scripts or visual effects might focus on universal themes rather than preserving the unique cultural elements intrinsic to Indian cinema. Additionally, AI-driven casting decisions could marginalize actors who represent specific cultural or regional identities, impacting the industry's ability to portray diverse voices. To mitigate these risks, the Indian film industry needs to establish ethical guidelines for AI use that honor and preserve its cultural values. This involves designing and applying AI tools in ways that support rather than compromise the rich heritage of Indian cinema. Collaboration between technologists and cultural experts is essential to ensure that AI solutions align with and enhance the industry's artistic and cultural goals.

As AI technologies continue to advance rapidly, the need for comprehensive regulatory and ethical frameworks becomes increasingly apparent. Such frameworks should address critical issues related to intellectual property, bias, and cultural preservation, providing clear guidelines for the responsible use of AI in filmmaking. Regulatory bodies, industry associations, and cultural representatives must collaborate to create standards that ensure the ethical application of AI technologies. This includes developing protocols for intellectual property rights concerning AI-generated content and mechanisms to address and mitigate biases in audience targeting and content creation. Additionally, ethical guidelines must be established to ensure that AI applications respect cultural values and contribute positively to the industry's diverse narrative traditions. Ongoing dialogue among filmmakers, technologists, regulators, and cultural experts will be crucial in adapting these frameworks to the evolving landscape of AI in cinema. By fostering a collaborative approach, the industry can proactively address ethical challenges and ensure that technological advancements enhance rather than detract from the creative and cultural essence of filmmaking.

Indian Film Industry and AI: Mapping Future Projections

The Indian film industry is on the brink of a revolutionary shift, fuelled by the rapid evolution of artificial intelligence (AI). As AI technologies become increasingly sophisticated, their integration across various facets of filmmaking is set to drive profound changes in production, distribution, and audience engagement. In script-writing, AI is poised to transform narrative development through advancements in natural language processing and machine learning. By analysing vast datasets that include historical box office trends, audience preferences, and thematic patterns, AI can generate fresh and compelling storylines and dialogues tailored to specific audience segments. This data-driven approach not only enhances creativity but also aligns narratives more closely with market demands, potentially increasing the commercial success of films.

The pre-production phase will also see significant benefits from AI, particularly through predictive analytics. AI tools can analyse historical data on actor performance and financial metrics to aid in making informed casting decisions and budget allocations. These predictive capabilities extend to risk assessment, offering insights that can mitigate financial uncertainties and bolster project viability. This strategic approach to pre-production is expected to streamline decision-making processes and enhance overall project planning. During production, AI-driven technologies will streamline workflows and enhance efficiency. Automated scene analysis and real-time script adjustments are just a few examples of how AI can expedite the production process while maintaining high creative standards. By handling routine tasks and providing valuable insights, AI will allow filmmakers to focus more on creative aspects and less on administrative details. The post-production phase will benefit immensely from AI advancements in visual effects (VFX), editing, and sound design. AI algorithms are anticipated to revolutionize VFX creation by automating complex tasks such as motion capture and scene integration, thus reducing both the time and costs associated with high-quality visual effects. In editing, AI will accelerate turnaround times by handling routine tasks like scene selection, colour correction, and sound mixing, enabling editors to concentrate on more pronounced creative decisions. Additionally, AI will enhance sound design by generating realistic soundscapes and automating audio adjustments, contributing to a more immersive cinematic experience. Audience engagement and content distribution are also set to undergo transformative changes through AI. Advanced data analytics will enable AI to offer highly personalized content recommendations, improving viewer satisfaction by aligning suggestions with individual preferences and viewing habits. AI-powered marketing strategies will enhance the targeting of promotional content, thereby increasing its effectiveness and reach among specific demographic groups. Furthermore, AI's impact on content distribution will be profound, with sophisticated recommendation engines and intelligent content curation transforming how viewers access and discover films. This will cater to the diverse tastes and regional preferences across India, making content more accessible and engaging.

CONCLUSION

The integration of artificial intelligence (AI) into the Indian film sector represents a significant evolution that spans the entire spectrum of filmmaking, from production to distribution. AI technologies have ushered in efficiencies, expanded creative possibilities, and broadened storytelling methods, effectively bridging traditional practices with innovative approaches. AI's impact is palpable across various facets of filmmaking, including scriptwriting, actor selection, and special effects creation, demonstrating its potential to revolutionize creative workflows while enhancing productivity. Moreover, AI tools have democratized access to filmmaking, lowering barriers for new voices and narratives to emerge and flourish within the industry. This inclusivity is crucial for representing the diverse cultural fabric of India on screen and empowering previously marginalized/subaltern voices (Khan, Khan & Mukherjee, 2024). However, as AI continues to evolve, challenges arise concerning the balance between technological augmentation and human creativity. It is essential to employ AI in ways that augment rather than replace human intuition and emotional depth in filmmaking. Ethical considerations, such as data privacy, algorithmic bias, and the socio-economic impact on industry professionals, must be carefully addressed to maintain a fair and equitable filmmaking environment. Looking forward, the future trajectory of Indian cinema hinges on effectively harnessing AI's potential to innovate storytelling, enhance audience engagement, and diversify content creation. Embracing AI not only optimizes filmmaking processes but also enriches viewer experiences, setting the stage for a dynamic and inclusive cinematic landscape.

Recommendations

a) **Investment in Research and Development**: Foster robust collaboration between academia, research institutions, and the film industry to pioneer AI applications tailored for Indian cinema. This partnership will drive cutting-edge innovations in narrative techniques, production efficiencies, and audience engagement strategies. By supporting research initiatives, India can lead the way in leveraging AI to redefine storytelling paradigms and elevate the quality of cinematic experiences.

b) **Comprehensive Skill Development Initiatives**: Launch comprehensive training programs aimed at upskilling filmmakers, technicians, and artists with a profound understanding of AI technologies. These initiatives should emphasize practical applications of AI in script analysis, visual effects, post-production processes, and audience analytics. By nurturing AI literacy across the sector, India can empower its creative workforce to harness technology responsibly, fostering a new generation of filmmakers' adept at integrating AI seamlessly into their artistic vision.

c) **Advancement of Diversity and Inclusivity**: Champion initiatives that harness AI-driven platforms to amplify diverse voices and narratives within Indian cinema. By promoting cultural representation and inclusivity, these efforts will enrich storytelling by capturing broader perspectives and resonating with global audiences. Embracing AI to curate content and enhance outreach strategies will ensure that the Indian film industry remains a beacon of cultural diversity and artistic expression on the global stage.

d) **Establishment of Ethical Guidelines and Regulatory Frameworks**: Develop sound ethical standards and regulatory frameworks that govern the responsible use of AI in filmmaking. These guidelines should address concerns related to data privacy, algorithmic bias, and intellectual property rights, thereby safeguarding creative integrity and ensuring sustainable industry practices. By establishing clear frameworks, India can foster trust among stakeholders and uphold its commitment to ethical AI adoption, thereby bolstering long-term industry growth and innovation.

e) **Promotion of Collaborative Partnerships**: Cultivate strategic partnerships between AI developers, filmmakers, and artists to co-create innovative solutions that enhance creative expression and audience engagement. By fostering interdisciplinary collaboration, these partnerships will drive the development of AI-powered tools and technologies that optimize production workflows, personalize viewer experiences, and expand market reach. Embracing collaborative innovation will position India at the forefront of AI-driven filmmaking advancements, reinforcing its reputation as a global hub for cinematic excellence and technological innovation.

By embracing these recommendations, the Indian film sector can harness AI as a transformative force, driving innovation, creativity, and inclusive growth. Through strategic investments, comprehensive training initiatives, and ethical frameworks,

India can unlock the full potential of AI to redefine the future of storytelling and consolidate its position as a global leader in cinematic excellence.

REFERENCES

Bedingfield, W. (2023, July 07). *How Indiana Jones and the Dial of Destiny De-Aged Harrison Ford*. Wired. https://www.wired.com/story/indiana-jones-and-the-dial-of-destiny-de-aging-tech/

Chase, N. (2024, March 30). *Artificial Intelligence In Film: Impact & Influence for 2024+*. Neil Chase Film. https://neilchasefilm.com/artificial-intelligence-in-film/

Chow, P.-S. (2020). Ghost in the (Hollywood) machine: Emergent applications of artificial intelligence in the film industry. *NECSUS European Journal of Media Studies, 9*(1), 193-214. https://doi.org/DOI: 10.25969/mediarep/14307

Coleman, F. (2019, October 3). *Can Fiction Introduce Empathy Into AI? Do We Want It To?* Literary Hub. https://lithub.com/can-fiction-introduce-empathy-into-ai-do-we-want-it-to/

Coyle, J. (2023, September 28). *In Hollywood writers' battle against AI, humans win (for now)*. AP. https://apnews.com/article/hollywood-ai-strike-wga-artificial-intelligence-39ab72582c3a15f77510c9c30a45ffc8

Datta, A., & Goswami, R. (2021). The Film Industry Leaps into Artificial Intelligence: Scope and Challenges by the Filmmakers. In Rathore, V. S., Dey, N., Piuri, V., Babo, R., Polkowski, Z., & Tavares, J. M. R. S. (Eds.), *Rising Threats in Expert Applications and Solutions. Advances in Intelligent Systems and Computing* (Vol. 1187). Springer., DOI: 10.1007/978-981-15-6014-9_80

Dayo, F., Memon, A. A., & Dharejo, N. (2023). Scriptwriting in the Age of AI: Revolutionizing Storytelling with Artificial Intelligence. *Journal of Media & Communication*, 4(1), 24–38. https://jmc.ilmauniversity.edu.pk/arc/Vol4/i1p2

Fikri, M. A., & Fitria, Y. (2022). Development Of Learning Media Based On Wondershare Filmora Software On Integrated Thematic Learning Elementary School. *Indonesian Journal of Learning Education & Counselling*, 4(2), 1–9. https://journal.ilininstitute.com/index.php/IJoLEC/article/view/1574/569

Ghosh, M. A. (2023). Artificial Intelligence as an Innovation in the Film Industry. *Research Inspiration*, 3(3), 12–16.

Haenlein, M., & Kaplan, A. (2019). A Brief History of Artificial Intelligence: On the Past, Present, and Future of Artificial Intelligence. *California Management Review*, 61(4), 5–14. DOI: 10.1177/0008125619864925

HLEGAI. (2019). *A definition of AI: Main capabilities and disciplines*. European Commission. Brussels. https://ec.europa.eu/newsroom/dae/document.cfm?doc_id=56341

Islam, M. M. (2022). Artificial intelligence in Indian films: Anukul and AI ethics. *Short Film Studies*, 12(2), 183–192. DOI: 10.1386/sfs_00082_1

Khan, S. U., Khan, S., & Mukherjee, T. (2024). The "Subaltern" Will Speak: Investigating Portrayals in the Acclaimed OTT Series of India and Pakistan. In Kalorth, N. (Ed.), *Exploring the Impact of OTT Media on Global Societies* (pp. 1–24). IGI Global., DOI: 10.4018/979-8-3693-3526-0.ch001

Khanna, A. (2024, February 21). From Script To Distribution: AI's Role In The Film World. *Forbes*. https://www.forbes.com/sites/forbestechcouncil/2024/02/21/from-script-to-distribution-ais-role-in-the-film-world/

Kumar, K. S. (2024,10 April). *The Role of AI in Rajmouli Films: Redefining Cinematic Excellence*. seamedu. https://www.seamedu.com/blog/the-role-of-ai-in-rajamouli-films

Li, C., & Bantourakis, M. (2023, August 2). *6 ways AI could disrupt the entertainment industry*. World Economic Forum. https://www.weforum.org/agenda/2023/08/hollywood-strike-synthetic-voice-digital-avatar-ai-entertainment/

Mahna, V. (2024, April 17). *A Brief Review on the Status of Artificial Intelligence in Cinema*. Exploratio. https://exploratiojournal.com/a-brief-review-on-the-status-of-artificial-intelligence-in-cinema/

Mathur, V. (2023, March 31). *Explained: How Artificial Intelligence in Hollywood movies like Blade Runner and The Matrix has been a game-changer.* Firstpost. https://www.firstpost.com/entertainment/explained-how-artificial-intelligence-in-hollywood-movies-like-blade-runner-and-the-matrix-has-been-a-game-changer-12383272.html

McMillan, K. (2021, September 6). *REVIEW: Look Designer 2 by ColourLab.ai.* Provideo Coalition. https://www.provideocoalition.com/review-look-designer-2-by-colourlab-ai/

Moore, S. (2019, April 13). Why Film Budgets Are Important, Beyond The Cost Of Production. *Forbes*. https://www.forbes.com/sites/schuylermoore/2019/04/13/the-importance-of-film-budgets/

Moviemaking platform largo.ai is about to help change advertising forever! (2021, September 02). Largo.ai. https://home.largo.ai/leading-ai-assisted-moviemaking-platform-largo-ai-is-about-to-help-change-advertising-forever/

Nair, V. (2024, April 09). *The Audio of This Bollywood Song was Generated by AI*.AIM. https://analyticsindiamag.com/the-audio-of-this-bollywood-song-was-generated-by-ai/

O'Shaughnessy, M. (2022, October 6). *One of the Biggest Problems in Regulating AI Is Agreeing on a Definition.* Carnegie Endowment for International Peace. https://carnegieendowment.org/posts/2022/10/one-of-the-biggest-problems-in-regulating-ai-is-agreeing-on-a-definition?lang=en

Parikh, P. (2019, April 16). *AI Film Aesthetics: A Construction of a New Media Identity for AI Films* [Masters Thesis, Chapman University].Chapman University Digital Commons. https://digitalcommons.chapman.edu/cgi/viewcontent.cgi?article=1007&context=film_studies_theses

Quthor (2024, January 27). *2024's Top AI Music Generators: Mubert, Aiva, and Beatoven Comparison.* Quick Creator. https://quickcreator.io/seo/2024-top-ai-music-generators-mubert-aiva-beatoven-comparison/

Salazar, D. (2023, May 15). *This K-pop artist sings fluently in 6 languages. His secret? Voice AI.* Fast Company. https://www.fastcompany.com/90896187/hybe-bts-kpop-midnatt-supertone-ai-lee-hyun

Sarkar, S. (2024, January 15). Does AI-produced film 'Maharaja in Denims' mark a shift in Indian cinema? *South China Morning Post*. https://www.scmp.com/week-asia/lifestyle-culture/article/3248487/does-ai-generated-film-maharaja-denims-mark-shift-indian-cinema

Sathyan, J. (2023, September 01). *Smart VFX: How AI Is Empowering Visual Effects*. India Art Review. https://indiaartreview.com/stories/smart-vfx-how-ai-is-empowering-visual-effects/

Shah, D. (2023, December 19). *Bollywood: How AI may affect India's vast film industry.* BBC News. https://www.bbc.com/news/world-asia-india-67657873

Sheikh, H., Prins, C., & Schrijvers, E. (2023). Artificial Intelligence: Definition and Background. In Mission, A. I. (Ed.), *Research for Policy*. Springer., DOI: 10.1007/978-3-031-21448-6_2

Singh, H., Kaur, K., & Singh, P. P. (2023, January). Artificial intelligence as a facilitator for film production process. In *2023 International Conference on Artificial Intelligence and Smart Communication (AISC)* (pp. 969-972). IEEE. DOI: 10.1109/AISC56616.2023.10085082

Sun, P. (2024). A Study of Artificial Intelligence in the Production of Film. *SHS Web of Conferences*. EDP Sciences.

Tamandehrou, A., & Khan, S. U. (2015). Assessing the importance of globalisation and new media technology in 21st century: An analytical overview. *International Journal of Multifaceted & Multilingual Studies*, 1(4).

Townsend, S. (2024, March 03). *Exploring the Impact of AI on Film Production in 2024*. Medium. https://medium.com/@channelasaservice/exploring-the-impact-of-ai-on-film-production-in-2024-f02da745af00

Vilenkin, R. (2024, April 11). *The Role of AI Voice Cloning in Virtual Reality and Immersive Environments*. respeecher. https://www.respeecher.com/blog/ai-voice-cloning-virtual-reality-immersive-environments

ADDITIONAL READINGS

Auer, R. M., Elflein, D., Kunas, S., Rhnert, J., & Voigts, E. (2024). *Artificial Intelligence - Intelligent Art? Human-machine Interaction and Creative Practice (Digital Society)*. Transcript Verlag.

Connock, A. (2022). *Media Management and Artificial Intelligence: Understanding Media Business Models in the Digital Age*. Routledge. DOI: 10.4324/9781003213611

Drennan, M., Baranovsky, Y., & Baranovsky, V. (2018). *Scriptwriting for Web Series: Writing for the Digital Age*. Routledge. DOI: 10.4324/9781351237857

Goraga, Z. (2024). *AI and ML Technological Solutions for the Film Industry*. Dr. Zemelak Goraga.

Heras, D. C. (2024). *Cinema and Machine Vision: Artificial Intelligence, Aesthetics and Spectatorship*. Edinburgh University Press. DOI: 10.1515/9781399514736

Hodges, A. (2014). *Alan Turing: The Enigma: The Book That Inspired the Film The Imitation Game*. Vintage.

Millar, I. (2022). *The Psychoanalysis of Artificial Intelligence (The Palgrave Lacan Series)*. Springer Nature Switzerland AG.

Pizzo, A., Lombardo, V., & Damiano, R. (2023). *Interactive Storytelling: A Cross-Media Approach to Writing, Producing and Editing with AI*. Routledge. DOI: 10.4324/9781003335627

Rice, J. (2017). *Kubrick's Story, Spielberg's Film: A.I. Artificial Intelligence*. Rowman & Littlefield.

Sarkar, S. (2024). *Artificial Intelligence and the Art of Digital Filmmaking: A Film Directors' Handbook for the Digital Era*. Notion Press.

KEY TERMS AND DEFINITIONS

Algorithm: A set of rules or instructions designed for computational problem-solving or data processing, fundamental in programming, AI, and cryptography.

Artificial Intelligence: Advanced computational systems that mimic human cognitive functions, enabling tasks such as problem-solving, learning, and decision-making, often used in automation and machine learning applications.

Computer-Generated Imagery (CGI): Digital graphics created using computers to generate realistic or stylized visual content, extensively used in movies, video games, and simulations.

Editing: The process of assembling and refining raw footage or content into a coherent sequence, essential in filmmaking, video production, and multimedia projects.

Hollywood: A colloquial term referring to the American film industry centered in Los Angeles, renowned globally for producing mainstream movies and entertainment.

Meta AI: Advanced AI systems that not only perform tasks but also analyze and improve their own processes, leading to enhanced learning and decision-making capabilities.

Screenplay: A detailed script for a movie or television show, outlining dialogue, actions, and settings to guide production and performance.

Script: The written text of a play, movie, or broadcast, including dialogue, stage directions, and other elements essential for production and performance.

Storyboard: A sequence of illustrations or images arranged to visualize a narrative, used in film, animation, and advertising to plan and convey scenes.

VFX: Visual Effects involve digitally manipulating or creating imagery to enhance or create new visuals, integral in filmmaking, advertising, and multimedia productions.

Chapter 8
Research on the Potential of Digital Image-Generating Artificial Intelligence Applications in Movie Poster Production

Özlem Delal Abanoz
https://orcid.org/0000-0002-3653-5838
Ondokuz Mayıs University, Turkey

Melike Sinem Yılmaz
https://orcid.org/0000-0002-6567-719X
Ondokuz Mayıs University, Turkey

ABSTRACT

The development of artificial intelligence technologies has brought about significant changes and transformations in many fields with its rapid and effective use in content production. These changes and transformations have also significantly affected the movie industry. The poster design process, which is of great importance in the promotion of a movie, has had the chance to gain a new dimension with speed, ease and low cost thanks to artificial intelligence applications. This article examines the potential of artificial intelligence in the reproduction of animated movie posters. The study aims to evaluate how image-generating AI applications can be used to create animated movie posters. Using semiotic analysis, original movie posters are compared with those made using depictions of different AI applications. The study

DOI: 10.4018/979-8-3693-3916-9.ch008

concluded that generative artificial intelligence applications can be successful in producing movie posters.

INTRODUCTION

Artificial intelligence, which we often hear about today, is used intensively as a technology that will make human life easier in many fields. Artificial intelligence applications used in many fields, such as health, education, technology, and automotive, are designed to fulfill difficult and complex tasks thanks to systems that mimic the human brain. In our daily lives, many artificial intelligence applications transform human life, whether we realize it or not.

One of the areas where these transformations are felt the most is the movie industry. Artificial intelligence applications, which bring significant developments in film production, distribution, and consumption processes such as script writing, editing, visual effects, sound processing and dubbing, audience analysis, and personalization, also have significant potential in producing movie posters.

Artificial intelligence applications that can produce visuals can be a turning point for poster creation processes that require a creative process and can enable a joint creation process with human-machine cooperation. In this creation process, the machine can overcome human limitations, and humans can overcome machine limitations.

Artificial intelligence in movie poster production can greatly benefit filmmakers and designers by accelerating creative processes and making them more accessible. In addition, AI applications that offer a wide range of possibilities to produce more effective and remarkable posters that appeal to the audience can also enrich the field with creative visual effects.

In this study, which was conducted to reveal the potential of image-generating artificial intelligence applications to produce movie posters, firstly, what artificial intelligence is was mentioned. Then, the concept of generative artificial intelligence is examined. In addition to information about examples of AI applications that can generate images, AI is also discussed in creative industries.

The methodology section gives the study's purpose, importance, scope, limitations, and methodology. In the analysis section of the study, the potential of artificial intelligence to produce movie posters was analyzed using the semiotic analysis method.

What is Artificial Intelligence?

Artificial intelligence, a concept we often hear about today, refers to a structure in which computers can imitate the human brain. By mimicking the cognitive functions associated with the human mind through machine learning, AI uses algorithms to perform complex tasks. What we see in AI today is primarily the capacity to match patterns and look at data sets (Parisse-Brassens 2021:4).

Marvin Lee Minsky was one of the first scientists to define artificial intelligence, which fulfills complex tasks in different fields in a short time with technological developments. In 1956, Minsky defined artificial intelligence as "the science of getting machines to do things that would require intelligence if done by humans." according to Minsky, this concept requires high-level mental processes such as perceptual learning, memory, and critical thinking (Dugal and Davey 2024).

Although it was defined in the 1950s, the dream of developing machines that mimic human cognition dates back centuries. In the 1890s, science fiction writers such as HG Wells began exploring the concept of robots and other machines thinking and acting like humans. However, the idea of artificial intelligence started to take shape in the early 1940s. After Alan Turing proposed the theory of computation, other researchers began to explore ways to build AI frameworks. In 1956, researchers gathered at Dartmouth College to develop a practical application of AI. Interest in these AI applications, which also taught computers to play checkers in a way that could beat many humans, waxed and waned over the following decades (Greengard 2019).

Today, however, artificial intelligence has become a technology we use effectively in every aspect of our lives, whether we realize it or not. Artificial intelligence applications have become indispensable, from smart cars to vacuum cleaners, health applications to education, voice assistants on mobile devices, and e-commerce. This technology, which refers to computational tools that can replace human intelligence in performing specific tasks, is advancing at a dizzying pace in the late 20th century (Fay and Trenholm n.d.).

Artificial intelligence is concerned with designing intelligent computer systems that mimic human intelligence, such as visual perception, speech recognition, decision-making, and language translation. The ability of machines to process, learn, and plan natural language makes it possible for intelligent systems to perform new tasks. The main goal of AI is to mimic human cognitive functions and perform activities typically performed by a human (Sadiku et al. 2021).

Artificial intelligence is generally classified as data-driven artificial intelligence and knowledge-based artificial intelligence. In the last decade, data-driven AI has played a crucial role in robotics and computer foresight. With the help of a given large data set, the computer builds a model that optimizes its predictions. It is based on the simple principle that the computer program makes the predictions. However, the program's behavior is adjusted to minimize errors if the projections are wrong during training.

Moreover, if the predictions made by the program are correct, it adapts its behavior so that the exact predictions are made with higher probability. Knowledge-based AI systems, on the other hand, derive their knowledge from conceptual structures created by humans. Therefore, the computer is a text-processing machine or a simple programmed computation in knowledge-based AI. Knowledge-based AI systems use an inference engine rather than an algorithm to derive their data (Malhan et al. 2023:58).

Generative Artificial Intelligence and Visual Generating Artificial Intelligence Applications

The concept of artificial intelligence has developed rapidly since the first idea of artificial intelligence emerged. Artificial intelligence applications, incredibly productive artificial intelligence, which includes systems that everyone can easily use in daily life, work on the principles of "machine learning," a branch of artificial intelligence that enables machines to learn from data. Utilizing deep generative models, generative AI can produce a wide range of new and realistic content for various domains based on primary user requests (Banh and Strobel 2023:63). Deep learning is designed to discover complex structures in large datasets by using a back-propagation algorithm to specify how a machine should modify its internal parameters used to calculate the representation at each layer from the representation at the previous layer. While deep networks have revolutionized image, video, speech, and audio processing, recurrent networks have shed light on sequential data such as text and speech.

Generative AI systems that can autonomously generate new content such as text, images, audio, and video (Lv 2023) take a user instruction (a prompt) as input and develop content that fulfills the instruction (Messer 2024). These AI systems can generate content to identify objects in images, transcribe speech into text, match news, posts, or products to users' interests, and select relevant search results (LeCun, Bengio, and Hinton 2015:436).

Generative artificial intelligence models can perform many functions, such as creating images from text (DALL-E, MidJourney, Stable Diffusion, Leonardo, Ideogram, Copilot, Gemini, Claude, etc.), creating 3D models from the text (Dreamfusion and Magic3D, etc.), making videos from the text (Phenaki and Soundif, etc.) (Gozalo-Brizuela and Garrido-Merchan 2023). These applications, which are very simple to use, are used extensively thanks to their ease of use that does not require technical knowledge.

ChatGPT is today's most widely known productive artificial intelligence application capable of generating text from text or images. ChatGPT is an artificial intelligence language model developed by OpenAI. It is built on the GPT-4 architecture and trained on an extensive text database. Thanks to its natural language processing capabilities, ChatGPT can have natural and meaningful conversations with users, answer questions, make suggestions, and perform various text-based tasks. ChatGPT continuously learns as it interacts with users and improves its performance based on user feedback. However, it cannot think or feel exactly like a human but generates human-like responses over text data (ChatGPT-4o, 2024).

ChatGPT was developed with a technique called "Reinforcement Learning from Human Feedback" to train its language model. This feature makes ChatGPT a writing assistant (Ali et al. 2023:1701). Nevertheless, the website states, "ChatGPT sometimes writes answers that sound logical but are wrong or nonsensical." A few examples also present the user with obvious errors, such as referring to a scientific study that does not exist (Thorp 2023).

Another artificial intelligence application developed by Open AI is DALL-E. DALL-E can produce creative and valuable visual content as an AI model that can generate high-quality images based on natural language descriptions. This image generator provides instant visual realization of innovative concepts. Authors can bring stories' characters, settings, and scenes to life through AI-generated images. These visualizations can reveal new facets, revealing details not apparent when left to text descriptions alone. For graphic content creators, such as video producers, DALL-E's ability to generate original images from short text prompts makes developing compelling visual components much more accessible. Beyond typing, it enables prototype design, advertising concept visuals, icon creation, and more based on annotations alone (Ali et al. 2023).

The name 'DALL-E' is a merger of the artist Salvador Dalí and Pixar's animated film WALL-E (2008), about a sentient robot picking up trash on a dehumanized Earth (O'Meara and Murphy 2023:1071).

Gemini, formerly known as Bard, was developed by Google AI. Gemini, a multimodal generative AI application, can process data from text, image, audio, and video inputs and create various types of content (Imran and Almusharraf, (Imran and Almusharraf 2024). Google's DeepMind Gemini is the latest text-based AI to challenge OpenAI's ChatGPT. Gemini includes multiple large language models (LLMs) of various sizes, each bringing multimodal capabilities to the Google AI suite.

Copilot is an AI-based digital assistant developed by Microsoft. It can complete user-authored text, write code, translate, answer questions, and more. Microsoft makes Copilot an artificial intelligence-based assistant that is available in its operating systems and programs. It learns the user's habits and preferences and offers suggestions accordingly Lan (Anon n.d.).

Ideogram AI is a highly effective tool designed to do the following. Unlike other image-generating AI tools, Ideogram allows text to be added to images to easily create stunning artwork logos and designs with a user-friendly interface. Ideograms can produce posters, advertisements, and infographics thanks to the ability to add text to the image. This feature has yet to be developed from other artificial intelligence applications, allowing you to choose styles such as anime, graffiti, or fantasy (Asif 2024).

Creativity and Artificial Intelligence

Artificial intelligence has been central to technological advances in recent years and plays a vital role in creativity. Creativity, traditionally considered unique to humans, has gained a new dimension with artificial intelligence, and its meaning has expanded. By training AI-supported systems on large datasets, they can mimic and sometimes even surpass human creativity. The impact and assistance of artificial intelligence in the implementation of artistic production practices where creative processes such as art, literature, music, and design are at the forefront is increasing.

The concept of creativity, which has been the basis of theological and sociological issues since ancient times, *derives from* the Latin verb "create," meaning to create, to bring into being, to give birth, and has evolved into the English word "creativity." There have been various definitions of creativity, a system of thought that aims to produce new concepts, ideas, and products throughout history. According to Thornton, the starting point of a creative work is the observation that creativity involves creating something new. This observation is supported by the observation that creation from nothing is logically impossible. (You cannot create something out of nothing.) Creativity must, therefore, be the creation of something new out of things that already exist. In other words, it confirms the theories suggesting that to produce something new, different things that already exist must be combined (Dartnall 1994:44). Jacques Séguél (1997) defines it as 'creation is an instinct, a force that lives within you and that you can only write about without speaking out.' Creativity, the raw material of the design process in creative industries, is the ability to establish relationships, present new and original ideas, and generate solutions.

Although it seems to belong to a human being, creativity is also an essential concept regarding artificial intelligence in today's technology. When studies created with artificial intelligence are examined, it can be said that although they differ from human intelligence and perspective, artificial intelligence also produces creative productions by feeding on various data.

Prof. Margaret Ann Boden, a researcher in computer science, artificial intelligence, psychology, and philosophy, continues to work on understanding the problematics of creativity and artificial intelligence. In her book *The Creative Mind Myths and*

Mechanisms, Boden defines creativity as the miracle of the human mind in three different forms. The first is *combinational* creativity, which refers to the unusual combinations of ideas that exist in the human mind; the second is *exploratory* creativity, which refers to the exploration of a preconfigured conceptual space and the new ideas produced after that, and the third is *transformational* creativity, which involves one or more transformations of a conceptual research space (Boden 2004:3–6).

AARON is one of the most prominent creative studies of artificial intelligence and one of the first in the field. Painter and computer scientist Harold Cohen developed AARON in the late 1950s and early 1960s. At the intersection of artificial intelligence and art, AARON is a software designed to produce artworks by computer systems and to research the artworks produced. This software, which can make abstract drawings, has been developed over time, enabling the production of more complex artworks. While AARON creates artistic productions within the framework of specific rules and algorithms as a working practice, it has been continuously developed over time, increasing the creative capabilities and complexity of the program. AARON is among the first studies to show that artificial intelligence is not limited to calculations and data analysis but can also be used in creative processes. In this sense, it opened the doors to the potential of artificial intelligence in the field and inspired AI-based art and creativity projects developed over the years. Artificial intelligence-supported programs in creative processes have become widespread, bringing revolutionary changes in art, literature, music, design, cinema, and many other fields. Artificial intelligence has become capable of producing new and original works by creative professionals trained in music, fashion design, architecture, literature, and other fields that require creativity, such as the production of works that enable the discovery of new styles and techniques that accelerate and diversify the creative process of artists in the field of visual arts, analyzing various design options and offering the most appropriate solutions to achieve specific goals in the field of design.

The impact of artificial intelligence, especially on creative industries, has been a topic of great interest in recent times. The increasing use of artificial intelligence in video production and artistic content creation has revealed this technology's role in evaluating and producing creative elements. These technologies, which imitate human intelligence or are designed as a new example of intelligence, have gained a significant place in many points, such as saving time and cost compared to the work produced by humans, minimizing human errors, offering innovative solutions, and providing significant progress and improvements in various sectors.

METHODOLOGY

Purpose of the Study

Today, artificial intelligence technologies have been used in many fields and have led to radical changes in human life. Artificial intelligence technologies have brought changes and transformations not only in business sectors such as medicine and information systems but also in business areas that require creativity. Creative applications have gained significant importance in exploring the synergy between human intelligence and artificial intelligence and utilizing the potential of these technologies by creative professionals in their production. While these applications offer artists and designers a wide range of creative potential, they also provide unique experience opportunities suitable for the purpose and target audience by creating the correct prompts. It is possible to evaluate AI-supported visual production tools as a technological development in related fields and as a universe of experience that expands the boundaries of creativity and aesthetic perspectives. This study examines the potential of AI-supported visual production tools in designing movie posters.

Movie posters are graphic design products visually prepared to promote a movie. Posters are essential in marketing and promotion, such as announcing the movie, reaching the movie's audience, and reinforcing brand awareness. In this context, this study aims to evaluate the competencies and potential of artificial intelligence in the field of art and design by transforming the descriptions created by artificial intelligence applications about the six most well-known and award-winning films of the famous anime artist, director, and screenwriter Hayao Miyazaki into posters using artificial intelligence-supported visual production tools. In this study, the posters produced in line with the results obtained with different artificial intelligence applications on the same movie summaries will be semiotically analyzed, and the extent to which the posters reflect the content and atmosphere of the movie will be evaluated.

Significance of the Study

Artificial intelligence technologies have started to play an essential role in creative processes. Artificial intelligence has significantly impacted the film industry in recent years, as in many other sectors. However, it is still being determined how successful artificial intelligence is in creative works and to what extent it can approach human creativity. This study titled "*An Investigation on the Potential of Artificial Intelligence Applications Creating Digital Visuals in Movie Poster Production*" is of critical importance in terms of contributing to the literature by filling the gaps in the related fields with the new doors it will open in terms of how artificial intelligence-supported visual production tools are integrated into design fields, the opportunities they offer for designers and the innovative approaches they develop. This study will evaluate the performance of artificial intelligence applications in movie poster design and reveal how effective these technologies can be in the movie industry.

Scope and Limitations

This study focuses on the most well-known and award-winning works of director and screenwriter Hayao Miyazaki, globally recognized and respected as one of the leading figures in Japanese animation cinema. As one of the founding members of Studio Ghibli, Miyazaki has created many unforgettable works with his distinctive artistic style, unique creativity, and excellent storytelling skills. Miyazaki's treatment of universal themes, the details in his films, the color palette, character designs, and cultural references have made him one of the few directors and screenwriters who have left their mark on the animation world.

This study analyzed six (6) of Miyazaki's films that received awards in various categories. The films subject to the survey are Princess Mononoke, Spirited Away, The Walking Castle, Ponyo, The Wind Rises, and The Boy and the Heron.

The 1997 film Princess Mononoke was nominated for many awards and was awarded by the Japanese Film Academy in the "Film of the Year" category.

The 2001 film Spirited Away was nominated for "Best Animated Film of the Year" at the Academy Awards, "Outstanding Direction in an Animated Production" and "Outstanding Screenplay in an Animated Production" at the Annie Awards, "Golden Bear" at the Berlin International Film Festival, "Best Film" at the Japanese Academy Awards, and "Best Animated Film" at the National Board of Review Awards, It won "Best Motion Picture, Animated or Mixed Media" at the Satellite Awards, "Best Animated Film" at the Saturn Awards, "Notable Entry - Japanese Film", "Animation of the Year," "Best Director," "Best Screenplay," "Best Character Design" at the Tokyo Anime Awards.

2004's The Walking Castle won "Best Screenplay" at the Nebula Awards, "Best Motion Picture, Animated or Mixed Media" at the Satellite Awards, "Best Director" and "Animation of the Year" at the Tokyo Awards.

2008's Ponyo won 4 awards at the Tokyo Anime Awards in the categories of "Noteworthy Entry-Japanese Film," "Animation of the Year," "Best Director," and "Best Original Story." At the Venice Film Festival, it was awarded the "Mimmo Rotella Foundation Award" and the "Future Film Festival Digital Award-Special Mention."

2013's The Wind Rises won "Outstanding Achievement in Screenwriting in an Animated Production" at the Annie Awards, "Best Animated Feature Film" at the Japanese Academy Awards, "Best Animated Feature Film" at the National Board of Review Awards, “Best Motion Picture, Animated or Mixed Media” at the Satellite Awards, “Animation of the Year” and “Best Screenplay/Original Story” at the Tokyo Anime Awards.

The 2024 film The Boy and the Heron won the “Best Animated Feature Film” category at the Academy Awards.

The study's limitations are that only specific artificial intelligence applications were used to create the descriptions and generate the visuals. Only Hayao Miyazaki's award-winning films were selected for analysis. In addition, the accuracy and reliability of the data used in the research (IMDB summaries, AI outputs) may affect the research results.

METHOD

In this study, which includes investigating the potential of artificial intelligence in producing movie posters for six award-winning films by Hayao Miyazaki and analyzing AI-supported movie poster designs, firstly, the summaries of Hayao Miyazaki's films were accessed from IMDB. These summaries were used as a database to be converted into posters by artificial intelligence applications. The collected movie summaries were given to artificial intelligence applications named Gemini, Copilot, and ChatGPT, and they were asked to create poster depictions based on these summaries. The movie posters depicted by the artificial intelligence applications were entered into an image-generating artificial intelligence application named Ideogram, and new and original posters were created. The obtained posters were analyzed according to the principles of Swiss linguist Saussure's semiotic analysis method, and the signifier, signified, signified, technical, and symbolic codes of each movie were processed into tables under the titles of the movie separately.

Semiotics is the branch of science that studies signs and elements of signs. Following the mid-20th century, it was developed with the works of thinkers such as Ferdinand de Saussure, Roland Barthes, Charles Sanders Peirce, and Umberto Eco. Saussure structured this science by associating two essential elements, the *signifier and the signified* (Saussure 1959:65). Barthes states that the signifier and the signified are not just two words that come one after the other. Still, they relate to each other, and their sum constitutes Alan's sig(Barthes 1996:182). Semiotic analysis is frequently used in literature, visual arts, media, and communication studies. This method examines the signs, signifiers, and signifieds in a text or a visual. This type of analysis helps to establish an in-depth interpretation process by exploring how language and visual elements are interpreted, revealing the underlying meanings of texts and visuals.

FINDINGS AND COMMENTS

Princess Mononoke

The movie summary of Princess Mononoke was accessed from IMDB and then uploaded to the artificial intelligence applications ChatGPT, Gemini, and Copilot with the command "From now on, act as a graphic designer who experienced on the movie poster. Create a one-paragraph description for the movie poster from the summary I'll provide you." The descriptions in text form taken from these applications were converted into visuals in the artificial intelligence application named Ideogram, which can produce visuals.

The summary of the movie from IMDB is as follows: On a journey to find the cure for a Tatarigami's curse, Ashitaka finds himself in the middle of a war between the forest gods and Tatara, a mining colony. In this quest, he also meets San, the Mononoke Hime. While protecting his village from a rampaging boar-god/demon, a confident young warrior, Ashitaka, is stricken by a deadly curse. To save his life, he must journey to the forests of the West. Once there, he's embroiled in a fierce campaign that humans waged on the forest. The ambitious Lady Eboshi and her loyal clan use their guns against the gods of the forest, as does a brave young woman, Princess Mononoke, who was raised by a wolf-god. Ashitaka sees the good on both sides and tries to stem the blood flood. Both sides meet this with animosity as they see him supporting the enemy. Medieval Japan at the dawn of the Iron Age. Touched by the indelible stigma of darkness, noble defender of good Prince Ashitaka embarks on a long and perilous quest to face his destiny after a nearly fatal encounter with a raging demon. But with Mother Nature in disarray and his combat hand poisoned to the bone, the brave protector can only pray for a miracle to lift the deadly curse on his arm.

After all, murderous ambition and senseless extermination ravage the land. As life slowly succumbs to chaos and barren landscapes replace the lush green forests of old, Ashitaka soon finds himself caught in the middle of a destructive conflict between humankind and omnipotent nature's ancient gods. Lady Eboshi, the bellicose leader of the Iron Town, stands in the way of resolution. With the future of all living things hanging by a thread, can the banished young warrior count on the feral Wolf Girl to restore peace? Ashitaka is infected with an incurable disease by a possessed boar/god. He is to die unless he can find a cure to rid the curse from his body. His only hope is to travel to the Far East. When he arrives to get help from the deer god, he finds himself in the middle of a battle between the animal inhabitants of the forest and an iron mining town exploiting and killing the forest. Princess Mononoke, a human raised by wolves, leads the forest animals in the struggle.

Table 1. Princess Mononoke original poster

Signifier	

Sign A girl dressed in primitive clothing, holding a sword, on a wild wolf. Forest in the background, and a sky is visible through the trees. Daytime scene.	**Signified** The concept of savagery can define the posture and expression of the wolf figure. The figures' facial expressions can be interpreted as defiant and ready to attack. While all the signs evoke danger and hostility, they also express power.

ChatGPT has made a very detailed description of the movie Princess Mononoke:

Concept and Visual Elements:
Central Image:
Ashitaka: Positioned at the center, Ashitaka is depicted with a determined and resolute expression, his cursed arm prominently visible, glowing faintly with dark, ominous energy.
San (Princess Mononoke): Beside Ashitaka, San is shown in her wolf-skin cloak, fierce and ready for battle, with her wolf companions subtly appearing in the background.
Background:
Forest and Iron Town Contrast: The poster features a stark contrast between the lush, vibrant forest on one side, filled with ancient gods and natural beauty, and the industrial, smoky Iron Town on the other, symbolizing the conflict between nature and human ambition.

Forest Gods: Ghostly images of the forest gods, like the Deer God and the Boar God, are integrated into the forest side, emphasizing their ethereal and powerful presence.
Lady Eboshi: In the Iron Town background, Lady Eboshi stands with a determined look, overseeing her industrious and armed followers.
Color Palette:
Nature's Greens and Browns: Dominating the forest side, these colors represent life, growth, and the ancient beauty of nature.
Industrial Grays and Reds: Dominating the Iron Town side, these colors represent the harshness, ambition, and destruction human progress brings.
Accents of Gold and Dark Purple: Highlighting the mystical elements and the curse affecting Ashitaka.
Text and Typography:
Title: "Princess Mononoke" in a bold, ancient Japanese-style font, positioned at the top center.
Tagline: "In the struggle between nature and humanity, one warrior stands for balance." Placed below the title in a smaller, italicized font.
Credits: Displayed at the bottom, featuring the director's name, main cast, and Studio Ghibli's logo.
Additional Elements:
Spirit Creatures: Small, ethereal Kodama spirits are scattered around the forest, adding a touch of magic and mystery.
Ashitaka's Bow: Ashitaka is holding his bow, ready to protect and mediate, symbolizing his role as a peacekeeper.
San's Dagger: San gripped her dagger, showcasing her readiness to defend the forest.

Overall Design: The poster artfully balances the epic struggle between nature and industrialization, highlighting the central characters and their roles in this conflict. The duality of the lush forest and the industrial Iron Town sets the stage for the film's themes of environmentalism and the clash between progress and preservation. Using vivid and contrasting colors and including mystical elements creates a visually stunning and emotionally resonant poster that captures the essence of "Princess Mononoke." This design invites viewers into the world of medieval Japan, where the fate of nature and humanity hangs in the balance, and one warrior's quest for peace holds the key to the future.

Table 2. Princess Mononoke poster created with ChatGPT prompt

Signifier	

Sign A girl with a wolf's head in the center, behind her, a male figure with a right arm covered in fire. Behind the statistics are wolves, supernatural beings, and human figures. Forest is in the background, and smoke is coming from the factory. The place is the forest.	**Signified** The girl and boy figure positioned in the center represent power, war, and enmity. Various animal and human figures in the background represent spiritual aspects, mystical powers, and human intervention.

Gemini, like ChatGPT, gave a very detailed description of the movie Princess Mononoke:

Concept: A dynamic and symbolic design that captures the clash between nature and humanity.

Visuals:

- **Foreground:**

Ashitaka stands tall and resolute, wielding his bow and arrow. He is adorned with a warrior's attire and his arm is visibly marked by the curse (darkened or wrapped).

San, the Mononoke Hime, crouches on the ground, facing Ashitaka. Untamed hair, animalistic features, and a spear in hand emphasize her wild demeanor.

- **Background:**

The left side depicts a lush green forest with towering trees and roaming animals bathed in warm sunlight.

The right side portrays a fiery industrial scene with billowing smoke from the Tatara ironworks, gears of machinery, and flames licking the sky.

Text:

- Title: "Princess Mononoke" in a bold, stylized font, with the "M" shaped like a wolf's head.
- Tagline: "Nature Fights Back." This tagline is positioned below the title in a robust and impactful font.

Color Palette:

- A vibrant and contrasting palette is used to highlight the conflict.
- The forest side is dominated by greens, browns, and blues, representing life and harmony.
- The Tatara side uses oranges, reds, and blacks, symbolizing destruction and industry.
- Ashitaka's attire reflects a neutral palette, showcasing his role as a mediator.

Additional Details:

- A mystical deer spirit could be seen faintly amidst the trees, representing the forest gods.
- Subtle wisps of the curse's dark energy could emanate from Ashitaka's arm, creating a sense of urgency.

Overall Tone: The poster aims to be visually striking, drawing viewers in with the beauty of nature and the stark contrast of industrial destruction. It sets the stage for the epic conflict between humans and the natural world, with Ashitaka caught in the middle.

Table 3. Princess Mononoke poster created with Gemini prompt

<table>
<tr><th colspan="2">Signifier</th></tr>
<tr><td colspan="2">
</td></tr>
<tr><td>Sign
In the center, male and female figures wear clothes with primitive motifs. Behind the statistics is a background of green forest and red industrial elements.
The setting is the forest, and the time is sunset or sunrise.</td><td>Signified
The facial expressions and postures of the figures evoke attack and war. The depiction of the sky in the background is thought to be a sunrise or sunset. The use of the factory image and the forest together suggests the imbalance between nature and industrialization and questions the relationality of the two.</td></tr>
</table>

Unlike the others, the depiction of the Copilot does not have much detail: In a mystical world torn between nature and industry, Prince Ashitaka embarks on a dangerous quest to cure a deadly curse. Caught in the crossfire between forest gods and a ruthless mining colony, he encounters San, the fierce Mononoke Hime. As Ashitaka grapples with conflicting loyalties, he must navigate a war threatening humanity and ancient nature. With Lady Eboshi's ambition driving the conflict and his life hanging in the balance, Ashitaka seeks redemption and peace. But can the feral Wolf Girl, Princess Mononoke, bridge the gap between worlds?"

Table 4. Princess Mononoke poster created with Copilot prompt

<table>
<tr><td colspan="2">Signifier
</td></tr>
<tr><td>Sign
A composition positioned in the center. There is a man in the foreground, a woman behind him and a wolf figure at the very back. A dark forest scene. San and Ashitaka in a dynamic action pose with a large wolf.</td><td>Signified
When we look at the positions of the figures, it gives information about the bond between the characters. The postures and facial expressions of the figures can be interpreted as a defense position.</td></tr>
</table>

All posters of Princess Mononoke, created by Ideogram, an artificial intelligence application, contain the essential elements of the movie. The characters of San and Ashitaka and forest-related indicators are used in all posters.

The original poster of the film establishes the basic narrative emphasizing the duality between nature and industrialization. Like the film's own poster, the poster produced with the Copliot script depicts the main characters of the movie in a forest and focuses on character relationships and action. On the other hand, the posters created with the ChatGPT and Gemini commands give more space to different themes in the movie. The ChatGPT image, which emphasizes the conflict between forest and industrialization, also highlights the spiritual and mystical dimensions of the story.

Typography, an essential element in poster design, uses the Latin alphabet in the original poster. ChatGPT and Gemini also used the Latin alphabet. However, Gemini did not successfully write the name "Princess Mononoke". In the image created with the Copilot command, Japanese spelling is used. The typography used is compatible with the movie, which is in the Japanese anime genre.

Spirited Away

ChatGPT was given the prompt, "From now on, act as a graphic designer experienced in movie posters. Create a one-paragraph description for the movie poster from the summary I will give you."

The movie summary of Spirited Away was accessed from IMDB. Then this summary was uploaded to the artificial intelligence applications ChatGPT, Gemini, and Copilot with the command "From now on, act as a graphic designer who experienced on the movie poster. Create a one-paragraph description for the movie poster from the summary I'll provide you." The descriptions in text form taken from these applications were converted into visuals in the artificial intelligence application named Ideogram, which can produce visuals.

The summary of the movie from IMDB is as follows: During her family's move to the suburbs, a sullen 10-year-old girl wanders into a world ruled by gods, witches, and spirits, where humans are changed into beasts. The fanciful adventures of a ten-year-old girl named Chihiro, who discovers a secret world when she and her family get lost and venture through a hillside tunnel. When her parents undergo a mysterious transformation, Chihiro must fend for herself as she encounters strange spirits, assorted creatures, and a grumpy sorceress who seeks to prevent her from returning to the human world. A young girl named Chihiro becomes trapped in a mysterious place after her parents accidentally enter a seemingly abandoned amusement park. As Chihiro navigates this strange realm, she embarks on a journey to return to her world. To do so, she must adapt and overcome challenges while displaying resilience and determination. Chihiro encounters various spirits throughout her adventure, some friendly and others less so. Annoyed about moving to a new home, 10-year-old scaredy-cat Chihiro finds herself stuck in the leather back seat of her parent's car while en route to an unknown neighborhood. However, today, of all days, the girl's father is feeling adventurous. As a result, he takes a shortcut through a dense forest. And one fine summer day like no other, a strange, mystical wind pulls the family into a mournful town--an ethereal place balancing between reality and fantasy, the natural and the supernatural. Now separated from her mum and dad, Chihiro has no choice but to pluck up the courage she never knew she had to find a way out. It sounds impossible, but Chihiro must confront her fears and the grotesque, menacing shadows hiding from the light for the first time in her life. Can life's frightening lessons help Chihiro find her identity in this eerie spiritual journey to the mysterious wonderland?

Table 5. Spirited Away Original Poster

<table>
<tr><th colspan="2">Signifier

</th></tr>
<tr><td>Sign
Main Character: A young girl in a pink dress with short hair, looking towards the viewer in a magical or mysterious setting.
Background: A pig next to the main character and a second less visible pig in the lower left of the frame, a fence separating the pigs and the main character, two spirits blurred behind the pigs, nighttime, surrounded by traditional Japanese architecture.
Text: Japanese text is prominent</td><td>Signified
The young girl expresses innocence, vulnerability and possibly a sense of adventure. The pig can represent magic, the spirits indicate that there is a fantastical element in the story. The fence between the pig and the character could represent two different worlds.
The traditional architecture and the Japanese text indicate a cultural context and provide information about the production.</td></tr>
</table>

Here is ChatGPT's description of the film from the synopsis: For the movie poster of this enchanting film, envision a scene where a young girl, Chihiro, stands at the threshold of a mystical tunnel, her expression a mix of awe and determination. The backdrop features an ethereal town with a blend of whimsical spirits, gods, and looming shadows, hinting at the extraordinary adventures awaiting her. The poster should capture the story's eerie beauty and fantastical elements, with Chihiro's figure illuminated by a soft, otherworldly glow. Her subtly transformed parents can be seen in the distance, symbolizing the mysterious transformation that sets her on this challenging journey. The title, "Spirited Away," should be bold and enigmatic, drawing viewers into the mystical world where courage and resilience lead to self-discovery.

Table 6. Spirited Away poster created with ChatGPT prompt

<table>
<tr><td colspan="2">Signifier

</td></tr>
<tr><td>Sign
Main Character: A young girl dressed in traditional Japanese dress, with a bewildered expression, surrounded by mystical elements and spirits.
Background: A detailed, complex environment with various spirits and figures, surrounded by an ethereal, glowing frame.
A passage with a stone and various creatures that allows us to see the main character and the background.
Text: English title "Spirited Away."</td><td>Signified
The girl in traditional dress expresses a connection to cultural elements and traditional values.
The glowing frame and ghostly figures express the boundary between the ordinary and the supernatural, a journey into a mystical world.
The title "Spirited Away" provides information about the production and stylistically expresses movement and the supernatural, reinforcing the fantasy genre.</td></tr>
</table>

The description produced by Gemini is as follows: A young girl, Chihiro, stumbles into a world of magic and mystery hidden within a seemingly ordinary forest. With her parents mysteriously transformed, Chihiro must navigate this fantastical realm filled with friendly and not-so-friendly spirits. To find her way back home, she'll need to overcome challenges, face her fears, and discover a courage she never knew she had.

Table 7. Spirited Away poster created with Gemini prompt

Signifier	

Sign Main Character: A young girl dressed in a blue outfit with folkloric elements, holding a glowing orb, surrounded by ghostly figures. Background: Dark, wooded setting, eerie atmosphere	**Signified** The brightness of the girl holding the glowing orb signifies purity, the potential to transcend the darkness and to be protected by a force. The ghostly figures and the dark forest express danger, fear and the unknown. The overall composition expresses the struggle between two worlds.

Copilot described the movie Spirited Away as follows: "Chihiro's Journey" captures the enchanting tale of a 10-year-old girl named Chihiro, who stumbles into a hidden world teeming with gods, witches, and spirits. After her parents undergo a mysterious transformation, Chihiro must navigate this strange realm, facing challenges, resiliently seeking a way back to her own world. Along the way, she encounters both friendly and enigmatic spirits, all while unraveling the secrets of her identity. The poster evokes wonder, mystery, and courage, inviting audiences to join Chihiro on her extraordinary adventure.

Table 8. Spirited Away poster created with Copilot prompt

<table>
<tr><th colspan="2">Signifier</th></tr>
<tr><td colspan="2">
</td></tr>
<tr><td>Sign
Main Character: A young girl holding a lantern, surrounded by a magical and fantastic atmosphere.
Background: A darker, fantastical setting, various creatures, and a moonlit sky.
Text: Title “Chihiro's Journey.”</td><td>Signified
The girl holding a lantern represents hope and possibly the light that comes with it.
The dark, fantastical setting and creatures in the background signify danger, adventure and the unknown.
The title “Chihiro's Journey,” formally expresses adventure, while the intersection with the light emanating from the lantern in the main character's hand emphasizes the character's progress towards the light.</td></tr>
</table>

As a result of the preliminary studies, all posters produced by the artificial intelligence application Ideogram for the movie Spirited Away carry elements and elements related to the movie. Central themes such as transformation, adventure, and the intersection of the ordinary and the magical were used in all posters. The standard features of the movie posters obtained through different artificial intelligence applications are the positioning of the main character, Chihiro, in the center of the composition, the placement of supernatural, glowing elements around the character, and the image of a magical universe. The movie's original poster features the main character, Chihiro, and a pig figure. Although the pig figure is an essential element of the film, it was not included in the images obtained. Folkloric elements and traditional architecture are in the foreground in the original poster. The ChatGpt visual was more successful than the other posters with features such as prioritizing design values, including folkloric features, metaphorically giving the concept of transition, and arousing curiosity.

ChapGpt and Copilot emphasize the mystical journey and supernatural elements with glowing frames and ghostly figures. The Gemini image, which focuses on the struggle between two worlds full of light and darkness, features a more intense depiction of the supernatural.

The use of typography, which complements the poster design, is successfully applied by ChapGpt and Copilot. However, no typographic element was found in the Gemini visual.

Howl's Moving Castle

Here is the summary of the movie from IMDB: When an unconfident young woman is cursed with an old body by a spiteful witch, her only chance of breaking the spell lies with a self-indulgent yet insecure young wizard and his companions in his legged, walking castle.

With her country's peace constantly under threat, Sophie, a lively but unloved milliner, catches the attention of an unexpected defender. But as the wide-eyed damsel in distress crosses paths with handsome Howl, a talented young magician with excess emotional baggage, a fit of jealousy turns the hat maker's world upside down forever. Now, stained by the indelible mark of the wicked Witch of the Waste, Sophie must move mountains to break the pitiless spell, including facing her fears and the mysterious sorcerer. However, has anyone ever set foot in Howl's impenetrable home, a walking wonder powered by a fiery heart, and lived to tell the tale?

It is a love story between an 18-year-old girl named Sophie, cursed by a witch into an older woman's body, and a magician named Howl. Under the curse, Sophie seeks her fortune, taking her to Howl's strange moving castle. In the castle, Sophie meets Howl's fire demon, named Karishifâ. Seeing that she is under a curse, the demon makes a deal with Sophie--if she breaks the contract he is under with Howl, then Karushifâ will lift the curse that Sophie is under, and she will return to her 18-year-old shape.

The Witch of the Waste curses a young woman named Sophie, turns into an older woman, and cannot tell anyone of her plight. Unable to continue her job at her mother's hat shop, she goes to the ambulatory castle of the notorious wizard Howl and insinuates herself into his household. Sophie befriends Calcifer, the fire demon who powers the castle, and is bound to Howl by a contract, the terms of which Calcifer cannot reveal. They promise to help each other with their problems. Like Calcifer, Howl can also see through the Witch's spell, and he and Sophie fall in love. Sophie helps Howl confront his former teacher and the Witch of the Waste.

The Witch of the Waste curses young Sophie Hatter and becomes an old hag. Ashamed of how she looks, she flees into the hills, where a moving castle roams the hills. It is said to belong to the young and handsome wizard Howl, who has a bad reputation. Within the castle, Sophie befriends the fire demon Calcifer, who promises to help her become young again. One catch: she must help Calcifer to be free of Howl, and Calcifer cannot tell her how. However, Sophie agrees to stay and tries to find out about the contract through other ways. Still, Howl can see that Sophie is under a spell like Calcifer can, and he falls in love with her for who she is and not for what she looks like. Sophie manages to bring life to the moving castle, and she helps Howl to face his former tutor, Madame Suliman.

Table 9. Howl's Moving Castle Original Poster

<table>
<tr><td colspan="2">Signifier

</td></tr>
<tr><td>Sign
Image of a giant mechanical house with legs. Dark and moody sky.
Japanese text is written in spot color.</td><td>Signified
An image of a house where magic and machines coexist, a blend of fantasy and industrial elements. The smoke coming out of the chimneys of the castle is an indication that it is still in operation. The intricate castle suggests a detailed and elaborate world.
While the Japanese text gives information about the construction, the complex composition and text are separated by the color used in the text.</td></tr>
</table>

Here is ChatGPT's description of the film from the synopsis: In this enchanting movie poster, we capture the magical and transformative journey of Sophie, a young milliner cursed into an old woman's body by a spiteful witch. Central to the composition is Howl's legged, walking castle, towering majestically in the background, symbolizing the fantastical adventure ahead. Sophie, depicted in her dual forms—young and old—stands resolutely at the forefront, her determined gaze reflecting her unyielding spirit. Beside her is the enigmatic and handsome wizard Howl, exuding vulnerability and charm. The fiery heart of Calcifer, the fire demon, glows warmly, casting a mystical light that hints at his crucial role in the unfolding drama. The poster's color palette combines warm and cool tones, illustrating the contrast between the characters' external battles and internal growth. This visually arresting poster not only hints at the magical elements of the story but also underscores the themes of love, transformation, and courage.

Table 10. Howl's Moving Castle poster created with ChatGPT prompt

Signifier	

Sign The figure of a girl in a red hat and a male figure in the foreground with arms outstretched are followed by bright red fantasy lines and a similarly composed heart image. Behind the male figure is a girl with a red hat in a lumbar plan, and behind her is an older male figure with a severe expression of her head plan. At the back is an image of a massive castle with legs, surrounded by fantastic elements. Dark space.	**Signified** The posture and facial expression of the male figure in the foreground can be interpreted as inviting and confident. The red hat and the girl's expression evoke innocence and adventure. The older man can represent wisdom and a protective figure. Fantastic elements such as the castle and the glowing heart emphasize the mystical nature of the story.

The description of Gemini includes the following statements: A whimsical adventure unfolds as Sophie, an unassuming young woman cursed with an old woman's body, finds herself entangled with the enigmatic wizard Howl and his peculiar moving castle. Together, they must navigate a world of magic, pacts with fire demons, and looming war, as Sophie discovers true courage and an unlikely love that transcends appearances.

Table 11. Howl's Moving Castle poster created with Gemini prompt

<table>
<tr><th colspan="2">Signifier</th></tr>
<tr><td colspan="2">
</td></tr>
<tr><td>Sign
A young girl in a blue dress. A prominent, old male figure and fantastic creatures and elements surround these two figures. Fairytale castles. Image of mountains and sky. English text.</td><td>Signified
The young girl signifies innocence and the beginning of an adventure.
The older male figure implies that he may be a wise person who is a protector or guide. The facial expression of the figures suggests a happy story.</td></tr>
</table>

Copilot's description is as follows: In a world where magic and curses intertwine, Sophie, an unloved milliner cursed to an old woman's body, stumbles upon Howl's enigmatic moving castle. With her country's fate hanging in the balance, Sophie must navigate treacherous spells, face her fears, and unravel the secrets of the fiery-hearted wizard. As love blossoms amidst magical turmoil, the castle's legs carry them toward an unforgettable adventure.

Table 12. Howl's Moving Castle poster created with Copilot prompt

Signifier	

Sign A young girl in a hat surrounded by figures of middle-aged men and women. A large castle built on fantastic legs. A magical, fairytale world with various creatures surrounding the castle. Japanese text above and below the composition.	**Signified** The fact that the figure of the girl is located on a brightly lit background separates the figure from the other elements and brings it to the foreground. From the placement of the composition, it can be interpreted that the story is progressed with the girl figure at the center. The images of the castle, the creatures and the fire surrounding the composition reinforce a magical, fantastic environment. Blue and orange tones create a mystical and fairytale-like atmosphere.

All posters produced for Howl's Moving Castel reinforce the story's fantasy world through elements such as a fantastic castle and magic. The posters include details that may give clues to the audience about the characters at the center of the story and their roles. All posters' vibrant, mystical colors (blues, oranges, and reds) evoke a sense of magic and fantasy. Although the posters have visual combinations produced in different styles and techniques, they all use elements that evoke the concepts of fantasy, adventure, and magic. Unlike the other posters, the ChatGpt image puts the castle in the background, and the characters in the foreground, but the hierarchical order used in the placement of the characters does not match the story. The artistic style and technique used in the Copilot and Gemini visuals are created in such a way that they succeed in attracting the viewer's attention. Despite the differences in style and technique, each poster conveys the enchanting and mystical essence of "Howl's Moving Castle."

Regarding typography, the Copilot image, like the original poster, is written in Japanese, thus directly hinting at the cultural origin. It is seen that the Gemini visual contains typographic elements created with the Latin alphabet, while the ChapGpt visual does not contain any typographic elements. For this reason, within the typography framework, the ChatGpt image was unsuccessful compared to the other posters.

Ponyo

"From now on, pretend you are a graphic designer experienced in movie posters. Create a one-paragraph description for the movie poster from the summary I will give you." ChatGPT, Gemini and Copilot were given the following movie summary: A five-year-old boy develops a relationship with Ponyo, a young goldfish princess who longs to become a human after falling in love with him. The son of a sailor, 5-year-old Sosuke lives a quiet life on an oceanside cliff with his mother Lisa. One fateful day, he finds a beautiful goldfish trapped in a bottle on the beach and upon rescuing her, names her Ponyo. But she is no ordinary goldfish. The daughter of a masterful wizard and a sea goddess, Ponyo uses her father's magic to transform herself into a young girl and quickly falls in love with Sosuke, but the use of such powerful sorcery causes a dangerous imbalance in the world. As the moon steadily draws nearer to the earth and Ponyo's father sends the ocean's mighty waves to find his daughter, the two children embark on an adventure of a lifetime to save the world and fulfill Ponyo's dreams of becoming human. With humankind polluting the ocean and abusing its not-so-abundant resources, young Sosuke, a bright boy living on a cliff, has a chance encounter with Ponyo, the sea's most unexpected inhabitant. Without a second thought, the adventurous lad rescues the mysterious creature resembling a bizarre goldfish, and just like that, an exciting friendship begins. But there's more to the curious, strangely amiable marine animal than meets the eye. When Ponyo's surprising secret eventually comes to light, Sosuke and his new companion must restore the fragile balance between the bustling terrestrial world and the lively underwater kingdom. If things go as planned, will Ponyo get her wish?

Table 13. Ponyo original poster

<table>
<tr><th colspan="2">Signifier</th></tr>
<tr><td colspan="2">
</td></tr>
<tr><td>Sign
The figure of a little girl with red hair, half submerged in water. Image of a jellyfish surrounding the girl's head.
A ship and boat in the background.
Japanese text is written in color at the bottom.</td><td>Signified
A connection is made between the red-haired girl figure and the sea. The ship and the boat show the marine environment, emphasizing the themes of adventure and the sea.
The Japanese text shows the cultural origin of the movie and information about the movie.</td></tr>
</table>

The description of ChatGPT includes the following statements: The movie poster for "Ponyo" beautifully captures the enchanting and whimsical essence of this heartwarming tale. At the center, a young boy, Sosuke, and the vibrant goldfish-turned-girl, Ponyo, are depicted in a joyous moment of discovery and friendship. The backdrop features the serene oceanside cliff where Sosuke lives, transitioning into the magical underwater realm filled with vibrant marine life and mystical elements. The poster uses a harmonious color palette of deep ocean blues and bright, warm tones to reflect the magical transformation and the brewing imbalance caused by Ponyo's powerful sorcery. Above, the moon looms larger than life, symbolizing the approaching peril. Gentle waves and intricate bubbles frame the characters, highlighting the adventure and the delicate balance between the human world and the underwater kingdom. The title "Ponyo" is elegantly displayed in a whimsical font at the top, with a tagline below: "A magical friendship. An adventure of a lifetime." This poster promises a captivating and visually stunning journey, appealing to audiences of all ages.

Table 14. Ponyo Poster created with ChatGPT prompt

<table>
<tr><th colspan="2">Signifier</th></tr>
<tr><td colspan="2">
</td></tr>
<tr><td>Sign
In the center, a colorful fish and a male figure. The two figures are in contact, and the fish smiles at the male figure—a fantastic mermaid figure in the right corner.
The significant wave to the left of the composition refers to Hokusai's "The Great Wave of Kanagawa."
Bright, vibrant colors and underwater background.
English text.</td><td>Signified
The waves and the underwater environment symbolize the connection with the ocean and its mysteries.
The male figure and the fish holding hands symbolize the fish's connection with the human world.
The use of bright colors expresses a sense of adventure and magic. The wave reinforces the folkloric elements, which resembles the Great Wave of Kanagawa.</td></tr>
</table>

Gemini gave a promt of a few sentences: The poster bursts with vibrant colors, capturing the wonder of a magical ocean adventure. A young boy, Sosuke, stands hand-in-hand with a goldfish with bright, curious eyes (Ponyo in disguise). Sparkling waves crash against a towering cliff house, hinting at the powerful connection between land and sea. The tagline, "A Boy, a Fish, and a World to Change," playfully highlights the extraordinary friendship and its potential impact.

Table 15. Ponyo Poster created with Gemini prompt

<table>
<tr><td colspan="2">Signifier

</td></tr>
<tr><td>Sign
The figure of a boy with his back turned, holding the hand of a yellow fish—a giant wave approached behind the statistics. In the background, a house is visible through the waves.
It is a calm but dynamic composition with a predominance of blue.
Text in English.</td><td>Signified
The gigantic wave hints at impending adventure or danger. It can also be said to contain cultural clues. The child and the yellow fish-holding hands symbolize the union of the human and underwater worlds. The text is placed in warm tones of blue, creating a cozy poster.</td></tr>
</table>

Copilot gave the command as follows: From the enchanting world of Studio Ghibli comes 'Ponyo,' a heartwarming tale of love, magic, and the delicate balance between land and sea. When 5-year-old Sosuke rescues a trapped goldfish named Ponyo, he discovers that she is no ordinary fish—she's a young princess longing to become human. As their bond grows, Ponyo's transformation into a girl sets off a chain of events that threatens the very fabric of existence. With the moon drawing closer and the ocean's fury unleashed, Sosuke and Ponyo embark on an extraordinary adventure to save their world. Featuring breathtaking animation and unforgettable characters, 'Ponyo' is a timeless tale of wonder and courage.

Table 16. Ponyo Poster created with Copilot prompt

Signifier	

Sign Two figures of children, one older. The older child figure shows, the younger child figure a figure of a mermaid traveling underwater. A large moon and giant waves circling the moon. Sea creatures and underwater elements in shades of blue and orange surround the figures. Text in English.	**Signified** The moon and the waves symbolize adventure and the story's magical elements. The figures' facial expressions and relaxed postures give the impression of a happy story. The underwater image surrounding the composition and the presence of sea creatures reinforce it and emphasize the film's theme of marine life.

All Ponyo posters feature the movie's main characters, Ponyo the fish and the boy characters. Ocean elements (waves, underwater scenes, sea creatures) emphasized the marine environment as repetitive signs, which was observed in all posters.

In the movie's original poster, Ponyo's curiosity, eagerness, and excitement to become human is reflected more. In contrast, in the other posters, a narrative is built on the friendship of Ponyo and her human friend. In the poster created with the ChatGPT command, the colors are more vivid, and the ocean waves are more dynamic. The friendship between fish and humans is emphasized in the poster designed by Gemini. In contrast, the poster produced with the Copliot command emphasizes the feeling of impending challenge or adventure with the massive wave and the house on the cliff. The images created with the ChatGPT and Copilot commands also feature other characters from the movie. Gemini has a design that only has the leads.

Looking at the typography on the posters, it was observed that the Japanese alphabet was used in the movie's original poster. In contrast, the Latin alphabet was used in the posters created with the commands of artificial intelligence applications. In addition to the Latin alphabet, the posters produced by ChatGPT and Copilot also include Japanese expressions in smaller font sizes. The use of Japanese typographic writings in these Japanese anime productions shows that cultural elements are incorporated into the visuals.

Although each poster is unique in its visual approach, it is consistent with the central theme of the movie: Ponyo's magical journey and her integration into the human world.

The Wind Rises

The IMDB summary of the movie is as follows: Jiro Horikoshi studies assiduously to fulfill his aim of becoming an aeronautical engineer. As WWII begins, fighter aircraft he designed end up getting used by the Japanese Empire against its foes. Jiro dreams of flying and designing beautiful airplanes, inspired by the famous Italian aeronautical designer Caproni. Nearsighted from a young age and unable to be a pilot, Jiro joins a major Japanese engineering company in 1927 and becomes one of the world's most innovative and accomplished airplane designers. The film chronicles much of his life, depicting key historical events, including the Great Kanto Earthquake of 1923, the Great Depression, the tuberculosis epidemic and Japan's plunge into war. Jiro meets and falls in love with Nahoko, and grows and cherishes his friendship with his colleague Honjo. An aviation-obsessed engineer named Jirô Horikoshi has loved the aesthetics, spirit, and science of flight for as long as he can remember. For years, he's been designing and building his dream plane, the Mitsubishi A6M Zero, and it's finally completed. But Jiro's dreams come crashing down when he learns, to his horror, that his creation will be used for combat in World War II. Forced to abandon his childhood dream to become a pilot, young Jiro Horikoshi pursues a career as an aeronautical engineer instead. And just like his idol, the Italian aircraft designer Giovanni Battista Caproni, the visionary youth goes to engineering school after saving a young girl during the 1923 Great Kanto Earthquake. As Jiro finds new purpose and meaning in life, his untamed creativity and love for aviation pave the way for his magnum opus, the legendary Mitsubishi A6M Zero fighter aircraft. But with WWII and the involvement of the Imperial Japanese Army looming, is the highly accomplished aeroplane designer prepared to confront life's tragedies and sacrifice everything for the glory of Japan?

Table 17. The Wind Rises original poster

<table>
<tr><td colspan="2">Signifier

</td></tr>
<tr><td>Sign
The protagonist has a hat and a drawing board.
An airplane in the sky.
Soft, bright color palette.
Open space and sky.
Text in Japanese.</td><td>Signified
The protagonist's passion for aviation and design.
The beauty and tranquility of nature.
The historical and emotional journey of the character.</td></tr>
</table>

ChapGPT's prompt for the movie The Wind Rises is as follows:

Concept and Visual Elements

1. **Central Image:**

   Jiro Horikoshi: Positioned prominently, Jiro is depicted with a contemplative expression, holding a blueprint of the Mitsubishi A6M Zero. His figure is framed by a mix of engineering tools and drafting instruments, showcasing his dedication and innovation.

   Mitsubishi A6M Zero: The iconic fighter plane is shown above Jiro, symbolizing his greatest achievement and the tragic use of his creation in war. The plane casts a shadow over Jiro, hinting at the moral and emotional weight he carries.

2. **Background:**

Historical Context: The backdrop features a collage of significant historical events:

- **The Great Kanto Earthquake:** A cracked earth and rising smoke to the left side.
- **The Great Depression:** Depicted through a somber, sepia-toned section on the right.
- **WWII:** Dark, ominous clouds and distant explosions represent the impending conflict.

Caproni's Influence: A ghostly image of Caproni's planes and his figure, faintly visible in the sky, symbolizing Jiro's inspiration and dreams.

3. **Color Palette:**

   Dreamy Sky Blues and Whites: Representing Jiro's aspirations and the beauty of flight.

   Muted Earth Tones: Depicting the historical and wartime elements, grounding the narrative.

   Accents of Red: Symbolizing Japan, passion, and the turbulence of war.

4. **Text and Typography:**

   Title: "The Wind Rises" in an elegant, flowing font reminiscent of aeronautical blueprints, positioned at the top center.

   Tagline: "Dreams take flight amidst the winds of change." Placed below the title in a smaller, italicized font.

   Credits: Displayed at the bottom, featuring the director's name, voice actors, and Studio Ghibli's logo.

5. **Additional Elements:**

   Nahoko and Honjo: Smaller vignette images of Nahoko and Honjo integrated into the side margins, emphasizing personal connections and their roles in Jiro's life.

   Imaginary Elements: Subtle, dreamlike elements, such as floating paper airplanes and whimsical clouds, illustrate the blend of reality and dreams.

   Wind Motif: Gentle, swirling lines representing the wind, weaving through the design, symbolizing change and inspiration.

Overall Design: The poster artfully combines the dual aspects of Jiro's life: his unrelenting pursuit of aviation dreams and the harsh realities of the world he navigates. It balances the aesthetics of innovation and personal growth with Jiro's journey's historical context and emotional depth, creating a compelling visual narrative that invites viewers into the poignant and inspirational story. The poster highlights Jiro's engineering brilliance and underscores the emotional and ethical dilemmas he faces, making it a thought-provoking visual piece.

Table 18. The Wind Rises poster created with ChapGPT prompt

<table>
<tr><th colspan="2">Signifier</th></tr>
<tr><td colspan="2">
</td></tr>
<tr><td>Sign
Portrait of a man holding blue drawings.
An airplane in flight.
Elements of war and machinery.
Pale color palette.
Text in English.</td><td>Signified
The protagonist's role is that of an engineer and designer.
Technical and war-related aspects of his work.
A more severe and historical focus than the original.</td></tr>
</table>

Gemini also depicted a detailed promt:

Concept: The poster will be a dramatic and thought-provoking design that captures the duality of Jiro's dream and its unintended consequences.

Visuals:

- **Foreground:** A young Jiro stands in a three-quarter pose, gazing upwards with a determined expression. He wears period clothing appropriate for the 1920s.
- **Background:** A majestic Mitsubishi A6M Zero fighter aircraft soars diagonally across the top right corner, with a plume of smoke trailing

behind it. The sky behind the plane is a gradient of blue fading into dark orange, hinting at a coming storm.

- **Center:** A single, transparent wing from a biplane (representing Jiro's childhood dream of flight) overlaps the bottom half of the Zero, creating a visual contrast.

Text:

- Title: "Jiro Horikoshi" in a bold, serif font with a slight upward tilt to echo the aspiration of flight.
- Tagline: "A Dream Takes Flight. A Nation Goes to War." This tagline is positioned under the title in a smaller, yet impactful, font.

Color Palette:

- The poster will use a muted color palette to evoke a sense of history and contemplation.
- Jiro's clothing will be brown and grey, highlighting his grounded nature.
- The Zero will be a dark metallic grey, emphasizing its power and potential for destruction.
- The background gradient will transition from a calm blue to a fiery orange, symbolizing the beauty of flight turning into the horrors of war.

Additional details:

- Cherry blossoms, a symbol of Japan, could be subtly incorporated around Jiro's feet, hinting at the beauty and fragility of life.
- The biplane wing could be slightly transparent, revealing a glimpse of the young Jiro looking out at the world with wonder.

Overall Tone: The poster aims to be visually arresting while prompting reflection on the complexities of ambition and the unintended consequences of innovation.

Table 19. The Wind Rises poster created with Gemini prompt

<table>
<tr><th colspan="2">Signifier</th></tr>
<tr><td colspan="2">
</td></tr>
<tr><td>Sign
A young man standing on top of an airplane.
There is a clear distinction between old and modern airplanes.
A bright and hopeful color palette.
Text in English.</td><td>Signified
The evolution of aviation technology.
The protagonist's dreams and goals.
A hopeful and inspiring tone.</td></tr>
</table>

Copilot prompt is as follows: In a world on the brink of war, Jiro Horikoshi, an aeronautical engineer, dreams of soaring skies and designing exquisite airplanes. His nearsightedness prevents him from becoming a pilot, but his passion leads him to create the legendary Mitsubishi A6M Zero fighter aircraft. As historical events unfold—the Great Kanto Earthquake, the Great Depression, and Japan's plunge into conflict—Jiro's life intertwines with love, friendship, and the pursuit of innovation. But as WWII looms and his creation becomes a weapon of war, Jiro faces a moral dilemma: can he reconcile his dreams with the harsh realities of combat?

Table 20. The Wind Rises poster created with Copilot prompt

<table>
<tr><th colspan="2">Signifier</th></tr>
<tr><td colspan="2">
</td></tr>
<tr><td>Sign
Silhouette of a man with airplanes flying overhead.
Dark, smoky background.
Intense and dramatic tones.
Text in English.</td><td>Signified
The intense and dark side of aviation and war.
The protagonist's struggles and the dangers he faces.
A more dramatic and serious interpretation.</td></tr>
</table>

Inspired by a true-life story, the original poster for The Win Rises uses an animated drawing. The original poster for the film, which tells the story of Japanese aeronautical engineer Jiro Horikoshi, uses soft, peaceful colors and a pastoral scene to evoke a sense of tranquility and creativity. In contrast, the AI-generated posters emphasize the historical and technical aspects of the story with more intense colors and elements of war. While the original poster focused on a peaceful setting, symbolizing the artistic side of the side character in the film, the other posters created a more intense atmosphere by emphasizing his technical skills and the wartime context. In addition, the visuals, which are also produced by artificial intelligence with artificial intelligence housing, consist of drawings closer to reality. It has been observed that these posters of movies in which a real-life story is told are closer to reality.

When we look at typography in movie posters, it is observed that the Japanese alphabet was used in the movie's original poster. Latin letters were used in the visuals produced with ChatGPT, Copilot, and Gemini commands. ChatGPT's poster also includes the company's name where the main character works. Although there are spelling mistakes, concepts such as “dedicate” and “achievement” are successfully emphasized in these visuals. In the visual produced with the command Gemini, the organization where the protagonist of the film works is included in small fonts. On the other hand, Copilot used the phrase “War II” in the poster since the movie is set during World War II.

Although different from the original visual of The Wind Rises, it was determined that the visuals produced were related to the movie's subject.

The Boy and The Heron

The IMDB summary of the 2024 film The Boy and the Heron is as follows: In the wake of his mother's death and his father's remarriage, a headstrong boy named Mahito ventures into a dreamlike world shared by both the living and the dead.

A new critically-acclaimed fantasy adventure comes from the legendary Studio Ghibli and Academy Award®-winning director Hayao Miyazaki (Spirited Away). After losing his mother during the war, young Mahito moves to his family's estate in the countryside. A series of mysterious events lead him to a secluded, ancient tower home to a mischievous gray heron. When Mahito's new stepmother disappears, he follows the gray heron into the tower and enters a fantastic world shared by the living and the dead. As he embarks on an epic journey with the heron as his guide, Mahito must uncover the secrets of this world and the truth about himself. He features the voices of Christian Bale, Dave Bautista, Gemma Chan, Willem Dafoe, Karen Fukuhara, Mark Hamill, Robert Pattinson, and Florence Pugh.

Mahito's mother is killed in World War 2. A few years later, his father remarries and moves his family to the country. With no friends, Mahito withdraws into his world. The only thing that seems interested in him is a large heron. Turns out the heron is more than it appears to be.

Table 21. The Boy and The Heron original poster

<table>
<tr><th colspan="2">Signifier</th></tr>
<tr><td colspan="2">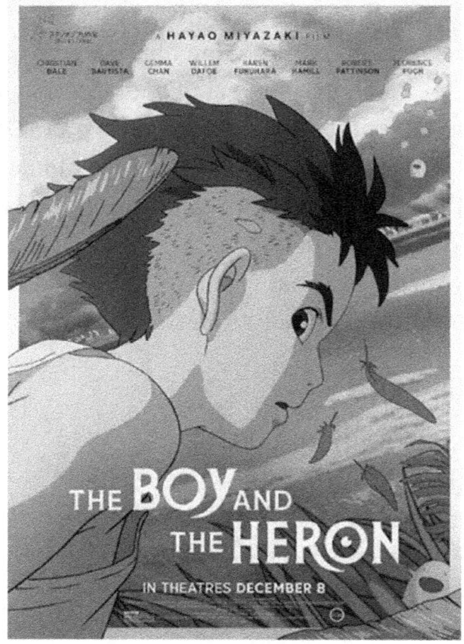
</td></tr>
<tr><td>Sign
The figure of a boy with hair cut on the right side in a striking style. Feathers of birds flying around the figure of a boy. Green and blue nature, the image of an overcast sky.
Text in English.</td><td>Signified
Looking at the child's hair, it is seen that there is a wound between the cut hair. The facial expression of the figure suggests that the character is worried. The feathers of birds flying around indicate the union between nature and the child.
The setting and the character emphasize the connection with nature, implying an adventure.</td></tr>
</table>

ChatGPT has described it as follows: The movie poster captures the ethereal and poignant journey of Mahito, a young boy navigating the complexities of life and loss. Central to the design is the ancient, secluded tower, shrouded in mystery and intrigue, standing against a backdrop of a serene countryside estate. Mahito, depicted with determination and vulnerability, is shown venturing toward the tower, symbolizing his quest for understanding and self-discovery. Beside him, the mischievous gray heron, with its enigmatic presence, hints at the story's fantastical elements. The poster's color scheme blends muted earth tones with dreamlike blues and purples, creating a sense of the boundary between the living world and the realm of the dead. Featuring the voices of renowned actors, the names are elegantly displayed at the top, highlighting the star-studded cast. This visually captivating poster encapsulates the essence of Studio Ghibli's magical storytelling, inviting viewers into a world of fantasy, adventure, and emotional depth.

Table 22. The Boy and The Heron poster created with ChapGPT prompt

Signifier	

Sign The figure of a boy walking towards a tower and a heron standing beside him. A scene of dense greenery and an old, rustic building. An image of a frame formed by greenery. English text above and below the poster.	**Signified** The color, the tower, and the setting may symbolize adventure or the adventure path. The heron accompanying the figure of the boy symbolizes a guide or protector on his journey. The rustic building reinforces the element of adventure, alluding to historical or mystical themes. The typographic elements below the title "Mahito" and at the top of the poster are thought to contain information about the movie.

Gemini gives a shorter description: A heartfelt Studio Ghibli adventure awaits. Enter a breathtaking world where the living and the dead coexist, as a young boy named Mahito embarks on a magical quest guided by a mysterious heron. Uncover the secrets of this fantastical realm and the truth about himself in a coming-of- age story that celebrates life, loss, and the enduring power of hope.

Table 23. The Boy and The Heron poster created with Gemini prompt

<table>
<tr><th colspan="2">Signifier</th></tr>
<tr><td colspan="2">
</td></tr>
<tr><td>Sign
The figure of a boy with a light and two herons, one large. Sunrise or sunset with a dramatic, vivid landscape.
Text in Japanese and English. Studio Ghibli credits.</td><td>Signified
The light in the child's hand symbolizes hope and discovery.
The herons behind the child can act as protectors and guides.
Sunset or sunrise may imply a transformation or climax in the narrative.</td></tr>
</table>

Copilot's description includes the following sentences: From the legendary Studio Ghibli and Academy Award®-winning director Hayao Miyazaki (Spirited Away) comes a new critically-acclaimed fantasy adventure. After losing his mother during the war, young Mahito moves to his family's estate in the countryside. There, a series of mysterious events lead him to a secluded and ancient tower, home to a mischievous gray heron. When Mahito's new stepmother disappears, he follows the gray heron into the tower, and enters a fantastic world shared by the living and the dead. As he embarks on an epic journey with the heron as his guide, Mahito must uncover the secrets of this world, and the truth about himself. Featuring the voices of Christian Bale, Dave Bautista, Gemma Chan, Willem Dafoe, Karen Fukuhara, Mark Hamill, Robert Pattinson, and Florence Pugh.

Table 24. The Boy and The Heron poster created with Copilot prompt

Signifier	

Sign The figure of a boy with a large heron to his right. Figures of women, men, and fantastic creatures behind the character. Behind the statistics is a high tower with stone walls and an image of the sky. Mystical creatures and birds surround the composition. English text and Studio Ghibli inscription.	**Signified** The centrality of multiple characters and fantastical elements implies various side stories in the film. With its size and posture, the heron plays the role of a protective figure. The tower and mystical creatures imply mystery, adventure, and the depiction of a magical world. The typographic elements under the title "Mahito" and at the top of the poster are thought to contain information about the movie.

In all movie posters created for The Boy and The Heron, the use of natural and mystical environments, the positioning of the main character, the boy figure in the center, and the presence of the heron figure accompanying the main character were identified as standard features. The consistency of the signs commonly used in the posters conveys a similar signified in the posters. Although only the main character and the setting are included in the movie's original poster, the heron figure, rustic architecture, side characters, and mystical creatures in the other poster designs obtained in the study reinforce the story. At the same time, they also give the viewer various clues about the story. The recurring heron figures in the posters symbolize guidance and a mystical element. The positioning of the herons as large and right next to the main character reflects that they are the protector of the main character.

When evaluated typographically, it is seen that the Copilot image contains Japanese spelling, while the ChatGpt and Gemini images are created with the Latin alphabet. In the Copilot and Gemini images, Studio Ghibli is included in addition to the title. Compared to Gemini images, typography is used more intensely in ChatGpt and Copilot images.

CONCLUSION

When the visuals produced in the study were evaluated in terms of design and creativity, it was seen that the details, such as the visual elements used in poster designs, the harmony of the color palette, the use of typography, and the use of symbols were created like a professional graphic designer.

Although the commands given to Ideogram did not specify an expected style, style, or technique to be produced, posters were mainly produced in a style and style appropriate to the content concerning the words and sentences in the descriptions given. It was observed that illustration, 3d rendering, and photo manipulation were mainly used.

Aesthetic concerns were evident in all of the visuals, and the layout and composition of the poster were balanced in each of them. In addition, it is seen that the visuals obtained are not similar to the original posters of the films. Nevertheless, all the visuals are consistent with the themes of the films.

It is seen that typography was used in the majority of the visuals produced. However, it was observed that typography was used in a planned manner as a design element in Gemini visuals. Typographic elements such as form, color, and typeface used in the visuals created with Gemini commands overlap with the content of the films. This situation stood out as an element that enriches the design.

In line with the findings obtained in the study, artificial intelligence applications that produce visuals can help professionals working in creative industries. It has been observed that artificial intelligence has many advantages, such as accelerating design processes, offering new composition suggestions, color palettes, style experiments, reducing costs, and being accessible to everyone. However, using artificial intelligence applications in visual production has disadvantages in addition to these advantages. Since artificial intelligence works on existing data, it sometimes has limitations in producing creative and original works. These applications may have difficulty producing original and innovative ideas like a designer. It has been observed that these applications may only sometimes produce the desired and correct results due to algorithms and technical errors. It has been observed that artificial intelligence cannot replace human touch in establishing an emotional and aesthetic connection, which is of great importance in design.

Although researchers and scientists have used artificial intelligence effectively for many years, it has only recently entered ordinary human life. Especially productive artificial intelligence applications such as chatbots and visual generation tools have been made available to everyone without requiring design knowledge or technical skills. However, entering the correct command is a skill required for these applications to be used effectively. Artificial intelligence applications can produce incorrect results if the wrong commands are given to the user. At this point, the user's competence in entering prompts will directly affect the use of these applications in the field of creativity.

REFERENCES

Ali, A. H., Alajanbi, M., Yaseen, M. G., & Abed, S. A. (2023). Chatgpt4, DALL·E, Bard, Claude, BERT: Open Possibilities. *Babylonian Journal of Machine Learning*, 17–18, 17–18. Advance online publication. DOI: 10.58496/BJML/2023/003

Anon. n.d. "copilot nedir." *Bing*. Retrieved July 5, 2024 (https://www.bing.com/search?q=copilot+nedir&toWww=1&redig=98F5A3365CC34881AE6A4514A7CBEF96)

Asif, A. W. (2024). "İdeogram AI İncelemesi: Onu Farklı Kılan Nedir?" *MSPoweruser*. Retrieved July 5, 2024 (https://mspoweruser.com/tr/ideogram-ai-review/)

Banh, L., & Strobel, G. (2023). Generative Artificial Intelligence. *Electronic Markets*, 33(1), 63. DOI: 10.1007/s12525-023-00680-1

Barthes, R. (1996). *Çağdaş Söylemler*. Metis Yayınları.

Boden, M. A. (2004). *The Creative Mind: Myths and Mechanisms* (2nd ed.). Routledge. DOI: 10.4324/9780203508527

Dartnall, T. (1994). *Artificial Intelligence and Creativity: An Interdisciplinary Approach*. Springer Science & Business Media. DOI: 10.1007/978-94-017-0793-0

de Saussure, F. (1959). *Course in General Linguistics*. Philosophical Library.

Dugal, M., & Davey, O. (2024). *Welcome to AI*. Wide Eyed Editions.

Fay, R., & Trenholm, W. n.d. "The Cyber Security Battlefield." *Centre for International Governance Innovation*. Retrieved July 3, 2024 (https://www.cigionline.org/articles/cyber-security-battlefield/)

Gozalo-Brizuela, Roberto, and Eduardo C. Garrido-Merchan. (2023). "ChatGPT Is Not All You Need. A State of the Art Review of Large Generative AI Models."

Greengard, S. 2019. "What is Artificial Intelligence & How Does It Work?" *Datamation*. Retrieved July 4, 2024 (https://www.datamation.com/artificial-intelligence/what-is-artificial-intelligence/)

Imran, M., & Almusharraf, N. (2024). Google Gemini as a next Generation AI Educational Tool: A Review of Emerging Educational Technology. *Smart Learning Environments*, 11(1), 22. DOI: 10.1186/s40561-024-00310-z

LeCun, Y., Bengio, Y., & Hinton, G. (2015). Deep Learning. *Nature*, 521(7553), 436–444. DOI: 10.1038/nature14539 PMID: 26017442

Lv, Z. (2023). Generative Artificial Intelligence in the Metaverse Era. *Cognitive Robotics*, 3, 208–217. DOI: 10.1016/j.cogr.2023.06.001

Malhan, S., Mewafarosh, R., Agnihotri, S., & Gupta, D. (2023). "Emergence of AI in Education: A Way Forward for Societal Development." Pp. 56–68 in *Artificial Intelligence and Society 5.0*. Boca Raton: Chapman and Hall/CRC.

Messer, U. (2024). Co-Creating Art with Generative Artificial Intelligence: Implications for Artworks and Artists. *Computers in Human Behavior: Artificial Humans*, 2(1), 100056. DOI: 10.1016/j.chbah.2024.100056

O'Meara, J., & Murphy, C. (2023). Aberrant AI Creations: Co-Creating Surrealist Body Horror Using the DALL-E Mini Text-to-Image Generator. *Convergence (London)*, 29(4), 1070–1096. Advance online publication. DOI: 10.1177/13548565231185865

Parisse-Brassens, J. (2021). *Future Impact of AI on Culture*. White Paper.

Sadiku, M. N. O., Ashaolu, T. J., Ajayi-Majebi, A., & Musa, S. M. (2021). Artificial Intelligence in Social Media. *International Journal Of Scientific Advances*, 2(1), 15–20. DOI: 10.51542/ijscia.v2i1.4

Seguela, J. (1997). *Eğlenceli Şeydir Şu Reklamcılık*. Doğan Kitap.

Thorp, H. H. (2023). ChatGPT Is Fun, but Not an Author. *Science*, 379(6630), 313–313. DOI: 10.1126/science.adg7879 PMID: 36701446

Chapter 9
The Synthesis Between Artificial Intelligence and Editing Stories of the Future

Serhat Erdem
https://orcid.org/0000-0002-3782-0147
Atatürk Üniversitesi, Turkey

ABSTRACT

The study employs a documentary method from qualitative research methods through a literature review. Different examples are used within the scope of purposive sampling to demonstrate the synthesis of artificial intelligence and editing: The selected examples show how artificial intelligence technologies are used in different areas and how they affect the editing processes. Examining each example will help to better understand the impact of the synthesis of artificial intelligence and editing on the film industry. It can be stated that studies on the synthesis of artificial intelligence and editing offer an important perspective on how future storytelling and visual art may be shaped. The aim of this study is to reveal the potential to further optimize creative processes, develop new opportunities for artists, and provide more impactful experiences for audiences

INTRODUCTION

Video editing determines the flow of a story and guides the emotions of the audience. By transitioning between interconnected scenes, editing draws the audience into the events and keeps their attention engaged. Editing, combined with visual

DOI: 10.4018/979-8-3693-3916-9.ch009

aesthetics, offers viewers an unforgettable experience. By carefully considering every detail, harmony is achieved between images and sounds, and the resulting coherence takes the audience on an impactful journey. Video editing, as a form of art, communicates with the audience through emotion and thought. This art, which appeals to viewers from all walks of life, enables a story to be told in a compelling way.

Traditional video editing is an ancient art form used to convey people's emotions, thoughts, and stories by harnessing the power of visual storytelling. Although traditional video editing initially involved manually cutting and pasting film strips, it has become more modern with the development of digital technology and the use of computer-based software. However, this transition preserves the core purpose of editing: to tell a compelling story and transport the audience to different worlds. Traditional video editing has the potential to leave deep cultural impressions by allowing people to form emotional and intellectual connections.

In the traditional art of editing, both in film and television, the process relied on the skills, experience, and aesthetic sensibilities of human editors. However, with the advancement of artificial intelligence technologies, this process is undergoing significant transformation. Now, AI algorithms can automatically analyse scenes, detect emotional tones, and even create the most effective edits to convey a specific emotional state.

In our era of rapidly advancing technology, the convergence of artificial intelligence and human creativity is ushering in a new epoch in storytelling and editing within visual fields, just as in many other domains. As Öcal (2020) notes, "Thanks to the applications revealed by digital technology, individuals, captivated by 'augmented' realities, can easily enter a mental process where they accept the reality of the 'virtual' and 'artificial' without question" (p. 1). The deep learning and natural language processing capabilities of artificial intelligence allow it to analyse vast datasets, directly influencing creative processes, while human creativity and emotional intelligence imbue stories with soul and meaning. The synthesis of these two elements makes it possible for future storytelling to become richer, more diverse, and more impactful than ever before.

Artificial intelligence today represents a rapidly advancing process, closely tied to technological developments, and is one of the key topics of discussion across various disciplines. At its core, artificial intelligence aims to make machines more autonomous and intelligent (Bolat, 2023, p. 44). AI has started to be used as a tool, particularly in editing software. Its algorithms can scan existing scripts, stories, and literary works to create new script templates and plotlines. This can spark writers' creativity, helping them generate new ideas or develop existing ones. For instance, AI-based writing assistants enable writers to quickly draft according to given themes, characters, and settings, thus accelerating the creative process and allowing more stories to emerge. Additionally, AI can analyze reader and viewer preferences to produce personalized visual content. This facilitates interactive and dynamic visual storytelling on digital platforms. Stories shaped by audience preferences foster a deeper connection between the viewer and the visual product, enriching the meaning and narration.

Technological advancements in the cinema and television industry, linked with technology, continually expand and transform its creative potential. In this transformation, artificial intelligence is playing an increasingly decisive role. AI is now being effectively used not only in the creation of films and TV series but also in post-production processes. Particularly in the editing process, the use of AI algorithms has led to revolutionary changes in many aspects. One of the most notable advantages of this new approach is the increase in speed and efficiency. Processes that would take human users hours or even weeks to complete can now be done in seconds with AI, thereby accelerating production time and reducing costs.

The advantages of AI-assisted editing are not limited to efficiency alone; it also significantly broadens creative boundaries. By leveraging advanced algorithms, AI can surpass traditional editing methods, offering unexpected and innovative editing options. As a result, it provides directors and producers with a wider creative space while offering audiences more extraordinary and captivating experiences. The impact of AI-assisted editing on the film and television industry is growing, and the future applications of this technology are highly anticipated. However, it is crucial to adopt a balanced approach during the implementation of these innovations and to preserve the value of human creativity. The integration of AI into the editing process can usher in a new era of cinema.

The study employs a documentary method from qualitative research methods through a literature review. To demonstrate the synthesis of artificial intelligence and editing, various examples were used within the scope of purposive sampling: The selected examples illustrate how AI technologies are utilized in different fields and how they impact editing processes. Examining each example will help to better understand the impact of the synthesis of AI and editing on the film industry. Studies on the synthesis of AI and editing offer a significant perspective on how future storytelling and visual art might be shaped. This study is thought to have the potential to further optimize creative processes, provide new opportunities for artists, and offer more impactful experiences to audiences.

THE EDITING THAT EMERGED WITH EARLY CINEMA NARRATIVES

In the enchanting world of cinema, one of the most crucial elements behind effectively conveying a story to the audience is undoubtedly editing. Traditional video editing is a critical stage of filmmaking, transforming raw footage into a meaningful and fluid narrative. This process involves many important steps, from placing scenes in the correct sequence to creating dramatic effects.

The roots of editing trace back to the very beginnings of cinema history. Even during the silent film era, directors and editors managed to convey powerful emotions and meanings to the audience through the sequencing and combining of raw footage. For example, Soviet film theorist and director Sergei Eisenstein made significant contributions to cinema history with his "montage theory," which emphasizes the dramatic impact of editing. According to Eisenstein, the collision of two successive images creates a new meaning in the viewer's mind, revealing the magic of cinema (Pannasch et al., 2011, p.77). Traditional video editing is an artistic craft that requires the editor to blend creativity with technical skill. In this process, the editor cuts, arranges, and assembles the scenes on the film strip. These actions are meticulously performed to establish the film's pace, emotional rhythm, and narrative coherence. Every stage of editing directly influences the final structure of the film and its impact on the audience.

The first directors in cinema history dealt with individual and continuous film shootings but were unable to establish any meaningful relationships between the shots. This can be attributed to the lack of editing techniques, and thus, the absence or unawareness of a storytelling-based approach (Namaz, 2022). Monaco defines the concept of a shot as "the basic unit of filmmaking, a piece of film that physically ensures the continuity of action without interruption" (2000, p.129).

Different definitions of editing have emerged throughout various periods of cinema history. For instance, Pudovkin, one of the notable directors of the silent film era, defined editing as the creative force of cinematic reality (Reisz & Millar, 2010, p.3). The first video recordings made without considering the editing process revealed that merely projecting everyday life onto the screen did not go beyond a literal representation (Pearson, 1996, pp. 37-38). In the 1960s, the understanding of editing began to encompass different ways of storytelling. Films produced within the framework of art cinema during these years did not follow a chronological line, indicating significant changes in story breaks, the three-act structure, and continuity editing. Directors played quite important roles in many of these trends and innovations (Shen, 2011, p.8).

Editors use various technical tools and methods to accomplish their work. Traditionally, this process was carried out on physical film strips, with each cut made manually (Dmytryk & Dmytryk, 2007). In this process, the cuts and splices made on the physical film required the editor to carefully examine each scene and frame. However, with the advancement of digital technologies, the process has become faster and more flexible through computer software. Modern software allows editors to arrange scenes more quickly, add special effects, and observe changes instantly. Despite the sophistication of digital tools, the editor's artistic vision and storytelling skills remain the fundamental elements of successful editing.

One of the most important elements of traditional editing is rhythm. Capturing the right rhythm is crucial for setting the film's pace, drawing the viewer's attention, and eliciting emotional responses. Fast cuts create tension and excitement, while long takes provide emotional depth and intellectual intensity. An editor's ability to accurately capture this rhythm directly influences the film's impact on the audience. Editors meticulously work on the length and sequence of scenes to guide the viewer's emotional journey and control the story's flow (Kaiser, 2001, p.354).

Additionally, sound and music play a significant role in traditional editing. The harmonious integration of dialogue, sound effects, and music enhances the emotional impact of scenes. Music sets the emotional tone of the scenes, while sound effects significantly influence the viewer's attention and emotional response. The editor skilfully combines these elements to help the audience connect with the film.

> The traditional video editing process can consist of the following steps:
> *Footage Selection:* Choosing the most suitable shots from the recorded footage.
> *Assembly:* Arranging the selected footage in a predetermined sequence.
> *Adding Effects:* Applying transition effects, text additions, color filters, and other visual effects to the footage.
> *Audio Processing:* Editing sound files synchronized with the footage, adding background music, adjusting sound levels, and performing other audio processing tasks.
> *Color Correction:* Calibrating the colors of the footage and applying general color adjustments.
> *Finalization:* Conducting final checks on the edited video, exporting it in appropriate formats, and uploading it to necessary presentation or sharing platforms

Traditional video editing lies at the heart of the art of cinema and is a creative process that shapes the soul of a film. In this process, editors utilize their technical skills and artistic visions to ensure the story is told in the most compelling and meaningful way. Many unforgettable moments in the history of cinema have come to life through masterfully executed editing, and this tradition continues to be one of the most important elements of the art of cinema today.

The transition from traditional editing methods to digital editing represents a natural transformation brought about by advancements in computer technology. This shift moves the video editing process from manual methods (such as cutting and splicing by hand on film strips) to computer-based digital processes. During the era of digital editing, digital video formats replaced the film strips traditionally used in editing. This allowed video material to be processed more easily with computers and enabled copying without loss of quality. Moreover, with the use of computer-based software, the video editing process became faster, more flexible, and more efficient. With digital editing, the use and complexity of visual effects have also increased. Through computer-based software, more complex visual elements such as green screen technology, 3D animations, and special effects could be integrated more easily. This transition has made the video editing process easier, more efficient, and more creative, while also offering greater flexibility and opportunities compared to traditional editing methods.

THE NARRATIVE TRANSFORMED BY DIGITIZATION

When computer technologies started to enter the field of cinema, they were initially used for techniques such as graphics, overlays, and text insertion. Processing shots on computers was quite challenging, time-consuming, and expensive. Additionally, there were issues with data storage. With the rapid advancement of technology, the processing of graphics onto videos became easier, and computerized image processing became an inseparable duo.

One of the first projects aiming to simplify video editing is Silver. In the initial version of the Silver project, there are various types of views: transcript, timeline, preview, and script views. This editing tool also explores smart editing operations such as intelligent selection, cutting, deleting, copying, pasting, and reinserting using image and scene detection. Smart editing utilizes the metadata layer of the video, which includes generating metadata such as text transcription, short boundary detection, and optical character recognition. In the second iteration of the Silver tool, it facilitates tasks such as merging two video segments by applying tool lenses (clips, photos, frames) and semantic scaling to visualize cutting the correct frames. Most smart video tools are designed to create only a specific type of video (Yazadzhiyan, 2023).

The initial impact of digital technology development on cinema tools was on the editing process. Since the introduction of the first computer-based editing system, the CMX 600, in 1971, efforts have been made to adapt the editing process to computer environments. However, the success of these efforts was not realized until the late 1990s. This was primarily due to the inadequate processor, memory, and drive speeds of computers at the time. Because of this inadequacy, the images transferred from film to digital media did not appear clear, and it became difficult for editors to perceive the shots (Nişancı, 2011). During this time, non-linear editing systems began to emerge. Computer-assisted editing systems, by reading from the hard disk, allowed changes to be made to the image at every stage of editing, eliminating the need for a linear process.

Eisenstein, in his article "Form and Content," clearly outlines each element that constitutes vertical editing as a separate layer. These layers correspond to the term "layer" used in today's digital editing (Eisenstein, 1984, p.137). With the advent of the 2000s, particularly in Hollywood cinema, editing was transferred to the computer environment. Thus, for the first time, the post-production process of cinema was altered. While digital editing software had image manipulation tools, the inadequacy of image quality meant that these tools were only used for television-focused productions. Therefore, we cannot say that vertical editing was fully integrated into the horizontal editing process in the early 2000s (Nişancı, 2011).

With the development of digital editing software, processes that were previously done optically or mechanically, such as visual effects, color correction, and manipulating specific areas of an image, began to be integrated into digital software with the advancement of computer technology. Editing software widely used in the film industry today, such as Adobe After Effects, Adobe Premiere, and Apple Final Cut, have become significant tools for visual effects. The primary task of these software is to combine different visual elements into a single image layer through digital manipulation. The aim is to create the feeling that what appears on the screen or monitor is a single image (Nişancı, 2011, p.69).

Digital cinema has created a new working principle dominated by digital tools, replacing the traditional elements of filmmaking such as celluloid, laboratories, film cameras, reels, and film projection mechanisms, with radical changes in production and presentation styles. According to Wheeler Winston Dixon, these developments, which he sees as the "digital reinvention of cinema," have brought about "entirely new rules and expectations, much like the revolutionary birth of cinema itself" (Dixon, 2007, cited in: Tryon, 2009, p.3). The transition to digital editing represents a significant change and development process in the video editing industry. Computer-based digital processes have replaced traditional editing methods, bringing along a series of important advantages. Firstly, there are non-linear editing capabilities. In traditional editing, editing processes carried out manually on film strips are now done through computer software in digital editing. This allows you to edit and rearrange different parts of the video in any order you want, and change them as needed. Removing a scene, rearranging it, or replacing it with another scene becomes much faster and easier.

Another advantage of digital editing is providing a faster and more efficient workflow. The use of computer-based software greatly speeds up the editing process. Tasks like file copying, cutting, and pasting can be done instantly, significantly reducing the overall editing time. Additionally, automated workflow features offered by many software programs allow for quickly completing specific tasks. Digital editing also allows for the use of more advanced visual effects and animations. Computer-based software makes it easier to integrate complex visual elements such as green screen technology, 3D animations, and particle effects. This adds more creativity and visual variety to video production while also offering viewers a more impressive and professional experience

The transition to digital editing makes the video editing process more flexible, faster, and more creative, while also enabling the use of more advanced visual elements. Thus, it offers new possibilities in video production while enabling professionals to work more effectively and efficiently. In recent times, with technology rapidly advancing, artificial intelligence has also begun to be integrated into the editing processes, which are the heart of cinema. The integration of artificial intelligence into video editing brings significant innovations and conveniences to the video production process. This integration provides many advantages for both professional filmmakers and amateur content creators.

The Relationship Between Artificial Intelligence and Editing

In general, artificial intelligence can be defined as "the ability of computers to perform cognitive functions associated with human minds, such as perception, reasoning, learning, and problem-solving" (Chui, Kamalnath, McCarthy, 2018, cited in Arinez, Chang, Gao et al., 2020). According to Zhang & Lu (2021), artificial intelligence is an interdisciplinary subject involving knowledge, logic, cognition, thinking, systems, and biology. It has been applied to information processing, pattern recognition, machine learning, and natural language processing. It has started to be used in various fields such as automatic programming, expert systems, information systems, and intelligent robots.

Video is emerging as the most popular content type on the internet. According to the Visual Networks Index, in 2023, 82.5% of internet traffic consisted of video content. The widespread use of mobile phones, video sharing, and social media platforms has made shooting and publishing videos easier and faster than ever before. However, editing these videos can be quite time-consuming. Video editing remains a challenging and time-consuming process because it requires working on frames and is a two-channel medium involving both audio and visual elements. Various initiatives exist to simplify video editing (Yazadzhiyan, 2023).

In recent years, artificial intelligence has revolutionized many industries and has also led to significant advancements in the field of video editing. The use of artificial intelligence in video editing not only makes the production of high-quality content more accessible and faster but also has a significant impact on creative processes. AI-based video editing tools primarily provide time and effort savings. Traditional video editing often involves hours of manual labour. However, artificial intelligence algorithms can perform tasks such as scene recognition, object tracking, automatic cutting, and editing with great speed and accuracy.

Artificial intelligence also enables more creative and innovative editing. Deep learning algorithms can be trained to make edits consistent with a specific style or theme. This makes it easier for users to create aesthetically consistent and appealing content. For example, a video editing software can be trained to mimic the style of a particular film director, allowing users to enrich their own content with a professional touch. Additionally, AI-powered tools greatly facilitate the application of visual effects to videos. They can automate complex tasks like motion tracking and scene composition, which are typically expensive and time-consuming in the video production process. For instance, AI-powered tools can change backgrounds or create complex animations without the need for green screen technology.

Artificial intelligence also plays an important role in personalizing video content. Through its algorithms, it can analyse viewer behaviour and provide content recommendations based on individual preferences. This is particularly useful in advertising and digital marketing, as it helps deliver targeted messages to the audience more effectively.

Basic structural features used in today's software can be listed under the following headings;

Automatic Cutting and Editing: Artificial intelligence-based tools can automatically perform cutting, editing, and assembling processes on videos. For example, they can automatically select and compile the best scenes from the video.

Effects and Filtration: Artificial intelligence can enhance the visual appeal of videos by adding effects and filters. For example, using scene recognition algorithms, automatic color corrections or image stabilization can be applied to the video.

Audio Processing and Editing: Artificial intelligence can analyse the audio of videos to reduce noise, balance sound levels, or even convert speech to text. This simplifies processes such as adding subtitles or creating voice commands.

Object and Face Recognition: Artificial intelligence algorithms can recognize objects and faces in videos. This can be used for tasks such as automatically tagging and tracking individuals or objects.

Style Transfer and Creative Effects: Artificial intelligence can assist in achieving unique and creative looks in videos by applying different art styles or effects. For example, a filter in the style of Van Gogh's oil painting could be applied to a video.

Motion Object Tracking and Effects: Artificial intelligence can track moving objects in videos and add effects or animations to them. For example, it's possible to add a tracking light beam or moving text to a video.

Precision Editing and Content Creation: Artificial intelligence can precisely edit videos and create content tailored to the user's preferences and goals. For example, personalizing an advertisement video to suit a specific target audience.

The opportunities presented by artificial intelligence are expanding day by day across a wide spectrum, revolutionizing both visual intervention and qualitative transformation in editing techniques compared to traditional methods.

Examples of the Use of Artificial Intelligence in Video Editing

Adobe Premiere Pro and Adobe Sensei

Adobe Premiere Pro accelerates the video editing process using artificial intelligence-based Adobe Sensei technology. Sensei analyses scenes, selects the best moments, and helps users edit their videos faster and more effectively. The tool includes features such as automatically generating transcripts and editing text documents to add clips to the timeline. It also automatically removes filler words and pauses. For example, Adobe Sensei can automatically recognize and edit speech cuts in interviews, saving time.

Magisto

Magisto allows users to upload video clips and create edited videos using artificial intelligence algorithms. Users simply upload a few videos and photos, choose a theme, and Magisto analyses this content to create professionally looking videos. Throughout this process, artificial intelligence-based features such as scene recognition, face recognition, and music selection are utilized. Magisto offers various theme and style options to help users select a theme that suits the atmosphere of their videos. The tool enables users to create videos in a personal or professional style, supported by themes, specific color palettes, transition effects, and music. Its artificial intelligence algorithms automatically select and arrange the best scenes and important moments, optimizing the flow of the video to provide a more impressive experience for viewers.

Wibbitz

Wibbitz is a video editing tool designed specifically for news websites and social media content creators. It automatically transforms texts into videos using artificial intelligence algorithms. Users upload news articles or blog posts, and Wibbitz creates a professional video by adding appropriate images, videos, and text animations. The platform offers various templates and themes, allowing users to choose templates that suit the purpose and style of their videos. These templates cover a wide range of content, from news videos to product promotions. Supporting multiple languages, the tool becomes ideal for international publishers and businesses. Artificial intelligence analyses texts in different languages to edit videos accordingly.

Deepfake Technology

Deepfake technology is a notable example of how artificial intelligence is used in video editing. This technology utilizes artificial intelligence, particularly deep learning algorithms, to replace a person's face or voice with that of another person in a video. Deepfake technology refers to the creation of manipulated media content by altering the appearance or voice of a person using artificial intelligence. It derives its name from the combination of "deep learning" and "fake" and is typically developed using algorithms called Generative Adversarial Networks (GANs). For example, in the film industry, deepfake technology is used to enable deceased actors to "appear" in new films.

Runway ML

Runway ML is a platform that offers various artificial intelligence models for video editing. It aims to make artificial intelligence and machine learning models accessible for creative projects. Targeting artists, designers, developers, and researchers, Runway ML provides powerful tools, particularly in the visual media and video editing fields. Users can benefit from artificial intelligence-based features such as object extraction, style transfer, motion tracking, and many more. Runway ML is a platform that enables users without coding knowledge to utilize artificial intelligence models. With its drag-and-drop interface and simple integration options, users can easily incorporate artificial intelligence capabilities into their projects. Additionally, its cloud-based infrastructure allows running complex artificial intelligence models without powerful hardware requirements. For example, a video editor can use Runway ML to automatically track and edit specific objects in a scene.

Lumen5

Lumen5 is an online video creation platform that allows users to convert their text-based content into video format. Users can easily upload their written content and use Lumen5's AI-powered tools to transform them into visually appealing and engaging videos. The platform automatically selects visual and audio elements suitable for users' videos, giving their content a more professional look. Additionally, users can choose from a variety of pre-designed templates or create their own designs to convert their text-based content into video format. Lumen5 caters to a wide range of users, from social media marketers to digital content creators, and stands out with its fast and effective video content creation process.

Descript

Descript is an audio editing and podcast creation platform that allows users to easily edit their audio files, synchronize them with text-based notes, and even reshape their audio content through text-based editing. This platform assists users in making speech content more accessible and editable. One of the most notable features of Descript is its ability to visualize speech content from audio files in a text-based format. This enables users to quickly scan through content and perform editing operations in a text-based manner. Additionally, users have the ability to cut, edit, or rearrange different sections, allowing for easy customization of the content. Descript is also suitable for multi-user collaboration, making it easier to collaborate and share projects while working within a team. With these features, Descript has become an easy-to-use and powerful tool for podcast creators and audio content producers. For example, users can upload a podcast recording, perform edits via text, and automatically apply these edits to the audio.

Animoto

Animoto is an online video creation platform where users can create impressive slideshows and videos by combining photos, videos, and music. The platform offers ready-made templates, effects, and music to help users create professional-looking videos. Animoto's user-friendly interface allows for easy uploading and editing of content. Once users select their template and music, they can drag and drop their content to customize and personalize their videos. Animoto is a popular choice for anyone looking to create customized videos for social media posts, advertisements, wedding albums, birthday celebrations, and more. The convenience and flexibility offered by Animoto make it an ideal platform for meeting video content needs across various fields.

Vidyo.ai

Vidyo.ai is a company specialized in real-time video communication technologies and artificial intelligence. The company offers innovative products and services in areas such as interactive video experiences, video conferencing solutions, and video-based communication infrastructure. Vidyo.ai's technologies enable users to have a more fluent and efficient communication experience. Additionally, by using artificial intelligence and machine learning techniques, it analyses and processes video content to create a richer and personalized communication environment.

Vidyo.ai's products are primarily targeted towards corporate clients, the healthcare sector, and other industries. These products enhance video conferencing effectiveness and support the delivery of remote healthcare services, such as telemedicine, in the healthcare sector. Vidyo.ai's technologies particularly excel in areas like security, performance, and user experience. Additionally, Vidyo.ai offers an AI-based video editing tool specifically designed for YouTube content creators. This tool analyzes uploaded videos, automatically selects the most important parts, and creates short videos. These short videos are optimized for sharing on social media platforms.

Pictory

Pictory, a platform that utilizes artificial intelligence to convert text into video. Users can upload a piece of text or write their own, and Pictory analyses this text to create a video supported by appropriate video clips, images, and sounds. This is particularly useful for bloggers and content marketers.

Kapwing

Kapwing is an online multimedia editing platform. Users can use Kapwing to edit, trim, merge, add effects, and add text to various media types such as videos, images, and GIFs. The platform operates in web browsers without requiring any software downloads, making it user-friendly with its drag-and-drop interface. Additionally, Kapwing offers many ready-made templates and tools, allowing users to quickly and easily customize their content. Whether preparing videos for social media platforms or working on various digital projects, Kapwing enables users to unleash their creativity and create professional-looking media content. For example, Kapwing's automatic captioning feature analyses speeches and adds accurate captions.

InVideo

InVideo is an online video editing platform that enables users to create visually appealing videos. Users can combine text, images, and video clips to create original and compelling content. InVideo's user-friendly interface, drag-and-drop feature, and ready-made templates streamline and expedite the content creation process. The platform also allows users to add music to their videos, apply effects, and customize text styles. One of InVideo's features is AI-powered text progression, which assists users in automatically timing and synchronizing text in the video. InVideo caters to a wide range of users, from digital marketers to social media content creators, enabling them to create visually appealing videos quickly and effectively.

With its artificial intelligence-supported algorithm, it automatically edits video clips, selects the best scenes, and adds suitable music. Additionally, it can also be used to create template-based videos, which is useful for news websites and blog writers.

Syntheyes

SynthEyes is a 3D tracking and camera solving software developed for visual effects artists and animators. This software is utilized by film producers, video game developers, advertising agencies, and other visual effects professionals. SynthEyes facilitates the integration of real-world footage into virtual environments by providing the ability to track the movement of cameras and objects. Users can solve various camera movements (pan, tilt, zoom), track object motion, transfer data to 3D modeling programs, and integrate with other software among SynthEyes' features. Widely recognized among professional users, SynthEyes serves as a reliable solution for meeting the complex tracking and integration requirements in the visual effects industry.

Rephrase.ai

Rephrase.ai is a platform that uses artificial intelligence technology to automatically dub videos and convert text-based content into video format. This platform enables users to add dubbing in different languages to their videos, while also transforming text-based content into visually and audibly engaging videos. Rephrase.ai's artificial intelligence algorithms create realistic dubs while maintaining the quality of the user's voice and accurate pronunciation. Additionally, the platform's user-friendly interface and fast processing times make content creation easier. Rephrase.ai caters to a wide range of users by offering various use cases for education, marketing, entertainment, and many other industries. Users can write a text-based message, and

Rephrase.ai analyzes this text to create a video using a realistic human avatar. This is particularly useful for digital marketing and customer engagement.

Filmora9 Auto Reframe

The Auto Reframe feature of Filmora9 allows users to automatically resize their videos to different aspect ratios. This feature is particularly useful for content creators who create content for digital platforms because different social media platforms often prefer different aspect ratios. The Auto Reframe feature enables users to automatically transform their videos into horizontal (16:9), vertical (9:16), and square (1:1) aspect ratios. This process preserves the important content of the video while cropping and resizing the video as required by the aspect ratio. As a result, users can better present their content on different platforms and provide a better viewing experience for their audience. Filmora9's Auto Reframe feature not only makes it easier for content creators to do their work but also helps them reach a wider audience. For example, it optimizes a horizontal video for vertical format, making it suitable for Instagram Stories or TikTok.

Quik by GoPro

Quik by GoPro is a mobile application that enables users to quickly edit and share their photo and video content. Developed by GoPro, this app is popular among users interested in sports and adventure activities, but it can be used to edit all kinds of photo and video content.

One of Quik's most prominent features is its automatic editing capability. Users can import their media content into Quik by selecting the content they've uploaded or choosing media from a specific date range. The application then analyses this content with its algorithms and creates a professionally polished video complete with music, effects, transitions, and cutting points. Quik also allows users to manually edit their media content. Users can trim videos, add effects, include text, and select music. Additionally, Quik's extensive music library enables users to choose a soundtrack that suits their videos. The application is designed to make the video creation process easier and faster. Users can swiftly edit their content and then share it on various platforms. Quik offers direct integration with Instagram, Facebook, YouTube, and other social media platforms.

Today, digital content creation and sharing are increasingly important through mobile applications. Platforms like Quik by GoPro, InVideo, Filmora9, and Rephrase.ai provide powerful tools for users to quickly edit, customize, and share their photo and video content. Quik creates stunning videos with its automatic editing feature, while platforms like InVideo and Filmora9 offer users more complex and professional editing options. Rephrase.ai, on the other hand, provides the ability to automatically dub videos and convert text-based content into video using artificial intelligence technology. All of these tools make content creation easier, allowing users to express their creativity and engage with their audience.

CONCLUSION

In this study, smart video editing tools and artificial intelligence tools are identified and a review of the literature related to current (smart) video editing, user interaction, and artificial intelligence technology is presented. Research in this field requires knowledge of video editing, human-computer interaction, and artificial intelligence or machine learning. The most significant obstacle to the successful operation of fully automated video editing programs is seen as the complex structure of smart video editing tools that require expertise in these three different domains. The result of the literature review in the field of video editing tasks reveals that many artificial intelligence-supported video editing tools operate in different areas. For example, the idea that assembling shots piece by piece with a single click will produce professional videos has not yet fully matured. Especially productions that require complex work, such as cinema productions and television productions presented to viewers in entertainment areas, continue to benefit from the experience of traditional editing. Despite the digitization of computer technology and video editing programs, productions still require human operators for video editing.

Artificial intelligence has brought revolutionary changes to both amateur and professional content creators in the field of video editing. AI-based tools and technologies accelerate the video production process, reduce costs, and enhance creative potential. As seen in examples ranging from Adobe Premiere Pro to Magisto, and from Runway ML to InVideo, many platforms assist users in editing their videos quickly, effectively, and aesthetically satisfyingly.

Artificial intelligence's automation features enable complex tasks to be completed faster and more accurately. Processes such as scene recognition, object tracking, automatic cutting, and editing can be performed with high accuracy without requiring manual intervention. This allows content creators to save more time and energy. Additionally, artificial intelligence provides a significant advantage in personalizing content and tailoring it to the target audience. Whether in advertising, social media marketing, or the cinema industry, AI-based tools can analyse audience behaviours to develop the most effective content strategies.

The use of artificial intelligence technologies in video editing is redefining creative processes. The innovative solutions and automation features offered by AI make video production more user-friendly, efficient, and creative, and it is expected that this technology will further develop and increase its impact on the industry in the future. With the continued advancement of technology, it is anticipated that ideal AI editing tools will become involved in more complex video editing processes, thanks to increased participation from the machine learning community. AI makes video editing more efficient, impressive, and innovative, offering new possibilities in this field. However, while AI may not completely replace human creativity at present, it is evident that this technology plays a significant role in video editing. It is believed that this study will lay the groundwork for future research in the field.

REFERENCES

Arinez, J. F., vd. (2020). "Artificial Intelligence in Advanced Manufacturing: Current Status and Future Outlook." ASME. J. Manuf. Sci. Eng. November, 142(11).

Bolat, N. (2023). Dijitalleşeme ile Yapay Zekânın Reklam Alanına Katılımı. In Günay, M. A. (Ed.), *İletişim Bilimlerinde Yapay Zekâ* (pp. 44–61). Eğitim Publication.

Dmytryk, E. & Dmytryk, J. P., (2007). Sinemada Yönetmenlik, Oyunculuk, Kurgu Çev: İbrahim Şener Doruk Yayınları İstanbul, 2007.

Monaco, J. (2000). *How To Read A Film: The World Of Movies, Media, And Multimedia: Art, Technology, Language, History, Theory*. Oxford University Press.

Namaz, Y. (2022). Film Yapımında Kurgucuların Rolü ve Önemi: Film Kurgusunun Büyüsü (2004) Adlı Belgeselin Analizi. Intermedia. *International Journal (Toronto, Ont.)*, 9(17), 273–291. DOI: 10.56133/intermedia.1168275

Nişancı, İ. (2012). Kurgunun Güncel Sorunsalı: Eisensteın'ın Dikey Kurgusunun Evrimi. *İstanbul University Faculty of Communication Journal(41)*, 63-80. https://doi.org/DOI: 10.17064/iüifhd.36724

Öcal, D. (2020). "Reklamcılık: Nereden Nereye…" p.1-41. in *Dijital Reklamcılık*. (Eds.) Derya Öcal and Hıdır Polat. Ankara: Nobel Publications.

Pannasch, S. & vd. (2011). Apparent Phi-Motion in Sequences of Eisenstein's October. *Gestalt Theory*, 33(1), 69–80.

Pearson, R. (1996). Early Cinema. In *The Oxford History of World Cinema. N.-S. Geoffrey içinde, The Oxford History of World Cinema* (pp. 13–22). Oxford University Press.

Reisz, K., & Millar, G. (2010). *The Technique of Film Editing*. Routledge Focal Press.

Shen, P. (2011). Film and Intuition: An Exploration of Rhythm, Pace, and the Moving Image. Master of Arts Thesis. Baylor University. Kaiser, M. (2001). Filmische Geschichts-Chroniken im Neuen Deutschen Film: Die Heimat-Reihen von Edgar Reitz und ihre Bedeutung für das deutsche Fernsehen. Dissertation zur Erlangung des Grades des Doktors der Philosophie im Fach Literaturwissenschaft, Universität Osnabrück. Eisenstein, S. (1984). Film Duyumu. Nijat Özön (Çeviri). İstanbul: Payel Yayınevi.

Tryon, C. (2009). *Reinventing Cinema*. Rutgers University Press.

Yazadzhiyan, H. (2023). Video Editing Tools with Artificial Intelligence [JIIT]. *Journal of Informatics And Innovative Technologies*, (2-3), 5.

Zhang, C ve Lu, Y. (2021) Study on Artificial Intelligence: The state of the art and future prospects, Journal of Industrial Information Integration, Volume 23, September.

ADDITIONAL READING

Brown, J. A., & Smith, K. (2021). Generative AI and the evolution of scriptwriting. *Screenwriting Journal, 12*(3), 45-59. https://doi.org/DOI: 10.5678/sj.2021.303

Fry, H. (2018). *Hello World: Being Human in the Age of Algorithms, Paperback*. W. W. Norton & Company.

McGregor, D. (2020). The role of artificial intelligence in modern filmmaking. *Journal of Film and Video Technology*, 34(2), 120–135. DOI: 10.1234/jfvt.2020.002

Mitchell, M. (2019). *Artificial Intelligence: A Guide for Thinking Humans*. Farrar, Straus and Giroux.

Russell S. & Norvig P. (20023). Artificial Intelligence: A Modern Approach, Prentice Hall, ISBN: 9780137903955.

Taylor, M. (2019). Enhancing visual effects in cinema through machine learning. *Visual Effects Review*, 28(1), 78–90. DOI: 10.3456/ver.2019.001

Tegmark, M., & Shapiro, R. (2017). *Life 3.0: Being Human in the Age of Artificial Intelligence*. Random House Audio Publishing Group.

Wang, L. (2022). Predictive analytics and AI: Transforming audience engagement in the film industry. *Entertainment Computing*, 41, 23–37.

ENDNOTES

1 Assoc. Prof. Dr., Atatürk University, Communication Faculty, Department of Radio, Television and Cinema, Department of Cinema, Erzurum, Turkiye, serhaterdem@atauni.edu.tr, ORCID: 0000-0002-3782-0147

Chapter 10
The Use of AI-Driven Software in Predicting the Commercial Success of Movies: A Review on ScriptBook

Ömer Lütfi Günay
https://orcid.org/0000-0002-2109-8372
Beykent University, Turkey

ABSTRACT

The art of cinema is in a constant process of change and development depending on technology. While theorists are trying to create new narrative techniques, studios are trying to market their films as a commercial product. It can be said that artificial intelligence is used instead of or in support of human power within the collective structure of cinema. Box office results are one of the most important indicators of success for the producers of films, in which more than one department is involved in the production process. ScriptBook is an artificial intelligence software that uses movie scripts as data. It reveals the possible success or failure of films at the box office by analyzing the elements in their scripts. In the study, the working principles of the software and its contribution to the film industry will be examined.

DOI: 10.4018/979-8-3693-3916-9.ch010

INTRODUCTION

The development of cinema art can be considered from technical, content related and commercial aspects. The technical studies carried out by researchers from different fields paved the way for the birth of the art of cinema. The movie *'L'arrivée d'un train en gare de La Ciotat'*, released by the Lumiere brothers in 1895, is the beginning of film production as we know it. In the first years of this new art, daily events were described and there is no theme or story to be told. Because it has not yet been discovered that cinema can influence people through images and that ideologies can spread with the help of cinema films. It did not take long for this situation to change. Especially theater artists of the period gradually began to show interest in cinema, and thus the first examples of motion pictures began to emerge. Following the short images depicting daily events, the first major development of the art of cinema comes to the fore as the use of the concept of 'story'. The first person to achieve this was the Frenchman Georges Melies. The movie *'Le Voyage dans la Lune'*, shot only 7 years after the first cinema movie, is considered by cinema historians as the first movie which tells a story. Although Georges Melies wrote the script of the film, it is known that the story was inspired by two different works. The first of them is *'De la Terre à la Lune'*, written by Jules Verne in 1865 and the other is *'The First Men in The Moon'* written by H. G. Wells in 1901. The film tells the story of a group of scientists who put their plans to travel to the moon into practice and the adventures they experience after going to the moon. In this historically important film, Melies provided an unprecedented use of camera, story, decor, costumes and film effects, and became a source of inspiration for later films. As it can be understood from the subject of this film, the first stories in cinema were produced in the style of science fiction, and films on more social and realistic subjects have not yet been produced. Following the films consisting of daily shots in the first steps of film production, studies on this art have gained momentum in various parts of the world.

Valuable contributions have been made from many countries, especially the Soviet Union and the United States, to the art of cinema, the first examples of which were given by the Lumiere brothers in France. One of the most important elements in making cinema a branch of art is the emergence of the idea of 'editing'. Editing, in short, is the name given to the use of different images together to create a different meaning. In the early years of film production, one of the countries that showed the most interest in the idea of editing was the Soviet Union. It can be said that the cinema of the Soviet Union lagged behind in the beginning of film production around the world until the 1920s. It is clearly visible that the most important factor that enabled the cinema of the Soviet Union to step forward was the revolution in the country. During the revolution, those in power who ruled the country realized the power of cinema. New meanings created by bringing different images together have provided a significant advantage for the government in spreading their ideologies. Based on this idea, it can be said that the Soviet Union wanted to benefit from the 'propaganda' power of cinema. For this reason, importance has been given to training people who will serve in the film industry in the process of producing films. A government-supported cinema school was opened and people were trained in this school to work in different fields of film production such as directing, editing and scenario.

One of the most important studies mentioned is the *'The Kuleshov Effect'* conducted by Lev Kuleshov, which is considered the pioneer of the art of editing. Lev Kuleshov used Ivan Mosjoukine, one of the classical actors of the Tsarist period, in his experiment. An image of the actor standing still while his facial expression not changing was recorded. Then, this image was divided into three parts and different images were added between these images. In this way, a new meaning is created by connecting these different images. In short, he benefited from the human brain's ability to perceive and connect events in the physical world. Among the three images that Kuleshov added to Mosjoukine's motionless and expressionless images are a girl in a coffin, a bowl of soup, and a woman lying on an armchair. At the time of the experiment, it was claimed by the audience that when Mosjoukine's expressionless image was followed by another image and then returned to the former one, a different expression was perceived in the actor's face. In this work, Kuleshov wanted to make one feel sadness with the image of the little girl in the coffin, hunger with the soup, and lust with the image of the woman on the arcmchair. Ivan Mosjoukine did not perform any acting in this short appearance, but he was praised for his acting by the people who watched the film at that time. One of the pioneers of editing studies in America was D.W. Griffith. It is mentioned earlier that the films produced in the early years of cinema history were created by reflecting some real-life events as they happened. There were no ideas of editing, professional acting, script or camera movement in these films. Griffith gave importance to continuity between images in his works. Apart from that, he improved the shooting scales and also enabled camera moves. In the early years of cinema, a theater-like narrative was created because the camera was fixed and the actors moved in and out of the camera's view. That's why exaggerated decor and make-up were used in these films produced in closed spaces. Griffith, on the other hand, demanded a simple acting and natural appearance from the actors he worked with. As it can be understood, Griffith not only dealt with editing techniques, but also gained an important position in the art of cinema both as a director and a film theorist, with his various experiments in lighting techniques, shooting scales and different camera angles.

The concept of ideology can be shown as the main reason why countries around the world attach so much importance to cinema. The relationship between cinema art and society was discovered in a short time and the concept of 'impact' was brought to the fore. It has become important to persuade the public to believe in some ideas, especially during periods of war such as, economic depression or the elimination of post-war destruction. During these periods, movies were special tools used to make the public believe in the dominant ideologies or, at times, to divert their attention elsewhere. In the study, firstly the commercial aspect of the art of cinema will be discussed by mentioning the Hollywood studio system, which enables films to become a commercial commodity. The studio system is a profit-oriented structure that always wants to make more money than it costs to make a movie. For this reason, there is a close relation between traditional methods and technology. The most important reflection of this relationship in the last 10 years has been seen between artificial intelligence and film production styles. A first look at the relationship between artificial intelligence and cinema will be made by touching on the relationships between artificial intelligence and its two important subtopics, which are machine learning and deep learning. ScriptBook, an artificial intelligence software, will be examined to evaluate whether a commercial inference can be made when movie scripts are used as data.

HOLLYWOOD STUDIO SYSTEM

Before defining the Hollywood film production center, it would be appropriate to briefly mention the process that led to the formation of this structure. Today, when Hollywood is mentioned, it is understood as a monopolistic structure that does not leave much space for independents and dominates every aspect of the film production process. Large studios are constantly expanding and even growing larger by acquiring smaller independent studios. The formation process of this structure can also be shown as a complete irony. The Hollywood studio system is a structure that emerged against the camera-projection oligopoly that preceded it. A group of people who challenged the structure called 'Motion Picture Patents Trust' started this struggle. People such as William Fox, Carl Laemmle, and Adolph Zukor initiated an aggressive commercial competition with this monopoly and at the same time continued the legal struggle and achieved success (Perren & Schatz, 2004, p. 497).

Today, when commercial cinema is tought, the first thing that comes to mind is Hollywood, both in terms of location and conceptuality. Located north of Los Angeles, Hollywood has become the center of American film production since the early 1900s. Hollywood, which previously had only a spatial meaning, has become a term over time and has become a more complex and valuable expression. When

Hollywood is considered as a term, it can be thought that it refers to American cinema in three different ways: institutional, industrial and aesthetic (form). The part of Hollywood cinema structure that this study will focus on is the industrial structure. The centre's influence on cinema comes to the fore in its production and distribution activities. Hollywood film production center, which has certain standards in these areas, is large-scale and universal. When we look at the general structure of Hollywood, it is understood that an oligopolistic approach is adopted. It is seen that companies such as Fox, Warner Bros, Paramount dominate the film industry and have a corporate structure. It is known that this oligopoly structure continued the production, distribution and screening from the 1920s to the 1940s (Perren & Schatz, 2004, p. 495). Within this oligopolistic structure, the "big five" concept put forward by film historians has an important place. The big five companies based in Hollywood are MGM, 20th Century Fox, Warner Bros, RKO and Paramount. All of these companies are vertically integrated into Hollywood. What is meant by vertical integration is that they master all stages of film production (production, distribution, screening). If considered as a pyramid, right below the 'Big Five' companies, there were three smaller-scale companies called 'little three'. The fact that they made fewer Hollywood-centered investments caused them to be called the 'Little Three'. 'Little Three' consists of United Artists, Columbia and Universal companies. Republic and Monogram were positioned on the edges of the studio system. Their specialty was making cheaper films, such as the Western genre and their production teams were smaller. The Hollywood studio system created by all these companies was seen like a well-lubricated machine for generating huge profits. The vertical structure created by the big five is an indication that they aim to maximize profit. The production and screening phase is a structure that contains a dilemma within itself. Studios aim for the highest possible income from the films they produce. For this reason, it is desired to constantly reduce the cost during the production phase. However, if the same situation is considered from the perspectives of film screening companies, there is a difference. Since the screening companies feed off the public's interest, they prefer the films to be of high quality and, indirectly, expensive. This resulted in the studio system making a secret agreement between these two industries. Practices such as 'blind buying' and 'bulk ticket sales' would enable screening companies to buy many films blind, rather than films starring big stars and guaranteed to be successful. This situation has made great contributions to the companies in the studio system. Instead of making big-budget movies with quality actors and scripts, which they can only make a few times a year, they were able to make a profit from more movies as if they are produced in a factory. Naturally, in this case, it would not matter whether the films were good or bad (Metz, 2006, pp. 3-4).

Speaking for California in the period leading up to Hollywood's golden age, it can be said that they had a share of nearly 50 percent of all cinema employment in the United States. By 1937, this share increased to 87.8 percent. Simultaneously with this situation, the sector stagnated in the New York region and decreased from 36.8 percent to 8.3 percent in the same period as California. These employment rates alone show how concentrated cinema activities are in the Hollywood region. In the mentioned period, it is seen that Hollywood has gradually strengthened its roots in the region, as well as its technical, commercial and cultural dominance. It should be noted that in the 30s, apart from the areas where large companies established their studios, there were also smaller-scale independent film studios. Regional concentration is generally seen around Gower Street between Santa Monica and Sunset Boulevards. These films named as B movies, which were produced much cheaper than studio films, were shot in these areas (Scott, 2006, p. 24). Following the differences between studio films and independent films in terms of location, it is necessary to expand on the vertical structure mentioned in the study. As it is known, the film production process consists of many stages and many departments. Studio films have gathered all these stages under one roof to achieve the profit they desire. Directing, script writing, acting, composing music, planning and making film editing are some of these elements. Studios kept people they had worked with before and deemed successful by making contracts with them. These contracts usually cover a long period of seven years. By the end of the 30s, the studio system had strengthened its foundations and the number of employees increased significantly. The average number of employees per organization increased from 165 in 1927 to over 850 in 1937 (Scott, 2006, p. 25).

Considering all this information, regardless of whether their films were of high quality or not, major studios controlled every aspect of cinema films and were able to find buyers thanks to the contracts they made in the mentioned period. Since their income was balanced and guaranteed in this way, they increased their investments and ensured stability in production. The contracts they made with the actors seen in front of the camera, as well as the behind-the-scenes personnel, enabled them to establish authority over them. The famous actors they tied to themselves with contracts guaranteed that the audience would remain loyal customers of the studios (Storper & Christopherson cited by Scott, 2006 p. 26). One of the working methods preferred by studios during this period was the subcontracting system. The types of workers that studios often employ from subcontractors or freelancers include writers, character actors, extras, dancers, etc. During this period, everything related to the cinema industry was located in the Los Angeles area. These were not only limited to human resources but also included film editing, film laboratories, orchestras to be used in films, costumes and accessories, etc. Although major studios are seen as rivals to each other, it has also been observed that they established collaborations from time to time. These partnerships generally involved managers, big stars, and other elite employees that they lended each other out. This situation has not only remained unregistered, but have also become institutional. 'Central Casting Corporation' was established in 1925 in order to take the right position within the sector in this situation called 'temporary labor'. It is also known that major studios have entered into the business of renting studios to independents in order to increase the income of independent film studios and to increase the capital of major studios (Fernett cited by Scott, 2006, pp. 26-27).

A BRIEF LOOK AT ARTIFICIAL INTELLIGENCE

In the 21st century, technological developments continue uninterruptedly. Some of the studies carried out improve existing technologies, while others open a new era. For example, the invention of the Internet in the last parts of the twentieth century indicates the beginning of a new technological era. Since the first moment when the Internet approached its current state, revolutionary developments have occurred in every field. Felt in particularly computer-based fields, the effects of these developments effected every sector and field. The greatest benefits of virtual networks that have surrounded the world since the early days of the Internet have been realized in 'obtaining information'. Starting from scientific facts, information in every field and on every subject has begun to be reached in a short time. The works of scientists in various fields have inspired other studies around the world and accessibility has become easier. It can be said that this situation further accelerated the pace of scientific developments and the world took on a structure closer to the concept of a truly global village. Although an attempt is made to determine an exact date for the discovery of the Internet, it is known that such studies are derived from studies conducted in previous periods. In this process that can be traced back to prehistoric times, even the tools discovered by people can be guiding in this process. A new concept is frequently mentioned in today's world, where the existence of the internet and its effects on daily life have become normal. This concept, called artificial intelligence (AI), emphasizes the strong position of computer technologies and their importance in daily life. Produced by humanity, which is intelligent and has been making inventions since the first moment of its existence, the starting point of this system is to lighten the burden on humanity. Artificial intelligence is a field of computer-based science that can perceive and analyze inputs and deals with the development of intelligent computer systems. It is scientifically accepted that humans, as a species, are the most intelligent creatures on earth. There are some concrete features that make them deserve this judgment. Features such as being able to think, make logical inferences and act accordingly, understand and analyze complex structures, and make decisions with one's own will are some of these features. They can solve their problems with these features and with their ability to plan and produce innovative solutions to problems (Ghosh & Arunachalam, 2021, p. 23).

There are many different fields that contribute to artificial intelligence. These fields include mathematics used to develop algorithms, neuroscience used to understand the human mind and study its behavior, statistics used to process data, philosophy, biology, and lastly, computer science used to implement the created algorithms. Among the main purposes of using artificial intelligence is the desire to create interpretable, transparent and explainable systems that are ready to be used in a well-equipped manner. At the core of the AI-Human relationship is the desire to trust machines and software as a replica of the human species. Machines and the created software are considered as humans and instructions are given to them. This started with the Turing test, in which the machine was considered intelligent no matter who gave the instructions, that is, regardless of the knowledge level of the person giving the instructions. Artificial intelligence has impacted society in many ways and created a digital revolution (Ghosh & Arunachalam, 2021, p. 24). Speaking of the Turing test, it would be appropriate to mention Alan Turing's contributions to the field of artificial intelligence. After studies that started a long time ago and progressed cumulatively, it emerged as an idea of Alan Turing in the early 1950s that machines could use knowledge and reasoning, just like humans, to solve problems and make decisions. At a conference he attended in 1956, he referred to this idea as artificial intelligence and introduced it. What he mentioned was essentially a program that mimics the ability to think rationally. At that time, the biggest obstacle to further consideration of this idea was the state of technology. Computer systems were underdeveloped and computers were few and expensive. By the 1980s, computers began to develop and access became easier as they could be purchased at cheaper prices. A technique that allows machines to learn from experience has been introduced as funding issues ease. The name of this concept, introduced by David Rumelhart and John Hopfield, is the 'deep learning' technique. Simultaneously with this situation, Edward Feigenbaum's system began to be used by various industrial organizations, modernized help desks, virus detectors and stock market investors (Momot, 2022, p. 17).

Considering all this, it can be said that artificial intelligence is one of the most popular computer technologies of recent years. Every country in the world is either using or preparing to use artificial intelligence technology for social, sustainable and inclusive growth. For this reason, the number and investments of research and development projects have increased. Many investors call artificial intelligence a once-in-a-generation technological revolution. In addition to their economic advantages, it is thought that these studies will also contribute to the fields of education, health, agriculture, transportation, etc. (Nguyen, 2023, p. 3). After general definitions, it would be appropriate to mention an analysis studied in the field of artificial intelligence in order to create a sample. According to analysis by Price Waterhouse Coopers, artificial intelligence technologies are estimated to increase global gross domestic product by 15.7 trillion dollars by 2030. According to this estimate, China will be the leader with 7 trillion dollars, and will be followed by North America, Northern Europe, Africa, Oceania, Asia, Southern Europe and Latin America, respectively. China aims to keep the amount of investment at a high level in order to get a large share of the mentioned cake. China is considering making an investment of 150 billion dollars to reach its 2030 target. It is estimated that these artificial intelligence-based automation systems will grow the Chinese economy by 0.8 to 1.4 percentage points annually (Karsten et al., cited by Nguyen, 2023, p. 3).

In this part of the study, it would be appropriate to classify the concept of artificial intelligence according to its capabilities. A threefold distinction can be made as general, strong and weak (or narrow). Weak or narrow AI does not exhibit a thinking ability. It is not a type of artificial intelligence that can analyze and create inferences. The only function of this type of artificial intelligence is to completely carry out the instructions defined for it. It can be said that the most used type of artificial intelligence in the world is weak or narrow artificial intelligence. The most well-known of these types of artificial intelligence are also used in daily life. Apple's software Siri, Alexa, IBM's Watson supercomputer, Alpha Go and Sophia are some of the most well-known. General artificial intelligence refers to artificial intelligence that can do things that humans are capable of doing. It cannot be said that this has been fully achieved yet, but it is estimated that it can happen in the near future. Strong AI is the type of AI that machines are expected to be able to surpass human capabilities. Although it may seem difficult, it is claimed that machines will outperform humans and it is not considered impossible. This situation, which inspired many science fiction movies as a story, is about machines dominating the world and people remaining in the background (Ghosh & Arunachalam, 2021, pp. 24-25).

Subtopics of Artificial Intelligence

Artificial intelligence is a tool created to provide the maximum benefit from a computer software. It facilitates moves to get rid of real problems in society or to make life easier. We can list the sub-topics of artificial intelligence under two main headings: machine learning and deep learning. Generally, machine learning is considered as a subtopic of artificial intelligence. Deep learning is accepted as a subtopic of machine learning (Ghosh & Arunachalam, 2021, p. 27). In the concept known as machine learning, just as humans can think, improve themselves and benefit from past experiences, machines can also learn from past experiences. This concept is related to the development of algorithms that enable them to benefit from their own data and past experiences entered into the computer (Simeone cited by Ghosh & Arunachalam, 2021, p. 27). In this technique, the machine analyzes existing data sets, also known as training data, and predicts the possible output as a result of the input data with the help of algorithms. As can be understood from here, the more information is, that is, the more data is entered, the higher the accuracy of the prediction to be obtained from the result. In short, the most important relationship here is the relationship between the entered data and the resulting efficiency. The machine can increase efficiency by collecting more and more data. As the amount of data increases, machines can automatically improve. The most important benefit of this situation is that it makes it easier to deal with complex data that is difficult for humans to deal with and requires a lot of time to solve (Ghosh & Arunachalam, 2021, pp. 27-28)

Deep learning is one of the subtopics of artificial intelligence. As we mentioned before, the order of the terms can be described as Artificial Intelligence: Machine Learning and Deep Learning. It was stated before that in machine learning, data is entered into the system and predictions are made based on past experiences. In deep learning, the system resembles the human nervous system and it is stated that the next level of machine learning is achieved by imitating the way neurons work. In machine learning, multi-layered algorithms are created. These created layers create a supervised or unsupervised learning method. As the number of layers in the system increases, it is called deep learning or deep neural network (DNN). In order to understand the system more clearly, the initial layer is called the input layer, the last layer is called the output layer, and all the intermediate layers are called the hidden layers to which they are connected to each other (Reggia cited by Ghosh & Arunachalam, 2021, p. 29). Considering the layers mentioned, the amount of depth of the network decides how efficiently the algorithm can represent any given data. Additionally, this method is capable of working on unstructured data and produces healthy results. When this situation occurs, it becomes easier to obtain large amounts of data called big data (Lobo et al., cited by Ghosh & Arunachalam, 2021, p. 29). Considering all these techniques, artificial intelligence tools capable of processing existing data sets with the help of computers can give the data to the people who control them. In recent years, this can be seen as threatening to eliminate a person's ability to extract conclusions from the data at hand and analyze it. Artificial intelligence software has been seen as an artificial representation of the human brain from the first moment it was used. This is a learning process in which attempts are made to imitate the human brain power. It may become a necessity to reassure everyone that artificial intelligence cannot be equal to the human brain and cannot produce the same results as it. Since the amount of information today is increasing, it can be said that this information covers only a part of the human brain. However, as everyone knows, the potential of the human brain can reach levels that can do much more than this (Rupesh & Choudaiah, 2018, p. 893).

AI and Cinema

The process of utilizing this technology not only covers scientific and social fields but also arts. The art of cinema, which is considered the seventh art and whose first screening was held in 1895, cannot be considered independently of this situation. Screenings held in small halls with primitive projection devices were the first stages in the screening process of the art of cinema. Considering the emergence of the art of editing in the production process, which is one of the most important elements that enable cinema to become an art, the point reached in a short time is remarkable. The process of bonding the films on film reels together with scissors and various chemicals enabled both classical editing and the emergence of the first effects (and transitions). As it is known, the filmmaking process is literally a team effort. There are many departments in front of the camera and behind the camera, and the work is divided. Artificial intelligence can be used in countless areas, from script writing to casting, from editing styles to effect preferences. After the introduction of artificial intelligence software into the film industry, it is also used in promotional activities effectively along with effective trailers and film production activities (Ali et al., cited by Nassar, 2024. p. 207). Machine learning is known to help the film industry predict the nature of individuals and enable effective decisions to be made while film production processes are ongoing (Nassar, 2024, p. 207).

Today, Hollywood's major film studios analyze their scripts using artificial intelligence and data analysis techniques and solve production-related problems quickly and effectively (Yasen & Tedmori cited by Nassar, 2024, p. 207). Cappello makes some suggestions about the reasons for using artificial intelligence in the filmmaking process. In this entire process, AI can be used as a tool to ensure routine task automation and to efficiently bring the cost of the film production process to the desired level. In the film production process, as in all other commercial fields, support may be needed to determine some goals with strategic approaches. Artificial intelligence can be used to create a data-aware culture centered around measurable goals. Apart from cost optimization and achieving measurable goals, it can be said that the use of artificial intelligence can contribute to content production. It can be used to create and assist creative processes to create unique contents. (Cappello cited by Momot, 2022, p. 22). In the film production process, artificial intelligence is used in different stages such as pre-production, production and post-production processes. As it is known, the first stage of the film production process is the pre-production stage, which also includes the approval process. There are some important elements in the approval process. Since cinema has a commercial structure in addition to its artistic nature, it is important to determine its potential success. This approval process is firmly grounded by analyzing the successes of previous films by similar writers, directors and actors. In this process, audience profiles gain importance. Planning is done by taking into account the characteristics of the target audience such as age, education, place of residence, gender, etc. (Mariani, 2024, p. 4). When the production stage begins, the film takes on a visibly lively structure. Film crew in the filmmaking process make visible and specific interventions. The director of the production applies technical choices in areas such as shooting angles, camera use, and light use according to his personal preferences. Therefore, when receiving artificial intelligence assistance, the data entered must be both high in quantity and trained in order to fully understand this cinematic structure. The cooperation between the machine and the human species, which is the basis of artificial intelligence, is also valid in film production (Mariani, 2024, p. 8). When filming is completed, this does not mean that the film production process has come to an end. Many works such as editing, adding music, designing and applying special effects are included in the post production process. For example, editing is the process of selecting and arranging the shots that will form the scenes in the script in the desired order. The editing process requires a lot of personnel and time, starting from the editing director and his/her subordinates. The use of artificial intelligence in the cinema industry has pleased the people working in the industry. One of the most important reasons for this situation is the potential to produce alternative solutions to existing problems. Also, the fact that the energy, time and all kinds of resources to be spent will decrease significantly makes the use of AI more attractive. Thanks to computer software, tasks that a large team of people can handle in weeks or even months can be accomplished in a few minutes or even seconds (Mariani, 2024, p. 12).

It can be said that artificial intelligence-based software is important in the film production process in two respects. The first one is the use of AI for possible market research in cinema films, which have commercial value as well as artistic value. One of these software will be mentioned in the study. Basically, this type of software, which evaluates the entered data and tries to estimate the possible market value, gives more reliable results day by day. The second area of use of artificial intelligence is its involvement in the film production process. It has begun to be used in addition to or instead of manpower at every stage of production. This situation can be exemplified with scenario writing and editing processes. By using artificial intelligence software in script writing, one of the most difficult stages of film production can be facilitated. One of the concrete examples of this is the artificial intelligence-based software Benjamin developed by Ross Godwin. Godwin developed this software during his artificial intelligence research at New York University. The said software wrote the science fiction short film called *Sunspring,* and this scenario was shot in 2016 under the direction of Oscar Sharp. In order for the script to be written successfully by artificial intelligence, the scripts of many films of the same type were added to the Benjamin software as data input. These films include familiar works such as *The Fifth Element, Stargate: SG-1, Star Trek, Futurama*. After the script was created, it was brought to life by the producers and actors in full compliance with the text. Working with the director of the film, Oscar Sharp, on machines that can write scripts, Godwin developed a neural network called 'Long Short Term Memory' (LTSM) and brought Benjamin to the level of script writing (Bloomberg cited by Zengin, 2020, pp. 161-162). The most important element that creates the meaning in cinema films is the shots, which are pieces of visuals. Realizing the power of the meaning created by images, film theorists in the Soviet Union and the United States focused on fiction studies. In the early periods of cinema history, editing work was done in the form of cutting, shortening and pasting in a room. With the introduction of computer technologies, editing can be done by saving a large amount of time and effort. With desktop editing programs becoming easier to access, shots taken with all kinds of devices can be edited quickly. Artificial intelligence-based software, which provides convenience at every stage of movie production, has also been effective in the editing processes of movies. These processes, which require a large number of people and a large amount of labor, have become easier with the use of software.

The first artificial intelligence-based program used in the editing process, which begins after the shooting of the films is completed, was created by IBM. Software called Watson created the trailer for 20th Century Fox's movie *Morgan*. Data set entry, which is the main source of artificial intelligence software, is also used here. The command given to the software is about what kind of moments in the scenes should be included in a horror movie trailer. In order for the software to decide this situation, 100 horror movies were analyzed by it. This analysis includes elements such as the images, composition and sounds used of the 100 selected trailers (Boxofficebuz cited by Zengin, 2020, p. 167). There are two important elements within the scope of these examinations carried out by artificial intelligence. The first of these relates to how AI emphasizes the relations between the use of music and sound effects and emotions in certain scenes (Businessinsider cited by Zengin, 2020, p. 168). The facial expressions of the people in the trailer, the use of colors and their relationships with objects are important. The second part is about how scenes are traditionally constructed and their composition. In the conclusion part, after all data entries were made, the software called Watson watched the *Morgan* movie and the software created a 6-minute trailer. Since 6 minutes is long for a trailer, this time was shortened by the producers (Boxofficebuz cited by Zengin, 2020, p. 167). According to Amelia Hethman, although an editing director is needed to create a story and connect the scenes with each other, editing processes that usually take up to a month are reduced to 24 hours with this software (Wired cited by Zengin, 2020, p. 168). As Zengin emphasizes in his study, the involvement of artificial intelligence in the post-production process of a film can also be seen as a marketing and advertising activity. Considering the relationship between artificial intelligence and the commercial success of films, which is the main subject of this study, announcing the presence of artificial intelligence in the editing process, as in Zengin's study, means that the film advertises itself.

Predicting Commercial Success of Films

One of the important purposes in the establishment of Hollywood film studios is the desire to make a certain area the center of film production. It was aimed to create a structure where employees in the sector can be together and the processes progress faster, as opposed to being spread across the country. Considering the general structure of film production, it is known that more than one expert is needed in more than one field. Considering this requirement, industry experts must be in contact with the studios to be available at any time. This is one of the starting points of Hollywood's view of films as a commercial structure. In this process, the best experts in various departments in the industry such as directors, writers, actors, musicians, editors, set designers, etc. began to be connected to the studios with a contract. It is clear that for this system, studios must have large budgets and they must obtain high profits from the films. To understand these commercial relations, it is necessary to understand the structure of Hollywood's film production system. Wayne examined this situation in terms of different aspects. High investments are also made in the advertising campaigns of the films they produce, and for this reason, it becomes difficult to compete with studio films. Investments also include adding the best experts in the film industry around the world. The horizontal and vertical monopolization of Hollywood film studios has a truly capitalist nature. Due to the strong local dominance of this structure, this dominancy can also be achieved throughout the world. As film studios grow, their opportunities to obtain low-cost loans from banks increase, and as a result, their investments within the sector can become stronger. Since these studios are among the most powerful film producers in the world as a result of all these advantages, the chance of other countries to compete with Hollywood is greatly reduced (Wayne cited by Yüksel, 2018, p. 334).

Hollywood movie studios apply previously tried and successful formulas to generate profits. These formulas can be applied in the selection of successful human resources, as well as scenario and genre selection. In other words, in addition to the re-use of directors, screenwriters and actors whose previous films were successful, it is known that previously successful genres and story structures are also used. Considering the relationship between artificial intelligence and cinema, it is known that some studies have been carried out for marketing and advertising activities as well as the production processes of films. Predicting the possible success of films and the desire to invest according to the income they will bring can be seen as the underlying idea of this situation. In order to achieve maximum profit, artificial intelligence can be used in many areas, from the selection of production team to the selection of scenario type. In this study, ScriptBook software will be mentioned within the scope of movie studios' desire to obtain maximum profit. Basic features such as how the software works and the success rates after entering the data will be discussed. This study will help to explain the accuracy rates of artificial intelligence, which is in constant development, in its predictions about the commercial success of films.

A Review on ScriptBook

Artificial intelligence software is designed separately for various parts of the film production process. Within the scope of this study, the focus will be on a AI software that analyzes the 'scenario' in determining the commercial success of films with artificial intelligence-based programs. The concept of scenario has been one of the important elements in terms of the quality of films since the beginning of storytelling with moving images in the history of cinema. This creative element in dividing film stories into scenes is open to continuous development. The transition from hand-written scenarios on paper to digital scenario softwares is an important turning point. Screenwriting applications such as Celtx and StudioBinder are in an important position to set a standard for the industry. These types of programs have provided permanence and universality in terms of form in the writing of movie scripts. This consistency in scripting style is a factor to consider in understanding the suitability and potential of AI software. This issue becomes a starting point for analyzing and creating original texts with AI tools with clear indications of the elements such as location, dialogue, characters and actions (Frohlick, 2020, pp. 5-6). In this context, it would be appropriate to evaluate how the scenario analysis made by ScriptBook, an artificial intelligence software, will shape the industry. On ScriptBook's website, it is stated that artificial intelligence software cannot be avoided in sectors that require creativity, as in every sector in the world. As a result of the developments in the field of artificial intelligence, especially in the last 10 years, it can be said that there is an increasing use of these software in sports, finance, consultancy systems, etc. The analysis formula used by ScriptBook to reach a reliable result can be given as 'Scriptbook = Hindsight + Foresight + Insight' (Url 1: Scriptook Website: Technology).

Figure 1. The working principle of ScriptBook as it defines itself (Url 1).

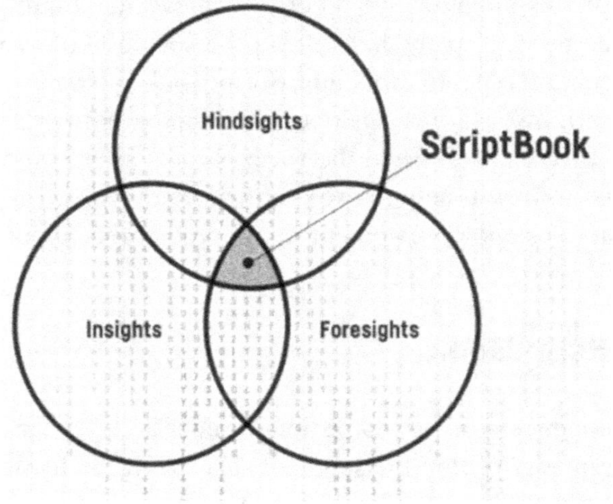

Hindsight refers to learning from past mistakes to develop expertise, which is a fundamental aim of artificial intelligence. This concept includes the phenomenon of critical thinking required to combine information obtained from past experiences with other available resources. Data mining used in this concept refers to the methods used to collect, process and analyze large amounts of textual data, that is, movie scripts, as in this example (Url 1: Scriptook Website: Technology). Foresight is about machine learning, which is mentioned in the study. Machine learning evaluates completed events. It enables the computers where the data is entered to 'learn' by analyzing the data of the events whose results are known. It is seen that machines that learn data make predictions about the future, as ScriptBook aims to do. The model that emerges after all data entry and data analysis is used to predict the commercial success of new movie scripts. Insight can be seen as a hybrid structure. It is the combination of hindsight and foresight to create information that can be used in decision-making. One of the most important efforts in ScriptBook's work is spent on engineering features that focus on the story. Story-based features need to be created manually at that stage. Manual entries have a structure that can be seen as a disadvantage. In this structure, a lot of time is spent with data, that is, real movie scenarios. However, it is necessary to reveal possible problems in the data and consider how the obtained data can be adapted to modeling algorithms based on predictions (Url 1: Scriptook Website: Technology).

ScriptBook software focuses its attention on an important concept in the process of understanding the content of movie scripts: Story awareness. The artificial intelligence of the software shows awareness of the features of the characters in the scenario, the content and writing style of the produced content after the thematic selection.

For character awareness it uses a feature obtained from ScriptBook's decision support tool. This way, every time a character speaks or moves, the model is aware of that character's profile. A scenario can be created by constantly updating character profiles to create consistent behavioral patterns (ScriptBook: "Man and Machine: AI as (co)-creator in Storytelling." Medium. cited by Frohlick, 2020, p. 7). As with most new technologies, in the early days of ScriptBook, there were question marks in some parts of the industry about the functions of the software. Michiel Ruelens, who works as a data scientist under ScriptBook, stated that the transformation in the industry is noticeable. He emphasized that when they first entered this industry four years ago, they were doubted in their negotiations with major film studios. The basis of the mentioned skepticism is the idea that "how can the machine/software tell us what to do?", by stating that the officials of the major film companies have decades of experience in this industry. Over time, this perception began to change after what the software revealed. As the accuracy rates in the predictions increased, they started to trust the algorithm. At this point, ScriptBook technology began to gain acceptance (The Verge cited by Zengin, 2020, p. 161). When ScriptBook's website is examined, it is seen that the projects analyzed for customers are transparently placed on the home page. The service offered is for three different phases. The first one is for customers whose projects are still in the development phase. The second is for customers whose projects were analyzed during the pre-production process. The third is for the customers who have their projects analyzed before they are shown. The home page also includes a proof of concept of ScriptBook and technological details of Scriptbook technology (Url 3: ScriptBook: Webpage) As proof of concept, the results of the company's work with a Hollywood film studio are cited without using the studio name. This is a verification exercise with a Hollywood studio. This verification study is a small-scale project consisting of 50 films released in 2018. The result of this study is that most of the movies that are in a good position in the USA - Box Office charts are given the greenlight by the software, even though the only element entered as a data set is the script (Url 2: ScriptBook: Proof).

Figure 2. Profit-loss and true-false forecast chart for the verification study taken from ScriptBook's website (Url 2).

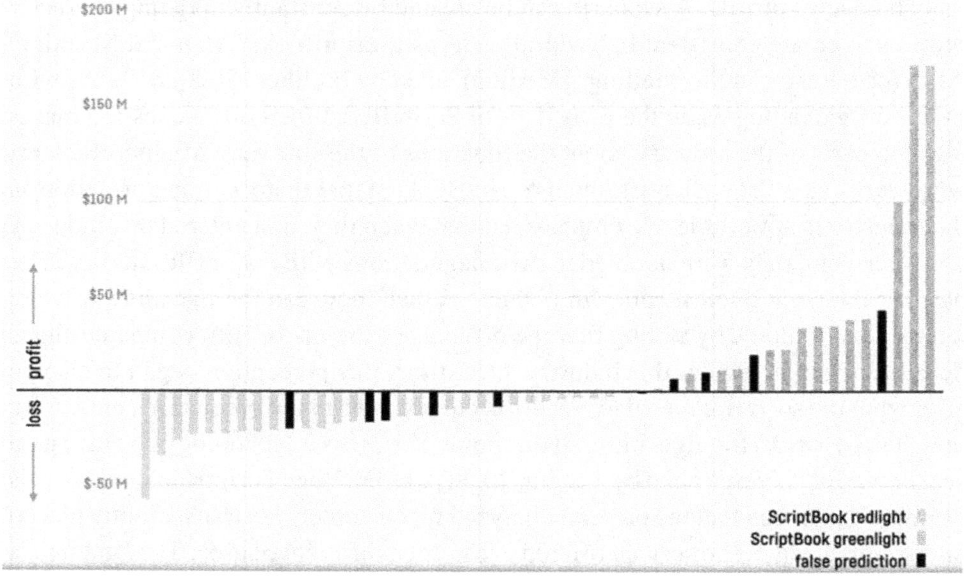

The chart above shows the results of the 50 projects analyzed. As can be seen from the chart, ScriptBook's predictions have a high accuracy rate. As a result of the predictions made by the software, 14 correct green lights are seen. This shows that the projects that were predicted to be successful by software were successful according to the box office results. In addition to this, it was concluded that 26 projects that the software claimed would not be successful and gave a red light were not successful. Despite successful predictions, it is seen that the software gave the wrong green light to 6 projects and the wrong red light to 4 projects. When all these results are evaluated, it is seen how successful Scriptbook is in eliminating projects that received false greenlight from the industry. After all these analyses, it is seen that the ScriptBook software is 80 percent successful (Url 2: ScriptBook: Proof). The fact that 4 out of every 5 projects are analyzed correctly by ScriptBook software is a very important development for the sector. Considering that the success rate of prediction increases as the number of data entries in software based on artificial intelligence increases, it can be better understood that ScriptBook, which can be considered a new initiative, can fill a very important gap in the field. The study results shown in the table represent a small-scale study conducted at that time. Currently, the hit rate and the number of projects in the database have changed positively. According to the current information obtained from ScriptBook's website, the number of scenarios in the database has exceeded 30,000. The time required for the software to examine a scenario file and make a 360° analysis is only 6 minutes. In the study of 50 films, the financial performance prediction accuracy, which was 80 percent, reached 87 percent. Considering all these data, it is seen that the software is well ahead of the forecast rates of stakeholders of the sector (Url 2: ScriptBook: Proof).

Future Research Directions

ScriptBook, which allows the possible box office success to be predicted from the script in order to meet the financial expectations of the producers, has been found open to development as an example of software that demonstrates impressive success in this regard. As mentioned in the study, it is predicted that as the data input increases, the prediction success will also increase. In future studies, artificial intelligence software that can be used in terms of both data percentages and prediction statistics and different movie elements can be studied. Because it is already foreseeable that movie studios will definitely use artificial intelligence software when deciding to make movies.

CONCLUSION

The first films, consisting of short shots depicting daily events, paved the way for cinema to become the seventh art. After these films, 'storytelling' with moving images was discovered in a short time and it was understood that it was actually a great power. The basis of this great power is the idea that a new meaning will emerge by bringing different images together. When we look at this relatively new art from the perspective of the viewer, we can describe it as a fascinating journey. Film production process is one of the art forms that requires the most intense and collective power among all branches of art. This process, which is divided into three as pre-production, production and post-production, is a process that requires both a long time and a lot of manpower. In the first place, by having recording devices, it was relatively easy to take shots that people made individually and did not have any technical quality or script. However, when the storytelling process begins, the professionalization process for departments in story, scenario, actors, location, editing staff, image-related units (sound was also included here in the following processes), etc. has begun. The production of a film, which is mentioned in the study as a collective product, requires many experts from every field. The studio system has helped facilitate access to these experts both in terms of location and cost. One of the last things film producers want is for the film industry to spread over a wide geography. Because, for example, not every expert may want to work with every producer or every producer may not want to work with every actor for various reasons. In this case, it may be difficult to create human resources in an increasingly commercial structure such as the film industry. Based on this idea, some precautions have been taken to obtain maximum profit from the screening of films. The leading actors of the industry, such as directors, writers and actors, have been tied to studios with contracts, making film production costs affordable. From that moment on, a demand for rights, which is still ongoing, began for both sides. In order to gain maximum profit, film studios began to see people as workers, not artists. This is a correct thought to some extent. Because artists are creative individuals who should have certain rights, just like normal workers. The artists of the said period were constantly in conflict with the studios to improve their employee rights and social rights, as well as to improve their income per film. The unions established or joined by sector stakeholders like directors, writers, actors are the most obvious examples of this situation. When all these processes are evaluated, the studio system and the artists and set workers working under it have been evaluated in a relationship of claiming - granting rights for approximately 100 years.

Artificial intelligence is one of the technologies that enable saving time and manpower while doing all kinds of work today. After mentioning the emergence process of artificial intelligence in the study, the concepts of machine learning and deep learning, which are two important subtopics of AI, are mentioned. These subtopics, which constitute the working principles of software using artificial intelligence, enable the production of outputs suitable for the desired purpose by using the data sets at hand. As with every technology, artificial intelligence is a progressive structure. The suitability of the available data for the purpose and their quantitative status are important for the result. If efficient results are to be achieved in any field, artificial intelligence must input as much data as possible regarding that field. One of the areas where artificial intelligence is used is cinema. As mentioned in the study, the use of artificial intelligence can be seen in every process of film production. For example, we can say that there are attempts to make artificial intelligence write scripts and more positive results are obtained day by day. After the type of scenario to be written is determined and other scenarios of that type are entered into the system, artificial intelligence is expected to produce scenarios. Artificial intelligence is not limited to the production of films. Software that can be designed for a purpose and is based on artificial intelligence also relates to the commercial aspects of films. The ScriptBook software mentioned in the study is a system that allows artificial intelligence to make inferences by simply adding movie scripts. This software predicts the possible success or failure of films by taking advantage of all kinds of elements in the scenario. The main purpose of this system is to be effective in getting a green light or red light for a project by making predictions in advance. In the study, by using the information on ScriptBook's web pages, it was seen that artificial intelligence passed a very successful test regarding the commercial aspect, which is among the most important elements of cinema. As the number of data entered into the system increases, that is, as the number of scenarios entered into the system increases, as in this example, the success rate increases day by day. Since all kinds of results, from the number of data entered into the system to the number of projects inferred and from how many of these projects received a green light or a red light to how accurate the predictions were, are presented in a concrete way, the results are not much open to interpretation. The main issue here is to what extent the processes can be shortened in terms of how quickly the produced software can collect more data and make more accurate inferences. Predicting the commercial success of films while they are still in the project stage, that is, before they go on set, is also closely related to the status of the investments that the studios will make. It can be seen as a very obvious inference to say that the success and number of these softwares will increase in the near future.

REFERENCES

Frohlick, A. (2020). Artificial Intelligence and Contemporary Film Production: A Preliminary Survey. https://www.researchgate.net/publication/342978310_Artificial_Intelligence_and_Contemporary_Film_Production_A_Preliminary_Survey

Ghosh, M., & Arunachalam, T. (2021). Introduction to Artificial Intelligence. Artificial Intelligence for Information Management: A Healthcare Perspective. *Studies in Big Data*, 88, 23–44.

Mariani, L. (2024). Cinema e Intelligenza Artificiale (Cinema and Artificial Intelligence). Cinemafocus. https://www.cinemafocus.eu/Studi%20sul%20cinema/IA.html

Metz, C. (2006). Hollywood Cinema. *The Cambridge Companion to Modern American Culture.* 374-391

Momot, I. (2022). Artificial Intelligence in Filmmaking Process: Future Scenarios. *Jamk: School of Business. Degree Programme in International Business.*

Nassar, S. (2024). Futuristic Scenarios: Utilization of AI Technological Settings to Foster the Filmmaking Visual Creation & Mass Production. *The International Design Journal*, 14(2), 207–212. DOI: 10.21608/idj.2024.258755.1110

Nguyen, Q. (2023). AI Representation in Cinema: A Quantitative Content Analysis. ttps://www.researchgate.net/profile/Quynh-Nguyen-431/publication/377410844_AI_REPRESENTATION_IN_CINEMA_A_Quantitative_Content_Analysis/links/65a56a5a5582153a6828704d/AI-REPRESENTATION-IN-CINEMA-A-Quantitative-Content-Analysis.pdf

Perren, A., & Schatz, T. (2004). Hollywood. Georgia State University Communication Faculty Publications. Published in The Sage Handbook of Media Studies. 495-515.

Rupesh, G., & Choudaiah, S. (2019). Artificial Intelligence and its Role in Near Future. *International Journal of Scientific Research*, 8, 893–898.

Scott, A. J. (2006). Origins and Growth of the Hollywood Motion Picture Industry: The First Three Decades. *Cluster Genesis: Technology-Based Industrial Development.* 17–37.

ScriptBook. (ScriptBook Formula and Chart)._https://www.scriptbook.io/#!/scriptbook/technology (Url 1). (Visited 11.06.2024).

ScriptBook. (Webpage). https://www.scriptbook.io/#!/scriptbook (Url 3). (Visited 12.06.2024).

Scriptbook: (Proof). https://www.scriptbook.io/#!/scriptbook/proof (Url2). (Visited 12.06.2024).

Yüksel, S. E. (2018). Küreselleşmenin Sinema Endüstrisine Etkileri: Türkiye'de Üretim-Dağıtım-Gösterim İlişkileri Üzerine Bir İnceleme. *Selçuk İletişim*, 11, 331–348. DOI: 10.18094/josc.346618

Zengin, F. (2020). Akıllı Makine Çağı Sinemasına Giriş: Sinema Sanatında Yapay Zeka Teknolojilerinin Kullanımı. *İletişim Çalışmaları Dergisi,* 6, 151-177.

ADDITIONAL READING

Boden, M. A. (2018). *Artificial Intelligence: A Very Short Introduction*. Oxford University Press. DOI: 10.1093/actrade/9780199602919.001.0001

Murphy, P. (2024). *AI in the Movies*. Edinburgh University Press. DOI: 10.1515/9781474448604

Schio, C. F. (2023). Artificial Intelligence on the Big Screen: How Hollywood is Tackling the Future.

Wooldridge, M. (2018). Artificial Intelligence: Everything You Need to Know About the Coming AI.

KEY TERMS AND DEFINITIONS

Hollywood Studio System: It is the name of the system established by those who want to take part in the film industry and have the means to achieve this, after settling in the Hollywood region, to dominate phases of film production such as production, distribution and screening.

Machine Learning: It is a concept examined within the scope of the study and is also important for the ScriptBook software. It can be considered as a subtopic of artificial intelligence. It is a structure that learns according to the data entered into it and thus improves its performance.

Motion Pictures: A term describing the number of photographs displayed per second for the eye to perceive as movement. If a sufficient number of photographs are shown at a sufficient speed within 1 second, the human eye will perceive it as a moving picture.

Oligopoly: It is a market structure where similar or differentiated products are offered and there are a small number of sellers. In oligopoly markets, a small number of rulers determine the prices of the entire market. Hollywood Studios at the time it was founded is an example of this situation.

Scenario/Script: The text used during the production phase to produce a film. The scenario is, in a sense, a flow text. Shows scenes. In the scenario, there are elements such as information about images, transitions, camera movements, dialogues, etc.

Chapter 11

Leveraging Personalized AI Recommendations to Enhance User Experience in Streaming Services (OTT Platform): An Empirical Evaluation of Recommendations

Dwijendra Nath Dwivedi
https://orcid.org/0000-0001-7662-415X
Krakow University of Economics, Poland

Ghanashyama Mahanty
https://orcid.org/0000-0002-6560-2825
Utkal University, India

ABSTRACT

Sophisticated recommendation systems are crucial in the dynamic digital content consumption environment to improve user engagement and content discoverability. This work provides an in-depth analysis of different recommendation models such as User-based Collaborative Filtering, NMF-based Content Filtering, and a Hybrid Model. It uses a detailed dataset of user interactions with a streaming platform to evaluate their performance. We utilized User-based Collaborative Filtering to utilize similarities among users for content recommendations, NMF-based Content Filtering to break down the user-item interaction matrix and reveal hidden features, and a Hybrid Model that combines the advantages of both methods to offer more tailored

DOI: 10.4018/979-8-3693-3916-9.ch011

and precise recommendations. The results demonstrate the intricate strengths and weaknesss of each model, with the Hybrid Model displaying a favorable combination of customisation and accuracy. The findings from this work provide valuable contributions to the discussion on recommendation systems and also have practical implications for streaming platform

1. INTRODUCTION

In the changing world of digital media consumption, the need for advanced recommendation algorithms is more important than ever. The rise of streaming services and the vast amount of content available has led to a situation where customers face a dilemma of choice. This has prompted the need for sophisticated algorithms that can tailor content experiences to individual preferences. This research study investigates and combines different recommendation system approaches, specifically analyzing a viewership dataset from a streaming platform. Our study aims to improve user happiness by providing tailored content recommendations and assist streaming services in optimizing content delivery and engagement. This inquiry relies heavily on analyzing a detailed viewership dataset that includes various user interactions with material, such as watching preferences, durations, and trends. The dataset's many characteristics, including user demographics, content metadata, and contextual information, offer an excellent opportunity to study the complexities of content consuming behavior.

Our exploration focuses on three main models of recommendation systems: User-based Collaborative Filtering, NMF-based Content Filtering, and a Hybrid Model. User-based Collaborative Filtering relies on the assumption that people who have similar patterns of consuming content are likely to have comparable preferences. This methodology utilizes the resemblance among user profiles to create content suggestions, promoting a feeling of personalized and significance. The NMF-based Content Filtering model takes a detailed approach by breaking down the user-item interaction matrix to reveal hidden information related to user preferences and content qualities. This approach sheds light on the many, often imperceptible, elements that impact the attractiveness of content and user contentment, offering a detailed comprehension of the suggestion environment.

We have made a significant advancement in the industry by creating a Hybrid Model that combines the predictive abilities of User-based Collaborative Filtering with NMF-based Content Filtering. This model is created to combine the qualities of the above approaches, reducing their particular limitations and improving the overall quality of recommendations. This study thoroughly details the theoretical basis of each recommendation model, the methodological framework used in their implementation, and the comparative analysis of their performance. We seek to enhance the current discussion on recommendation systems by providing insights on their ability to revolutionize content consumption experiences in the digital era. The results have significance for both scholarly investigation and real-world use, offering a guide for upcoming advancements in the field of tailored content selection.

Literature Study

In recommendation systems, one of the most fundamental approaches is known as collaborative filtering. It is important to note that the Netflix Prize competition, which resulted in substantial advancements in collaborative filtering algorithms, is considered a classic research. An program called BellKor's Pragmatic Chaos was presented by Bell et al. (2007). This algorithm demonstrated the significance of ensemble approaches in terms of improving the accuracy of recommendations. This study is a famous example of collaborative filtering and its applications to recommendation systems. Although the work of Bell et al. (2007) is not directly related to over-the-top (OTT) platforms, it is an excellent example of them. Y. Koren's (2009) research investigates temporal dynamics in collaborative filtering, which may be applicable to the process of recording user preferences in over-the-top (OTT) platforms over more time. In the publication that was written by Koren, Y., and others in 2009, matrix factorization techniques were discussed. These approaches are frequently utilized in collaborative filtering algorithms. With a particular emphasis on motion pictures, Bansal and Belcastro (2020) describe a collaborative filtering algorithm that has the potential to be modified in order to promote material on over-the-top (OTT) platforms. An autoencoder-based collaborative filtering strategy that can be used to recommend material on over-the-top (OTT) platforms is presented by Sedhain et al. (2015). AutoRec is a collaborative filtering approach. The study that was written by B. Sarwar and his colleagues in 2002 on item-based collaborative filtering algorithms is relevant for the purpose of recommending content on over-the-top (OTT) platforms. A discussion is presented in Christakopoulou, K. et al. (2016) regarding an effective implementation of the SVD++ algorithm. This approach extends the conventional matrix factorization for the purpose of enhancing collaborative filtering. In content-based filtering, item features are utilized to make recommendations for things that are comparable to those that the consumer has previously enjoyed. In the process of developing content-based recommendations, researchers have investigated the possibility of including textual information, visual elements, and audio data. It is important to note that the study that Covington et al. (2016) wrote about YouTube's recommendation system, which blends deep learning and content-based algorithms, is a noteworthy endeavor. In the article "Covington, P. et al. (2016)," the authors address the application of deep neural networks to the YouTube platform in order to make content-based recommendations. Cantador, I., et al. (2011) conducted a study that investigates the diversity of recommendations, which is essential for over-the-top (OTT) platforms in order to guarantee a diverse selection of material. In their study, Feng, J. and colleagues proposed a content-based recommendation algorithm that makes use of attention processes for short video platforms. These platforms are common in over-the-top (OTT) services. In their 2011 study, Baltrunas, L. and colleagues addressed context-aware recommendation, which is relevant for the purpose of providing individualized content suggestions. Alt-hough not being particular to OTT, Recurrent neural networks (RNNs) were investigated by Jannach, D., and Ludewig, M. (2017) for the purpose of session-based recommendations. These RNNs are capable of being converted to over-the-top (OTT) platforms. In their 2017 work, Deldjoo, Y. and colleagues investigate the use of deep learning approaches to improve content-based and hybrid recommendation systems. These techniques have the potential to be applied to over-the-top (OTT) content.

Hybrid recommendation systems integrate a number of different methods in order to capitalize on their respective advantages. A hybrid model that combines collaborative filtering and deep learning was proposed by Ma et al. (2019) for the purpose of improving suggestions in e-commerce environments. In his 2002 article, Burke, R. offered a detailed survey of hybrid recommendation systems and discussed the benefits and challenges associated with these systems. A contextual bandit strategy was proposed by Li, L., et al. (2010). This approach has the potential to be utilized for hybrid suggestions on over-the-top (OTT) platforms. In their 2018 study, Feng, Y, and colleagues suggested a hybrid recommendation algorithm for over-the-top (OTT) platforms that combines topic modeling with collaborative filtering. A hybrid recommendation approach that has the potential to be applicable to over-the-top (OTT) platforms was presented by Yu, F. et al. (2016). For the purpose of enhancing suggestions, Ma, H. et al. (2019) introduced a hybrid model that combines collaborative filtering and deep learning. The importance of context-aware suggestions was explored by Adomavicius, G., and Tuzhilin, A. (2015). These recommendations can be useful for hybrid techniques in over-the-top (OTT) distribution platforms. The time, location, and behavior of the user are examples of contextual information that can be used to improve recommendations. Within their 2015 publication, Adomavicius and Tuzhilin presented a detailed overview of the strategies and issues associated with context-aware recommendation. As a result of deep learning, several other industries, including recommendation systems, have been transformed. The Neural Collaborative Filtering (NCF) framework was presented by He et al. (2017). This framework combines matrix factorization and neural networks in order to capture complicated user-item interactions. It has been demonstrated that recommendation systems can benefit from the application of reinforcement learning, which approaches suggestion as a sequential decision-making problem. A contextual bandit technique was presented by Li et al. (2010) for the purpose of providing personalized suggestions for news articles. It is exceptionally important to guarantee that recommendations are both fair and diverse. A approach to promote content diversity was proposed by Beutel et al. (2019), who examined algorithmic biases in YouTube's recommendation engine and proposed a solution to the problem.

2. DATA AND UNIVARIATE ANALYSIS

The dataset frokm Kaggle contains 456,548 entries and spans across various features related to food orders from a meal delivery service. Each entry represents a unique meal order, with details about the week of order, meal specifications, pricing, promotional activities, and the number of orders placed.

- id: Unique identifier for each order.
- week: The week number when the order was placed.
- center_id: Unique identifier for the food center from where the meal is dispatched.
- meal_id: Unique identifier for the meal.
- checkout_price: Price of the meal after any discount applied.
- base_price: Original price of the meal without any discount.
- emailer_for_promotion: Indicates if an emailer was sent for promotion (1 for yes, 0 for no).
- homepage_featured: Indicates if the meal was featured on the homepage (1 for yes, 0 for no).
- num_orders: Number of orders received for the meal.

3. RESULTS

Exploratory Data Analysis: Distribution of Viewing Durations

The distribution of viewing durations is right-skewed, with most viewing sessions being short and fewer extended sessions. This suggests that shorter content or brief viewing periods are more common among viewers.

Figure 1. Distribution of duration

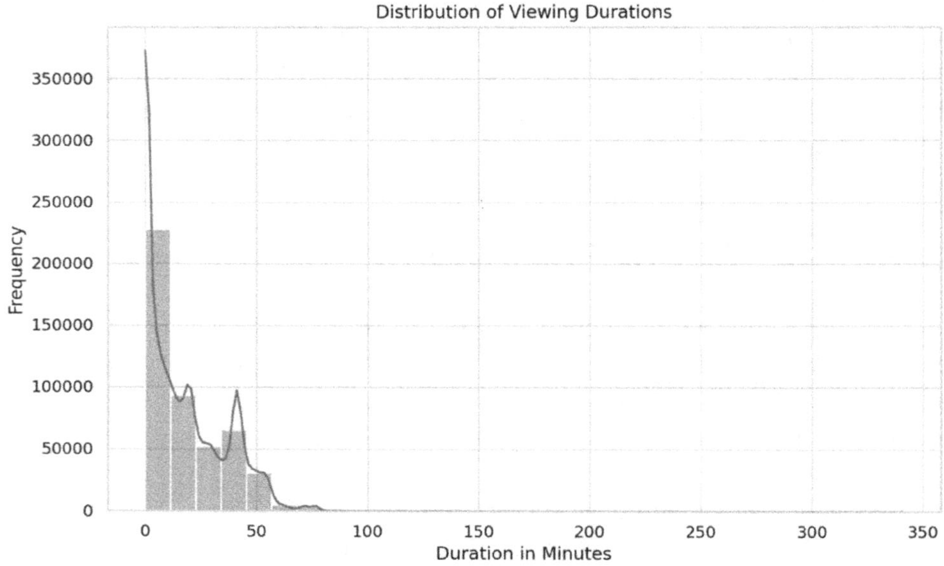

Platform Usage: The count plot for platform usage indicates the relative popularity of different platforms among the viewers. This provides insights into where viewers prefer to consume content.

Figure 2. Platfrom usage

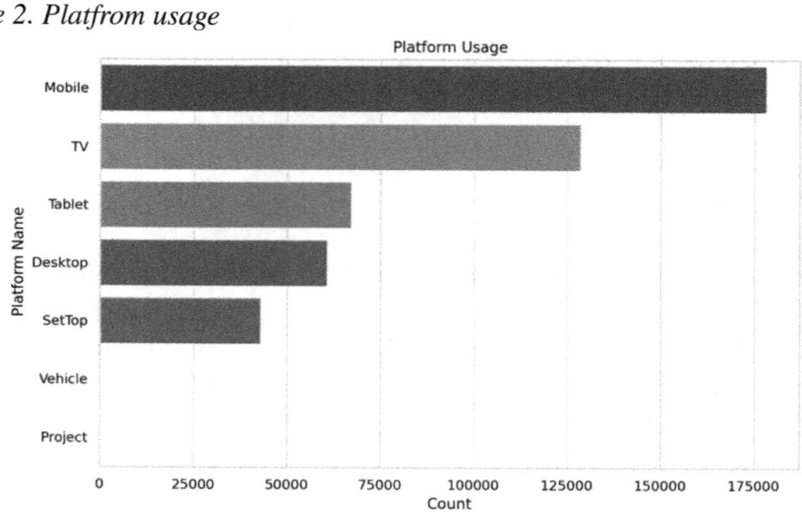

Viewing Duration by Platform: The viewing duration by platform box plot illustrates how different platforms compare in terms of viewer engagement, as measured by viewing duration

Figure 3. Platfrom usage by viewing

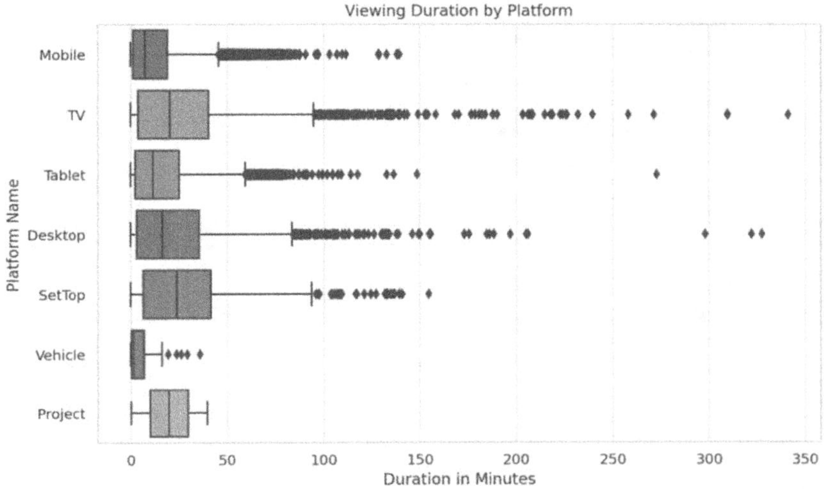

Viewing Duration by Country: The box plot below shows the distribution of viewing durations across the top 10 countries, highlighting differences in viewer engagement..

Figure 4. Viewing by country

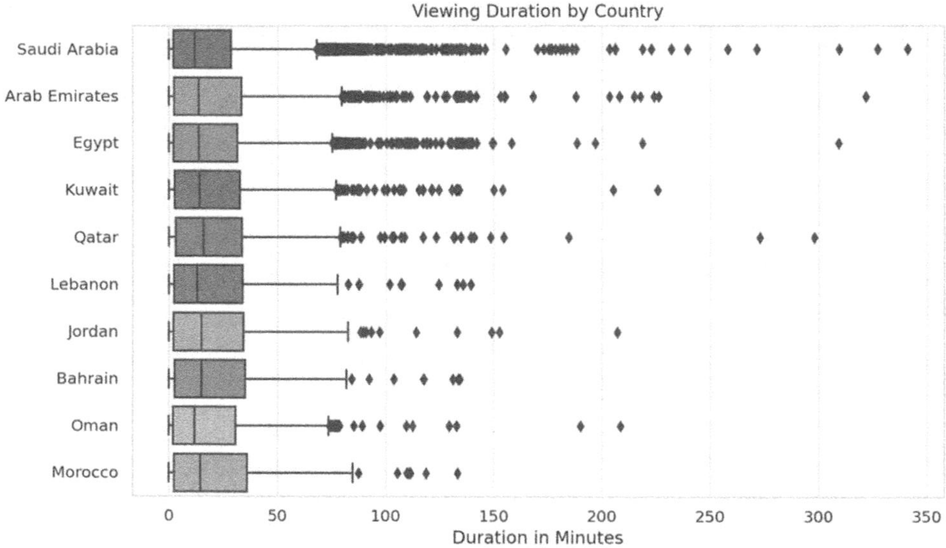

Box Plot Analysis of viewing hours: The box plot provides a visual summary of the distribution of viewing durations, highlighting the median, quartiles, and outliers. Outliers are typically defined as observations that fall below Q1 - 1.5*IQR or above Q3 + 1.5*IQR, where IQR is the interquartile range (Q3-Q1).

Figure 5. Boxplot of bviewing hours

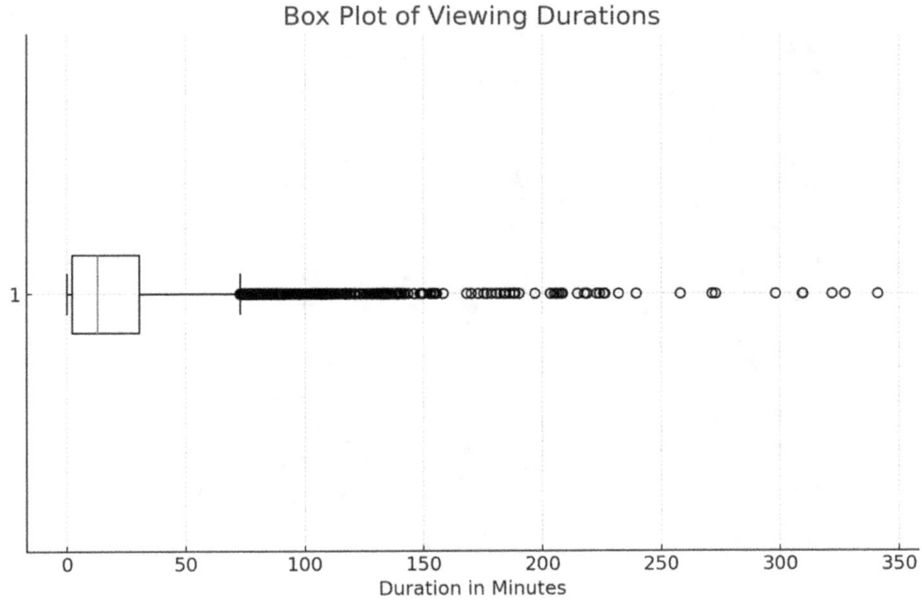

User Similarity Heatmap: The following heatmap shows the similarity scores between a subset of viewers, calculated using cosine similarity. A higher score indicates greater similarity in content preferences between viewers. This visualization is crucial for understanding how the recommendation engine identifies viewers with similar viewing habits.

Figure 6. Viewer heatmap

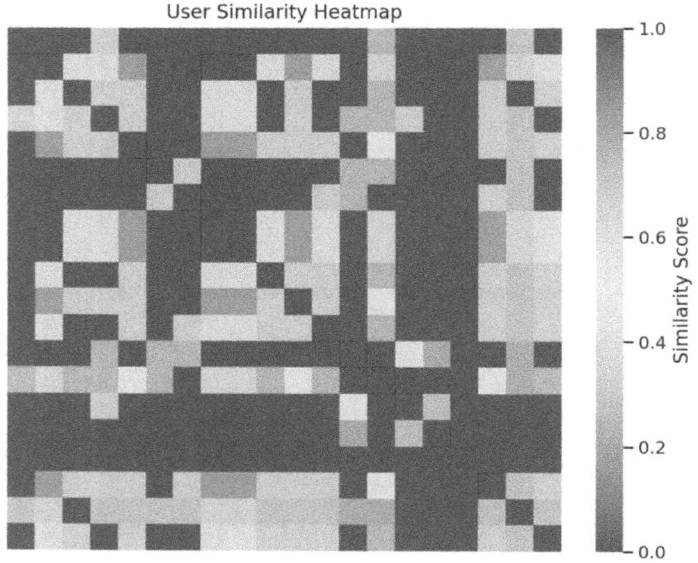

User-Item Interaction Heatmap: The heatmap below illustrates the interactions between a subset of viewers and content titles. Each cell represents whether a viewer (row) has watched a specific content title (column). This visualization helps in understanding the diversity and range of content preferences among viewers.

Figure 7. User item interaction heatmap

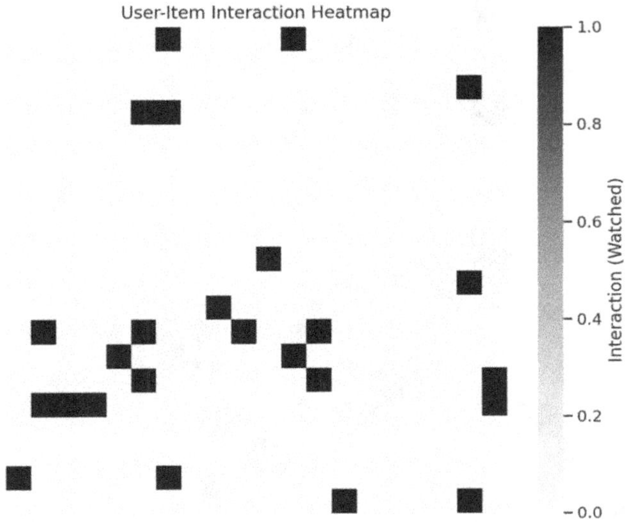

User-based Collaborative Filtering Recommendation System: We prepared the data by creating a user-item matrix where rows represent unique users, columns represent unique items (titles), and the values are binary indicators showing whether a user has selected an item. Below is a heatmap representing a sample of the user-item interactions. Each cell indicates whether a user has selected an item, providing a visual overview of the data sparsity and user preferences. We built a User-based Collaborative Filtering model using cosine similarity to compute similarities between users. Recommendations are made by identifying items that similar users have selected but the target user has not. For a sample user, the model recommended the following items: THE LAST OF US, GAME OF THRONES, HOUSE OF THE DRAGON, THE WHITE LOTUS, and YELLOWSTONE.

Figure 8. User intearaction heatmap

NMF-based Content Filtering Recommendation: outlines the process of building an NMF (Non-Negative Matrix Factorization)-based Content Filtering Recommendation System using a viewership dataset. The system aims to recommend items to users based on the latent features extracted from the user-item interactions . An NMF model with 15 latent factors was built to decompose the user-item matrix into user and item matrices. These matrices represent the latent features of users and items, respectively. Below is a heatmap representing the latent features of items extracted by the NMF model. Each row represents a latent feature, and each column represents an item.

Figure 9. Residual plot

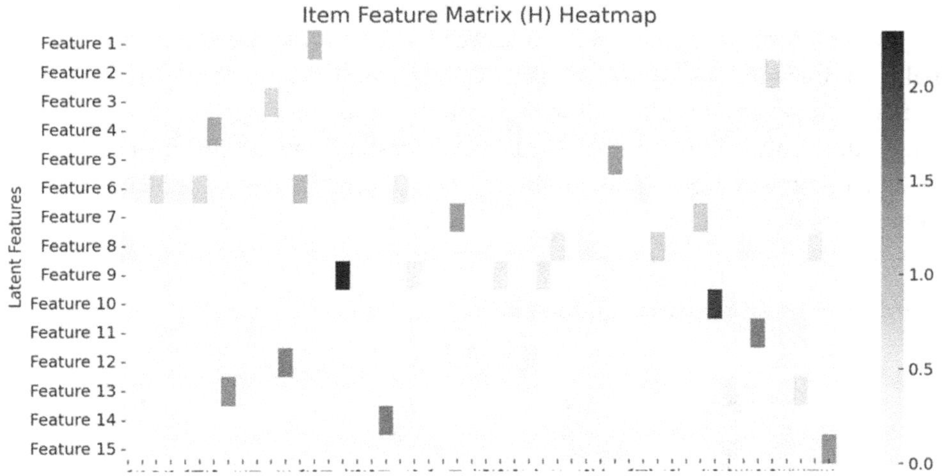

Below is a heatmap representing a sample of user latent features extracted by the NMF model. Each row represents a user, and each column represents a latent feature.

Figure 10. User Feature Matrix (W) Heatmap

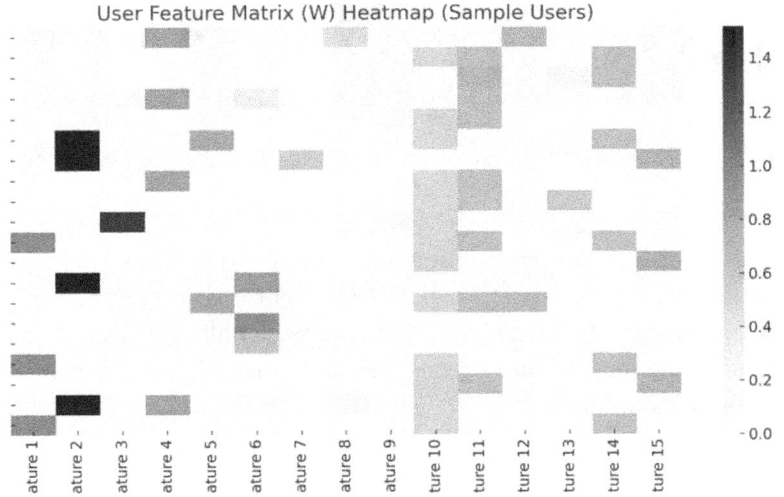

Hybrid Recommendation System: The system integrates User-based Collaborative Filtering and NMF-based Content Filtering approaches to provide more accurate and personalized recommendations. The Hybrid Recommendation System integrates the results from both the User-based Collaborative Filtering model and the NMF-based Content Filtering model. This integration leverages the strengths of both models to improve the recommendation quality. Recommendations are generated by averaging the predicted scores from both models for each item. The final recommendations are the items with the highest average scores that the user has not yet interacted with. Below is a visualization showing the contribution of each model (Collaborative Filtering and NMF-based Content Filtering) to the final hybrid recommendations. This highlights how the integrated approach combines the strengths of both models.

Figure 11. Hybrid recommendation model

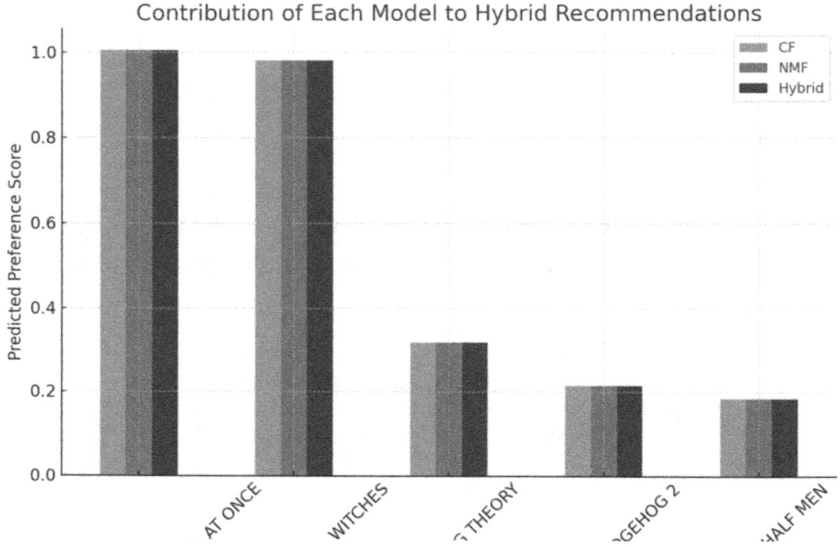

Comparison of Recommendation Models: here we provide a comparison of three recommendation models: User-based Collaborative Filtering, NMF-based Content Filtering, and a Hybrid Model that integrates both approaches. The comparison includes the models' approaches, key strengths, potential limitations, and example recommendations.

Table 1. Model comparison

Model	Approach	Key Strengths	Potential Limitations	Example Recommendations
User-based Collaborative Filtering	Similarity between users	Personalization based on user similarity	Sparsity of data can affect performance	THE LAST OF US, GAME OF THRONES, ...
NMF-based Content Filtering	Decomposition of user-item matrix	Captures latent features of items and users	May not capture all nuances of user preferences	THE BIG BANG THEORY, TWO AND A HALF MEN, ...
Hybrid Model	Combination of CF and NMF approaches	Leverages strengths of both CF and NMF	Complexity in combining and tuning models	Hybrid of CF and NMF recommendations

5. SUMMARY

The research article thoroughly examines recommendation systems in a streaming platform's viewership dataset, comparing three models: User-based Collaborative Filtering, NMF-based Content Filtering, and a new Hybrid Model. The paper is organized to lead the reader through the steps of data analysis, model development, assessment, and comparison, resulting in valuable insights for the personalized content recommendations area. Analysis and preparation of data involve a thorough review of the viewership information, encompassing various user behaviors such content choices, viewing times, and dates. Viewer ID, content titles, and device information are emphasized for their significance in comprehending user preferences and behavior. The dataset's intricate and diverse nature laid the foundation for the later creation of recommendation algorithms. The main focus of the paper is the Hybrid Model, which combines the advantages of User-based Collaborative Filtering with NMF-based Content Filtering. The research describes a new method of combining these models to counteract their specific drawbacks, with the goal of improving the precision and customization of recommendations. The Hybrid Model's performance is thoroughly assessed, showing its exceptional capability to meet a wide range of user preferences and scenarios. An evaluation and comparison of three models is carried out using several metrics to measure their effectiveness in suggestion relevancy, user happiness, and system efficiency. The study offers a detailed examination of the models' advantages and disadvantages, offering unique perspectives on their suitability in various situations. The paper ends by discussing the wider significance of the findings for recommendation systems. It highlights the effectiveness of combining several methods to find a middle ground between customization and precision, indicating directions for future studies and advancements. The research supports future exploration of multi-model integration and the use of advanced machine learning techniques to enhance recommendation systems. The paper provides a thorough examination of recommendation models, combining theoretical concepts with real-world implementations. It is a significant resource for researchers and practitioners in data science and recommendation systems, leading to future advancements in personalized content curation.

4. CONCLUSION

This research article delved into recommendation algorithms, specifically focusing on viewing statistics from a streaming network. We meticulously constructed and evaluated three models: User-based Collaborative Filtering, NMF-based Content Filtering, and a Hybrid Model, to understand user preferences and content interactions. This study emphasizes the complex nature of recommendation systems and showcases the possibility of improving personalization and accuracy by integrating models. The User-based Collaborative Filtering model confirmed the importance of using user similarities to anticipate content preferences, providing a tailored method for content suggestion. Yet, its effectiveness was sometimes limited by the scarcity of user-item interactions, a typical obstacle in collaborative filtering methods. The NMF-based Content Filtering model offered excellent insights into the latent features that determine content preferences, uncovering the fundamental aspects that impact user decisions. The model excels in identifying complex patterns in the data, which helps to enhance comprehension of content characteristics and user preferences. The Hybrid Model, central to this research, showed an impressive capacity to combine the predictive powers of the User-based and NMF-based models. The Hybrid Model combined the capabilities of two approaches to establish a greater balance between personalization and suggestion accuracy, thereby boosting the user experience on the streaming platform..

This work adds to the developing field of recommendation systems by providing a thorough examination of three models and presenting a Hybrid Model that demonstrates the advantages of combining different approaches. The constant change in user preferences and technical improvements poses a perpetual challenge and opportunity for researchers and practitioners. The way ahead requires creative solutions that address consumers' varied needs and also expand the limits of what can be achieved in content suggestion.

REFERENCES

Adomavicius, G., & Tuzhilin, A. (2015). Context-Aware Recommender Systems. *ACM Transactions on Intelligent Systems and Technology.*

Baltrunas, L., & Ricci, F. (2011). Context-Aware Event Recommendation in Event-based Social Networks. *User Modeling and User-Adapted Interaction.*

Bell, R. M., Koren, Y., & Volinsky, C. (2007). "Modeling the Relationship Between a User and Her Mobile Phone." *International Conference on Machine Learning.*

Beutel, A., Covington, P., Jain, S., Kothakota, V., Lu, J., Ramakrishnan, R., & Xin, J. (2019). "Fairness-aware Ranking in Search & Recommendation Systems with Application to LinkedIn Talent Search." *ACM SIGKDD Conference on Knowledge Discovery and Data Mining.*

Burke, R. (2002). Hybrid Recommender Systems: Survey and Experiments. *User Modeling and User-Adapted Interaction*, 12(4), 331–370. DOI: 10.1023/A:1021240730564

Cantador, I., Fernández-Tobías, I., & Bellogín, A. (2011). "A New Approach to Diversity for Recommender Systems: A Case Study in the Tourism Domain." *International Conference on User Modeling, Adaptation, and Personalization.*

Christakopoulou, K., Karypis, G., & Gunopulos, D. (2016). SVD++: An Efficient Implementation of the SVD++ Algorithm. *ACM Transactions on Intelligent Systems and Technology.*

Covington, P., Adams, J., & Sargin, E. (2016). "Deep Neural Networks for YouTube Recommendations." *ACM Conference on Recommender Systems.* DOI: 10.1145/2959100.2959190

Deldjoo, Y., Burke, R., & Zhang, M. (2017). Enhancing Content-Based and Hybrid Music Recommendation Using Deep Learning. *ACM Transactions on Internet Technology.*

Dwijendra, N. (2022). *Benchmarking of traditional and advanced machine Learning modelling techniques for forecasting in book.* Visualization Techniques for Climate Change with Machine Learning and Artificial Intelligence.

Dwivedi, D., Batra, S., & Pathak, Y. K. (2023). A machine learning based approach to identify key drivers for improving corporate's esg ratings. *Journal of Law and Sustainable Development*, 11(1), e0242. DOI: 10.37497/sdgs.v11i1.242

Dwivedi, D., Kapur, P. N., & Kapur, N. N. (2023). Machine Learning Time Series Models for Tea Pest Looper Infestation in Assam, India. In Sharma, A., Chanderwal, N., & Khan, R. (Eds.), *Convergence of Cloud Computing, AI, and Agricultural Science* (pp. 280–289). IGI Global., DOI: 10.4018/979-8-3693-0200-2.ch014

Dwivedi, D., & Vemareddy, A. (2023). Sentiment Analytics for Crypto Pre and Post Covid: Topic Modeling. In Molla, A. R., Sharma, G., Kumar, P., & Rawat, S. (Eds.), Lecture Notes in Computer Science: Vol. 13776. *Distributed Computing and Intelligent Technology. ICDCIT 2023*. Springer., DOI: 10.1007/978-3-031-24848-1_21

Dwivedi, D. N. (2024). The Use of Artificial Intelligence in Supply Chain Management and Logistics. In Sharma, D., Bhardwaj, B., & Dhiman, M. (Eds.), *Leveraging AI and Emotional Intelligence in Contemporary Business Organizations* (pp. 306–313). IGI Global., DOI: 10.4018/979-8-3693-1902-4.ch018

Dwivedi, D. N., & Anand, A. (2021). Trade Heterogeneity in the EU: Insights from the Emergence of COVID-19 Using Time Series Clustering. *Zeszyty Naukowe Uniwersytetu Ekonomicznego w Krakowie*, 3(993), 9–26. DOI: 10.15678/ZNUEK.2021.0993.0301

Dwivedi, D. N., & Anand, A. (2021). The Text Mining of Public Policy Documents in Response to COVID-19: A Comparison of the United Arab Emirates and the Kingdom of Saudi Arabia. Public Governance / Zarządzanie Publiczne, 55(1), 8-22. DOI: 10.15678/ZP.2021.55.1.02

Dwivedi, D. N., & Anand, A. (2022). A Comparative Study of Key Themes of Scientific Research Post COVID-19 in the United Arab Emirates and WHO Using Text Mining Approach. In Tiwari, S., Trivedi, M. C., Kolhe, M. L., Mishra, K., & Singh, B. K. (Eds.), *Advances in Data and Information Sciences. Lecture Notes in Networks and Systems* (Vol. 318). Springer., DOI: 10.1007/978-981-16-5689-7_30

Dwivedi, D. N., & Batra, S. (2024). Case Studies in Big Data Analysis: A Novel Computer Vision Application to Detect Insurance Fraud. In Darwish, D. (Ed.), *Big Data Analytics Techniques for Market Intelligence* (pp. 441–450). IGI Global., DOI: 10.4018/979-8-3693-0413-6.ch018

Dwivedi, D. N., Batra, S., & Pathak, Y. K. (2024). Enhancing Customer Experience: Exploring Deep Learning Models for Banking Customer Journey Analysis. In Sharma, H., Chakravorty, A., Hussain, S., & Kumari, R. (Eds.), *Artificial Intelligence: Theory and Applications. AITA 2023. Lecture Notes in Networks and Systems* (Vol. 843). Springer., DOI: 10.1007/978-981-99-8476-3_39

Dwivedi, D. N., & Gupta, A. (2022). Artificial intelligence-driven power demand estimation and short-, medium-, and long-term forecasting. In *Artificial Intelligence for Renewable Energy Systems* (pp. 231–242). Woodhead Publishing., DOI: 10.1016/B978-0-323-90396-7.00013-4

Dwivedi, D. N., & Mahanty, G. (2024). Mental Health in Messages: Unravelling Emotional Patterns Through Advanced Text Analysis. In Rai, M., & Pandey, J. (Eds.), *Using Machine Learning to Detect Emotions and Predict Human Psychology* (pp. 187–208). IGI Global., DOI: 10.4018/979-8-3693-1910-9.ch009

Dwivedi, D. N., & Mahanty, G. (2024). AI-Powered Employee Experience: Strategies and Best Practices. In Rafiq, M., Farrukh, M., Mushtaq, R., & Dastane, O. (Eds.), *Exploring the Intersection of AI and Human Resources Management* (pp. 166–181). IGI Global., DOI: 10.4018/979-8-3693-0039-8.ch009

Dwivedi, D. N., Mahanty, G., & Pathak, Y. K. (2023). AI Applications for Financial Risk Management. In M. Irfan, M. Elmogy, M. Shabri Abd. Majid, & S. El-Sappagh (Eds.), The Impact of AI Innovation on Financial Sectors in the Era of Industry 5.0 (pp. 17-31). IGI Global. https://doi.org/DOI: 10.4018/979-8-3693-0082-4.ch002

Dwivedi, D. N., Mahanty, G., & Vemareddy, A. (2022). How Responsible Is AI?: Identification of Key Public Concerns Using Sentiment Analysis and Topic Modeling. [IJIRR]. *International Journal of Information Retrieval Research*, 12(1), 1–14. DOI: 10.4018/IJIRR.298646

Dwivedi, D. N., Mahanty, G., & Vemareddy, A. (2022). How Responsible Is AI?: Identification of Key Public Concerns Using Sentiment Analysis and Topic Modeling. [IJIRR]. *International Journal of Information Retrieval Research*, 12(1), 1–14. DOI: 10.4018/IJIRR.298646

Dwivedi, D. N., Mahanty, G., & Vemareddy, A. (2023). Sentiment Analysis and Topic Modeling for Identifying Key Public Concerns of Water Quality/Issues. In: Harun, S., Othman, I.K., Jamal, M.H. (eds) Proceedings of the 5th International Conference on Water Resources (ICWR) – Volume 1. Lecture Notes in Civil Engineering, vol 293. Springer, Singapore. DOI: 10.1007/978-981-19-5947-9_28

Dwivedi, D. N., Pandey, A. K., & Dwivedi, A. D. (2023). Examining the emotional tone in politically polarized Speeches in India: An In-Depth analysis of two contrasting perspectives. SOUTH INDIA JOURNAL OF SOCIAL SCIENCES, 21(2), 125-136. https://journal.sijss.com/index.php/home/article/view/65

Dwivedi, D. N., Pandey, A. K., & Dwivedi, A. D. (2023). Examining the emotional tone in politically polarized Speeches in India: An In-Depth analysis of two contrasting perspectives. SOUTH INDIA JOURNAL OF SOCIAL SCIENCES, 21(2), 125-136. https://journal.sijss.com/index.php/home/article/view/65

Dwivedi, D. N., & Pathak, S. (2022). Sentiment Analysis for COVID Vaccinations Using Twitter: Text Clustering of Positive and Negative Sentiments. In Hassan, S. A., Mohamed, A. W., & Alnowibet, K. A. (Eds.), *Decision Sciences for COVID-19. International Series in Operations Research & Management Science* (Vol. 320). Springer., DOI: 10.1007/978-3-030-87019-5_12

Dwivedi, D. N., & Patil, G. (2023). Climate change: Prediction of solar radiation using advanced machine learning techniques. In Srivastav, A., Dubey, A., Kumar, A., Narang, S. K., & Khan, M. A. (Eds.), *Visualization Techniques for Climate Change with Machine Learning and Artificial Intelligence* (pp. 335–358). Elsevier., DOI: 10.1016/B978-0-323-99714-0.00017-0

Dwivedi, D. N., Tadoori, G., & Batra, S. (2023). Impact of women leadership and ESG ratings and in organizations: A time series segmentation study. *Academy of Strategic Management Journal*, 22(S3), 1–6.

Dwivedi, D. N., Wójcik, K., & Vemareddyb, A. (2022). Identification of Key Concerns and Sentiments Towards Data Quality and Data Strategy Challenges Using Sentiment Analysis and Topic Modeling. In Jajuga, K., Dehnel, G., & Walesiak, M. (Eds.), *Modern Classification and Data Analysis. SKAD 2021. Studies in Classification, Data Analysis, and Knowledge Organization*. Springer., DOI: 10.1007/978-3-031-10190-8_2

Feng, J., Zhao, Z., & Qian, X. (2019). A Content-Based Recommendation Algorithm for Short Video Platforms Based on Attention Mechanism. *IEEE Access : Practical Innovations, Open Solutions*.

Feng, Y., Lv, J., & Zhao, K. (2018). Hybrid Recommendation Algorithm for OTT Users Based on Topic Model and Collaborative Filtering. *IEEE Access : Practical Innovations, Open Solutions*.

Gupta, A. et al., 2021. Understanding Consumer Product Sentiments through Supervised Models on Cloud: Pre and Post COVID. Webology, 18(1), pp.406â€“415. Available at: .DOI: 10.14704/WEB/V18I1/WEB18097

Gupta, A., Dwivedi, D. N., & Shah, J. (2023). *Artificial Intelligence Applications in Banking and Financial Services: Anti Money Laundering and Compliance*. Springer Nature. DOI: 10.1007/978-981-99-2571-1

Gupta, A., Dwivedi, D. N., & Shah, J. (2023). Overview of Money Laundering. In: Artificial Intelligence Applications in Banking and Financial Services. Future of Business and Finance. Springer, Singapore. https://doi.org/DOI: 10.1007/978-981-99-2571-1_1

Gupta, A., Dwivedi, D. N., & Shah, J. (2023). Financial Crimes Management and Control in Financial Institutions. In: Artificial Intelligence Applications in Banking and Financial Services. Future of Business and Finance. Springer, Singapore. https://doi.org/DOI: 10.1007/978-981-99-2571-1_2

Gupta, A., Dwivedi, D. N., & Shah, J. (2023). Overview of Technology Solutions. In: Artificial Intelligence Applications in Banking and Financial Services. Future of Business and Finance. Springer, Singapore. https://doi.org/DOI: 10.1007/978-981-99-2571-1_3

Gupta, A., Dwivedi, D. N., & Shah, J. (2023). Data Organization for an FCC Unit. In: Artificial Intelligence Applications in Banking and Financial Services. Future of Business and Finance. Springer, Singapore. https://doi.org/DOI: 10.1007/978-981-99-2571-1_4

Gupta, A., Dwivedi, D. N., & Shah, J. (2023). Planning for AI in Financial Crimes. In: Artificial Intelligence Applications in Banking and Financial Services. Future of Business and Finance. Springer, Singapore. https://doi.org/DOI: 10.1007/978-981-99-2571-1_5

Gupta, A., Dwivedi, D. N., & Shah, J. (2023). Applying Machine Learning for Effective Customer Risk Assessment. In: Artificial Intelligence Applications in Banking and Financial Services. Future of Business and Finance. Springer, Singapore. https://doi.org/DOI: 10.1007/978-981-99-2571-1_6

Gupta, A., Dwivedi, D. N., & Shah, J. (2023). Artificial Intelligence-Driven Effective Financial Transaction Monitoring. In: Artificial Intelligence Applications in Banking and Financial Services. Future of Business and Finance. Springer, Singapore. https://doi.org/DOI: 10.1007/978-981-99-2571-1_7

Gupta, A., Dwivedi, D. N., & Shah, J. (2023). Machine Learning-Driven Alert Optimization. In: Artificial Intelligence Applications in Banking and Financial Services. Future of Business and Finance. Springer, Singapore. https://doi.org/DOI: 10.1007/978-981-99-2571-1_8

Gupta, A., Dwivedi, D. N., & Shah, J. (2023). Applying Artificial Intelligence on Investigation. In: Artificial Intelligence Applications in Banking and Financial Services. Future of Business and Finance. Springer, Singapore. DOI: 10.1007/978-981-99-2571-1_9

Gupta, A., Dwivedi, D. N., & Shah, J. (2023). Ethical Challenges for AI-Based Applications. In: Artificial Intelligence Applications in Banking and Financial Services. Future of Business and Finance. Springer, Singapore. https://doi.org/DOI: 10.1007/978-981-99-2571-1_10

Gupta, A., Dwivedi, D. N., & Shah, J. (2023). Setting up a Best-In-Class AI-Driven Financial Crime Control Unit (FCCU). In: Artificial Intelligence Applications in Banking and Financial Services. Future of Business and Finance. Springer, Singapore. https://doi.org/DOI: 10.1007/978-981-99-2571-1_11

He, X., Liao, L., Zhang, H., Nie, L., Hu, X., & Chua, T. S. (2017). "Neural Collaborative Filtering." *WWW Conference*.

Jannach, D., & Ludewig, M. (2017). "When Recurrent Neural Networks meet the Neighborhood for Session-Based Recommendation." *ACM Conference on Recommender Systems*. DOI: 10.1145/3109859.3109872

Koren, Y. (2009). Collaborative Filtering with Temporal Dynamics. *Communications of the ACM*.

Koren, Y., Bell, R., & Volinsky, C. (2009). "Matrix Factorization Techniques for Recommender Systems." Computer. Bansal, T., & Belcastro, L. (2020). "Movie Recommendation System using Collaborative Filtering Algorithm. *International Journal of Advanced Computer Science and Applications*.

Li, L., Chu, W., Langford, J., & Schapire, R. E. (2010). "A Contextual-Bandit Approach to Personalized News Article Recommendation." *ACM International Conference on World Wide Web*. DOI: 10.1145/1772690.1772758

Ma, H., Yang, H., Lyu, M. R., & King, I. (2019). Learning to Recommend with Personalized Feature Enhancement for E-commerce. *ACM Transactions on Information Systems*.

Ma, H., Yang, H., Lyu, M. R., & King, I. (2019). Learning to Recommend with Personalized Feature Enhancement for E-commerce. *ACM Transactions on Information Systems*.

Pozzi, F. A., & Dwivedi, D. (2023). ESG and IoT: Ensuring Sustainability and Social Responsibility in the Digital Age. In Tiwari, S., Ortiz-Rodríguez, F., Mishra, S., Vakaj, E., & Kotecha, K. (Eds.), *Artificial Intelligence: Towards Sustainable Intelligence. AI4S 2023. Communications in Computer and Information Science* (Vol. 1907). Springer., DOI: 10.1007/978-3-031-47997-7_2

Pozzi, F. A., & Dwivedi, D. (2023). ESG and IoT: Ensuring Sustainability and Social Responsibility in the Digital Age. In Tiwari, S., Ortiz-Rodríguez, F., Mishra, S., Vakaj, E., & Kotecha, K. (Eds.), *Artificial Intelligence: Towards Sustainable Intelligence. AI4S 2023. Communications in Computer and Information Science* (Vol. 1907). Springer., DOI: 10.1007/978-3-031-47997-7_2

Sarwar, B., Karypis, G., Konstan, J., & Riedl, J. (2001). "Item-Based Collaborative Filtering Recommendation Algorithms." *WWW Conference*.

Sedhain, S., Kawale, J., & Kumar, S. (2015). "AutoRec: Autoencoders Meet Collaborative Filtering." *World Wide Web Conference*. DOI: 10.1145/2740908.2742726

Yu, F., Ren, X., Luo, J., & Sun, G. (2016). A Hybrid Recommendation Model for Streaming Services in a Smart Home. *IEEE Transactions on Consumer Electronics*.

Ziska Fields, I. G. I. (Ed.). (2023). *Dwivedi, DwijendraNath, and Ghanashyama Mahanty. "Human Creativity vs. Machine Creativity: Innovations and Challenges." Multidisciplinary Approaches in AI, Creativity, Innovation, and Green Collaboration* (pp. 19–28). Global., DOI: 10.4018/978-1-6684-6366-6.ch002

Ziska Fields, I. G. I. (Ed.). (2023). *Dwivedi, DwijendraNath, and Ghanashyama Mahanty. "Human Creativity vs. Machine Creativity: Innovations and Challenges." Multidisciplinary Approaches in AI, Creativity, Innovation, and Green Collaboration* (pp. 19–28). Global., DOI: 10.4018/978-1-6684-6366-6.ch002

CONFLICT OF INTEREST

The authors whose names are listed immediately below certify that they have NO affiliations with or involvement in any organization or entity with any financial interest (such as honoraria; educational grants; participation in speakers' bureaus; membership, employment, consultancies, stock ownership, or other equity interest; and expert testimony or patent-licensing arrangements), or non-financial interest (such as personal or professional relationships, affiliations, knowledge or beliefs) in the subject matter or materials discussed in this manuscript.

AUTHOR BIOGRAPHY

Dr. Dwijendranath Dwivedi is PhD. from Krakow university of economics.
Dr. Ghanashyama Mahanty is PhD from Utkal University, India.

Compilation of References

A very short history of cinema I National Science and Media Museum. (n.d.). National Science and Media Museum. https://www.scienceandmediamuseum.org.uk/objects-and-stories/very-short-history-of-cinema#:~:text=The%20first%20to%20present%20projected,film%20printer%20all%20in%20one

Adomavicius, G., & Tuzhilin, A. (2015). Context-Aware Recommender Systems. *ACM Transactions on Intelligent Systems and Technology.*

AI-Writer.comTM - The only AI writing platform built to be trusted. (n.d.). https://ai-writer.com/

Ali, A. H., Alajanbi, M., Yaseen, M. G., & Abed, S. A. (2023). Chatgpt4, DALL·E, Bard, Claude, BERT: Open Possibilities. *Babylonian Journal of Machine Learning*, 17–18, 17–18. Advance online publication. DOI: 10.58496/BJML/2023/003

All Time Worldwide Animated Box Office. (n.d.). The Numbers. https://www.the-numbers.com/box-office-records/worldwide/all-movies/cumulative/all-time-animated

Al-sa'di, A., & Miller, D. (2023). Exploring the Impact of Artificial Intelligence language model ChatGPT on the User Experience. *International Journal of Technology* [IJTIM]. *Innovation and Management*, 3(1), 1–8. DOI: 10.54489/ijtim.v3i1.195

Al-Zaghir, Z., Matroud, A. A., Abdalgader, K., & Alnaqbi, N. (2023). Exploring opportunities and challenges of using ChatGPT in professional writing instruction. *2023 IEEE International Conference on Teaching, Assessment and Learning for Engineering (TALE)*. DOI: 10.1109/TALE56641.2023.10398234

Anadolu, B. (2019). *Dijital Hikâye Anlatıcılığı Bağlamında Yapay Zekanın Sinemaya Etkisi: Sunspring ve It's No Game Filmlerinin Analizi*. Erciyes İletişim Dergisi / Journal of Erciyes Communication.

Anantrasirichai, N., & Bull, D. (2022). Artificial intelligence in the creative industries: A review. *Artificial Intelligence Review*, 55(1), 589–656. DOI: 10.1007/s10462-021-10039-7

Anderson, N., McGowan, A., Galway, L., Hanna, P., Collins, M., & Cutting, D. (2023). Implementing generative AI and large language models in education. *2023 7th International Symposium on Innovative Approaches in Smart Technologies (ISAS)*.

Anon. n.d. "copilot nedir." *Bing*. Retrieved July 5, 2024 (https://www.bing.com/search?q=copilot+nedir&toWww=1&redig=98F5A3365CC34881AE6A4514A7CBEF96)

APA. (2021). The promise and challenges of AI

Arinez, J. F., vd. (2020). "Artificial Intelligence in Advanced Manufacturing: Current Status and Future Outlook." ASME. J. Manuf. Sci. Eng. November, 142(11).

Aristoteles. (1987). Poetika. (Çev. İsmail Tunalı). Remzi Kitabevi.

Arslantepe, Mehmet (2012). Sinema Okuryazarlığı. Kocaeli: Umuttepe Yayınları

Asif, A. W. (2024). "İdeogram AI İncelemesi: Onu Farklı Kılan Nedir?" *MSPoweruser*. Retrieved July 5, 2024 (https://mspoweruser.com/tr/ideogram-ai-review/)

Azzarelli, A., Anantrasirichai, N., & Bull, D. R. (2024). Reviewing Intelligent Cinematography: AI research for camera-based video production. *arXiv preprint arXiv:2405.05039*.

Baheti, P. (2021, September 8). Neural Style Transfer: Everything You Need to Know [Guide]. V7. https://www.v7labs.com/blog/neural-style-transfer

Baltrunas, L., & Ricci, F. (2011). Context-Aware Event Recommendation in Event-based Social Networks. *User Modeling and User-Adapted Interaction*.

Banh, L., & Strobel, G. (2023). Generative Artificial Intelligence. *Electronic Markets*, 33(1), 63. DOI: 10.1007/s12525-023-00680-1

Barthes, R. (1996). *Çağdaş Söylemler*. Metis Yayınları.

Bedingfield, W. (2023, July 07). *How Indiana Jones and the Dial of Destiny De-Aged Harrison Ford*. Wired. https://www.wired.com/story/indiana-jones-and-the-dial-of-destiny-de-aging-tech/

Befores & Afters (2023). The AI, volumetric and animation tools that helped make Pixar's 'Elemental' possible.

Bekeš, E. R., & Galzina, V. (2023). Exploring the pedagogical use of AI-powered chatbots educational perceptions and practices. *2023 46th MIPRO ICT and Electronics Convention (MIPRO).*

Bell, R. M., Koren, Y., & Volinsky, C. (2007). "Modeling the Relationship Between a User and Her Mobile Phone." *International Conference on Machine Learning.*

Bermudez, L., Dabby, N., Lin, Y. A., Hilmarsdottir, S., Sundararajan, N., & Kar, S. (2021). A Learning-Based Approach to Parametric Rotoscoping of Multi-Shape Systems. In *Proceedings of the IEEE/CVF Winter Conference on Applications of Computer Vision* (pp. 776-785). DOI: 10.1109/WACV48630.2021.00082

Beutel, A., Covington, P., Jain, S., Kothakota, V., Lu, J., Ramakrishnan, R., & Xin, J. (2019). "Fairness-aware Ranking in Search & Recommendation Systems with Application to LinkedIn Talent Search." *ACM SIGKDD Conference on Knowledge Discovery and Data Mining.*

Bin-Hady, W. R. A., Al-Kadi, A., Hazaea, A., & Ali, J. K. M. (2023). Exploring the dimensions of ChatGPT in English language learning: A global perspective. *Library Hi Tech.* Advance online publication. DOI: 10.1108/LHT-05-2023-0200

Biswas, S. (2023). *Role of ChatGPT in the film industry: According to ChatGPT.* Qeios., DOI: 10.32388/NABVHA

Boden, M. A. (2004). *The Creative Mind: Myths and Mechanisms* (2nd ed.). Routledge. DOI: 10.4324/9780203508527

Bolat, N. (2023). Dijitalleşeme ile Yapay Zekânın Reklam Alanına Katılımı. In Günay, M. A. (Ed.), *İletişim Bilimlerinde Yapay Zekâ* (pp. 44–61). Eğitim Publication.

Boords. (n.d.). AI Storyboard Generator (Try for Free) | boords.com. https://boords.com/ai-storyboard-generator

Bordot, F. (2022). Artificial intelligence, robots and unemployment: Evidence from OECD countries. *Journal of Innovation Economics & Management*, (1), 117–138. DOI: 10.3917/jie.037.0117

Bozkurt, A., Karadeniz, A., Baneres, D., Guerrero-Roldán, A. E., & Rodríguez, M. E. (2021). Artificial intelligence and reflections from educational landscape: A review of AI Studies in half a century. *Sustainability (Basel)*, 13(2), 800–812. DOI: 10.3390/su13020800

Brecht, B. (1975) "Sesli Sinema" Çağdaş Sinema Dergisi, Birlik Matbaası, Sayı 7: İstanbul.

Brookings Institution. (2021). How to regulate AI-generated deepfakes

Burke, R. (2002). Hybrid Recommender Systems: Survey and Experiments. *User Modeling and User-Adapted Interaction*, 12(4), 331–370. DOI: 10.1023/A:1021240730564

Campbell, J. (2008). *The Hero with a Thousand Faces*. New World Library.

Cantador, I., Fernández-Tobías, I., & Bellogín, A. (2011). "A New Approach to Diversity for Recommender Systems: A Case Study in the Tourism Domain." *International Conference on User Modeling, Adaptation, and Personalization*.

Carter, J. (2018). How artificial intelligence is creating new ways of storytelling. https://www.techradar.com/news/how-artificial-intelligence-is-creating-new-ways-of-storytelling

Cavazza, M., Charles, F., & Mead, S. J. (2001, November). AI-based animation for interactive storytelling. In Proceedings Computer Animation 2001. Fourteenth Conference on Computer Animation (Cat. No. 01TH8596) (pp. 113-120). IEEE.

Cetinic, E., & She, J. (2022). Understanding and creating art with AI: Review and outlook. [TOMM]. *ACM Transactions on Multimedia Computing Communications and Applications*, 18(2), 1–22. DOI: 10.1145/3475799

Chase, N. (2024, March 30). *Artificial Intelligence In Film: Impact & Influence for 2024+*. Neil Chase Film. https://neilchasefilm.com/artificial-intelligence-in-film/

Chatman, S. (2008). Öykü ve Söylem. Filmde ve Kurmacada anlatı Yapısı. (Story and Discourse: Narrative Structure in Fiction and film) Cornell University Press, 1978.

Chinonso, O. E., Theresa, A. M.-E., & Aduke, T. C. (2023). ChatGPT for teaching, learning and research: Prospects and challenges. *Global Academic Journal of Humanities and Social Sciences*, 5(02), 33–40. DOI: 10.36348/gajhss.2023.v05i02.001

Chow, P. S. (2020). Ghost in the (Hollywood) machine: Emergent applications of artificial intelligence in the film industry. *NECSUS_European Journal of Media Studies, 9*(1), 193-214.

Chow, P.-S. (2020). Ghost in the (Hollywood) machine: Emergent applications of artificial intelligence in the film industry. *NECSUS European Journal of Media Studies, 9*(1), 193-214. https://doi.org/DOI: 10.25969/mediarep/14307

Christakopoulou, K., Karypis, G., & Gunopulos, D. (2016). SVD++: An Efficient Implementation of the SVD++ Algorithm. *ACM Transactions on Intelligent Systems and Technology*.

Chubb, J., & Beer, D. (2023). *Establishing Counterpoints in the Sonic Framing of AI Narratives, AI and Ethics*. Springer.

Clayphan, A., Kay, J., & Weinberger, A. (2014). ScriptStorm: Scripting to enhance tabletop brainstorming. *Personal and Ubiquitous Computing*, 18(6), 1433–1453. DOI: 10.1007/s00779-013-0746-z

Coleman, F. (2019, October 3). *Can Fiction Introduce Empathy Into AI? Do We Want It To?* Literary Hub. https://lithub.com/can-fiction-introduce-empathy-into-ai-do-we-want-it-to/

Covington, P., Adams, J., & Sargin, E. (2016). "Deep Neural Networks for YouTube Recommendations." *ACM Conference on Recommender Systems*. DOI: 10.1145/2959100.2959190

Coyle, J. (2023, September 28). *In Hollywood writers' battle against AI, humans win (for now)*. AP. https://apnews.com/article/hollywood-ai-strike-wga-artificial-intelligence-39ab72582c3a15f77510c9c30a45ffc8

Cram, C. (2012). Digital cinema: The role of the visual effects supervisor. Film History. *International Journal (Toronto, Ont.)*, 24(2), 169–186.

Crawford, K., & Paglen, T. (2021). Excavating AI: The politics of images in machine learning training sets. *AI & Society*, 36(4), 1105–1116. DOI: 10.1007/s00146-021-01301-1

Dai, F., & Li, Z. (2024). Research on 2D Animation Simulation Based on Artificial Intelligence and Biomechanical Modeling. *EAI Endorsed Transactions on Pervasive Health and Technology*, •••, 10.

Dartnall, T. (1994). *Artificial Intelligence and Creativity: An Interdisciplinary Approach*. Springer Science & Business Media. DOI: 10.1007/978-94-017-0793-0

Das, S. (2023). The Evolution Of Visual Effects In Cinema: A Journey From Practical Effects To CGI. Kolkata India, Journal Of Emergıng Technologies and Innovative Research (JETIR) s, 303-309.

Datta, A., & Goswami, R. (2021). The Film Industry Leaps into Artificial Intelligence: Scope and Challenges by the Filmmakers. In Rathore, V. S., Dey, N., Piuri, V., Babo, R., Polkowski, Z., & Tavares, J. M. R. S. (Eds.), *Rising Threats in Expert Applications and Solutions. Advances in Intelligent Systems and Computing* (Vol. 1187). Springer., DOI: 10.1007/978-981-15-6014-9_80

Davies, J., Klinger, J., Mateos-Garcia, J., & Stathoulopoulos, K. (2020). *The art in the artificial AI and the creative industries*. Creat Ind Policy Evid Centre.

Dayo, F., Memon, A. A., & Dharejo, N. (2023). Scriptwriting in the Age of AI: Revolutionizing Storytelling with Artificial Intelligence. *Journal of Media & Communication*, 4(1), 24–38.

de Saussure, F. (1959). *Course in General Linguistics*. Philosophical Library.

DeepStory. (n.d.). https://deepstory.ai/

Deldjoo, Y., Burke, R., & Zhang, M. (2017). Enhancing Content-Based and Hybrid Music Recommendation Using Deep Learning. *ACM Transactions on Internet Technology*.

Deruvo, J. (2022). This Film Was Written and Directed by AI—Here's the How and What You Can Learn. https://nofilmschool.com/ai-generated-movie

Dewasiri, N. J., Baker, H. K., Banda, Y. K. W., & Rathnasiri, M. S. H. (2022), "The Dividend Decision Model: A Possible Solution for the Dividend Puzzle", Rana, S., Sakshi and Singh, J. (Ed.) Exploring the Latest Trends in Management Literature (Review of Management Literature, Vol. 1), Emerald Publishing Limited, Leeds, pp. 249-267. https://doi.org/DOI: 10.1108/S2754-586520220000001013

Dewasiri, N. J., Dharmarathna, D. G., & Choudhary, M. (2024). Leveraging Artificial Intelligence for Enhanced Risk Management in Banking: A Systematic Literature Review. Singh, R., Khan, S., Kumar, A., & Kumar, V. (Ed.) Artificial Intelligence Enabled Management: An Emerging Economy Perspective, De Gruyter, pp. 197–213, Berlin, https://doi.org/DOI: 10.1515/9783111172408-013

Dewasiri, N. J., Karunarathne, K. S. S. N., Menon, S., Jayarathne, P. G. S. A., & Rathnasiri, M. S. H. (2023a). Fusion of Artificial Intelligence and Blockchain in the Banking Industry: Current Application, Adoption, and Future Challenges; Saini, A. and Garg, V. (Ed.) Transformation for Sustainable Business and Management Practices: Exploring the Spectrum of Industry 5.0, Emerald Publishing Limited, pp. 293-307, Bingley, https://doi.org/DOI: 10.1108/978-1-80262-277-520231021

Dewasiri, N. J., Pigera, A. K. M., Karunarathne, K. S. S. N., & Rathnasiri, M. S. H. (2023), "Financial Services Employee Engagement and Attitude Toward Artificial Intelligence: Evidence From Sri Lanka", Saini, A. and Garg, V. (Ed.) Transformation for Sustainable Business and Management Practices: Exploring the Spectrum of Industry 5.0, Emerald Publishing Limited, Leeds, pp. 231-245. https://doi.org/ DOI: 10.1108/978-1-80262-277-520231017

Dhahir, M. Q., AL-hakeem, M. A. M., & Alshadoodee, H. A. A. (2022). Automatic camera control and artificial intelligence in the future of cinematography. *International Journal (Toronto, Ont.)*, 7(1).

Disney Research. (2022). Storyliving

Dmytryk, E. & Dmytryk, J. P., (2007). Sinemada Yönetmenlik, Oyunculuk, Kurgu Çev: İbrahim Şener Doruk Yayınları İstanbul, 2007.

Duc, A. N., Lønnestad, T., Sundbø, I., Johannessen, M. R., Gabriela, V., Ahmed, S. U., & El-Gazzar, R. (2023). *Generative AI in Undergraduate Information Technology Education — Insights from nine courses.* DOI: 10.48550/ARXIV.2311.10199

Dugal, M., & Davey, O. (2024). *Welcome to AI.* Wide Eyed Editions.

Dwijendra, N. (2022). *Benchmarking of traditional and advanced machine Learning modelling techniques for forecasting in book.* Visualization Techniques for Climate Change with Machine Learning and Artificial Intelligence.

Dwivedi, D. N., & Anand, A. (2021). The Text Mining of Public Policy Documents in Response to COVID-19: A Comparison of the United Arab Emirates and the Kingdom of Saudi Arabia. Public Governance / Zarządzanie Publiczne, 55(1), 8-22. DOI: 10.15678/ZP.2021.55.1.02

Dwivedi, D. N., Mahanty, G., & Pathak, Y. K. (2023). AI Applications for Financial Risk Management. In M. Irfan, M. Elmogy, M. Shabri Abd. Majid, & S. El-Sappagh (Eds.), The Impact of AI Innovation on Financial Sectors in the Era of Industry 5.0 (pp. 17-31). IGI Global. https://doi.org/DOI: 10.4018/979-8-3693-0082-4.ch002

Dwivedi, D. N., Mahanty, G., & Vemareddy, A. (2023). Sentiment Analysis and Topic Modeling for Identifying Key Public Concerns of Water Quality/Issues. In: Harun, S., Othman, I.K., Jamal, M.H. (eds) Proceedings of the 5th International Conference on Water Resources (ICWR) – Volume 1. Lecture Notes in Civil Engineering, vol 293. Springer, Singapore. DOI: 10.1007/978-981-19-5947-9_28

Dwivedi, D. N., Pandey, A. K., & Dwivedi, A. D. (2023). Examining the emotional tone in politically polarized Speeches in India: An In-Depth analysis of two contrasting perspectives. SOUTH INDIA JOURNAL OF SOCIAL SCIENCES, 21(2), 125-136. https://journal.sijss.com/index.php/home/article/view/65

Dwivedi, D. N. (2024). The Use of Artificial Intelligence in Supply Chain Management and Logistics. In Sharma, D., Bhardwaj, B., & Dhiman, M. (Eds.), *Leveraging AI and Emotional Intelligence in Contemporary Business Organizations* (pp. 306–313). IGI Global., DOI: 10.4018/979-8-3693-1902-4.ch018

Dwivedi, D. N., & Anand, A. (2021). Trade Heterogeneity in the EU: Insights from the Emergence of COVID-19 Using Time Series Clustering. *Zeszyty Naukowe Uniwersytetu Ekonomicznego w Krakowie*, 3(993), 9–26. DOI: 10.15678/ZNUEK.2021.0993.0301

Dwivedi, D. N., & Anand, A. (2022). A Comparative Study of Key Themes of Scientific Research Post COVID-19 in the United Arab Emirates and WHO Using Text Mining Approach. In Tiwari, S., Trivedi, M. C., Kolhe, M. L., Mishra, K., & Singh, B. K. (Eds.), *Advances in Data and Information Sciences. Lecture Notes in Networks and Systems* (Vol. 318). Springer., DOI: 10.1007/978-981-16-5689-7_30

Dwivedi, D. N., & Batra, S. (2024). Case Studies in Big Data Analysis: A Novel Computer Vision Application to Detect Insurance Fraud. In Darwish, D. (Ed.), *Big Data Analytics Techniques for Market Intelligence* (pp. 441–450). IGI Global., DOI: 10.4018/979-8-3693-0413-6.ch018

Dwivedi, D. N., Batra, S., & Pathak, Y. K. (2024). Enhancing Customer Experience: Exploring Deep Learning Models for Banking Customer Journey Analysis. In Sharma, H., Chakravorty, A., Hussain, S., & Kumari, R. (Eds.), *Artificial Intelligence: Theory and Applications. AITA 2023. Lecture Notes in Networks and Systems* (Vol. 843). Springer., DOI: 10.1007/978-981-99-8476-3_39

Dwivedi, D. N., & Gupta, A. (2022). Artificial intelligence-driven power demand estimation and short-, medium-, and long-term forecasting. In *Artificial Intelligence for Renewable Energy Systems* (pp. 231–242). Woodhead Publishing., DOI: 10.1016/B978-0-323-90396-7.00013-4

Dwivedi, D. N., & Mahanty, G. (2024). AI-Powered Employee Experience: Strategies and Best Practices. In Rafiq, M., Farrukh, M., Mushtaq, R., & Dastane, O. (Eds.), *Exploring the Intersection of AI and Human Resources Management* (pp. 166–181). IGI Global., DOI: 10.4018/979-8-3693-0039-8.ch009

Dwivedi, D. N., & Mahanty, G. (2024). Mental Health in Messages: Unravelling Emotional Patterns Through Advanced Text Analysis. In Rai, M., & Pandey, J. (Eds.), *Using Machine Learning to Detect Emotions and Predict Human Psychology* (pp. 187–208). IGI Global., DOI: 10.4018/979-8-3693-1910-9.ch009

Dwivedi, D. N., Mahanty, G., & Vemareddy, A. (2022). How Responsible Is AI?: Identification of Key Public Concerns Using Sentiment Analysis and Topic Modeling. [IJIRR]. *International Journal of Information Retrieval Research*, 12(1), 1–14. DOI: 10.4018/IJIRR.298646

Dwivedi, D. N., & Pathak, S. (2022). Sentiment Analysis for COVID Vaccinations Using Twitter: Text Clustering of Positive and Negative Sentiments. In Hassan, S. A., Mohamed, A. W., & Alnowibet, K. A. (Eds.), *Decision Sciences for COVID-19. International Series in Operations Research & Management Science* (Vol. 320). Springer., DOI: 10.1007/978-3-030-87019-5_12

Dwivedi, D. N., & Patil, G. (2023). Climate change: Prediction of solar radiation using advanced machine learning techniques. In Srivastav, A., Dubey, A., Kumar, A., Narang, S. K., & Khan, M. A. (Eds.), *Visualization Techniques for Climate Change with Machine Learning and Artificial Intelligence* (pp. 335–358). Elsevier., DOI: 10.1016/B978-0-323-99714-0.00017-0

Dwivedi, D. N., Tadoori, G., & Batra, S. (2023). Impact of women leadership and ESG ratings and in organizations: A time series segmentation study. *Academy of Strategic Management Journal*, 22(S3), 1–6.

Dwivedi, D. N., Wójcik, K., & Vemareddyb, A. (2022). Identification of Key Concerns and Sentiments Towards Data Quality and Data Strategy Challenges Using Sentiment Analysis and Topic Modeling. In Jajuga, K., Dehnel, G., & Walesiak, M. (Eds.), *Modern Classification and Data Analysis. SKAD 2021. Studies in Classification, Data Analysis, and Knowledge Organization*. Springer., DOI: 10.1007/978-3-031-10190-8_2

Dwivedi, D., Batra, S., & Pathak, Y. K. (2023). A machine learning based approach to identify key drivers for improving corporate's esg ratings. *Journal of Law and Sustainable Development*, 11(1), e0242. DOI: 10.37497/sdgs.v11i1.242

Dwivedi, D., Kapur, P. N., & Kapur, N. N. (2023). Machine Learning Time Series Models for Tea Pest Looper Infestation in Assam, India. In Sharma, A., Chanderwal, N., & Khan, R. (Eds.), *Convergence of Cloud Computing, AI, and Agricultural Science* (pp. 280–289). IGI Global., DOI: 10.4018/979-8-3693-0200-2.ch014

Dwivedi, D., & Vemareddy, A. (2023). Sentiment Analytics for Crypto Pre and Post Covid: Topic Modeling. In Molla, A. R., Sharma, G., Kumar, P., & Rawat, S. (Eds.), Lecture Notes in Computer Science: Vol. 13776. *Distributed Computing and Intelligent Technology. ICDCIT 2023*. Springer., DOI: 10.1007/978-3-031-24848-1_21

Dyer, T., Steele, J., & Mandernach, J. (2023). Three student-centered approaches to integrate ChatGPT in the online classroom: Effective eLearning (special series). *ELearn, 2023*(7). https://doi.org/DOI: 10.1145/3609266.3594546

Eldın, N. M. S. (2012). Visual Effects Cinematography the Cinematographer's Filmic Technique From Traditional to Digital Era. *Turkish Online Journal of Design Art and Communication*, 2(2), 115–122. DOI: 10.7456/10202100/016

Elnoshokaty, I. (2021). Cinema industry and artificial intelligency dreams. Prof. Ibrahim elnoshokaty.

Erdoğan, İ. (2005). *Sinema ve Müzik*. ERK Yayınları.

Fastcompany.com. (2024) Universal Music Group is Rewriting How Musicians are Paid in the AI era https://www.fastcompany.com/91041305/universal-music-group-most-innovative-companies-2024 (16.06.2024).

Fay, R., & Trenholm, W. n.d. "The Cyber Security Battlefield." *Centre for International Governance Innovation*. Retrieved July 3, 2024 (https://www.cigionline.org/articles/cyber-security-battlefield/)

Felix, C. V. (2020). The role of the teacher and AI in education. In *International perspectives on the role of technology in humanizing higher education* (pp. 33–48). Emerald Publishing Limited. DOI: 10.1108/S2055-364120200000033003

Feng, J., Zhao, Z., & Qian, X. (2019). A Content-Based Recommendation Algorithm for Short Video Platforms Based on Attention Mechanism. *IEEE Access : Practical Innovations, Open Solutions*.

Feng, Y., Lv, J., & Zhao, K. (2018). Hybrid Recommendation Algorithm for OTT Users Based on Topic Model and Collaborative Filtering. *IEEE Access : Practical Innovations, Open Solutions*.

Fernandez, P. (2023). "Through the looking glass: Envisioning new library technologies" AI-text generators as explained by ChatGPT. *Library Hi Tech News*, 40(3), 11–14. DOI: 10.1108/LHTN-02-2023-0017

Fikri, M. A., & Fitria, Y. (2022). Development Of Learning Media Based On Wondershare Filmora Software On Integrated Thematic Learning Elementary School. *Indonesian Journal of Learning Education & Counselling*, 4(2), 1–9. https://journal.ilininstitute.com/index.php/IJoLEC/article/view/1574/569

Fischer, H., Dres, M., & Seidenstricker, S. (2023). *Application of ChatGPT in Design Thinking*. AHFE International. DOI: 10.54941/ahfe1004312

Forbes. (2022). How AI is changing the future of film production

Fraiwan, M., & Khasawneh, N. (2023). *A review of ChatGPT applications in education, marketing, software engineering, and healthcare: Benefits, drawbacks, and research directions*. DOI: 10.48550/ARXIV.2305.00237

Friedman, D., & Feldman, Y. A. (2006). Automated cinematic reasoning about camera behavior. *Expert Systems with Applications*, 30(4), 694–704. DOI: 10.1016/j.eswa.2005.07.027

Frohlick, A. (2020). Artificial Intelligence and Contemporary Film Production: A Preliminary Survey. https://www.researchgate.net/publication/342978310_Artificial_Intelligence_and_Contemporary_Film_Production_A_Preliminary_Survey

Gerges, F. A. (2017). Pre-Production Movie Rating Prediction Using Machine Learning (Doctoral dissertation, LEBANESE AMERICAN UNIVERSITY).

Gervacio, M.Jr. (2023). Breaking barriers in academic writing: The uses of Chat AI models in empowering international TESOL students. *International Journal of Asian Education*, 4(4), 256–264. DOI: 10.46966/ijae.v4i4.361

Ghiassi, M., Lio, D., & Moon, B. (2015). Pre-production forecasting of movie revenues with a dynamic artificial neural network. *Expert Systems with Applications*, 42(6), 3176–3193. DOI: 10.1016/j.eswa.2014.11.022

Ghose, S., & Ve Prevost, J. J. (2020). AutoFoley: Artificial Synthesis of Synchronized Sound Tracks for Slient Videos with Deep Learning. *IEEE Transactions on Multimedia*.

Ghose, S., & Ve Prevost, J. J. (2021). FoleyGAN: Visually Guided Generative Adversarial Network-Based Synchonous Sound Generation in Silent Videos. *IEEE Transactions on Multimedia*, V, 25. DOI: 10.1109/TMM.2022.3177894

Ghosh, M. A. (2023). Artificial Intelligence as an Innovation in the Film Industry. *Research Inspiration*, 3(3), 12–16.

Ghosh, M., & Arunachalam, T. (2021). Introduction to Artificial Intelligence. Artificial Intelligence for Information Management: A Healthcare Perspective. *Studies in Big Data*, 88, 23–44.

Gong, Y. (2021). Application of virtual reality teaching method and artificial intelligence technology in digital media art creation. *Ecological Informatics*, 63, 101304. DOI: 10.1016/j.ecoinf.2021.101304

Goodfellow, I. J.. (2014). Generative adversarial Nets. *Advances in Neural Information Processing Systems*, 3(11). Advance online publication. DOI: 10.1145/3422622

GoodworksLabs (2019, May 2). How Machine Learning Gave "Thanos" a Soul in Avengers Endgame.

Gozalo-Brizuela, Roberto, and Eduardo C. Garrido-Merchan. (2023). "ChatGPT Is Not All You Need. A State of the Art Review of Large Generative AI Models."

Greengard, S. 2019. "What is Artificial Intelligence & How Does It Work?" *Datamation*. Retrieved July 4, 2024 (https://www.datamation.com/artificial-intelligence/what-is-artificial-intelligence/)

Gupta, A. et al., 2021. Understanding Consumer Product Sentiments through Supervised Models on Cloud: Pre and Post COVID. Webology, 18(1), pp.406â€“415. Available at: .DOI: 10.14704/WEB/V18I1/WEB18097

Gupta, A., Dwivedi, D. N., & Shah, J. (2023). Applying Artificial Intelligence on Investigation. In: Artificial Intelligence Applications in Banking and Financial Services. Future of Business and Finance. Springer, Singapore. DOI: 10.1007/978-981-99-2571-1_9

Gupta, A., Dwivedi, D. N., & Shah, J. (2023). Applying Machine Learning for Effective Customer Risk Assessment. In: Artificial Intelligence Applications in Banking and Financial Services. Future of Business and Finance. Springer, Singapore. https://doi.org/DOI: 10.1007/978-981-99-2571-1_6

Gupta, A., Dwivedi, D. N., & Shah, J. (2023). Artificial Intelligence-Driven Effective Financial Transaction Monitoring. In: Artificial Intelligence Applications in Banking and Financial Services. Future of Business and Finance. Springer, Singapore. https://doi.org/DOI: 10.1007/978-981-99-2571-1_7

Gupta, A., Dwivedi, D. N., & Shah, J. (2023). Data Organization for an FCC Unit. In: Artificial Intelligence Applications in Banking and Financial Services. Future of Business and Finance. Springer, Singapore. https://doi.org/DOI: 10.1007/978-981-99-2571-1_4

Gupta, A., Dwivedi, D. N., & Shah, J. (2023). Ethical Challenges for AI-Based Applications. In: Artificial Intelligence Applications in Banking and Financial Services. Future of Business and Finance. Springer, Singapore. https://doi.org/DOI: 10.1007/978-981-99-2571-1_10

Gupta, A., Dwivedi, D. N., & Shah, J. (2023). Financial Crimes Management and Control in Financial Institutions. In: Artificial Intelligence Applications in Banking and Financial Services. Future of Business and Finance. Springer, Singapore. https://doi.org/DOI: 10.1007/978-981-99-2571-1_2

Gupta, A., Dwivedi, D. N., & Shah, J. (2023). Machine Learning-Driven Alert Optimization. In: Artificial Intelligence Applications in Banking and Financial Services. Future of Business and Finance. Springer, Singapore. https://doi.org/DOI: 10.1007/978-981-99-2571-1_8

Gupta, A., Dwivedi, D. N., & Shah, J. (2023). Overview of Money Laundering. In: Artificial Intelligence Applications in Banking and Financial Services. Future of Business and Finance. Springer, Singapore. https://doi.org/DOI: 10.1007/978-981-99-2571-1_1

Gupta, A., Dwivedi, D. N., & Shah, J. (2023). Overview of Technology Solutions. In: Artificial Intelligence Applications in Banking and Financial Services. Future of Business and Finance. Springer, Singapore. https://doi.org/DOI: 10.1007/978-981-99-2571-1_3

Gupta, A., Dwivedi, D. N., & Shah, J. (2023). Planning for AI in Financial Crimes. In: Artificial Intelligence Applications in Banking and Financial Services. Future of Business and Finance. Springer, Singapore. https://doi.org/DOI: 10.1007/978-981-99-2571-1_5

Gupta, A., Dwivedi, D. N., & Shah, J. (2023). Setting up a Best-In-Class AI-Driven Financial Crime Control Unit (FCCU). In: Artificial Intelligence Applications in Banking and Financial Services. Future of Business and Finance. Springer, Singapore. https://doi.org/DOI: 10.1007/978-981-99-2571-1_11

Gupta, A., Dwivedi, D. N., & Shah, J. (2023). *Artificial Intelligence Applications in Banking and Financial Services: Anti Money Laundering and Compliance*. Springer Nature. DOI: 10.1007/978-981-99-2571-1

Habeb Al-Obaydi, L., Pikhart, M., & Klimova, B. (2023). ChatGPT and the general concepts of education: Can artificial intelligence-driven chatbots support the process of language learning? [IJET]. *International Journal of Emerging Technologies in Learning*, 18(21), 39–50. DOI: 10.3991/ijet.v18i21.42593

Haenlein, M., & Kaplan, A. (2019). A Brief History of Artificial Intelligence: On the Past, Present, and Future of Artificial Intelligence. *California Management Review*, 61(4), 5–14. DOI: 10.1177/0008125619864925

Harvard Business Review. (2020). AI bias: How to avoid it and ensure fairness

Hawanti, S., & Zubaydulloevna, K. M. (2023). AI chatbot-based learning: Alleviating students' anxiety in english writing classroom. *Bulletin of Social Informatics Theory and Application*, 7(2), 182–192. DOI: 10.31763/businta.v7i2.659

He, X., Liao, L., Zhang, H., Nie, L., Hu, X., & Chua, T. S. (2017). "Neural Collaborative Filtering." *WWW Conference*.

History of VFX. (2022, October 10). https://encyclopedia.pub/entry/28574

Hitsuwari, J., Ueda, Y., Yun, W., & Nomura, M. (2023). Does human–AI collaboration lead to more creative art? Aesthetic evaluation of human-made and AI-generated haiku poetry. *Computers in Human Behavior*, 139, 107502. DOI: 10.1016/j.chb.2022.107502

Hladum, O., Berko, A., Bublyk, M., Chyrun, L., & Schuchmann, V. (2021). Intelligent System for Film Script Transformation Based on Artbook Text and Big Data Analysis. *2021 IEEE 16th International Conference on Computer Sciences and Information Technologies (CSIT)*. https://doi.org/DOI: 10.1109/CSIT52700.2021.9648682

HLEGAI. (2019). *A definition of AI: Main capabilities and disciplines*. European Commission. Brussels. https://ec.europa.eu/newsroom/dae/document.cfm?doc_id=56341

Huang, P. (2024). Decoding Emotions: Intelligent Visual Perception for Movie Image Classification Using Sustainable AI in Entertainment Computing. *Entertainment Computing*, 50, 50. DOI: 10.1016/j.entcom.2024.100696

Huang, T., Le, V., Paine, T., Khorrami, P., & Tariq, U. (2014). Visual media: History and perspectives. *IEEE MultiMedia*, 21(2), 4–10. DOI: 10.1109/MMUL.2014.35

IBC (2023). Pixar's Elemental Lays Foundation for AI Powered Workflow.

Imran, M., & Almusharraf, N. (2024). Google Gemini as a next Generation AI Educational Tool: A Review of Emerging Educational Technology. *Smart Learning Environments*, 11(1), 22. DOI: 10.1186/s40561-024-00310-z

Inamdar, M.. (2023). Voice Cloning Using Artifical Intelligence and Machine Learning: A Review. *Journal of Advanced Zoology*, 44-7(S7), 419–427. DOI: 10.17762/jaz.v44iS7.2721

Irfan, M., Murray, L., & Ali, S. (2023). Integration of artificial intelligence in academia: A case study of critical teaching and learning in higher education. *Global Social Sciences Review*, VIII(I), 352–364. DOI: 10.31703/gssr.2023(VIII-I).32

Islam, M. M. (2022). Artificial intelligence in Indian films: Anukul and AI ethics. *Short Film Studies*, 12(2), 183–192. DOI: 10.1386/sfs_00082_1

Jannach, D., & Ludewig, M. (2017). "When Recurrent Neural Networks meet the Neighborhood for Session-Based Recommendation." *ACM Conference on Recommender Systems*. DOI: 10.1145/3109859.3109872

Jasper | AI copilot for enterprise marketing teams. (n.d.). https://www.jasper.ai/

Jayanthiladevi, A., Raj, A. G., Narmadha, R., Chandran, S., Shaju, S., & Prasad, K. K. (2020, December). AI in video analysis, production and streaming delivery. []. IOP Publishing.]. *Journal of Physics: Conference Series*, 1712(1), 012014. DOI: 10.1088/1742-6596/1712/1/012014

Jayawardena, N. S., & Dewasiri, N. J. (2023). *Food Acquisition and Consumption Issues of South Asian Countries: A Systematic Literature Review and Future Research Agenda*. FIIB Business Review., DOI: 10.1177/23197145231194113

Johnson, G. (2011). Spielberg your way to information literacy: producing educational movies and videos. In *Information Literacy* (pp. 151–183). Chandos Publishing. DOI: 10.1016/B978-1-84334-610-4.50007-0

Karnouskos, S. (2020). Artificial intelligence in digital media: The era of deepfakes. *IEEE Transactions on Technology and Society*, 1(3), 138–147. DOI: 10.1109/TTS.2020.3001312

Karunarathna, K. S. S. N., Dewasiri, N. J., Singh, R., & Rathnasiri, M. S. H. (2024). What Does Artificial Intelligence–Powered ChatGPT Bring to Academia? A Review. Singh, R., Khan, S., Kumar, A., & Kumar, V. (Ed.) Artificial Intelligence Enabled Management: An Emerging Economy Perspective, De Gruyter, pp. 3-13, Berlin, https://doi.org/DOI: 10.1515/9783111172408

Khanna, A. (2024, February 21). From Script To Distribution: AI's Role In The Film World. *Forbes*. https://www.forbes.com/sites/forbestechcouncil/2024/02/21/from-script-to-distribution-ais-role-in-the-film-world/

Khan, S. U., Khan, S., & Mukherjee, T. (2024). The "Subaltern" Will Speak: Investigating Portrayals in the Acclaimed OTT Series of India and Pakistan. In Kalorth, N. (Ed.), *Exploring the Impact of OTT Media on Global Societies* (pp. 1–24). IGI Global., DOI: 10.4018/979-8-3693-3526-0.ch001

Khurana, R., Yadav, M., Quttainah, M., Srivastava, A. P., Baludi, A., & Singh, P. K. (2023, November). Neural Networks in Recruitment: Trends and Future Directions. In *2023 International Conference on Ambient Intelligence, Knowledge Informatics and Industrial Electronics (AIKIIE)* (pp. 1-5). IEEE. DOI: 10.1109/AIKIIE60097.2023.10390017

Kim, Y., Park, J. Y., Hwang, E. J., Lee, S. M., & Park, C. M. (2021b). Applications of artificial intelligence in the thorax: A narrative review focusing on thoracic radiology. *Journal of Thoracic Disease*, 13(12), 6943–6962. DOI: 10.21037/jtd-21-1342 PMID: 35070379

Kiy, H. (2023). A study on writing experience with ChatGPT of college students. *Culture and Convergence*, 45(9), 853–868. DOI: 10.33645/cnc.2023.09.45.09.853

Kleist, K. (2023). *Machine Learning & Cinema: Color grading style classification through Vectorscopes and CNNs* (Doctoral dissertation, Politecnico di Torino).

Koren, Y. (2009). Collaborative Filtering with Temporal Dynamics. *Communications of the ACM*.

Koren, Y., Bell, R., & Volinsky, C. (2009). "Matrix Factorization Techniques for Recommender Systems." Computer. Bansal, T., & Belcastro, L. (2020). "Movie Recommendation System using Collaborative Filtering Algorithm. *International Journal of Advanced Computer Science and Applications*.

Kumar, K. S. (2024,10 April). *The Role of AI in Rajmouli Films: Redefining Cinematic Excellence*. seamedu. https://www.seamedu.com/blog/the-role-of-ai-in-rajamouli-films

Kunnumpurath, B., Menon, V. A., & Paul, A. (2024). ChatGPT and virtual experience. In *Advances in computational intelligence and robotics book series* (pp. 32–50). DOI: 10.4018/979-8-3693-4268-8.ch003

Lai, Y. (2023). The impact of AI-driven narrative generation, exemplified by ChatGPT, on the preservation of human creative originality and uniqueness. *Lecture Notes in Education Psychology and Public Media*, 26(1), 121–124. DOI: 10.54254/2753-7048/26/20230865

LeCun, Y., Bengio, Y., & Hinton, G. (2015). Deep Learning. *Nature*, 521(7553), 436–444. DOI: 10.1038/nature14539 PMID: 26017442

Lee, J. (2023). A case study on writing a self-introduction letter in university liberal education using ChatGPT. *Culture and Convergence*, 45(9), 193–208. DOI: 10.33645/cnc.2023.09.45.09.193

Li, C., & Bantourakis, M. (2023, August 2). *6 ways AI could disrupt the entertainment industry*. World Economic Forum. https://www.weforum.org/agenda/2023/08/hollywood-strike-synthetic-voice-digital-avatar-ai-entertainment/

Li, L., Chu, W., Langford, J., & Schapire, R. E. (2010). “A Contextual-Bandit Approach to Personalized News Article Recommendation.” *ACM International Conference on World Wide Web*. DOI: 10.1145/1772690.1772758

Loos, E., Gröpler, J., & Goudeau, M.-L. S. (2023). Using ChatGPT in education: Human reflection on ChatGPT’s self-reflection. *Societies (Basel, Switzerland)*, 13(8), 196. DOI: 10.3390/soc13080196

Loureiro, S. M. C., Guerreiro, J., & Tussyadiah, I. (2021). Artificial intelligence in business: State of the art and future research agenda. *Journal of Business Research*, 129, 911–926. DOI: 10.1016/j.jbusres.2020.11.001

Luan, L., Lin, X., & Li, W. (2023). *Exploring the cognitive dynamics of artificial intelligence in the post-COVID-19 and learning 3.0 era: A case study of ChatGPT*. DOI: 10.48550/ARXIV.2302.04818

Lv, Z. (2023). Generative Artificial Intelligence in the Metaverse Era. *Cognitive Robotics*, 3, 208–217. DOI: 10.1016/j.cogr.2023.06.001

Maayah, M.. (2023) "Using Context Specific Generative Adversarial Networks for Audio Data Completion" *Jordan International Joint Conference on Electrical Engineering and Information Technology*, Amman, Jordan. DOI: 10.1109/JEE-IT58638.2023.10185733

Ma, H., Yang, H., Lyu, M. R., & King, I. (2019). Learning to Recommend with Personalized Feature Enhancement for E-commerce. *ACM Transactions on Information Systems*.

Maher, M. L., Tadimalla, S. Y., & Dhamani, D. (2023). An exploratory study on the impact of AI tools on the student experience in programming courses: An intersectional analysis approach. *2023 IEEE Frontiers in Education Conference (FIE)*.

Mahna, V. (2024, April 17). *A Brief Review on the Status of Artificial Intelligence in Cinema*. Exploratio. https://exploratiojournal.com/a-brief-review-on-the-status-of-artificial-intelligence-in-cinema/

Malhan, S., Mewafarosh, R., Agnihotri, S., & Gupta, D. (2023). "Emergence of AI in Education: A Way Forward for Societal Development." Pp. 56–68 in *Artificial Intelligence and Society 5.0*. Boca Raton: Chapman and Hall/CRC.

Mannarsamy, N. (2023). Scripting imagination: The AI revolution in creative writing. *Shanlax International Journal of English*, 12(1), 33–36. DOI: 10.34293/english.v12i1.6727

Marechal, C.. (2019). Survey on AI-Based Multimodal Methods for Emotion Detection. In Kolodzjej, J., & Gonzalez-Velez, H. (Eds.), *High-Performance Modelling and Simulation for Big Data Applications*. Springer. DOI: 10.1007/978-3-030-16272-6_11

Mariani, L. (2024). Cinema e Intelligenza Artificiale (Cinema and Artificial Intelligence). Cinemafocus. https://www.cinemafocus.eu/Studi%20sul%20cinema/IA.html

Markauskaite, L., Marrone, R., Poquet, O., Knight, S., Martinez-Maldonado, R., Howard, S., Tondeur, J., De Laat, M., Buckingham Shum, S., Gašević, D., & Siemens, G. (2022). Rethinking the entwinement between artificial intelligence and human learning: What capabilities do learners need for a world with AI? *Computers and Education: Artificial Intelligence*, 3, 100056. DOI: 10.1016/j.caeai.2022.100056

Mashable.com. (2023) "Ghostwriter, the guy behind the viral Drake/Weeknd Song, Thinks AI Music is Like Fanfiction" https://mashable.com/article/ai-music-ghostwriter-drake (20.06.2024).

Mathur, V. (2023, March 31). *Explained: How Artificial Intelligence in Hollywood movies like Blade Runner and The Matrix has been a game-changer.* Firstpost. https://www.firstpost.com/entertainment/explained-how-artificial-intelligence-in-hollywood-movies-like-blade-runner-and-the-matrix-has-been-a-game-changer-12383272.html

Mckee, R. (1997). *Story: Substance, Structure, Style and the Principles of Screenwriting*. Regan Books.

McKinsey & Company. (2021). The real-world potential and limitations of artificial intelligence

McMillan, K. (2021, September 6). *REVIEW: Look Designer 2 by ColourLab.ai.* Provideo Coalition. https://www.provideocoalition.com/review-look-designer-2-by-colourlab-ai/

Meltzer, A. (2024) "AI-Generated Music In Film: Enhancing Emotional Impact" https://cassetteai.com/blog/ai-generated-music-in-film-enhancing-emotional-impact (25.06.2024).

Messer, U. (2024). Co-Creating Art with Generative Artificial Intelligence: Implications for Artworks and Artists. *Computers in Human Behavior: Artificial Humans*, 2(1), 100056. DOI: 10.1016/j.chbah.2024.100056

Metz, C. (2006). Hollywood Cinema. *The Cambridge Companion to Modern American Culture.* 374-391

Ming, X. M. Post-Production of Digital Film and Television with Development of Virtual Reality Image Technology-Advance Research Analysis.

Minsker, E. (2019) Holly Herndon, Weighs in on Grimes and Zola Jesus' Debate About AI and the Future of Music" https://pitchfork.com/news/holly-herndon-weighs-in-on-grimes-and-zola-jesus-debate-about-ai-and-the-future-of-music/ (19.06.2024).

Mishra, U., Rathnasiri, M. S. H., & Dewasiri, N. J. (2024). Net-Zero Economy and Energy Sustainability: A Nepalese Perspective. In Singh, R., Khan, S., Kumar, A., Luthra, S., & Chokshi, H. (Eds.), *Net Zero Economy, Corporate Social Responsibility and Sustainable Value Creation. CSR, Sustainability, Ethics & Governance* (pp. 145–161). Springer., DOI: 10.1007/978-3-031-55779-8_9

MIT Technology Review. (2019). The ethical dilemma of deepfakes

Momot, I. (2022). Artificial intelligence in filmmaking process: future scenarios.

Momot, I. (2022). Artificial Intelligence in Filmmaking Process: Future Scenarios. *Jamk: School of Business. Degree Programme in International Business.*

Monaco, J. (2000). *How To Read A Film: The World Of Movies, Media, And Multimedia: Art, Technology, Language, History, Theory*. Oxford University Press.

Moore, S. (2019, April 13). Why Film Budgets Are Important, Beyond The Cost Of Production. *Forbes*. https://www.forbes.com/sites/schuylermoore/2019/04/13/the-importance-of-film-budgets/

Moore, S. A. (2017). *The Rise of the Sound Designer: Northen California Film Sound in the 1960's and 1970's in Historical Journal of Film*. Radio and Television.

Moviemaking platform largo.ai is about to help change advertising forever! (2021, September 02). Largo.ai. https://home.largo.ai/leading-ai-assisted-moviemaking-platform-largo-ai-is-about-to-help-change-advertising-forever/

Murad, I. A., Surameery, N. M. S., & Shakor, M. Y. (2023). Adopting ChatGPT to enhance educational experiences. *International Journal of Information Technology and Computer Engineering*, 35(35), 20–25. DOI: 10.55529/ijitc.35.20.25

Murphy, G., Ching, D., Twomey, J., & Linehan, C. (2023). Face/Off: Changing the face of movies with deepfakes. *PLoS One*, 18(7), e0287503. DOI: 10.1371/journal.pone.0287503 PMID: 37410765

Nair, V. (2024, April 09). *The Audio of This Bollywood Song was Generated by AI*.AIM. https://analyticsindiamag.com/the-audio-of-this-bollywood-song-was-generated-by-ai/

Naji, A. K. (2024). Employing artificial intelligence techniques to make films. Al-Academy, 171-180.

Namaz, Y. (2022). Film Yapımında Kurgucuların Rolü ve Önemi: Film Kurgusunun Büyüsü (2004) Adlı Belgeselin Analizi. Intermedia. *International Journal (Toronto, Ont.)*, 9(17), 273–291. DOI: 10.56133/intermedia.1168275

Nassar, S. (2024). Futuristic Scenarios: Utilization of AI Technological Settings to Foster the Filmmaking Visual Creation & Mass Production. *International Design Journal*, 14(2), 207–212. DOI: 10.21608/idj.2024.258755.1110

Nguyen, Q. (2023). AI Representation in Cinema: A Quantitative Content Analysis. ttps://www.researchgate.net/profile/Quynh-Nguyen-431/publication/377410844_AI_REPRESENTATION_IN_CINEMA_A_Quantitative_Content_Analysis/links/65a56a5a5582153a6828704d/AI-REPRESENTATION-IN-CINEMA-A-Quantitative-Content-Analysis.pdf

Niloy, A. C., Akter, S., Sultana, N., Sultana, J., & Rahman, S. I. U. (2024). Is Chatgpt a menace for creative writing ability? An experiment. *Journal of Computer Assisted Learning*, 40(2), 919–930. DOI: 10.1111/jcal.12929

Nişancı, İ. (2012). Kurgunun Güncel Sorunsalı: Eisensteın'ın Dikey Kurgusunun Evrimi. *İstanbul University Faculty of Communication Journal(41)*, 63-80. https://doi.org/DOI: 10.17064/iüifhd.36724

Nofilmschool.com. (2016) How IBM's Watson Used AI to the Trailer for Upcoming AI Thriller 'Morgan' https://nofilmschool.com/2016/10/ibm-watson-edits-morgan-trailer (21.06.2024).

NVIDIA. (n.d.). *NVIDIA RTX: Ray Tracing*. Rendering, AI, & Deep Learning.

O'Meara, J., & Murphy, C. (2023). Aberrant AI Creations: Co-Creating Surrealist Body Horror Using the DALL-E Mini Text-to-Image Generator. *Convergence (London)*, 29(4), 1070–1096. Advance online publication. DOI: 10.1177/13548565231185865

O'Shaughnessy, M. (2022, October 6). *One of the Biggest Problems in Regulating AI Is Agreeing on a Definition.* Carnegie Endowment for International Peace. https://carnegieendowment.org/posts/2022/10/one-of-the-biggest-problems-in-regulating-ai-is-agreeing-on-a-definition?lang=en

Öcal, D. (2020). "Reklamcılık: Nereden Nereye…" p.1-41. in *Dijital Reklamcılık.* (Eds.) Derya Öcal and Hıdır Polat. Ankara: Nobel Publications.

Onaran, A. Ş. (1986). *Sinemaya Giriş*. Agora Kitaplığı/ Sinema Dizisi.

Optical Flow Algorithms Overview — Metavision SDK Docs 4.6.0 documentation. (n.d.). https://docs.prophesee.ai/stable/algorithms/optical_flow.html

Özön, N. (1964). *Sinema El Kitabı*. Elif Yayınları.

PALANIMURUGAN, P. (2024). Challenges and Solutions in Green Screen Post-Production: A Narrative Review.

Pannasch, S. & vd. (2011). Apparent Phi-Motion in Sequences of Eisenstein's October. *Gestalt Theory*, 33(1), 69–80.

Parikh, P. (2019, April 16). *AI Film Aesthetics: A Construction of a New Media Identity for AI Films* [Masters Thesis, Chapman University].Chapman University Digital Commons. https://digitalcommons.chapman.edu/cgi/viewcontent.cgi?article=1007&context=film_studies_theses

Paris, B., & Donavan, J. (2019). *Deep Fakes and Cheap Fakes Them Manipulation of Audio and Visual Evidence*. Data and Society.

Parisse-Brassens, J. (2021). *Future Impact of AI on Culture*. White Paper.

Pearson, R. (1996). Early Cinema. In *The Oxford History of World Cinema. N.-S. Geoffrey içinde, The Oxford History of World Cinema* (pp. 13–22). Oxford University Press.

Pecora, A. E. (2023). *Data Driven: AI Voice Cloning*. Politecnico Di Torino Masters Degree in Data Science and Engineering.

Penrose, R. (1997). *Bilgisayar ve Zeka*. Kralın Yeni Usu. Tübitak Yayınları.

Peres, F. (2024). Health literacy in ChatGPT: Exploring the potential of the use of artificial intelligence to produce academic text. *Ciencia & Saude Coletiva*, 29(1). Advance online publication. DOI: 10.1590/1413-81232024291.02412023 PMID: 38198321

Perren, A., & Schatz, T. (2004). Hollywood. Georgia State University Communication Faculty Publications. Published in The Sage Handbook of Media Studies. 495-515.

Pixar Post. (2023). *Elemental Fun Facts – 5 Things We Learned About the Film When Visiting Pixar*. And More Screencaps.

Polyzos, D. (2022). Critical Examination of the Use of Artificial Intelligence as a Creative Tool in Editing and its Potential as a Creator in its own.

Pozzi, F. A., & Dwivedi, D. (2023). ESG and IoT: Ensuring Sustainability and Social Responsibility in the Digital Age. In Tiwari, S., Ortiz-Rodríguez, F., Mishra, S., Vakaj, E., & Kotecha, K. (Eds.), *Artificial Intelligence: Towards Sustainable Intelligence. AI4S 2023. Communications in Computer and Information Science* (Vol. 1907). Springer., DOI: 10.1007/978-3-031-47997-7_2

Prajapat, S., Singh, A. K., Banerjee, A., & Bhatnagar, K. Role of AI and Video Technology in Sci-Fi Cinema.

Propp, V. (1985). *Masalın Biçimbilimi. (Çev. Mehmet&Sema Rifat)*. Bilim/Felsefe/Sanat Yayınları.

Pudovkin, V. I. (1965). *Sinemanın Temel İlkeleri*. Bilgi Yayınevi.

Purves, D.. (2004). *Neuroscience*. Sinauer.

Quthor (2024, January 27). *2024's Top AI Music Generators: Mubert, Aiva, and Beatoven Comparison*. Quick Creator. https://quickcreator.io/seo/2024-top-ai-music-generators-mubert-aiva-beatoven-comparison/

Ram, B., & Verma, P. (2023). Artificial intelligence AI-based Chatbot study of ChatGPT, Google AI Bard and Baidu AI. *World Journal of Advanced Engineering Technology and Sciences*, 8(1), 258–261. DOI: 10.30574/wjaets.2023.8.1.0045

Reddy, V. S., Kathiravan, M., & Reddy, V. L. (2024). Revolutionizing animation: Unleashing the power of artificial intelligence for cutting-edge visual effects in films. *Soft Computing*, 28(1), 749–763. DOI: 10.1007/s00500-023-09448-3

Reisz, K., & Millar, G. (2010). *The Technique of Film Editing*. Routledge Focal Press.

Ren, X., Tong, L., Zeng, J., & Zhang, C. (2023). AIGC scenario analysis and research on technology roadmap of Internet industry application. *China Communications*, 20(10), 292–304. DOI: 10.23919/JCC.fa.2023-0359.202310

Respeecher.com. (t.y.) "Respeecher Synthesized a Younger Luke Skywalker's Voice for Disney+'s The Mandalorian" https://www.respeecher.com/case-studies/respeecher-synthesized-younger-luke-skywalkers-voice-disneys-mandalorian (30.06.2024).

Riedl, M. O., & Young, R. M. (2010). Narrative Planning: Balancing Plot and Character. *Journal of Artificial Intelligence Research*, 39, 217–268. DOI: 10.1613/jair.2989

Ring, D., Barbier, J., Gales, G., Kent, B., & Lutz, S. (2019, July). Jumping in at the deep end: how to experiment with machine learning in post-production software. In *Proceedings of the 2019 Digital Production Symposium* (pp. 1-5). DOI: 10.1145/3329715.3338880

Ritala, P., Ruokonen, M., & Ramaul, L. (2024). Transforming boundaries: How does ChatGPT change knowledge work? *The Journal of Business Strategy*, 45(3), 214–220. DOI: 10.1108/JBS-05-2023-0094

Robinson, S. C. (2020). Trust, transparency, and openness: How inclusion of cultural values shapes Nordic national public policy strategies for artificial intelligence (AI). *Technology in Society*, 63, 101421. DOI: 10.1016/j.techsoc.2020.101421

Rose, S. (2020, January 16). "It's a war between technology and a donkey" – how AI is shaking up Hollywood. The Guardian. https://www.theguardian.com/film/2020/jan/16/its-a-war-between-technology-and-a-donkey-how-ai-is-shaking-up-hollywood

Rupesh, G., & Choudaiah, S. (2019). Artificial Intelligence and its Role in Near Future. *International Journal of Scientific Research*, 8, 893–898.

Russel, S. J., & Ve Norvig, P. (1995). *Artifical Intelligence A Modern Approach.* Prentice Hall Englewood Cliffs.

Ryu, S. (2024). *Media and Entertainment Industry Management: How to Integrate Business and Management with Creativity and Imagination*. Taylor & Francis. DOI: 10.4324/9781003271222

Sadiku, M. N. O., Ashaolu, T. J., Ajayi-Majebi, A., & Musa, S. M. (2021). Artificial Intelligence in Social Media. *International Journal Of Scientific Advances*, 2(1), 15–20. DOI: 10.51542/ijscia.v2i1.4

Salazar, D. (2023, May 15). *This K-pop artist sings fluently in 6 languages. His secret? Voice AI*. Fast Company. https://www.fastcompany.com/90896187/hybe-bts-kpop-midnatt-supertone-ai-lee-hyun

Sanjay, M., Vikas, S., & Prashant, D. (2023). ChatGPT: Optimizing text generation model for knowledge creation. *I-Manager's Journal on Software Engineering*, 17(3), 21. DOI: 10.26634/jse.17.3.19469

Sarkar, S. (2024, January 15). Does AI-produced film 'Maharaja in Denims' mark a shift in Indian cinema? *South China Morning Post*. https://www.scmp.com/week-asia/lifestyle-culture/article/3248487/does-ai-generated-film-maharaja-denims-mark-shift-indian-cinema

Sarwar, B., Karypis, G., Konstan, J., & Riedl, J. (2001). "Item-Based Collaborative Filtering Recommendation Algorithms." *WWW Conference*.

Sathyan, J. (2023, September 01). *Smart VFX: How AI Is Empowering Visual Effects*. India Art Review. https://indiaartreview.com/stories/smart-vfx-how-ai-is-empowering-visual-effects/

Schmidt, L., Piazza, A., & Wiedenhöft, C. (2023). "augmented brainstorming with AI" – research approach for identifying design criteria for improved collaborative idea generation between humans and AI. In *Frontiers in Artificial Intelligence and Applications*. IOS Press.

Scientific American. (2021). AI's Biggest Challenges Are Still Unsolved

Scott, A. J. (2006). Origins and Growth of the Hollywood Motion Picture Industry: The First Three Decades. *Cluster Genesis: Technology-Based Industrial Development*. 17–37.

ScriptBook. (ScriptBook Formula and Chart). https://www.scriptbook.io/#!/scriptbook/technology (Url 1). (Visited 11.06.2024).

ScriptBook. (Webpage). https://www.scriptbook.io/#!/scriptbook (Url 3). (Visited 12.06.2024).

Scriptbook: (Proof). https://www.scriptbook.io/#!/scriptbook/proof (Url2). (Visited 12.06.2024).

Sedhain, S., Kawale, J., & Kumar, S. (2015). "AutoRec: Autoencoders Meet Collaborative Filtering." *World Wide Web Conference*. DOI: 10.1145/2740908.2742726

Seguela, J. (1997). *Eğlenceli Şeydir Şu Reklamcılık*. Doğan Kitap.

Sengar, P. (2020). Big Data: Frame the Cinema from Viewership to Projection. *MediaSpace: DME Media Journal of Communication*, 1(01), 66–72.

Shah, D. (2023, December 19). *Bollywood: How AI may affect India's vast film industry*. BBC News. https://www.bbc.com/news/world-asia-india-67657873

Shan, M., Kuo, F.-F., Chiang, M.-F., & Lee, S.-Y. (2009). Emotion-based Music Recommednation by Affinity Discovery From Film Music [Elsevier.]. *Expert Systems with Applications*, 36(4), 7666–7674. DOI: 10.1016/j.eswa.2008.09.042

Sharma, A. (2023, October 2). A Deep Dive into Variational Autoencoders with PyTorch - PyImageSearch. PyImageSearch. https://pyimagesearch.com/2023/10/02/a-deep-dive-into-variational-autoencoders-with-pytorch/

Sheikh, H., Prins, C., & Schrijvers, E. (2023). Artificial Intelligence: Definition and Background. In Mission, A. I. (Ed.), *Research for Policy*. Springer., DOI: 10.1007/978-3-031-21448-6_2

Shen, P. (2011). Film and Intuition: An Exploration of Rhythm, Pace, and the Moving Image. Master of Arts Thesis. Baylor University. Kaiser, M. (2001). Filmische Geschichts-Chroniken im Neuen Deutschen Film: Die Heimat-Reihen von Edgar Reitz und ihre Bedeutung für das deutsche Fernsehen. Dissertation zur Erlangung des Grades des Doktors der Philosophie im Fach Literaturwissenschaft, Universität Osnabrück. Eisenstein, S. (1984). Film Duyumu. Nijat Özön (Çeviri). İstanbul: Payel Yayınevi.

Silva, A. de O., & Janes, D. dos S. (2021). The emergence of ChatGPT and its implications for education and academic research in the 21st century. *Review of Artificial Intelligence in Education*, 2(00), e06. DOI: 10.37497/rev.artif.intell.education.v2i00.6

Singer, J. B., Báez, J. C., & Rios, J. A. (2023). AI creates the message: Integrating AI language learning models into social work education and practice. *Journal of Social Work Education*, 59(2), 294–302. DOI: 10.1080/10437797.2023.2189878

Singh, H., Kaur, K., & Singh, P. P. (2023, January). Artificial intelligence as a facilitator for film production process. In *2023 International Conference on Artificial Intelligence and Smart Communication (AISC)* (pp. 969-972). IEEE. DOI: 10.1109/AISC56616.2023.10085082

Sklar, B. (2021). *Digital communications: fundamentals and applications*. Pearson.

Squibler: AI Story Writer. (n.d.). https://www.squibler.io/

Storyboard, A. I. - The AI Storyboard Generator from Shai - Shai Creative. (2024, April 17). Shai Creative. https://shaicreative.ai/ai-storyboard-generator/

Storyboarder.ai – Revolutionize Your Storyboarding Process. (n.d.). Storyboarder.ai. https://storyboarder.ai/

StudioBinder. (2024, January 30). Video, TV & Film Production Management Software | StudioBinder. https://www.studiobinder.com/

StudioBinder. (2024, March 25) What is Cinematography? Defining the Art and Craft. https://www.studiobinder.com/blog/what-is-cinematography/

Sudirman, I. D., & Rahmatillah, I. (2023). Artificial intelligence-assisted discovery learning: An educational experience for entrepreneurship students using ChatGPT. *2023 IEEE World AI IoT Congress (AIIoT)*.

Sun, P. (2024). A Study of Artificial Intelligence in the Production of Film. In *SHS Web of Conferences* (Vol. 183, p. 03004). EDP Sciences. DOI: 10.1051/shsconf/202418303004

Sun, P. (2024). A Study of Artificial Intelligence in the Production of Film. *SHS Web of Conferences*. EDP Sciences.

Sundar, S. S., & Liao, M. (2023). Calling BS on ChatGPT: Reflections on AI as a communication source. *Journalism & Communication Monographs*, 25(2), 165–180. DOI: 10.1177/15226379231167135

Susanto, H., Woo, D. J., & Guo, K. (2023). *The role of AI in human-AI creative writing for Hong Kong secondary students*. DOI: 10.48550/ARXIV.2304.11276

Szilas, N. (2007). A computational model of an intelligent narrator for interactive narratives. *Applied Artificial Intelligence*, 21(8), 753–801. DOI: 10.1080/08839510701526574

Tahoun, N. (2020). The utilization of artificial intelligence in online advertising and its perceived effectiveness.

Tamandehrou, A., & Khan, S. U. (2015). Assessing the importance of globalisation and new media technology in 21st century: An analytical overview. *International Journal of Multifaceted & Multilingual Studies*, 1(4).

Tapaswi, M., Rainer, S., Antonio, T. (2016). MovieQA: Understanding Stories in Movies through Question-Answering. Computer Vision and Pattern Recognition (CVPR), Conference Paper. https://www.researchgate.net/publication/286513348_MovieQA_Understanding_Stories_in_Movies_through_Question-Answering

Telefonicatech.com. (2024) "Behind the Scenes Algorithms: Hollywood and the AI Technology Revolution" https://telefonicatech.com/en/blog/behind-the-scenes-algorithms-hollywood-and-the-ai-technology-revolution (21. 06.2024)

Tenhundfeld, N. L. (2023). Two birds with one stone: Writing a paper entitled "ChatGPT as a tool for studying human-AI interaction in the wild" with ChatGPT. *Proceedings of the Human Factors and Ergonomics Society ... Annual Meeting. Human Factors and Ergonomics Society.Annual Meeting, 67*(1), 2007–2012. DOI: 10.1177/21695067231192916

Tholander, J., & Jonsson, M. (2023). Design ideation with AI - sketching, thinking and talking with generative machine learning models. *Proceedings of the 2023 ACM Designing Interactive Systems Conference*. DOI: 10.1145/3563657.3596014

Thorp, H. H. (2023). ChatGPT Is Fun, but Not an Author. *Science*, 379(6630), 313–313. DOI: 10.1126/science.adg7879 PMID: 36701446

Time (2023) "4 Ways AI Transformed Music, Movies and Art in 2023" https://time.com/6343945/ai-music-movies-art-2023/ (19.06.2024).

TinyWow. (n.d.). Free AI Writing Tools - No Sign-Up, No Limit - TinyWow. https://tinywow.com/tools/write

Townsend, S. (2024) Exploring the Impact of AI on Film Production in 2024 https://medium.com/@channelasaservice/exploring-the-impact-of-ai-on-film-production-in-2024-f02da745af00 (19.06.2024).

Townsend, S. (2024, March 03). *Exploring the Impact of AI on Film Production in 2024*. Medium. https://medium.com/@channelasaservice/exploring-the-impact-of-ai-on-film-production-in-2024-f02da745af00

Tran, N. V. (2023a). How to edit a manuscript with assistance of ChatGPT. *TTU Journal of Biomedical Sciences*, 2(1), 51–64. DOI: 10.53901/tjbs.2023.08.art06

Tran, N. V. (2023b). Utilizing ChatGPT in the process of crafting a research paper: A comprehensive guide. *TTU Journal of Biomedical Sciences*, 2(1), 41–50. DOI: 10.53901/tjbs.2023.08.art05

Trivedi, S. K., Vishnu, S., Singh, A., & Yadav, M. (2023). Research trends in sustainable E-payment systems: A study using topic modeling approach. *IEEE Transactions on Engineering Management*, 71, 7511–7525. DOI: 10.1109/TEM.2023.3280216

Tryon, C. (2009). *Reinventing Cinema*. Rutgers University Press.

Tseng, W., & Warschauer, M. (2023). AI-writing tools in education: If you can't beat them, join them. *Journal of China Computer-Assisted Language Learning*, 3(2), 258–262. DOI: 10.1515/jccall-2023-0008

Valente, D., Strand, O., Kryza, A., & Singer, M. (2024, January 12). 50 Best Disney Movies Of All Time For Family Film Night With The Kids. Time Out Worldwide. https://www.timeout.com/film/the-best-disney-movies-of-all-time

Vasconcelos, M. A. R., & dos Santos, R. P. (2023). *Enhancing STEM learning with ChatGPT and Bing Chat as objects to think with: A case study*. https://doi.org/DOI: 10.48550/ARXIV.2305.02202

Verschure, J. P. (1995) "The Challenge of Sound Restoration from 1927 to Digital" in Film History 7:3 pp.264-276.

Vicente-Yagüe-Jara, M. I., López-Martínez, O., Navarro-Navarro, V., & Cuéllar-Santiago, F. (2023). Writing, creativity, and artificial intelligence. ChatGPT in the university context. *Comunicar*, 31(77). Advance online publication. DOI: 10.3916/C77-2023-04

Vilenkin, R. (2024, April 11). *The Role of AI Voice Cloning in Virtual Reality and Immersive Environments*. respeecher. https://www.respeecher.com/blog/ai-voice-cloning-virtual-reality-immersive-environments

Virtual Producer. (2023). Generative AI and the future of filmmaking

Vogler, C. (2009). *Yazarın sonsuz Yolculuğu*. Okyan Us Yayınları.

Walt Disney Animation Studios - The Role Of Hand Drawn Animation In Disneys Moana. (n.d.). Walt Disney Animation Studios. https://disneyanimation.com/publications/the-role-of-hand-drawn-animation-in-disneys-moana/#:~:text=The%20art%20direction%20of%20Moana,CG%20and%20hand%2Ddrawn%20elements

Wang, C.-H., & Li, T.-Y. (2018). Design of an Intelligent Agent for Stimulating Brainstorming. *Proceedings of the 2018 10th International Conference on Machine Learning and Computing*. DOI: 10.1145/3195106.3195119

Warner, A. (2022) AI-powered Localization Startup Deephub Raises 20 Million Dolars in Series A Funding" https://multilingual.com/deepdub-funding-milestone/ (24.06.2024).

Weber, C. J., Burgkart, S., & Rothe, S. (2024, June). wr-AI-ter: Enhancing Ownership Perception in AI-Driven Script Writing. In *Proceedings of the 2024 ACM International Conference on Interactive Media Experiences* (pp. 145-156). DOI: 10.1145/3639701.3656325

Wegerif, R., McLaren, B. M., Chamrada, M., Scheuer, O., Mansour, N., Mikšátko, J., & Williams, M. (2010). Exploring creative thinking in graphically mediated synchronous dialogues. *Computers & Education*, 54(3), 613–621. DOI: 10.1016/j.compedu.2009.10.015

Weis, E. And Belton J. (1985) "Film Sound: Theory and Practise" in Film Quarterly 39:1 pp.46-48.

Welsh, A. P. (2019) "Is AI making it easier for everyone to become a musician?" https://www.redbull.com/se-en/how-ai-will-make-everyone-a-musician (19.06.2024).

Wenewsenglish.pk. (2024) Microsoft Develops AI Tool for Perfect Human Voice Clonning https://wenewsenglish.pk/microsoft-develops-ai-tool-for-perfect-human-voice-cloning/ (21.06.2024).

Weta Digital. (n.d.).. . *Technology*.

Wired. (2023). AI is making film. Will it steal human creativity soon?

Wu, X., & Wu, X. (2021). U.S. Patent No. 11,107,503. Washington, DC: U.S. Patent and Trademark Office.

Yadav, M., Khurana, R., Vihari, N. S., Mittal, A., Balodi, A., & Srivastava, A. P. (2023, November). Virtual Reality in Human Resource Management: Past, Present and Future Trends. In *2023 International Conference on Recent Advances in Science and Engineering Technology (ICRASET)* (pp. 1-5). IEEE. DOI: 10.1109/ICRASET59632.2023.10420290

Yao, L., Peng, N., Weischedel, R., Knight, K., Zhao, D., & Yan, R. (2019). Plan-and-write: Towards better automatic storytelling. *Proceedings of the ... AAAI Conference on Artificial Intelligence.AAAI Conference on Artificial Intelligence, 33*(01), 7378–7385. DOI: 10.1609/aaai.v33i01.33017378

Yazadzhiyan, H. (2023). Video Editing Tools with Artificial Intelligence [JIIT]. *Journal of Informatics And Innovative Technologies*, (2-3), 5.

Yeh, Y.-P., & Chang, T.-W. (2007). Playwright agent as adaptive scripts for organization-communication. In *Human-Computer Interaction. HCI Applications and Services* (pp. 816–824). Springer Berlin Heidelberg. DOI: 10.1007/978-3-540-73111-5_91

Yılmaz, A. (2022). *Yapay Zeka*. Kodlab.

Yudono, K. D. A. (2023). Keterbatasan Cerita Pendek Horor Karya Artificial Intelligence (AI) pada Perangkat Lunak ChatGPT. *DIDAKTIS: Jurnal Pendidikan Bahasa Dan Sastra Indonesia*, 1(2), 51–56. DOI: 10.33096/didaktis.v1i2.306

Yu, F., Ren, X., Luo, J., & Sun, G. (2016). A Hybrid Recommendation Model for Streaming Services in a Smart Home. *IEEE Transactions on Consumer Electronics*.

Yüksel, S. E. (2018). Küreselleşmenin Sinema Endüstrisine Etkileri: Türkiye'de Üretim-Dağıtım-Gösterim İlişkileri Üzerine Bir İnceleme. *Selçuk İletişim*, 11, 331–348. DOI: 10.18094/josc.346618

Zanzarella, I. (2020). The Problem of Musical Creativity and its Relevance for Ethical and Legal Decisions towards Musical AI.

Zengin, F. (2020). Akıllı Makine Çağı Sinemasına Giriş: Sinema Sanatında Yapay Zeka Teknolojilerinin Kullanımı. *İletişim Çalışmaları Dergisi,* 6, 151-177.

Zeng, R., & Zhang, H. (2023). *Analysis of film distribution methods based on artificial intelligence technology*. Applied Mathematics and Nonlinear Sciences.

Zhang, C ve Lu, Y. (2021) Study on Artificial Intelligence: The state of the art and future prospects, Journal of Industrial Information Integration, Volume 23, September.

Zhang, T., Kishore, V., Wu, F., Weinberger, K. Q., & Aetzi, Y. (2020). BERTSCore: Evaluating Text Generation with BERT. *arXiv (Cornell University)*. https://arxiv .org/pdf/1904.09675.pdf

Zhao, L. F. (2020). Data-driven approach for predicting and explaining the risk of long-term unemployment. In *E3S Web of Conferences* (Vol. 214, p. 01023). EDP Sciences. DOI: 10.1051/e3sconf/202021401023

Zhi, B. Et al. (2018) "Synthesizing Audio Using Genereative Adversarial Networks" CMSC723 University of Maryland Collgege Park fall 2018.

Zhu, Y., Kiros, R., & Richard, Z. Ruslan Salakhutdinov et. (2015). Aligning Books and Movies: Towards Story-like Visual Explanations by Watching Movies and Reading Books. https://arxiv.org/pdf/1506.06724

Ziska Fields, I. G. I. (Ed.). (2023). *Dwivedi, DwijendraNath, and Ghanashyama Mahanty. "Human Creativity vs. Machine Creativity: Innovations and Challenges." Multidisciplinary Approaches in AI, Creativity, Innovation, and Green Collaboration* (pp. 19–28). Global., DOI: 10.4018/978-1-6684-6366-6.ch002

Zylinska, J. (2020). *AI art: machine visions and warped dreams* (p. 181). Open humanities press.

About the Contributors

Uğur Kılınç received his undergraduate education in Radio, Television, and Cinema at Kocaeli University's Faculty of Communication, continuing his academic journey with a master's degree from the same university's Institute of Social Sciences in the Department of Radio, Television, and Cinema. He completed his doctorate in 2022 at Marmara University's Institute of Social Sciences, majoring in Cinema Studies and graduating with the highest GPA of 4.0. From 2015 to 2022, Dr. Kılınç served as a Research Assistant at the Faculty of Communication's Department of Radio, Television, and Cinema at Ondokuz Mayıs University. Since 2022, he has been contributing as an Associate Professor. As a full-time academic at the faculty, his work transcends academic teaching; he is also an accomplished author in the genres of gothic and horror, with works published by notable publishers such as İthaki Publishing, KaraKarga Publishing, Bilgi Publishing, and Dark Istanbul Publishings in Turkey. Dr. Kılınç lectures on an array of subjects at the undergraduate level, including Cinema History, Art History, Mythology, Independent Cinema, Screenwriting, Adaptations in Cinema, Film Production, and Video-Art. He offers courses in Visual Literacy, Nordic Cinema, and Horror Cinema at the graduate level. With a burgeoning interest in artificial intelligence, especially post-pandemic, Dr. Kılınç has pivoted to integrate this field into his area of expertise, delivering numerous seminars in universities and private institutions on the relationship between Artificial Intelligence and the film industry. In 2023, he authored a book chapter titled "Technological Transformations in the Cinema Industry: Where Does Artificial Intelligence Stand in Cinema?" in the Turkish publication "Artificial Intelligence in Communication Sciences. Dr. Kılınç has previously enjoyed the privilege of contributing to IGI Global's "Encyclopedia of Information Science and Technology, Fourth Edition" (2018), "Narrative Advertising Models and Conceptualization in the Digital Age" (2017), and "Handbook Of Research On Effective Advertising Strategies In The Social Media Age" (2015). His Turkish works focus on cinema, including published books such as "50 Essentials of Horror

Cinema," "Nordic Cinema," and "The Music of Mythology," as well as numerous articles, providing a profound knowledge base in the field of cinema.

***

Vishnu Achutha Menon is an independent journalist, writer, researcher, and an Indian percussionist. He is a recipient of the Junior Scholarship the Ministry of Culture awarded. His research interests are film studies, verbal & nonverbal communication, south Asian performances, Natyasastra, media studies, media analysis techniques, Laban Movement Analysis, and Ethnomusicology.

Shivam Ballewar epitomizes the dynamic essence of the media landscape, seamlessly blending a rich nexus of practical industry acumen with a profound academic journey. With an extensive background spanning over four years of immersive experience, he currently serves as an Assistant Professor at Symbiosis Institute of Media and Communication, Symbiosis International Deemed University, Pune, where he enriches the minds of aspiring media professionals with a wealth of insights. His academic journey, spanning five years, has served as a crucible for deepening his understanding of the intricate mechanisms governing media dynamics. At the nexus of his passions lies Photography, Visual Communication, and Audio-Video Production, where he showcases a formidable array of skills honed through years of dedicated practice. Beyond his professional pursuits, he embarks on a journey of intellectual expansion, pursuing a Ph.D. at Amity University Rajasthan.

Lakshmi D is presently designated as a Senior Associate Professor in the School of Computing Science Engineering and Artificial Intelligence and Assistant Director, at the Centre for Innovation in Teaching & Learning (CITL) at VIT Bhopal. From 2016 to 2021 served as an Educational Research Officer, at Vishnu Educational Development and Innovation Centre (VEDIC) Shri Vishnu Educational Society, Hyderabad She has 26 years of teaching experience. She has addressed innumerable guest lectures, acted as a session chair, and was invited as a keynote speaker at several international conferences. She has conducted FDPs that cover approximately ~1,00,000 plus faculty members including JNTU, TEQIP, SERB, SWAYAM, DST, AICTE, MHRD, ATAL, ISTE, Madhya Pradesh Government-sponsored, Malviya Mission Teacher Training, Central University of Gujarat and self-financed workshops across India as well as Misamis University, Philipines on Artificial Intelligence in Education: The Future and Futuristic Perspectives both theory and practical sessions. The other titles such as Modern Tools and Software in Teaching Learning Practices, Outcome Based Education, Scientific Educational Practices, Flipped Learning, Blended Learning, Activity Based Learning, Marching towards Quality and Excellence in Higher Educational Institutions, NEP 2022, Emotional Intelligence, Python Essential, Data Analytics, IoT, Machine Learning, Deep Learning, Cyber Security, AR/VR in Medicine, Architecture and Military Applications Instructional Strategies, Assessment techniques, Research Writing, etc. She has 20 international conference presentations, and 50 international journal papers and book chapters inclusive of SCOPUS & SCI. A total of 20 SCOPUS-indexed book chapters. A total of 24 patents are in various stages and 18 patents have been granted at both national and international levels. She was appointed as an external examiner for several Ph.D candidates at reputed universities. Under her supervision, one scholar has completed a Ph.D. at Annamalai University. One scholar is pursuing a Ph.D. right now at VIT Bhopal University. She has won two Best Paper awards at international conferences, one at the IEEE conference and another one at EAMMIS 2021 (First European, Asian, Middle Eastern North African Conference on Management & Information Systems). She received two awards in the year 2022 on the eve of Teacher's Day 1. Kamal Sharma Award of Academic Excellence - 2022 from Lexicon Group of Institutions, Pune for the Engaged Pedagogies. from the virtual ceremony. 2. Bharat Academic Excellence "UttamaAdyapika" Award from Braino Vision. She published a book on "Theory of Computation" in 2003, "Leading Education in the Age of Disruption" in 2021, and "Smart Cities: Disruptive Technologies Driving the Force", in 2023. In the last three editions, she acted as a SPOC for KAVACH and the Smart India Hackathon. She has created 15 hours of the high-quality "Python Essentials" online course at VITyarthi Online Learning Platform. She has 9 SCOPUS Indexed book edits with three CRS Press, Taylor, and Francis, four IGI Global, and two IEEE Rivers.

Özlem Delal Abanoz received her bachelor's, master's and doctorate degrees from Selçuk University, Institute of Social Sciences, Department of Journalism. She is currently working as a Dr. Research Assistant at Ondokuz Mayıs University, Faculty of Communication, Department of Journalism. Her research interests include new media, artificial intelligence and fact-checking journalism.

Dwijendra Nath Dwivedi is a professional with 20+ years of subject matter expertise creating right value propositions for analytics and AI. He currently heads the EMEA+AP AI and IoT team at SAS, a worldwide frontrunner in AI technology. He is a post-Graduate in Economics from Indira Gandhi Institute of Development and Research and is PHD from crackow university of economics Poland. He has presented his research in more than 20 international conference and published several Scopus indexed paper on AI adoption in many areas. As an author he has contributed to more than 8 books and has more than 25 publications in high impact journals. He conducts AI Value seminars and workshops for the executive audience and for power users.

Serhat Erdem, who was born in Kırıkkale in 1982, completed his high school education at Samsun Ondokuz Mayıs High School. In 2004, he was awarded a bachelor's degree from Atatürk University, Faculty of Communication, Department of Radio, Television and Cinema. In 2005, he took his first step into academic life as a Research Assistant at Atatürk University, Faculty of Fine Arts, Department of Cinema and Television. Erdem, who completed his master's degree in 2009 at Atatürk University Social Sciences Institute, Department of Journalism, with the thesis "A Study on the Transformations Revealed by the Application of Matte Paint in Cinema", started his doctoral studies at Istanbul University Social Sciences Institute, Radio, Television and Cinema Department in 2010. In 2015, he completed his PhD thesis titled "Use of Visual Effects in the Reconstruction of Reality: Space Construction in the Spartacus Television Series" and was entitled to receive the title of Doctor. Lecturer Working as a member, Erdem received the title of Associate Professor in the field of Visual Communication Design in 2022. Since February 2022, he has been continuing his academic studies at Atatürk University, Faculty of Communication, Department of Radio, Television and Cinema.

Ufuk İnal has received undergraduate and master degree from Radio, Television and Cinema department in Kocaeli University. He has started PHD study in communication sciences departmant in Kocaeli University. He's currently working in Radio, Television and Cinema department in Ondokuz Mayıs University. His current research interest are Radio Broadcasting and New Media Studies.

Amila Jayarathne is a Senior Lecturer in Marketing attached to the School of Leadership, Management and Marketing, De Montfort University (DMU), Leicester, the UK, Prior to this position she worked as a Professor in Marketing attached to the Department of Marketing Management, University of Sri Jayewardenepura (USJ), Sri Lanka. She obtained her Batcher's degree from the USJ, and Masters in Policy Studies from Japan and MSc in Management from USJ. She obtained her PhD at the Nottingham University Business School in UK. She was an ADB scholar, a Commonwealth scholar, and a Fellowship receiver. She has more than 50 publications in several international conferences, scholarly books, and in high-ranked indexed journals, she has been awarded several times for her outstanding research performance locally and internationally. She was the former Editor-in-Chief in the Vidyodaya Journal of Management, the founding Editor-in-Chief, the Asian Journal of Marketing Management, the Associate Editor of SLIIT Business Review, and a senior editor in the South Asian Journal of Marketing Management (an Emerald

Journal). She has engaged in several industrial based research projects individually and in collaboration with scholars in Sri Lanka, India, UK, Swidden, China and Australia, during her career in the higher education sector.

Sadaf Khan has extensive teaching experience of more than ten years. A core academician and a prolific researcher, she has done incredible work in the domain of English Literature, Film Studies, Cultural Studies, and Afghanistan Studies. Having an international teaching experience, she has been felicitated multiple times as 'Best Teacher' by various academic institutions in which she had worked. Besides, she has also served as the Joint Editor of Women's College Annual magazine of Aligarh Muslim University for the session 2007-2008.

Saad Ullah Khan has more than a decade long extensive experience at university level teaching and research. Dr. Khan has authored various research papers in journals of national as well as international repute. He was awarded 'Rajat Jayanti Vigyan Sancharak Fellowship-2009' by DST, Ministry of Science and Technology (Government of India) for his contribution to the field of communication and its social implications. Further he was bestowed with MANF Fellowship 2011 by UGC to carry out his research work. A PhD from prestigious Aligarh Muslim University, Dr. Saad Ullah Khan has presented 90 Research Papers in various National and International Conferences. He was awarded 'Best Researcher Award' twice (2020 & 2023) and 'Best Journalism Teacher Award' in 2021.

Mohan Kumar has a total of seven years of professional experience, both in the corporate sector and as an academician. Specifically, he has worked in the Public Sector Bank and State Government University, focusing on Marketing and Entrepreneurship Development. He has completed his PhD on the topic of "Motivational Factors and Challenges of Start-Ups in NCR" at the Institute of Management Studies and Research, Maharshi Dayanand University, located in Rohtak-124001, Haryana. He specializes in Marketing Management, Human Resource Management, Quantitative Analysis, and Entrepreneurship Development. He has published his research in various esteemed national and international journals. He has actively engaged in both national and international conferences, where he has showcased his research findings. In March 2022, he received the "Best Research Paper Award" at an international conference conducted by IITM, GGSIU, Delhi. He was awarded for his research paper titled "Psychological wellbeing before & during the COVID-19 Pandemic: A longitudinal sample study of creative writers and Directors." He has successfully participated in various other workshops as well.

Ghana Mahanty leads MENA Data science, UAE and Global Data Science Center of Excellent, India for Visa Inc. He is a data enthusiast with expertise in mobilizing the organization to deliver value out of data and specializing in business management, data transformation strategy, and machine learning and artificial intelligence solutions for Retail Banking and Payment industry. He has worked extensively across North America, Asia, Europe and Middle East regions. Currently pursuing PhD. in Economics from Department of Analytical and Applied Economics, Utkal University, Bhubaneswar, India. His research area of interests are machine learning, artificial intelligence, macro econometric and structural data modelling, panel modelling, money, banking and payments.

Dipandi Mishra is a dedicated academic with a strong foundation in finance and marketing, having earned an MBA with a specialization in these fields, where she graduated as a silver medalist. With over three and a half years of teaching experience at the university level, Dipandi has consistently demonstrated a commitment to education and research. In 2022, Dipandi was honored with the prestigious Manubhai M. Shah Memorial Award by the Indian Commerce Association for the best paper presentation, where she also received a gold medal. Currently, she has submitted her Ph.D. thesis at Indira Gandhi National Tribal University, one of the only two tribal universities in India, further contributing to their academic achievements. Dipandi's research interests are centered around green marketing, organic marketing, sustainable development, and the integration of artificial intelligence in these areas.

Sakalya Mitra is currently a pre-final year student at VIT Bhopal University, pursuing Integrated M.Tech in Computer Science with specialization in Artificial Intelligence and Machine Learning. He is an AI and ML enthusiast who wishes to pursue his career in the field of Data Science and Machine Learning. He has achieved the 2nd Position in BPlan Competition at IIT Kharagpur among 10K+ Teams and have also won 2nd prize at the WCE Hackathon. He aims to bring a revolutionary impact by harnessing the true power of AI based methodologies and contributing to the convergence of AI in different domains, shaping the future of automation.

Arjama Pal is student at VIT Bhopal University, specializing in Computer Science with a focus on Artificial Intelligence and Machine Learning. With a strong foundation in computational methodologies and machine learning principles, Arjama combines technical proficiency with a diverse set of creative and analytical skills.

Jayendra Prabhakar Rane is currently teaching on the post of Assistant Professor at Amity School of Communication, Amity University Rajasthan, Jaipur. His scholarly journey is determined by a profound specialization in the realms of Film and TV production, fortified by the attainment of a postgraduate degree in Mass Communication from the Shivaji University in Kolhapur, Maharashtra (India). Moreover, Mr. Rane has showcased his dedication and expertise by successfully clearing both the National Eligibility Test (NET) and the State Eligibility Test (SET) within his subject domain. Distinguished by a multifaceted academic repertoire, Mr. Rane's research pursuits converge on the intersections of Film Studies, Film Theories, Cinematography, and Documentary Production. Beyond the realms of academia, Mr. Rane's creative fervor finds expression in the domain of audio-visual storytelling, manifesting in his involvement in numerous documentary and fictional short film productions.

Shanika Rathnasiri is a Lecturer at the Department of Marketing Management, Faculty of Management Studies, Sabaragamuwa University of Sri Lanka. She obtained her BSc (Special) degree in Marketing Management from Sabaragamuwa University of Sri Lanka with a second class upper division in 2017. In 2019, she obtained an MSc in Business and Organization Psychology from Coventry University, United Kingdom, and an MBA from the Postgraduate Institute of Management (PIM), USJP, in 2022.

Anita Sahoo is Associate Professor of Faculty of Management Sciences at Siksha O Anusandhan Deemed University, Odisha, India. She is an M.Com, M.Phil, MBA and Ph.D. She has been teaching Post- Graduate Subjects for last thirteen years in the areas of Corporate Financial Reporting, Corporate Finance Management, Cost & Management Accounting, Security Analysis & Portfolio Management, Bank Management, and Financial Market & Services. She has published more than twenty articles in the journals of Indian repute. She has also presented more than fifteen papers in the national and international seminars.

Abdul Quadir Siddiquee is associated with Centre for Media and Mass Communication Studies, Jamia Hamdard-New Delhi. He was previously associated with the Amity School of Communication, Amity University Rajasthan-Jaipur. He has almost a decade of teaching and journalism experience in the field of Mass Communication and Journalism. He was associated with Network 18 and ETV. He produced several TV programs and documentaries on social issues. He received the Maulana Azad National Fellowship (MANF) for his PhD research from UGC. His area of research interest is semiotic analysis of Cinema and gender studies. He has done a TESOL Methodology course from the University of Maryland, Baltimore County (UMBC), USA Organized by FHI360 USA. He has presented more than fifteen research papers in National and International seminars. He is an author and Co-author of 10 research papers.

Mohit Yadav is an Associate Professor in the area of Human Resource Management at Jindal Global Business School (JGBS). He has a rich blend of work experience from both Academics as well as Industry. Prof. Mohit holds a Ph.D.

from Department of Management Studies, Indian Institute of Technology Roorkee (IIT Roorkee) and has completed Master of Human Resource and Organizational Development (MHROD) from prestigious Delhi School of Economics, University of Delhi. He also holds a B.Com (Hons.) degree from University of Delhi and UGC-JRF scholarship. He has published various research papers and book chapters with reputed publishers like Springer, Sage, Emerald, Elsevier, Inderscience etc. and presented research papers in national and International conferences both in India and abroad. He has many best paper awards on his credit too. He is reviewer of various international journals like Computers in Human Behavior, Policing etc. His areas of interest are Organizational Behavior, HRM, Recruitment and Selection, Organizational Citizenship Behavior, Quality of work life and role.

Melike Sinem Yılmaz is a lecturer at Ondokuz Mayıs University. She completed her undergraduate education at Gazi University, Faculty of Fine Arts, Department of Visual Communication Design. Yılmaz completed her master's degree in Media Design at Ankara Hacı Bayram Veli University and continues her proficiency in art in Media Design at the same university. Her research interests include visual design, advertising design, transmedia storytelling and perception manipulation. She has also participated in various academic projects and publications.

Index

G

H

I

M

N

P

R

S

T

U

V

www.ingramcontent.com/pod-product-compliance
Lightning Source LLC
LaVergne TN
LVHW080557300926
849162LV00005B/981
9798369339169